Daily Lives, and Wisdom of the Saints & Fasting Calendar

2018

On the Cover:

Icon of the Theotokos as the Abbess of the Holy Mountain

While the Panagia and St. John the Evangelist were sailing from Joppa to Cyprus to visit Lazarus, the ship was blown off course and was forced to drop anchor near the present-day monastery of Iveron on Mt. Athos. She walked ashore and was overwhelmed by the natural beauty. She blessed it and asked her Son that it be her garden, and a Voice was heard, saying, "Let this place be your inheritance and your garden, a paradise and a haven of salvation for those seeking to be saved." Mt. Athos is known as the Garden of the Panagia, and is out of bounds to any other women. There is a strong belief among the monks living on the Holy Mountain that through the centuries She continues to visit Athos to manifest herself as its Protectress.

RESEARCHED AND WRITTEN BY TOM AND GEORGIA MITRAKOS

ORTHODOX CALENDAR COMPANY ✠ PITTSBURGH, PENNSYLVANIA

Front cover with permission by the Orthodox Christian Network.

This calendar follows the Revised Julian Calendar (New Calendar). All listed commemorations and Scripture readings are according to the Greek Orthodox Church liturgical calendar.

The fasting guidelines are those prescribed by the Church. Fasting is a spiritual discipline and it is recommended that each Orthodox Christian consult with their spiritual father.

Fast-free—All foods allowed.

Strict Fast—Abstain from meat products, dairy products, fish, oil, and wine.

22nd Annual Edition

Orthodox Calendar Company
P. O. Box 11331, Pittsburgh, PA 15238
Tel: 412-736-7840
www.LivesoftheSaintsCalendar.com
Email: OrthodoxCalendarCompany@gmail.com
Facebook.com/OrthodoxCalendarCompany

ISBN-13: 978-0-9980817-1-7

Printed in the United States of America.

The Circumcision of Christ
Fast-free
Colossians 2:8-12; Luke 2:20-21, 40-52

January 1

God's will is to save us, and nothing pleases Him more than our coming back to Him with true repentance. It was precisely in order to show that there is nothing closer to God's heart than the divine Word of God lived among us in the flesh, and died, suffered, and said all that was necessary to reconcile us to God the Father, when we were at enmity with Him. He also taught us in many different ways that we should wish to imitate Him by our own kindness and genuine love for one another.

St. Maximos the Confessor

CLARUS OF VIENNE. Clarus was the name given to him from his youth because of his perception of the things of God. He was at first a monk in the abbey of St. Ferrêol and was highly thought of by the Archbishop of Vienne. Clarus was made the spiritual director of the convent of St. Blandina, where his mother and other widows became nuns. Later in life, he became the abbot of St. Marcellus at Vienne. The book, "A Latin Life," written about a hundred years later, relates many wonderful stories of the miracles that St. Clarus worked.

SAINTS OF THE DAY: Basil the Great, Archbishop of Caesarea; Gregory, Bishop of Nazianzus; Theodosius of Tryglia; Fulgentius, Bishop of Ruspe; Basil of Ancyra; Peter of the Peloponnesus; Platon of Revel, with Michael, Nicholas, and Alexander; Theodotos and Telemachos; Emilia, mother of St. Basil the Great; Athanasius, Bishop of Mogilev; New Hieromartyr Jeremiah; Clarus of Vienne; Fanchea of Killeany; Eugendus, abbot of Condat.

JANUARY 2

Hebrews 5:4-10; John 3:1-15

Have fear of God, and make a good beginning every day. Those of you who are stumbling, correct yourselves; and those of you who are not stumbling, govern yourselves by the grace of the Lord, so as not to fall—because it's not so easy to live, and it's very hard to die. All those who die forget this life, and in the hour of their death they see before their eyes only the things they have done, good or bad.

+*Elder Paisius of Sihla*

NEW MARTYR GEORGE (ZORZES) THE GEORGIAN. George was a Christian from eighteenth-century Georgia, formerly Iberia in southwest Russia. In his youth, he was sold as a slave to a Turk and was raised as a Muslim. George remained a Muslim until the age of seventy. One day his conscience provoked him to present himself before a judge, and taking off his turban, George declared that he was a Christian. The judge asked if he had lost his mind, and with further questioning, George remained immovable and determined. He was whipped, threatened with death, and publicly ridiculed; however, George endured all this with a quiet strength. His only words were, "I am a Christian; I want to die a Christian." The executioners hanged him.

SAINTS OF THE DAY: Cosmas I, Patriarch of Constantinople; Sylvester, Pope of Rome; Theogenes, Bishop of Parium; Gerasimus II, Patriarch of Alexandria; Theodota, mother of the first Sts. Cosmas and Damian; Sergius of Caesarea; Ammon of Tabennisi; Mark the Deaf; Righteous Theopemptos; Sylvester of the Kiev Caves; Juliana of Lazarevo; Martyr Theopistos; George (Zorzes) the Georgian; Nilos the Sanctified; Basil of Ancyra; Smaragda, abbess of Nezhinsk (Ukraine); Schottin, hermit of Ireland; Repose and second finding of the relics of St. Seraphim of Sarov.

WEDNESDAY **Fast-free**

JANUARY 3

Acts 10:44-48, 11:1-10; John 1:18-28

Nothing of this world is more desirable than the heavens and the earth, and nothing in the order of nature passes away more quickly than speech.

St. Gregory the Great

FINDING OF THE RELICS OF NEW MONK-MARTYR ST. EPHRAIM OF NEA MAKRI. On January 3, 1950, St. Ephraim revealed the location of his burial at the Monastery of the Annunciation in Nea Makri, Attica. He lived during the fifteenth century. Since 1965, he has often appeared to the monastery nuns and pilgrims, either in their sleep or directly before them, surrounded by a brilliant light and exuding a wonderful fragrance. What he tells them is consistent with various accounts of his life and martyrdom. He became a monk at the age of fourteen, and for thirty years lived the ascetical life. He was arrested by the Turks, who had killed all the other monks and then razed the monastery. They tortured Ephraim for about seven months and then hanged him upside down. His feet and head were nailed to a mulberry tree, and a fire set to his body. St. Ephraim often appeared to many and cured the sick. He heals people with incurable illnesses, helps those with wavering faith, saves others from danger, and comforts those troubled by bitterness by showing them the tortures he endured for the love of Christ. In 1982, St. Ephraim appeared with St. Raphael the New Martyr of Mytilene. It appears that the Lord through his saints pours out His grace to bolster the Church and comfort the faithful.

SAINTS OF THE DAY: Prophet Malachi; Genevieve of Paris; Peter of Atroa; Gordius at Caesarea; Euthymius, the Man of God of Tbilisi; Abelard of Belgium; Titus, Bishop of Tomis; Thomais of Lesbos; Findlugan of Islay; Three martyrs, a mother and her two children slain by fire; Finding of the relics of New Monk-martyr St. Ephraim of Nea Makri.

JANUARY 4

1 Corinthians 4:9-16; John 1:18-28

People give all sorts of reasons to excuse their lack of charity, their hardheartedness! Some say, "hard times." But if the times are hard for those who have a sufficiency, how much harder are they for the poor? This pretext alone should lead one to give all the more generously.

St. Theophan the Recluse

MARTYR ZOSIMAS THE HERMIT AND MARTYR ATHANASIOS THE COMMENTARIUS (SUPERINTENDENT OF PRISONERS) OF CILICIA. In fourth-century Cilicia, Zosimas was an ascetic living in the deserts and mountains together with the wild animals. He was sought out and arrested by the prefect Dometian. When Zosimas confessed Jesus as true God, he was burned through the ears with hot irons, thrown into a vat of boiling water, and later tied upside down with a large stone around his neck. By the power of God, Zosimas was preserved unharmed. The torturers taunted Zosimas, asking him to call upon the wild beasts to come, and then they would believe. Suddenly a large lion appeared and began to lift the stone around the saint's neck. Seeing this, the notary Athanasios was drawn to the faith. Zosimas was freed, and together with Athanasios, they returned to the desert. Athanasios was catechized and then baptized. One day a large stone miraculously parted, and upon entering both gave up their souls to God.

SAINTS OF THE DAY: Synaxis of the Seventy Apostles; Eustathios I, Archbishop of Serbia; Evagre, Ilia, and the disciples of the 13 Syrian Fathers of Georgia; Gregory, Bishop of Langres; Theoctistus, abbot of Cucomo; Euthymios the New of Thessalonica; Zosimas the Hermit and Athanasios the Commentarius of Cilicia; Aquila of the Kiev Caves; Euthymios and 12 monks of Vatopedi; Symeon of Smolensk; Holy Six Martyrs; Apollinaria of Egypt; Chrysanthos and Euphemia in Constantinople; Onuphrius of Gabrovo; Mark, Bishop of Sergievsk; Eustathius I, Archbishop of Serbia; The Ethiopian Eunuch of Queen Candace.

FRIDAY

Eve of the Theophany
Strict Fast

JANUARY 5

1 Corinthians 9:19-27; Luke 3:1-18

One must act in such a way that the soul does not turn to God only when you are standing in prayer, but should do so as far as possible throughout the day. It should be an unceasing offering of oneself to Him.

St. Theophan the Recluse

MARTYRS THEOPEMPTOS OF NICOMEDIA AND THEONAS. Bishop Theopemptos of Nicomedia was the first martyr of the persecutions of Emperor Diocletian. He was arrested and ordered to sacrifice to idols. Theopemptos defended the faith in Christ, and refused to offer the sacrifice. They threw him into a red-hot furnace, where he remained throughout the day and night. That night, Theopemptos appeared in Diocletian's bedchamber and told him that he was unharmed. The emperor and his soldiers went to the furnace and there saw the saint alive and praying to God. Diocletian called him a wizard and imprisoned him for twenty-two days without food or water, but Theopemptos remained in good spirits. A sorcerer named Theonas was found to combat Theopemptos. His evil was so great that with an incantation he caused a raging bull to split in half. He tried two times to poison Theopemptos, but it proved harmless, which caused Theonas to become a Christian. In the morning, Diocletian commanded him again to renounce Christ, but seeing that he would not, he ordered more tortures and sentenced St. Theopemptos to beheading. St. Theonas also refused to offer a sacrifice to the idols, so he was buried alive in a deep ditch.

SAINTS OF THE DAY: Syncletike of Alexandria; Phosterios and Menas of Sinai; Gregory at Akrita; Martyr Sais; Theopemptos of Nicomedia and Theonas; Martyr Theoeidos; Righteous Domnina; Righteous Tatiana; Romanos of Carpenision; Talida, abbess of Antinoe, and Taora; Romanus of Lacedaemonia; Theophan of the Rykhlovsk Monastery (Ukraine); Symeon of the Pskov Caves; Niphon, Bishop of Cyprus.

Holy Theophany
Fast-free

JANUARY 6

Titus 2:11-14, 3:4-7; Matthew 3:13-17

We must have our gaze fixed on heaven. Then nothing here can shake us.

+Elder Amphilochios Makris of Patmos

VENERABLE LAURENCE OF CHERNIGOV. Laurence was a good student, gifted in music, and at age fourteen was a choir director. He became a monk and went to the Chernigov-Trinity Monastery at the request of the archbishop who foresaw that Laurence would become a great man of prayer. He was made the abbot at the age of 27. He was always joyful and radiated love with everyone, which was the fruit of his prayer. When he visited his village, he had the spiritual insight to see which girls were inclined to monasticism, and he would pray for them and nurture their love for prayer. Once while building a monastery during bad weather, the stucco froze. Laurence made the sign of the cross, and it became pliable. During wartime, the enemy would not allow the monks to harvest the monastery wheat, but Laurence prayed, and it was permitted. He said, "When a person is wicked he has a demon within, but when you pray, the demon scampers away." He also said, "It's so difficult for a Christian to live in this world. The devil doesn't give him any peace." He told a girl not to enter a convent but to marry. When she objected, he said, "then who will give birth to priests and bishops." She married and had a son who became an archpriest. Laurence talked much about the end times and how the Antichrist will become the single world leader after a terrible war. "In the last times they will banish the true Christians," and the mark of the beast will be necessary to buy and sell, but "the Lord will not abandon His children. One mustn't fear!" He said the rivers and lakes would dry up, and grain will not grow, but those "under the powerful influence of the Jesus Prayer" will not see those false signs. After a few months with a short illness, Laurence died on the Feast of Theophany, in 1950.

SAINTS OF THE DAY: Andrew Zimin, Lydia, 3 daughters, and Domnica, of Russia; Romanus of Lacedemonia; Laurence of Chernigov.

Synaxis of St. John the Forerunner
Fast-free

Acts 19:1-8; John 1:29-34

JANUARY 7

All the conflicts in the world have their origin in unabated anger. One is angry and wounds the other, who then responds with greater violence and strength. Once this chain is begun, it cannot be stopped except through the appeal of prayer—genuine prayer.

+Elder George Calciu of Romania

CEDD, BISHOP OF LASTINGHAM. Cedd was the oldest of four brothers, born into a noble family in seventh-century Northumbria. The brothers all entered the priory school at an early age and learned the ways of Irish monks, and they all became priests. Cedd was consecrated Bishop of Essex and was sent to evangelize the people who were in need of spiritual guidance. He built churches and monasteries, baptized the locals, and ordained priests and deacons to help him. Together they gathered a large flock. King Ethelwald of Deira gave land to Cedd to build a monastery, but Cedd refused to lay the foundation stones until the place had first been cleansed through prayer and fasting. In 664, Cedd and his brother Cynibil fell sick from a great plague and died. Cedd was at first buried in the open air, but the 30 monks who attended his funeral also contracted the plague and died.

SAINTS OF THE DAY: Synaxis of St. John the Forerunner; Miracle of St. John the Baptist in Chios; Translation of the right hand of St. John the Baptist; New Martyr Athanasios of Attalia and Smyrna; Cedd, Bishop of Lastingham; Brannock (Brynach) of Braunton (England); Kentigerna of Loch Lomond; Paphnutius (Kostin) of Optina Monastery; Nicholas (Parfenov), Bishop of Atkarsk.

January 8

Romans 6:3-11; John 3:22-33

As bread is food for the body and virtue is food for the soul, so spiritual prayer is food for the mind.

St. Nilus of Mt. Sinai

NATHALAN OF TULLICH. Nathalan was from a noble family in seventh-century eastern Scotland. He decided to dedicate his life to God and distributed his large estate to the poor. He grew vegetables, which he gave to the poor during a disastrous famine. He said that plowing land was a sort of penance for him. He prayed, fasted, and led a solitary life. He also preached the Word of God to the pagans. He became a bishop in Scotland in the following manner. Once a violent wind ruined the saint's crop, and he began grumbling to God. Realizing his sin, he put one of his feet and his arms into irons and threw the key into the river. Then he made a pilgrimage to Rome to atone for his sin. Upon reaching the gates of the city, a youth sold him a fish, and the key to the irons was found in its stomach. When the pope of Rome learned this, he consecrated Nathalan a bishop. Nathalan built many churches and struggled against the heresy of Pelagianism, which stated that original sin did not taint human nature, and that mortal will is capable of choosing good or evil without divine aid. Nathalan is venerated as a chief apostle and patron in the Scottish county of Aberdeenshire.

SAINTS OF THE DAY: Carterios of Caesarea; Dominica of Carthage; Atticus and Cyrus, Patriarchs of Constantinople; George the Chozevite; Agathon of Egypt; Abo the Perfumer of Baghdad; Elias of Egypt; Julian, Basilissa, Marcionilla, Celsus, Anthony, Anastasius, 7 children, and 20 soldiers at Antinoe; Theophilus and Helladius in Libya; Prophet Shemaiah; Gregory of Ochrid; Gregory of the Kiev Caves, wonderworker; Gregory of the Kiev Caves, recluse; Paisius of Uglich; Macarius of Vatopedi; Isidore and 72 others at Yuriev; Severinus of Austria; Theodore of Constantinople; Pega of Peakirk; Wulsin of Sherborne; Erhard of Regensburg; Gudula of Brussels; Nathalan of Aberdeenshire; Severin of Cologne.

 Fast-free

January 9

2 Timothy 2:1-10; Mark 1:9-15

Sometimes we find ourselves at odds with another person, and we stubbornly insist: 'He is at fault. He's the one who became angry. He's the one who spoke to me rudely. He must humble himself. If he had spoken to me calmly and addressed me with respect, I would have been patient and not have been offended. Hence, He is to blame!' We must oppose such thoughts by responding: 'No, no! If I did not have egotism, I would not be bothered. Hence, I am to blame. My brother is not at fault.'

Elder Ephraim of Arizona

BERHTWALD, ARCHBISHOP OF CANTERBURY. Berhtwald was born around the middle of the seventh century. About 30 years later, he was made abbot of the Reculver monastery in Kent. Later, he was elected archbishop of Canterbury, a position which had remained vacant for two years because various kings had fought for control of the area. Berhtwald traveled to France for his consecration. He wanted to be certain that his consecration was supported by all the kings and bishops. He then traveled to Rome to obtain the support of the pope who in turn wrote to many kings and bishops to rally support for Berhtwald. It was during his tenure that the last pagan kingdom in England was converted. Berhtwald also believed that his see included the entire island of Britain. He secured the exemption of the Church from taxation and consecrated a number of bishops.

SAINTS OF THE DAY: Peter, Bishop of Sebaste, brother of Basil the Great and Gregory of Nyssa; Polyeuktos of Melitene in Armenia; Eustratios of Tarsus; Philip, Metropolitan of Moscow; Jonah, founder of Holy Trinity Monastery in Kiev; Adrian of Canterbury; Parthena of Edessa; Finian, Bishop of Lindisfarne; Berhtwald, Archbishop of Canterbury; Fillan, abbot of Strathfillan; Translation of the relics of St. Judoc, hermit of Ponthie.

 Strict Fast

JANUARY 10

Ephesians 4:7-13; Luke 3:19-22

True Christians flee the praise of men.

St. Nikolai Velimirovich

VENERABLE ANTIPAS OF ROMANIA. Antipas was born to a pious family in the twentieth century. He prayed to succeed in school and promised to dedicate himself to spiritual reading. Unable to find his place among the world, he begged God for help. He left home secretly and went to the monastery of Neamt. As he prayed before a wonderworking icon of the Virgin Mary, the curtains on both sides of the icon opened of themselves. He then went to Mt. Athos where he spent four years as a novice in the kitchen of Esphigmenou Monastery. Then Antipas followed his original dream to live the life of an ascetic in the desert. He found an uninhabitable hut and an old icon of the Panagia that was in very poor condition. As soon as he began to clean it, it cleaned itself and shone brightly. In time, it would be revealed as miracle-working. A hermit gave Antipas five gold coins, and he hired a carpenter to repair the hut. When the worker fell and was near death, Antipas placed the icon near him, and he was restored to health. Antipas was asked to help with the building of a Romanian skete on Mt. Athos. He was put in charge of the administration and the stores in the monastery, and was asked to go to Russia to raise money for the project. This work was not without problems. The boat that took the gifts from Russia sank, and another time the money he raised had to be converted into gold which was forbidden. However, Antipas prayed before the icon of the Panagia, and all went well. He said that although praying in church is a great thing, it will not happen if we do not complete our rule in our own cell.

SAINTS OF THE DAY: Gregory of Nyssa;Theophan the Recluse; Theosebia the Deaconess; Marcian of Constantinople; Dometian of Melitene; Ammon of Nitria; Paul of Obnora; Ephraim and 6 monks of Obnora; Macarius of Pisemsk; Peter of Radushino; Antipas of Romania; Macarius of Pisma; Miltiades of Rome; Antipas of Valaam; Anatole of Odessa; Arsenia, in Shuisk.

Fast-free

JANUARY 11

Hebrews 13:7-16; Matthew 11:27-30

The very sin that each person thinks is so bad in his neighbor is the one that accuses himself, the accuser.

St. Joseph of Optina

VENERABLE VITALIS OF THE MONASTERY OF ABBA SERID AT GAZA. For many years Vitalis lived as a monk in seventh-century Palestine. He went to Alexandria to labor for the salvation of women living as prostitutes. He worked as a laborer by day, but he only kept a tenth of his earnings for himself. At night, he would give the rest of his money to a prostitute on the condition that she does not give herself up to sin that night, but instead stay with him and pray for his salvation. He would make her promise to tell no one about this. Complaints of this scandal soon reached the patriarch, St. John the Merciful. But St. John knew Vitalis' good heart and did nothing. When Vitalis died, a tablet was found near his body, on which was written, "Inhabitants of Alexandria, judge not before the time, until the coming of the Day of the Lord." The women who had been converted from their immoral life by Vitalis came forward and told of his good deeds. The people honored him with a lavish funeral. Vitalis did everything he could to hide his virtues, and he counted himself more sinful than the fallen.

SAINTS OF THE DAY: Theodosios the Great, the Cenobiarch; Theodosios, Metropolitan of Trebizond; Theodosios of Antioch; Stephen of Placidian; Agapius of Apamea; Romilos the Hermit of Veddin; Vitalis of Abba Serid at Gaza; Michael of Klops Monastery; Joseph of Cappadocia; Martyr Mairus; Hyginus, Pope of Rome; Vladimir the Confessor of Minsk; New Martyrs Nicholas, Theodore and Vladimir; "Chernigov-Eletskaya" Icon of the Mother of God.

 Strict Fast

JANUARY 12

Acts 18:22-28; John 10:39-42

Refuse to listen to the devil when he whispers to you: give me now, and you will give tomorrow to God. No, no! Spend all the hours of your life in a way pleasing to God; keep in your mind the thought that after the present hour you will not be given another and that you will have to render a strict account for every minute of this present hour.

St. Nicodemus the Hagiorite

MARTYR TATIANA OF ROME. Tatiana was a young Christian woman that grew up in the catacombs of third-century Rome. Her father was a deacon there, and she later became a deaconess. The Virgin Tatiana was brought before Emperor Severos, who demanded that she sacrifice in the temple, but her prayers brought down the structure. Eight executioners tore away the skin on her face; however, four angels appeared and blinded them. This miracle caused the executioners to believe in Christ, and they became Christians, but the emperor ordered them to be killed. The emperor continued to humiliate Tatiana. Her head was shaved and her breasts removed. She was thrown into flames and to wild animals to be devoured, but she remained unharmed. Her limbs were mutilated. Angels appeared to her in prison and completely healed her. Exasperated, the emperor gave orders to behead her. Tatiana's last words were, "Loving thee O Savior, I am brought to the slaughter."

SAINTS OF THE DAY: Tatiana of Rome; Peter Absalom in Palestine; Eight Martyrs of Nicaea; Philotheus of Antioch; Mertius of Mauretania; Theodora of Alexandria; Eupraxia of Tabenna in Egypt; Philotheus of Antioch; Elias the Wonderworker, of the Paradise; John of Tula, fool-for-Christ; Galacteon and Martinian of White Lake; Martyr Euthasia; Benedict Biscop, abbot of Wearmouth; "The Milk-giver" and Hilander "Of the Akathist" Icons of the Mother of God.

Saturday after Theophany
Fast-free
Ephesians 6:10-17; Matthew 4:1-11

JANUARY 13

Many rich and powerful men would pay dearly to see the Lord or His Most Pure Mother, but God does not appear in riches, but in the humble heart… Any of the poorest of men can be humbled and come to know God. He needs neither money nor reputation to come to know God, but only humility.

St. Silouan the Athonite

VENERABLE MAXIMOS OF KAPSOKALYVIA SKETE, MT. ATHOS. Maximos lived during the fourteenth century. At the age of seventeen, he went to Mt. Athos and lived there for seventy-eight years. After the plunder of the Fourth Crusades, he helped to bring about the revival of Mt. Athos, along with others such as St. Gregory Palamas. He got his name 'Kapsokalyvia' by living for a short time in a hut of his making, burning it, and then building it again. He was thought to be a fool until St. Gregory of Sinai visited Mt. Athos and discerned that Maximos was a wonderworker and an angel in the flesh. The Theotokos appeared to Maximos, telling him that henceforth he would know spiritual perfection through the Holy Spirit. When his fame spread, crowds came for his blessing and healing. He gave up his soul at the age of 95. St. Maximos was glorified by many miracles during life and in death.

SAINTS OF THE DAY: James, Bishop of Nisibis; Hermylus and Stratonicus at Belgrade; Hilary, Bishop of Poitiers; Maximos of Kapsokalyvia, Mt. Athos; Peter of Anium; Irenarchus of Rostov; Martyrs Pachomius and Papyrinos in Greece; Remigius of Rheims; Eleazar of Anzersk Island at Solovki.

Sunday after Theophany
Fast-free

Ephesians 4:7-13; Matthew 4:12-17

JANUARY 14

We will see our Guardian Angel on the day of our departure from this life. But what kind of meeting this will be will depend upon us and our deeds. Will our Guardian Angel rejoice or will he sorrow at our careless life?

St. Sebastian of Optina

VENERABLE THEODOULOS OF SINAI. As a young boy, Theodoulos went to live with his father St. Neilos the Faster on Mount Sinai during the fifth century. Barbarians once attacked the monks there, and Theodoulos was taken prisoner. The pagans, who worshiped things created rather than the Creator, decided to sacrifice him to their god, the morning dawn. Neilos prayed for God's intercession, and the barbarians overslept, missing the sunrise. They took Theodoulos to the city of Eluza, and he was ransomed by the local bishop. Neilos found his son there, and they returned to Sinai, where they served the Lord until the end of their lives. Theodoulos wrote about the slaughter of the monks at Raithu Monastery. The relics of Sts. Neilos and Theodoulos were found incorrupt and were transferred to the Church of the Holy Apostles in Constantinople.

SAINTS OF THE DAY: Sava I, first Archbishop of Serbia; Nina (Nino), enlightener of Georgia; Holy Fathers slain at Sinai and Raithu: Isaiah, Sabbas, Moses, Moses, Jeremiah, Paul, Adam, Sergius, Domnus, Proclus, Hypatius, Isaac, Macarius, Mark, Benjamin, Eusebius, Elias, and others; Theodoulos of Sinai; Acacius, Bishop of Tver; Macrina, grandmother of St. Basil the Great; New Martyr Bishop Ambrose (Gudko) and others martyred at Sinai and Raitho Monastery near Kazan; John (Kevroletin) of Verkhoturye; Martyr Agnes; Meletius, Bishop of Ryazan; Stephen of Chenolakkos Monastery; Joseph Analytinus of Raithu Monastery; Felix of Nola, priest; Kentigern (Mungo) of Glasgow.

January 15

Galatians 5:22-26, 6:1-2; Luke 12:32-40

It is enough if you will often repeat from your whole heart: Lord, as it pleases Thee and as Thou knowest, have mercy on me. And if temptation comes upon you: Lord, help me! The Lord knows what is profitable for us and has mercy on us.

St. Macarius the Great

VENERABLE MAURUS, DISCIPLE OF ST. BENEDICT. Maurus was the son of a nobleman from sixth-century Rome. When he was about twelve years of age, his father put him under the care of St. Benedict at Subiaco. Though perfect in many virtues, obedience to his elder was his greatest virtue. God granted Maurus the gift of miracles. Once when St. Placid, a fellow disciple, fell into a lake and was carried away, Benedict ordered Maurus to run to him, and walking upon the water he dragged Placid out by the hair. Benedict attributed this to his obedience. Pope St. Gregory the Great also gave testimony to this miracle. The prayer of Maurus healed a boy who was crippled and mute. A certain vicar fell headlong from a high stairway and amputation of his arm was critical. With a relic of the True Cross and fervent, heartfelt prayers of Maurus, all the infected blood began to flow off from three different places in his arm, and his arm was cured. With the prayer, "In the name of Almighty God, arise and be cured," Maurus healed a man blind from birth and a companion who had fallen from a horse and crushed his leg.

SAINTS OF THE DAY: Paul of Thebes; John Calybites of Constantinople; Pansophios of Alexandria; Prochorus of Pshina in Bulgaria; Maurus, disciple of St. Benedict; Maximus, Bishop of Nola; Salome and Perozhavra of Sivnia, Georgia; Ita of Killeedy; Gabriel, founder of Lesnov Monastery; Gerasimos Palladas, Patriarch of Alexandria; Benjamin, Bishop of Romanov; Nectarius of Tobolsk.

JANUARY 16

Acts 12:1-11; John 21:14-25

Nothing humbles the soul more than the scarcity of bread and water. When the enemy wants to take a city, he first stops the food and water supplies, and they thus give themselves up even against their will. So is it for a monastic—unless he restrains his stomach with hunger and thirst, he cannot rid himself of evil thoughts.

St. Sarah of Egypt

JAMES OF TARENTAISE. James was a noble knight of Syria, and he served the king in fifth-century Persia. One day James witnessed the martyrdom of some Catholics, and he converted to Christianity. He entered the priesthood and was consecrated bishop. He was assigned to the region of the Alps where the people were descendants of the barbarian bands of Gaul who had battled the Romans. The village of Tarentaise had once been Christianized, but these teachings were lost due to the flood of barbarian pagans who constantly crossed the Alps. However, these people received James with fervor, and after his first sermon, they asked to be baptized. James began the construction of a church. Men were sent into the forest to cut wood, which was dragged by oxen to the site. One day a large bear killed one of the oxen and began to devour it. James approached the bear and commanded it in the name of Christ to take the place of the ox. The bear immediately bowed his head to receive the yoke of the ox it had killed. After the logging was complete, James ordered the bear to return to the forest and never to repeat such an act. James dedicated the church to St. Stephen the First Martyr.

SAINTS OF THE DAY: Veneration of the Precious Chains of Apostle Peter; Speusippus, Eleusippus, and Meleusippus, with Neon, Turbo, Leonilla, and Jonilla in Cappadocia; Honoratus, Archbishop of Arles; Danax the Reader; Damascene of Bulgaria; Maximus of Totma; New Martyr Nicholas of Mytilene; Romilos of Mt. Athos and Ravanica (Serbia), and with him Nestor, Martinius, Daniel, Sisoes, Zosimas, and Gregory; Sigebert, King of the East Angles; Fursey of Burgh Castle; James of Tarentaise.

WEDNESDAY

JANUARY 17

Abstain from meat and dairy products, and fish.
Hebrews 13:17-21; Luke 6:17-23

Live through lowliness of mind instead of going to your death through pretentious pride.

St. Dorotheos of Gaza

VENERABLE ACHILLES THE CONFESSOR. Achilles was an austere ascetic and anchorite who lived in the Egyptian desert of Scetis with other very ascetic fathers. The following is an example of their strict abstinence. Once when Father Achilles went to the cell of Father Esaias, he saw a bowl of water and some salt, of which Esaias had partaken. Esaias begged forgiveness for this, saying that he had been working in the intense heat, which caused his throat to hurt, so he dipped his dried bread into the salted water to be able to swallow without pain. Achilles then accused Esaias of indulging in this "soup" of water and salt. Another time one of the fathers insulted Achilles, but in order to remain at peace with the other, Achilles said nothing. The restraint he used to keep the resentment at bay caused his mouth to fill with blood. When Achilles spat out the blood, another father saw this and asked about it. Achilles said the blood was the word of one who had grieved him and that through prayer this is how God had removed the remembrance of it from him. When he spat out the blood, he forgot the sorrow and was again at rest. Once a certain father complained to Achilles about the power the demons have over us. Achilles replied that the only power they have is our own lack of will. The demons then act like an ax and cut us down.

SAINTS OF THE DAY: Anthony the Great; Theodosios the Great; George of Ioannina; Anthony the Roman of Novgorod; Macarius (Kalogeras) of Patmos; Achilles of Egypt; Anthony the New of Beroea in Macedonia; Anthony of Dymsk Monastery (Novgorod); Anthony of Chermoezersk Monastery; Anthony of Krasnokholmsk Monastery (Tver); Severus the Pious, Bishop of Bourges.

JANUARY 18

Hebrews 13:7-16; Matthew 5:14-19

Meekness is the fellow-worker with obedience, the guide of the brotherhood, a bridle for the enraged, a check for the irritable, a minister of joy, the imitation of Christ, something proper to angels, shackles for demons, a shield against bitterness.

St. John Climacus

MARTYR THEODULA OF ANAZARBUS AND COMPANIONS. The third-century persecutions of Diocletian and Maximian were brought to Cilicia by Governor Pelagius, who had Theodula arrested. Because she would not deny her Christian faith, Pelagius gave orders to suspend her by her hair and to burn her with skewers. She would not back down and did not seem affected by the torture. Instead, she chastised him and his idols. By her prayers, an idol fell and was smashed. Pelagius bargained with her to restore it, and he would believe. Through prayer, she restored the idol, and he recanted, but he did not know what to do with her. The commander Helladius vowed to convert her, promising his own life if he failed. He drove nails into her head but panicked when she remained steadfast. She prayed and converted him to Christianity, and for this, he was beheaded. She was thrown into a furnace, and again God preserved her. Another came forward, and he too was converted and soon beheaded. When Theodula was placed on a burning rack, the rack collapsed, and those watching were burned. Finally, Theodula and others were thrown into a large furnace, and she gave up her spirit.

SAINTS OF THE DAY: Cyril and Athanasios, Archbishops of Alexandria; Joachim, Patriarch of Turnovo; Maximus, Archbishop of Wallachia; Cyril and Maria, parents of Sergius of Radonezh; Martyr Xenia; Theodula, Helladius, Evagrius, Macarius, and Boethos of Anazarbus; Marcian of Cyrrhus in Syria; Silvanus of Palestine; Ephraim, Bishop of Mylasa; Ephraim the Lesser of Georgia; Leobardus of Gaul; Athanasius of Novolotsk Monastery; Alexis of Teklati, Georgia; Athanasius of Syadem; Ninnidh of Inismacsaint; Vladimir Zubkovich of Smolevichi (Belorussia).

JANUARY 19

Galatians 5:22-6:2; Matthew 19:16-26

The suffering that grips the heart as a result of sinning against love is sharper than all other tortures.

St. Isaac the Syrian

BLESSED THEODORE OF NOVGOROD, FOOL-FOR-CHRIST. Theodore was from a wealthy family in fourteenth-century Novgorod. His parents raised him with strict Christian piety. When he came of age, out of humility, he decided to live the life of an ascetic and a fool-for-Christ. He gave away all that he owned and lived his entire life without warm clothes or a home. In Novgorod, there were separate quarters of the city. When Theodore realized that there would be hostilities between his quarter of Torgov and the neighboring quarter of Sofia, which would usually end in bloodshed, Theodore and a fool-for-Christ living in Sofia began crossing over into each other's territories and pushing each other back. This was a lesson to the inhabitants to remind them of the foolishness of inciting each other to violence. The citizens of Novgorod always perceived Theodore as a man of God. Once when he foresaw a famine, he warned the people by telling them to look at their bread. Another time when he foresaw a fire, he told them that area would be bare. Theodore was forewarned of his own death and bade the people goodbye, saying that he was going far away. He asked to be buried at the porch of the church of Great Martyr George, where he would always go to pray, and the people built a chapel over his relics.

SAINTS OF THE DAY: Macarius the Great of Egypt; Mark Eugenikos of Ephesus; Arsenius of Corfu; Euphrasia of Nicomedia; Macarius of Alexandria; Meletios of Mt. Galesios; Anton the Stylite of Martgopi; Theodore of Novgorod; Macarius the Faster of the Kiev Caves; Macarius, Hierodeacon of the Kiev Caves; Macarius the Roman, and Chariton; Anthony Rawah the Qoraisite; Branwalader (Breward) of Cornwall; Peter Skipetrov of Petrograd; Translation of the relics of St. Gregory the Theologian; Uncovering of the relics of St. Sabbas of Zvenigorod.

JANUARY 20

2 Corinthians 4:6-15; Luke 6:17-23

There is no victory more glorious than to be victorious over one's self and sin. There is no crown or triumph without victory, and no victory without struggle against enemies.

St. Tikhon of Zadonsk

VENERABLE EUTHYMIOS THE GREAT. Euthymios was born to a barren couple that had prayed for a child. An angel of God appeared to them, naming the child Euthymios, which means exaltation. The bishop of their Armenian town of Melitene taught the boy Christian theology, and at the age of nineteen, he was ordained a priest. He soon became a monastic and later lived in a cave where he attracted many disciples who also became saints, including Cyriac the Hermit and Savvas the Sanctified. His prayers could drive out demons, produce water in the desert, multiply bread, prophesy, and heal the sick. Once, an Arab boy paralyzed by an accident, was brought to him. Euthymios knelt beside him and prayed, and the healed boy stood up. He converted tribes of Nomads to Christianity. He foretold the death of Empress Eudocia and rescued her from the Monophysite heresy. He created a large monastery by his cave that survived for hundreds of years. His admonition to the monks was that the gates should never close but always offer loving hospitality. He died peacefully at ninety-seven years of age. The crowds took a whole day to pass by and give him a last kiss. The patriarch of Jerusalem buried him in the fifth century.

SAINTS OF THE DAY: Euthymios the Great; Leo I, Emperor of Byzantium; Inna, Pinna, and Rimma in Scythia; Euthymius Kereselidze of Georgia; Bassos, Eusebius, Eutychios, and Basilides at Nicomedia; Martyrs Thyrsos and Agnes; Peter the Publican of Constantinople; Anna at Rome; Euthymius, Patriarch of Turnovo, Bulgaria; Euthymius the Silent of the Kiev Caves; Laurence the Recluse of the Kiev Caves; New Martyr Zacharias of Patras; Theodore Kuzmich of Tomsk; Euthymius of Syanzhemsk; Euthymius of Archangelsk; Paul Dobromyslov of Ryazan.

Fifteenth Sunday of Luke
Fast-free
Philippians 1:12-20; Luke 19:1-10

JANUARY 21

If you want to tune in to God so He listens to you when you pray, turn the knob to humility, for on this frequency God always operates, and humbly ask for his mercy.

St. Paisios the Athonite

VIRGIN-MARTYR AGNES OF ROME. Agnes was a young woman in early fourth-century Rome, who taught Christianity to other women. She was beautiful, wealthy, and pursued in marriage. She denied them all saying that she intended to remain a virgin and a Christian. These same men who would have married Agnes reported her when the Christian persecutions began, hoping that she would renounce her faith. When she was threatened and shown the instruments of torture, she remained in good cheer. They could not even compel her hand to offer incense to the idols, as she continually crossed herself. Finally, the governor sent her to a brothel for shaming. Miraculously long thick hair grew out of her head to cover her body, and a heavenly light shown on her, which blinded anyone who approached her. Only one attempted to violate her, the son of the governor, and he fell down dead. Through her fervent prayers, Agnes restored him to life before his father. The governor proclaimed, "There is One God in the heavens and on earth—the Christian God, and the other gods be but dust and ashes!" Witnessing this miracle, 160 men believed and were baptized, but they soon were martyred by the pagans. The pagan priests demanded that Agnes be tortured, claiming she was a witch. She remained unharmed in a fire while praying to God, but was then killed with the sword.

SAINTS OF THE DAY: Maximos the Confessor and Anastasius; Neophytos of Nicaea; Zosimas of Syracuse; Agnes of Rome; Maximus the Greek; Eugene, Candidus, Valerian, and Aquila at Trebizond; Neophytos of Vatopedi; 4 Martyrs of Tyre; Timon of Kostroma; Fructuosis of Spain; Synaxis of the Church of Holy Peace by the Sea, Constantinople; "Consolation" and "The Stabbed" Icons of the Mother of God.

JANUARY 22

2 Timothy 1:3-8
Matthew 10:32-33, 37-38, 19:27-30

A sure sign of the deadening of the soul is the avoidance of church services.

St. John Climacus

VENERABLE MACARIUS OF ZHABYNSK. Macarius became a monk at a young age, taking the name Onuphrius. At the age of forty-six, he founded a monastery dedicated to the Mother of God's Entry into the Temple. Thirty years later, Polish soldiers destroyed the monastery. Afterward, while walking in the forest near his monastery, Onuphrius heard a faint moaning and came across a dying Polish soldier leaning against a tree. He was thirsty and separated from his unit. With his prayer, Onuphrius struck the ground with his walking staff, and a spring of water gushed forth, and he gave the dying man a drink. When the monastery was rebuilt, Onuphrius entrusted its guidance to a disciple. Onuphrius took the schema with the name Macarius. He became a hermit along the river Zhabynka, where he continued his ascetic struggles in secret. He died eight years later and was buried across from the monastery, where a church was built dedicated to him. Almost two hundred years passed, and the monastery became deserted. However, the people of that area never lost their faith in Macarius. His relics were uncovered and found incorrupt. Late in the nineteenth century, the annual commemoration of the saint resumed. Later when a church was built and dedicated to the saint, Abbot Jonah of the monastery decided to uncover the saint's relics again. St. Macarius appeared to the abbot in a dream, warning him not to proceed with the uncovering, or there would be punishment.

SAINTS OF THE DAY: Apostle Timothy of the Seventy; Joseph Samakus the Sanctified of Crete; Anastasius the Persian; Manuel, Bishop of Adrianopole; Anastasius of the Kiev Caves; Macarius of Zhabynsk; Martyrs Manuel, George, Peter, Leontius, bishops, and Sionius, Gabriel, John, Leontus, and Parodus, presbyters, and 377 companions in Bulgaria; Brithwald of Wilton; Wendreda of March.

JANUARY 23

Philippians 2:20-21, 4:1-3; Mark 2:23-3:5

Be careful when you are in church.... You must know my child, that there are countless angels above the people in church and invisibly sing along with them. But when one of the faithful begins to joke, to talk about worldly things, or to comment about others, the angels who see him, drop the hymn and weep bitterly for his plight.

St. Nephon of Constantia

HIEROMARTYR CLEMENT, BISHOP OF ANCYRA, AND MARTYR AGATHANGELOS. Clement was born in Ancyra during the third century to a pagan father and a Christian mother. While still an infant, his father died, and at age twelve, his mother died. She predicted that Clement would receive a martyr's death for his belief in Christ. Clement was adopted and raised in the Christian faith. At age eighteen, he became a priest and was appointed bishop at the age of only twenty. He ate just bread and vegetables and had great restraint. Over 28 years, he was tormented by eleven different torturers, being taken from city to city as an example. Witnessing the saint's bravery and miraculous healings, many people believed in Christ. In prison, people flocked to him for guidance, healing, and Baptism. Clement's disciple Agathangelos wanted to suffer and die for Christ. After the death of Maximian, Agathangelos was beheaded, and Clement was set free from prison and taken to a cave church. He was soon killed by soldiers from the city of Ancyra who stormed the church. St. Clement was beheaded while offering Holy Communion.

SAINTS OF THE DAY: Clement, Bishop of Ancyra, and Agathangelos; Salamanes the Silent of the Euphrates; Dionysios of Olympus; Two Martyrs of Parion; Gennadius of Kostroma; Eusebius of Mt. Coryphe; Mausimas the Syrian; Seraphim, Eudokia, Ecaterine, and Militsa, of Moscow; Barlaam of Siberia; Commemoration of the Sixth Ecumenical Council; Translation of the relics of St. Theoctistus of Novgorod; Synaxis of All Saints of Kostroma.

JANUARY 24

Galatians 5:22-6:2; Mark 11:22-26

The fear of God makes a person wise. What is the fear of God? Not that one should be afraid of God, but to be afraid to sadden someone, to harm someone, to do them no wrong, and to not make accusations. This is wisdom. After all this, God will illumine you as to what to do in your life.

St. Sophia of Kleisoura

GERASIMUS, BISHOP OF PERM. Gerasimus was the third bishop of the newly-enlightened Zyryani people in the fifteenth century. He was a participant in the Church councils, condemning the Unia. He was relentless in caring and protecting his newly established flock that had suffered raids from the Novgorodians and the pagan Vogulians. Gerasimus would fearlessly show up in the enemy camps urging them to stop pillaging the villages of the Perm Christians who were defenseless. During a journey, Gerasimus was murdered by a Vogul servant, strangling him with his omophorion, according to tradition. Gerasimus was buried in the cathedral church of the first bishops of Perm.

SAINTS OF THE DAY: Babylas, Timothy, and Agapius of Sicily; Philo, Bishop of Carpasia; Zosimas of Cilicia; Gerasimus, Bishop of Perm; John of Kazan; Xenia, deaconess of Rome, and 2 female slaves; Xenia of St. Petersburg; Martyrs Hermogenes and Mamas; Neophytos the Recluse of Cyprus; Philip the presbyter and Barsimus of Syria and his two brothers; Paul, Pausirius, and Theodotian of Egypt; Macedonius of Mt. Silpius, near Antioch; Lupicinus of Gaul; Felician, Bishop of Foligno in Italy; Sophia of Shamordino Convent; Translation of the relics of St. Anastasius the Persian.

JANUARY 25

Hebrews 7:26-8:2; John 10:9-16

A pure heart passes through Heaven's gate with ease.

+Elder Amphilochios Makris of Patmos

GREGORY THE THEOLOGIAN, ARCHBISHOP OF CONSTANTINOPLE. Gregory's schoolmates in Athens included St. Basil the Great and Julian the Apostate. Gregory foretold on several occasions that Julian would one day persecute the Church. Following his education, Gregory was baptized, and together with Basil became monks. Gregory was later ordained to the priesthood. He helped his father who was the bishop of Nazianzus. Basil appointed Gregory bishop of Sasima, but Emperor Theodosius called him to Constantinople to head the reorganization of the Orthodox Church after the Arian heresy ravaged it. Gregory was bestowed the gift of words. He received the title of theologian for his theological writings on the Holy Trinity, interpretations of feast days, laudatory hymns, and discourses of reproach against various heretics, including: Macedonios, who taught that the Holy Spirit was created by God, Apollinacios, who taught that Jesus did not have a human soul, Julian the Apostate, and Arian. When Gregory participated in the Second Ecumenical Council, which was convened to resolve differences among prelates, he was voted Patriarch of Constantinople. When he wearied of the personal attacks against him, he retired to Nazianzus and wrote instructive books. He died peacefully at the age of seventy. His relics are in Rome and Moscow.

SAINTS OF THE DAY: Gregory the Theologian; Moses of Novgorod; Gabriel of Imereti; Castinus of Byzantium; Apollo of Thebes; Mares the Singer of Syria; Felicitas of Rome and 7 sons; Publius of Syria; Medula and companions; Bretanion of Romania; Demetrios Skevophylax of Constantinople; Anatole I of Optina; Gregory of Golutvin; Vladimir of Kiev; Auxentios of Constantinople; Praejectus of Clermont; Dwyn of Llandwyn; Athanasia (Lepeshkin) of Zosima Hermitage; Basil of Priluksk; Peter of Voronezh; Margaret (Gunaronulo) of Menzelino; "Assuage My Sorrow" and "Unexpected Joy" Icons of the Mother of God.

JANUARY 26

1 Peter 1:1-2:10; Mark 12:1-12

Love every man in spite of his falling into sin. Never mind the sins, but remember that the foundation of the man is the same—the image of God.

St. John of Kronstadt

NEW MARTYR MATUSHKA MARIA OF GATCHINA. Before the Russian Revolution of 1917, in the town of Gatchina, thirty miles from Petrograd, Maria suffered inflammation of the brain which left her whole body painfully immovable. She was in constant need of help but did not complain. She exhibited personality traits not characteristic of this illness. She became meek, humble, and submissive. She was in constant prayer. As a reward, the Lord sent her the gift of consoling those who sorrow. Unknown people with grief, despondency, and depression would visit her, and they would leave comforted and alleviated of their pain. Maria was tonsured and given the schema in the presence of many bishops, priests, and deacons. Her words helped many people. She said that depression is a spiritual cross. It is sent to help the penitents who do not know how to repent. One must either learn to repent or bear this cross with humility and gratitude to the Lord. When one comes to contrition, the depression gradually melts. On February 8, 1930, many monastics and believers throughout Russia were accused and arrested for counter-revolutionary propaganda. Maria was dragged from her bed on the second floor with her arms twisted behind her back. Her body was swung into the truck, and she was taken to Leningrad, where she remained two months before her death. Matushka Maria is buried in the Smolensk cemetery.

SAINTS OF THE DAY: Xenophon, Mary, John, and Arcadios of Constantinople; Symeon the Ancient; Ammon of Egypt; Ananias, Peter, and 7 soldiers in Phoenicia; Joseph of Thessalonica; Clement of Mt. Sagmation; David IV the Restorer of Georgia; Gabriel, at Jerusalem; Paula of Rome; 2 Martyrs of Phrygia; Xenophon of Novgorod; Joseph of Romania; Cyril of Kazan; Maria of Gatchina; Conon, on the Isle of Man.

JANUARY 27

Hebrews 7:26-8:2; John 10:9-16

It is better to err by excess of mercy than by excess of severity... Do you will to become a Saint? Be severe to yourself but kind to others.

St. John Chrysostom

DEMETRIUS KLEPININE OF PARIS. Demetrius was the priest and spiritual father of St. Maria of Paris in the twentieth century. He was from an educated and devout Orthodox family. His mother helped establish Orthodox schools in Odessa and provided help and support to the city's poor. The family left Russia after the Communist revolution and finally settled in Paris. Demetrius enrolled in the St. Sergius Theological Institute in Paris and later at the New York Protestant Theological Seminary. He returned to Paris married and was ordained to the priesthood. He was assigned as the parish priest at the shelter for the poor operated by St. Maria Skobtsova. During this timeframe, the German Nazis invaded France, and they began mass arrests of French Jews in 1942. Many Jews sought help and refuge at St. Maria's shelter. To avoid deportation to the concentration camps, many tried to obtain baptismal certificates from Father Demetrius. He reasoned, "If a man surprised by a storm takes shelter in a church, do I have the right to close the door?" The Gestapo realized what Father Demetrius was doing, so he turned himself into the authorities. He was sent to a prison camp and continued to function as a priest. After a year, he was sent to the Buchenwald concentration camp in Germany and then to the camp at Dora. With his health broken, and suffering from pneumonia, he died in 1944. His body was cremated at Buchenwald.

SAINTS OF THE DAY: Peter of Egypt; Marciana the Empress; Venerable Claudinus; New Hieromartyr Peter of Russia; Leonty of Ivanovo; New Martyr Demetrius at Constantinople; Demetrius Klepinine of Paris; Translation of the relics of St. John Chrysostom.

SUNDAY

Sunday of the Publican and Pharisee
Triodion Begins
Fast-free week

JANUARY 28

Galatians 5:22-6:2; Luke 18:10-14

Silence unites you to God Himself.

St. Isaac the Syrian

VENERABLE JACOB (JAMES) THE ASCETIC. In the fourth century, Jacob left all worldly things, and for fifteen years lived as an ascetic in a cave near the village of Porphyreon in Palestine. He led a life of prayer and mortification of the flesh, and God granted him the gift of miracle-working. He received many visitors. Lecherous men once sent a prostitute to him to incite him to sin. In order to resist the temptation, Jacob kept his left hand plunged in a fire. This caused the woman to repent and believe in Jesus Christ. Jacob's fame soon spread, and many more visitors came to see him. He soon fell into the sin of pride. About this time, a nobleman brought his demon-possessed daughter to the saint for healing. Jacob prayed, and she was immediately healed, but for fear that the demon might return, the father left his daughter and son in a nearby cave. Overcome with desire, Jacob violated the girl. To hide his sin, he killed the two and threw them into a nearby river. In complete despair and concerned for his salvation, Jacob hastened his return to the world. On his way, he met a pious elder who told him that God would have mercy. Jacob came upon an old sepulcher, and shut himself in and began to pray humbly. For ten years he suffered every type of torment and hardship. Only at night did he go out to eat some plants that grew nearby. Much later, when a severe drought struck the land, God directed the bishop of the city to find Jacob who was shut in a tomb, for only his prayer would end the drought. The bishop and all the people went to Jacob and convinced him to pray for them. As soon as he prayed, the rain began to fall. From this sign, Jacob received hope that his sin would be forgiven. He gave up his soul at the age of seventy-five.

SAINTS OF THE DAY: Ephraim the Syrian; Isaac the Syrian; Ephraim of Pereyaslavl; Palladius of Antioch; John of Reomans; Theodosius of Totma; Ignatius of Skopin; Leontius of Jablechna; Arsenius of Tashkent.

JANUARY 29

Hebrews 10:32-38; Mark 9:33-41

Who sits in solitude and is quiet hath escaped from three wars: hearing, speaking, seeing: yet against one thing shall he continually battle: that is, his own heart.

St. Anthony the Great

MARTYRS PHILOTHEOS, HYPERECHIOS, HABIB, JULIAN, ROMANOS, JAMES, AND PARIGOREAS AT SAMOSATA. These seven saints lived in the third-century town of Samosata in Turkey during the Christian persecutions of the ruthless Emperor Diocletian. Once before a battle against the Persians, all the citizens were required to worship at the Temple of Fortune. Philotheos and Hyperechios, magistrates of the city of Samosata, refused and went instead to pray at a chapel. With them was Habib, Julian, Romanos, James, and Parigoreas. When the emperor learned that Philotheos and Hyperechios did not offer the public sacrifice, soldiers were sent to apprehend them. All seven men were tortured, and still, they refused to sacrifice. Their arms and thighs were broken with thick rods, and their skin was flayed. They were stretched on the rack and given stripes. Bound in heavy chains, they were imprisoned. For over two months they were left in prison to starve. They were invited again to offer sacrifice, but they said they would not deny Jesus Christ. The emperor ordered seven crosses to be set up near the city gates. The martyrs were suspended, and their heads were nailed to the wood. Orders were given to throw their bodies in the river, but a Christian named Bassus bought their bodies and buried them by night.

SAINTS OF THE DAY: Silvanus of Emesa, Luke the Deacon, and Mocius the Reader; Sarbelos and Bebaia of Edessa; Barsimaeus the Confessor; Gerasimus, Pitirim, and Jonah, of Perm; Seven Martyrs of Samosata; Aphrahates of Persia; Laurence of the Kiev Caves; Ignatius of Smolensk; Demetrios of Chios; Ashot Kuropalates of Tao-Klardjeti; Righteous Acepsimas; Gildas of Brittany; Severus of Gaul; John, Leontius, Constantine, and 5 martyrs with them; Translation of the relics of St. Ignatius the God-bearer.

Tuesday

January 30

Synaxis of the Three Hierarchs
Fast-free
Hebrews 13:7-16; Matthew 5:14-19

Those who fear God are the furthest from telling lies because they have their conscience as an honest judge.

St. John Climacus

"TINOS" ICON OF THE MOTHER OF GOD. The Most Holy Mother of God once appeared to an old man on the island of Tinos, telling him to dig in a certain field to find her Annunciation icon in the foundation of an ancient church. Then she disappeared. Only two people in the town believed the old man, and they dug a whole night finding only a part of the church wall. Then St. Pelagia, who was then an 80-year-old nun, had the same dream three times. She was instructed to go to a wealthy man in the village named Mr. Kangades, to enlist his help in the search. Kangades went to Bishop Gabriel, who in turn wrote to all the churches of Tinos for their help. The foundation of the church was uncovered, but the money ran out, and no icon was found. Again, the Most Holy Mother of God appeared to Pelagia, and she went to the bishop. He went to the people to raise funds to build a new church on the old foundation. The church was built, and when the ground was being prepared for a stone floor, a worker's pick struck the icon splitting it in two. The icon was repaired, cleaned, and given to the bishop. This miraculous icon has been the source of a multitude of healings and deliverance from danger.

SAINTS OF THE DAY: Synaxis of the Three Hierarchs: Basil the Great, Gregory the Theologian, and John Chrysostom; Hippolytus of Rome, with Censorinus, Sabinus, Ares, Chryse, Felix, Maximus, and others, at Ostia; Zeno of Antioch; Zeno the Faster of the Kiev Caves; Grand Dukes Paul Alexandrovic and Dimitri Konstantinovich, and Eugene Poselianin; Adelgonda of Maubeuge; Demetrius of Sliven; Peter, King of Bulgaria; Hadji Theodore of Mytilene; Theophilus the New; Theophil, fool-for-Christ; Pelagia of Diveyevo; Bathild, Queen of France; "Tinos" Icon of the Mother of God.

JANUARY 31

1 Corinthians 12:27-13:8
Matthew 10:1, 5-8

Do not forsake prayer, for just as the body becomes weak when it is deprived of food, so also the soul when it is deprived of prayer draws nigh to weakness and noetic death.

St. Gennadios of Constantinople

NICETAS OF THE KIEV CAVES, BISHOP OF NOVGOROD. Nicetas was a monk at the end of the eleventh century in Russia. He learned about the dangers of being disobedient to one's spiritual father. He asked once if he could live alone, apart from the brothers. Even though he was denied permission, he departed. The devil deceived him by appearing as an angel of light, telling him to cease praying and begin reading books. Nicetas bowed down to him. Without a spiritual father with discernment, he followed the devil's instructions. He read the Old Testament but was physically restrained from reading the New Testament. When the brothers surmised that Nicetas was possessed, they prayed for him, and the devil was driven out. After this, Nicetas lived in strict fasting and prayer and practiced obedience and humility. Through the prayers of his elders, the Lord forgave Nicetas. After some time, he was made bishop in Novgorod. For his holy life, God granted him the gift to work miracles. He served his flock for thirteen years and died peacefully.

SAINTS OF THE DAY: Cyrus and John the Unmercenaries, and with them Martyrs Athanasia and her daughters Theoctiste, Theodota, and Eudoxia, at Canopus in Egypt; Tryphaina at Cyzicus; Victorinus, Victor, Nicephorus, Claudius, Diodorus, Serapion, and Papias of Egypt; Nicetas of the Kiev Caves; Marcella of Rome; Pachomius of Keno Lake; Athanasius, Bishop of Methone; Arsenius the New of Paros; New Martyr Elias Ardunis of Mt. Athos and Kalamata.

Let us consider the patience of holy men and women, how they willingly endured long periods of fasting, vigil and various other physical hardships as though they were not in the body, battling to the end against evil passions and all sorts of sin, in the invincible inner warfare against principalities, powers and spiritual wickedness.

St. Gregory Palamas

Forefeast of the Presentation
Fast-free
Romans 8:28-39; Luke 10:19-21

February 1

The Name of Jesus is sweet to utter. It casts out the demons and brings the angels back into the heart, into the mind, and you will bear yourself in meekness before others.

+Elder George Calciu of Romania

SEIRIOL, ABBOT OF PENMON. Seiriol was from fifth-century Wales. He was the son of King Owain Danwyn and the younger brother of King Cynlas of Rhos and King Einion of Lleyn. Seiriol became a monk in a small hermitage, in a place known today as Anglesey, Wales. His brothers later decided that his humble cell was too lowly for Seiriol, so they founded an important monastery around his cell. Seiriol became the first abbot of Penmon Priory, and this hermitage can still be seen there today. Other hermits and monks soon followed, and a small community of solitaries was created. This monastery was still attracting monastics six centuries later when Gerald of Wales visited Penmon with Archbishop Baldwin of Canterbury. In Gerald's "Journey Through Wales," he writes that when any discord arose within that monastery, a species of small mice that infested the island would eat all their provisions, but when the discord ceased, they were no longer molested. Seiriol became a great friend of St. Cybi who lived on the other side of the island. They often walked several miles to meet up for prayers at the center of the island. Seiriol walked with his back to the sun, so his skin remained fair. On the other hand, St. Cybi was tanned, as he walked in the opposite direction with his face to the sun. St. Seiriol died in the mid-sixth century at the age of fifty-six.

SAINTS OF THE DAY: Perpetua, Felicitas, Saturus, Revocatus, Saturninus, and Secundulus of Carthage; Basil, Archbishop of Thessalonica; Peter of Galatia; Tryphon of Campsada; Brigid of Kildare; Tryphon of Pechenga; Bendimianus of Bithynia; Martyr Carion; Theion with two children at Kariona; Elias the New of Damascus; Timothy the Confessor; David, Symeon, and George of Mitylene; Seiriol of Penmon; Tryphon, Bishop of Rostov; Anastasios at Nauplion.

FRIDAY

Presentation of Our Lord
Fast-free
Hebrews 7:7-17; Luke 2:22-40

FEBRUARY 2

The work of our salvation depends on our volition, on God's help, and on cooperation. But the latter will not follow if the first does not precede it.

St. Ambrose of Optina

PRESENTATION OF THE LORD IN THE TEMPLE. The custom of presenting a child to God forty days after its birth is one of the most ancient feasts of the Christian Church. St. John the Baptist's father, Zacharias, was the chief priest of the temple. A righteous man named Symeon lived in Jerusalem during this time. The Holy Spirit told him that he would not see death until he beheld Christ the Savior. It was revealed to him to go to the temple at the very moment that the Mother of God and Righteous Joseph brought the Infant Jesus. Symeon responded, "Lord, now You are letting Your servant depart in peace, according to Your word, for my eyes have seen Your salvation (Luke 2:29-30)." It was said that he was about 250 years old. Then Anna, who was a prophetess and widow of about eighty-four years of age, saw Jesus "And coming in that instant she gave thanks to the Lord, and spoke of Him to all those who looked for redemption in Jerusalem (Luke 2:38)." Soon after, an angel of God directed Joseph to take Jesus and the Theotokos into Egypt to escape Herod's soldiers, who were sent to kill the baby, Jesus.

SAINTS OF THE DAY: Anthimos of Chios; Agathodoros of Tyana in Cappadocia; New Martyr Gabriel at Constantinople; Jordan of Trebizond, at Constantinople.

FEBRUARY 3

Hebrews 9:11-14; Luke 2:25-38

The ladder to the Kingdom is hidden within you, and within your soul. Dive down into your self, away from sin, and there you will find the steps by which you can ascend.

St. Isaac the Syrian

VENERABLE WERBURGA OF CHESTER. Werburga was the daughter of King Wulfhere of Mercia. She was pious and virtuous and learned the Christian faith from her mother. Her beauty attracted many admirers, but she refused all her suitors. After much persuasion, Werburga received her father's permission to enter a convent. She traveled to the Abbey of Ely and was met at the gate by her aunt, the royal abbess Ethelreda, and her nuns. Werburga fell on her knees and asked to be received as a novice. She progressed well, and after many years was chosen to oversee all the convents of the kingdom. Under her guidance, they became models of monastic discipline. She also founded new convents and established the church of St. John the Baptist in Chester. Werburga converted many from a life of dissipation and vice. Her work was anchored on prayer and discipline. She ate one meal daily and recited the whole Psalter daily on her knees. Her example was the desert fathers. She lived into old age, and before her death, she visited all her convents to bid each farewell. Her shrine in Leicester attracted many pilgrims. Because of the invading Danes, her relics were moved to Chester, where a great church was later built over them. Deep niches remain near her tomb where pilgrims knelt to seek healing. The shrine was largely destroyed by King Henry VIII. Twelve English churches were dedicated to St. Werburga.

SAINTS OF THE DAY: Symeon the God-receiver and Anna the Prophetess; Prophet Azarias; James of Serbia; Nicholas of Japan; Symeon of Polotsk; Ansgar of Hamburg; Blaise of Caesarea; Papias, Diodorus, and Claudianus at Perga; Adrian and Eubulus at Caesarea; Sabbas of Ioannina; Paul the Syrian; Sviatoslav-Gabriel and Dimitry of Yuriev; Nicholas, Stamatios, and John of Chios; Romanus of Uglich; James of Serbia; Vladimir of Borisoglebsk.

SUNDAY

Sunday of the Prodigal Son
Fast-free

FEBRUARY 4

1 Corinthians 6:12-20
Luke 15:11-32

A bad word makes bad even the good, but a good word makes good even the bad.

St. Macarius the Great

HIEROMARTYR PHILEAS AND MARTYR PHILOROMUS THE MAGISTRATE. Phileas was a wealthy nobleman of Thmuis in Egypt. He was eloquent and learned. He was converted to Christianity and chosen the bishop of that city, but he was arrested and imprisoned in fourth-century Alexandria. From the dungeon, he wrote a letter about the suffering condition of his fellow prisoners, saying they were beaten by rods, whips, and clubs. They were torn with iron hooks and hung by one or both hands. No treatment was too bad for Christians. The governor who interrogated Phileas ardently wanted to spare him because Phileas had many riches. Phileas defended the divinity of Christ with proof of the Lord's many miracles. The governor pointed out the sorrow of Phileas' wife, but he replied, "Jesus Christ, the Savior of souls, calls me to his glory; and he can also, if he pleases, call my wife." He said it was his unchangeable resolution to die for Jesus. Then all the counselors present, the emperor's lieutenant, all the officers of justice, and his relations, fell down together at his feet, asking him to have compassion and not to abandon his children. But Phileas stood unmoved, saying the apostles and martyrs were his only kindred. A Christian named Philoromus spoke before the assembly defending Phileas. The whole assembly was outraged and condemned him to die with Phileas. At the site of the execution, Phileas prayed aloud, exhorting the faithful to constancy and perseverance, and the two were beheaded.

SAINTS OF THE DAY: Isidore of Pelusium; Nicholas the Confessor; Abramios of Arbela; Lucius, in Africa; Jadorus and Isidore; John of Irenopolis; Martyr Theoktistos; Iasimos, wonderworker; George of Vladimir; Joseph of Aleppo; Abraham and Coprius of Pechenga; Phileas and Philoromus; Evagrius of Tsikhedidi; Cyril of New Lake; Modan of Stirling; Aldate of Gloucester; Methodius of Petropavlovsk; Theodosios of Chudov.

FEBRUARY 5

1 John 2:18-29, 3:1-8; Mark 11:1-11

We are not battling with a man, whom you can kill in many ways, but with the powers and rulers of darkness. They are not fought with sweets and marshmallows, but with streams of tears, with pain of soul until death, with utter humility, and with great patience. Blood must flow from over-exhaustion in saying the prayer… And you must not give up the fight, until the demons are beaten and withdraw. Then you will receive freedom from the passions.

+Elder Joseph the Hesychast

HOLY MARTYR AGATHA OF PALERMO IN SICILY. Agatha was the daughter of rich and respected Christian parents from the third-century city of Palermo. During the Christian persecutions of Emperor Decius, the governor of the city, Centianus, heard about the beauty and wealth of the fifteen-year-old Agatha. He sent his soldiers to bring her to trial as a Christian. Through flattery and threats, she was urged to offer sacrifice to the pagan gods, but she refused. She was subjected to cruel tortures. The Apostle Peter appeared to her in prison, and healing her wounds he said, "I heal thee by the grace of Christ." The next day she was chained and thrown into burning coals. She prayed, and a violent earthquake struck the city. The people threatened the governor's life if he continued to torture Agatha. Fearing the people, he returned Agatha to prison, where she prayed and gave up her soul. When Centianus heard about her death, he went to take control of her lands. But while crossing a river on horseback with two soldiers, one of the horses reared up and struck Centianus, trampling him to death.

SAINTS OF THE DAY: Polyeuctus of Constantinople; Theodosius of Chernigov; Agatha of Palermo; Anthony of Athens; Theodosios of Skopelos; Agatha, Eugene, and Paramon of Belorussia; Gregory and Valeriu of Romania; Avitus of Vienne; Alexandra and Michael; "In Search of the Perishing," "Eletsk-Chernigov," and "Sicilian" Icons of the Mother of God.

February 6

Hebrews 7:26-8:2; John 10:9-16

Holy Scripture forbids the veneration of sculpted figures and deities. This prohibition refers to the veneration of idols. The law however does not forbid the veneration of certain signs and representations of God and His holy ones, since this honour does not pertain to the material from which they were constructed but rather, via the holy visage which is depicted, our thoughts ascend to God... Just as we are helped by the word to ascend beyond the word, so too are we led by the icons to rise above the icons. Correspondingly, just as God wants our hearing to be made holy through spiritual discourse, so too he wants our sight to be made holy via the holy icons, so that by way of these two superior senses there enters into the soul pure thoughts.

+Elder Cleopa of Romania

VENERABLE BUCOLOS, BISHOP OF SMYRNA. From his youth, Bucolos kept himself pure, and the Holy Spirit dwelled within him. He was a disciple of St. John the Theologian, who consecrated Bucolos as the first bishop of the Smyrna Church in Asia Minor. Bucolos enlightened the Greeks of Smyrna, baptizing them and freeing them from wild and dark demons. Then, seeing his own end, he consecrated St. Polycarp as his successor. At the grave of St. Bucolos, a myrtle tree grew, which healed the sick.

SAINTS OF THE DAY: Barsanuphius the Great and John the Prophet of Palestine; Bucolos, Bishop of Smyrna; Photios, Patriarch of Constantinople; Dorothea of Caesarea, and with her Christina, Callista, and Theophilus; James of Kyros; Julian of Emesa; Fausta, Evilasius, and Maximus at Cyzicus; Dorothea of Kashin; John of Thebes; Arsenius of Iqalto, Georgia; Amand, apostle of Maastricht; Vedast, Bishop of Arras; Mael, Bishop of Ardagh; Basil Nadezhnin of Moscow.

February 7

1 John 3:21-4:11; Mark 14:43-72, 15:1

Don't be deceived regarding the knowledge of what will be after your death: what you sow here, you will reap there. After leaving here, no one can make progress. Here is the work, there the reward; here the struggle, there the crowns.

St. Barsanuphius the Great

VENERABLE PARTHENIOS, BISHOP OF LAMPSACUS ON THE HELLESPONT. Parthenios was the illiterate son of a church deacon in the city of Melitopolis in Asia Minor. However, he comprehended Holy Scripture by attending church for the Divine services. He worked for a fisherman, and the money he earned he gave to the poor. For his virtuous life, God granted Parthenios the gift of miracles. At just the age of eighteen, he healed the sick and cast out demons. When Bishop Philip of Melitopolis saw the life Parthenios lived, he gave him an education and ordained him to the priesthood. During the reign of Emperor Constantine the Great, Parthenios was made the bishop of Lampsacus. Emperor Constantine received him with honor and assigned him the task of destroying pagan temples and replacing them with churches. Parthenios healed all the sick of bodily illnesses and unclean spirits. In the name of Christ, he cast out a host of demons from people and homes, thus showing the people the great power of faith in Christ. A multitude of idol-worshippers were converted. Parthenios died peacefully in the fourth century and was buried in the cathedral church of Lampsacus.

SAINTS OF THE DAY: Parthenios, Bishop of Lampsacus on the Hellespont; Aprionus, Bishop of Cyprus; Augulius, Bishop of Brittany; The 1,003 Martyrs of Nicomedia; Six martyrs of Phrygia; Mastridia of Jerusalem, woman ascetic of the desert; Luke of Mt. Steirion; Theopemptus and his brotherhood; Peter of Monovatia; Euthymius of Glinsk; New Martyr George of Crete; Richard, King of Wessex; Roman, Bishop of Kilmaronen; Barlaam Ryashentsev, Archbishop of Perm.

FEBRUARY 8

Ephesians 2:4-10; Matthew 10:16-22

When monks carry the prayer rope in their hands, it serves as a reminder of their obligation to pray unceasingly, in keeping with the commandment of the Holy Apostle Paul to "pray without ceasing." Anyone can keep a prayer rope in a pocket or some other discreet place where it can be easily used unnoticed when in situations where it is better to pray or remember prayer in secret, without attracting the attention of others. The prayer rope can also be placed over the head of our bed, in an automobile, with a small cross or icon, or in other appropriate places as a reminder of prayer and a kind of blessing and a holy and godly presence in our lives.

St. Ignatius Brianchaninov

SABBAS II, ARCHBISHOP OF SERBIA. Sabbas II lived in the thirteenth century. He was given the name Predislav at birth. He was the youngest son of the first crowned king of Serbia Stephen. His uncle was St. Sava IV, and together with the king built monasteries on Mt. Athos, Serbia, and the Holy Land. Following his uncle's example, Sabbas accepted monasticism and struggled as an ascetic in Jerusalem and on Mt. Athos. He was chosen to become the archbishop of Serbia following St. Arsenius. He ruled the Serbian Church with great love and was known for his humility and meekness. He died peacefully, and his relics are in the Serbian monastery in Pec.

SAINTS OF THE DAY: Theodore Stratelates the Commander, of Heraclea; Prophet Zechariah of the Twelve Minor Prophets; Sabbas II, Archbishop of Serbia; Conitus of Alexandria; Martha and Mary the sisters, and Lycarion the Child Martyr, of Egypt; Martyrs Nikephoros and Stephen; Martyrs Philadelphus and Polycarp; Martyr Pergetus; Macarios, Bishop of Paphos; John and Basil of the Kiev Caves; Lyubov of Ryazan, fool-for-Christ; Cuthman, hermit of Steyning; Kew, virgin of Cornwall; Agathangelus, Bishop of Damascus.

FRIDAY

Abstain from meat, dairy products, and fish.

FEBRUARY 9

2 John 1:1-13
Mark 15:20, 22, 25, 33-41

When the Enemy of your soul whispers, "you have lost all, you cannot be saved," answer him: "I do not despair of my salvation, for I have a compassionate and long-suffering God. And this conviction upholds me in my belief that He Who commanded that we forgive our fellow man for his transgressions against us even seven times seventy—that He, by the same token, will forgive the sins of all who with their whole souls turn to Him." With such reflections and with the Grace of God, most assuredly all warfare with Satan will depart from you.

St. Ephraim the Syrian

HIEROMARTYR PETER DAMASCENE OF DAMASCUS. Peter was an ascetic, living during the eighth-century reign of Constantine Copronymos. It is said that Peter collected wisdom as a bee collects honey. He never owned a book and was forced to borrow everything that he read. As bishop of Damascus, he spoke out forcefully against the heretical doctrines of the Arabs and Manichaeans, and for this, he was arrested by the caliph. His tongue was severed, and he was exiled to South Arabia. Miraculously he still spoke clearly and taught the true Faith, converting many. His life ended in martyrdom.

SAINTS OF THE DAY: Nicephorus of Antioch; Peter, Bishop of Damascus; Marcellus, Philagrius, and Pancratius, disciples of Apostle Peter; Aemilianus and Bracchio of Tours; Romanos the Wonderworker of Cilicia; Apollonia of Alexandria; Pancratius of the Kiev Caves; Gennadius and Nicephorus of Vazhe Lake (Vologda); Teilo, Bishop of Wales; Uncovering of the relics of St. Innocent of Irkutsk; Uncovering of the relics of St. Tikhon, Patriarch of Moscow and All Russia.

Commemoration of the Departed
Fast-free

FEBRUARY 10

2 Timothy 2:1-10
John 15:17-27, 16:1-2

The divine Scripture...says that the souls of the just are in God's hand and death cannot lay hold of them. For death is rather the sleep of the saints than their death... What then, is more precious than to be in the hand of God. For God is Life and Light, and those who are in God's hand are in life and light.

St. John of Damascus

VENERABLE PROCHOROS THE ORACH-EATER OF THE KIEV CAVES. Prochoros was a great ascetic at the Kiev-Pechersk monastery at the end of the eleventh century. Orach was a type of spinach grown in the mountains that was used to make bread during a famine that befell Russia. People were not able to eat this bread because of the bitterness. When Prochoros made this bread, he distributed it to the needy, and the bread was sweet. From that time, the spinach was only gathered with the blessing of Prochorus. This became known to people far and wide. At a time when there was a shortage of salt in Kiev, he blessed ashes, and they became salt, which he then gave to the needy. When the prince ordered Prochoros' stockpile of "salt" to be brought to him, they remained ashes. After three days, the prince discarded the ashes, but Prochoros blessed the people to take the ashes, and they became salt. This miracle converted the prince. Upon the death of St. Prochoros, the prince himself took the body and buried him in the Nearer Caves.

SAINTS OF THE DAY: Haralampus of Magnesia, and Porphyrius and Baptus; Anastasius II of Jerusalem; Anatole of Odessa; Zeno of Caesarea; Prochoros the Orach-eater; Ennatha, Valentina, and Paula of Palestine; John Chimchimeli of Bachkovo; Scholastica of Italy; Anna of Novgorod; Longinus of Vologda; Raphael and Ioannicius of Svatogorsk; Merwinna of Romsey; Synaxis of Novgorod Hierarchs: Joachim, Luke the Jew, Germanus, Arcadius, Gregory, Martyrius, Anthony, Basil, Moses, Symeon, Gennadius, Pimen, and Athonius; "Areovindus" Icon of the Mother of God.

SUNDAY

Meatfare Sunday
Fast-free

FEBRUARY 11

1 Corinthians 8:8-9:2
Matthew 25:31-46

Cleansing of our inner self cannot be accomplished without effort, as if we are just pushing buttons. The passions are not severed at once, just as the trunk of a large tree can't be severed with one stroke of the saw. The saw has to go back and forth for a long time before the trunk is cut through. And the work does not stop there. It takes so much work to turn the trunk into furniture! First, it has to be sawed into planks; and then worked and shaped by a skilled carpenter, in order to be made into useful furniture.

St. Paisios the Athonite

EMPRESS THEODORA, PROTECTRESS OF ORTHODOXY. Theodora was the wife of Emperor Theophilos the Iconoclast in ninth-century Constantinople. He favored the elimination of icons as he saw them as a form of idolatry. Theodora secretly kept the icons, praying before them. When the emperor died, Theodora governed the realm together with her minor son Michael III. She convened a Council to restore the veneration of icons, and the iconoclasts were anathematized. This marked the end of the 150-year war between the Iconophiles (supporters of icons) and the Iconoclasts. This decision started the celebration of the Triumph of Orthodoxy, which is celebrated the first Sunday of Great Lent. When Michael came of age, Theodora retired to a monastery, where she devoted herself to ascetic deeds and the reading of Divine books. She died peacefully. In the fifteenth century, the fragrant and incorrupt relics of St. Theodora were taken to Kerkyra, and remain there today in the Church of the Most Holy Theotokos Speliotissa. Every year on the Sunday of Orthodoxy, there is a procession of her holy relics throughout the city.

SAINTS OF THE DAY: Blaise, Bishop of Sebaste; Theodora the Empress; Lucius of Adrianopole; George of Kratovo; Demetrius of Priluki Monastery; Vsevolod (Gabriel) of Pskov; Gobnait of Ireland; Caedmon of Whitby; Benedict of Aniane; Finding of the relics of Prophet Zacharias, father of St. John the Baptist; "Corfu" Icon of the Mother of God.

 Abstain from meat products.

FEBRUARY 12

3 John 1:1-15
Luke 19:29-40, 22:7-39

Do we forgive our neighbors their trespasses? God also forgives us in His mercy. Do we refuse to forgive? God, too, will refuse to forgive us. As we treat our neighbors, so also does God treat us. The forgiveness, then, of your sins or un-forgiveness, and hence also your salvation or destruction, depend on you yourself, man. For without forgiveness of sins there is no salvation. You can see for yourself how terrible it is.

St. Tikhon of Zadonsk

MELETIOS, ARCHBISHOP OF ANTIOCH. Meletios was one of the main opponents of the Arian heresy in the fourth century. Arius, an Egyptian priest, convinced many that Jesus Christ had been created; therefore, His Divinity and the Holy Trinity were in question. Even the other bishops of Antioch were Arians and succeeded in removing Meletios as archbishop on three different occasions. However, Meletios convened and presided over the Second Ecumenical Council of Constantinople. Raising up his hand, he displayed three fingers, and conjoining together two fingers and bending the one, he blessed the people, proclaiming, "We apprehend three hypostatic-persons, and we speak about one self-same nature," and immediately a lightning bolt flashed from his fingers before the entire Council. During the time of this Council, Meletios gave up his soul. Arianism was condemned, and Arius excommunicated.

SAINTS OF THE DAY: Meletios, Archbishop of Antioch; Anthony II, Patriarch of Constantinople; Alexis, Metropolitan of Moscow; Meletius, Archbishop of Kharkov; Mary, called Marinus, and her father Eugene, at Alexandria; Alexius, Bishop of Voronezh; Martyrs Plotinus and Saturninus; Bassian of Uglich; Nicholas Dvali, Prochorus the Georgian, Luke of Jerusalem, and the Holy Fathers of the Georgian monasteries in Jerusalem; Chrestos at Constantinople; Meletios of Rhodes; Urbanus of Rome; Ethilwald of Lindisfarne; Gertrude of Nijvel; Callia of Serbia; Appearance of the "Iveron" Icon of the Mother of God (Mt. Athos).

 Abstain from meat products.

February 13

Jude 1:1-10
Luke 22:39-42, 45-71, 23:1

He who loves God will certainly love his neighbor as well. Such a person cannot hoard money, but distributes it in a way befitting God, being generous to everyone in need.

St. Maximos the Confessor

NEW HIEROMARTYR SILVESTER, BISHOP OF OMSK. Silvester graduated from the Kiev theological academy and was appointed diocesan missionary for Kiev and Poltava, and teacher in the theological seminary. He was also president of the diocesan council and inspector of church schools. Over the next twenty years, he served in many other capacities. He was consecrated bishop of Priluki in 1911 by Metropolitan Vladimir of Moscow, together with other hierarchs. Seven years later, he was raised to the rank of archbishop. In 1920, there was a decree on the separation of Church and State, and the Bolsheviks demanded that Silvester hand over the administration of the Church, its property, the building and its equipment, as well as the archbishop's residence. One night in February, an armed detachment of sailors began breaking down the doors of Silvester's house. When the Red Army arrived, they shot and killed Silvester's cell attendant. They seized Silvester at gunpoint, and without allowing him to put on warm clothing, they led him through the Siberian night. After enduring many sufferings, Silvester died in prison in Omsk.

SAINTS OF THE DAY: Eulogios I, Patriarch of Alexandria; Martinian of Caesarea in Palestine; Aquila and Priscilla, Apostles of the Seventy; Symeon the Myrrh-gusher of Hilander; Zoe of Bethlehem and Virgin Photina; Joseph of Volokolamsk; a father and son, crucified; Timothy, Patriarch of Alexandria; George, Archbishop of Mogilev; Modomnoc of Ossory; Castor of Karden, Germany; Huna of Huneya; Ermenhilda of Ely; Seraphim (Sobolev) of Bogucharsk; Silvester (Olshevsky) of Omsk; Translation of the relics of St. Edward, King of England.

 Abstain from meat products.

February 14

Joel 3:12-21; Joel 2:12-26

Oh, if you only knew what happened to the Lord on Wednesday and Friday, you would put nothing in your mouth. Neither bread, nor oil. Do not break the fast of Wednesday and Friday.

St. Sophia of Kleisoura

VENERABLE AUXENTIOS, MONK OF BITHYNIA. Auxentios was born into a military family. Known as a wise and learned man, he served at the court of Emperor Theodosius the Younger in the fifth century. He helped to fight off the invading barbarians who tried to overrun Constantinople. Troubled by worldly vanity, he resigned his commission and studied with clergy, theologians, and monastics. At last, he received monastic tonsure and found a solitary place on a mountain where he could struggle in asceticism. One day some shepherds stumbled upon Auxentios, and soon people began to come to him for healing. Out of humility, he would ask the others present to pray for the sick, always deflecting the attention away from himself. His prayers healed all manner of illness, and he drove out demons. Emperor Marcian invited Auxentios to the Fourth Ecumenical Council at Chalcedon, where he powerfully spoke against the Nestorian and Eutychian heresies. When the Council finished, he returned to his mountain. He died peacefully in great old age, leaving behind many disciples and monasteries that he founded.

SAINTS OF THE DAY: Auxentios of Bithynia; Cyril, Equal-to-the-Apostles and teacher of the Slavs; Peter, Patriarch of Alexandria; Abraham, Bishop of Charres; Philemon, Bishop of Gaza; Theodore of Chernigov; Maron of Syria; George the Tailor of Mytilene; Nicholas of Corinth; Hilarion the Georgian; Isaac of the Kiev Caves; Damian the New of Philotheou and Kissavos, at Larissa; Onisimus, Bishop of Tula; The 12 Greek Master-builders of the Dormition Cathedral in the Kievan Caves.

FEBRUARY 15

Philemon 1:1-25
Luke 23:1-31, 33, 44-56

How mistaken are those people who seek happiness outside of themselves, in foreign lands and journeys, in riches and glory, in great possessions and pleasures, in diversions and vain things, which have a bitter end! It is the same thing to construct the tower of happiness outside of ourselves as it is to build a house in a place that is consistently shaken by earthquakes. Happiness is found within ourselves, and blessed is the man who has understood this. Happiness is a pure heart, for such a heart becomes the throne of God. Thus says Christ of those who have pure hearts: "I will visit them, and will walk in them, and I will be a God to them, and they will be my people." (II Cor. 6:16) What can be lacking to them? Nothing, nothing at all! For they have the greatest good in their hearts: God Himself!

St. Nectarios of Aegina

VENERABLE EUSEBIOS THE HERMIT. Eusebios was a fifth-century hermit from Syria. He wisely began his monastic life under the direction of spiritual elders. He lived in solitude on a mountain and led a rigorous life. He endured the heat and cold, wearing only animal skins. His food was vegetables and beans. When people began to visit him, he moved to a nearby monastery and built himself a small enclosure, and dwelled there until his death at the age of ninety.

SAINTS OF THE DAY: Apostle Onesimos of the Seventy; Anthimos of Chios; Major of Gaza; Oswy, King of Northumbria; Eusebios of Syria; Paphnutius of the Kiev Caves; Dalmatus, abbot in Siberia; New Hieromartyrs Michael Piataev and John Kumin, priests; New Hieromartyr Priests Nicholas, Alexis, Alexis, and Simeon the deacon; New Hieromartyr Paul (Kozlov) of St. Nilus Hermitage (Tver) and Virgin-martyr Sophia; Theognius, Bishop of Bethelia; Synaxis of St. John the Theologian at Diaconissa; "Vilensk" and "Dalmatian" Icons of the Mother of God.

FEBRUARY 16

Zechariah 8:7:17; Zechariah 8:19-23

When a soul is distressed, it looks for comfort everywhere. The afflicted soul doesn't want to be concerned about many things. It only wants peace and stillness. It is content to be done with the present things, even if nothing else follows. So then, don't sink in your afflictions, but give thanks in everything so that you may profit from them and please God.

St. John Chrysostom

MARTYRS ELIAS, JEREMIAH, ISAIAH, SAMUEL, AND DANIEL, AT CAESAREA IN PALESTINE. The fourth-century emperors Maximian and Maximus continued the Christian persecutions begun by Emperor Diocletian in the third century. Five men from Egypt went to visit the Christians who had been condemned to work in the gold mines in Cilicia. On their return journey, they were detained and thrown into prison for confessing Christ. They were brought before the governor Firmilian, who questioned where they were from. They answered Jerusalem, meaning the heavenly Jerusalem, the country of all Christians, but Firmilian did not know this city Jerusalem since at this time it was named Eleia-Adrian. He ordered his soldiers to stretch the youths on the rack and to suffer all manner of torture. He asked them again to tell him the location of this unknown city and to deny their Christian faith. When they would not, the governor ordered their beheading by the sword.

SAINTS OF THE DAY: Pamphilus, Paul, Valens, Seleucus, Porphyrius, Julian, Theodoulos, Elias, Jeremiah, Isaiah, Samuel, and Daniel, at Caesarea in Palestine; Flavian, Archbishop of Antioch; Maruthas, Bishop of Martyropolis, and others with him in Mesopotamia; Macarius (Nevsky), Metropolitan of Moscow, apostle to the Altai; Flavian the Hermit; Romanus of Carpenision; Basil Gryaznov of Pavlovo-Posadsky; Mary the New of Byzia in Thrace; Persian martyrs under Shapur.

Saturday

February 17

Commemoration of the Departed
Abstain from meat products.
2 Timothy 2:1-10; Luke 20:46-21:4

*I*f we quarrel, let us be reconciled quickly! If we make peace with our enemy, our success is double: we have snatched both ourselves and him from the claws of the evil one.

St. John Chrysostom

NEW HIEROMARTYR MICHAEL OF PETROGRAD. Michael was the son of a priest in nineteenth-century Ryazan. He studied at the Ryazan Seminary and Kazan Theological Academy. He moved to Petrograd with his family and worked as a diocesan missionary and in the office of the Synod. He authored books, brochures, and journals, and lectured at religious gatherings. Fr. Michael was arrested on suspicion of counter-revolutionary activity and was held in solitary confinement many times. He wrote extensively of his days and nights in prayer and reading, and the agony of not knowing when and if he would be executed. His prison cell was seven feet wide and twice as long, with a peep hole the guards used to spy on him. He wrote of being deprived of the consolation of corporate worship and Holy Communion. One day one of the guards on duty quickly gave him a package that contained a four- to six-day portion of the Holy Gifts. Fr. Michael was overjoyed. He wrote that only in prison had he felt and experienced true satisfaction, true peace and joy in prayer and from prayer. After several years, he was released. His final imprisonment came about because he was the spiritual father of a certain countess. He was told that he would certainly be executed, and he said, "The Lord is calling me to Himself by this blessed way." As Fr. Michael was led to his death, he sang hymns of the Nativity of Christ. The next day, an order came from Moscow to release Fr. Michael for lack of evidence of a crime.

SAINTS OF THE DAY: Theodore the Tyro; Mariamne, sister of Apostle Philip; Hermogenes, Patriarch of Moscow; Emperor Marcian and Pulcheria; Auxibius of Soli; Theodosius the Bulgarian, and Romanus; Theodore the Silent of the Kiev Caves; Righteous Theosterictus; Theodore of Byzantium; Barnabas of the Gethsemane Skete; Theodore of Adjara.

SUNDAY

Foregiveness Sunday
Cheesefare Sunday
Abstain from meat products.

FEBRUARY 18

Romans 13:11-14:4; Matthew 6:14-21

Love the peace that comes from above at all costs. Make sure you are seeking the peace from above, not the peace from this world, which is unstable and not very safe.

+*Elder Sergei of Vanves*

LEO THE GREAT, POPE OF ROME. Pope Leo defended the Church against the heretics and saved Italy from destruction. He was born in Italy during the fifth century and received an excellent education. He yearned for the spiritual life and progressed from archdeacon to pope. Many heretics besieged the Church. Leo prevailed against Eutychius and Dioscoros who taught that there was only one nature in the Lord Jesus Christ. Almost twenty years later, Leo found it necessary to defend the Church against the Nestorians. He helped convene the Fourth Ecumenical Council at Chalcedon to condemn the heresy of the Monophysites. In a letter to the Council, he wrote about the Orthodox teaching on the two natures, Divine and human, in the Lord Jesus Christ. All the bishops present at the Council agreed with Pope Leo, and Eutychius and Dioscoros were excommunicated. In defending his homeland, Pope Leo personally went out to meet Attila the Hun who was pillaging the country. He also defended Rome from the leader of the Vandals, persuading him not to burn buildings and spill blood. St. Leo received foreknowledge of his death, and he fasted and prayed for forty days at the tomb of Apostle Peter before giving up his soul.

SAINTS OF THE DAY: Leo the Great, Pope of Rome; Leo and Paregorius of Patara; Nicholas the Catholicos of Georgia; Agapitus, Bishop of Synnada, and Martyrs Victor, Dorotheus, Theodulus, and Agrippa; Blaise of Mt. Athos; Martyr Piulius; Agapetus, Archbishop of Ekaterinoslav; Cosmas of Yakhromsk; Colman, Bishop of Lindisfarne; Commemoration of the New Martyrs who suffered during the "Holy Night" in St. Petersburg.

MONDAY

Clean Monday—Great Lent Begins
Strict Fast

FEBRUARY 19

Isaiah 1:1-20; Genesis 1:1-13
Proverbs 1:1-20

Bringing one soul close to God by repentance is much better, in the eyes of God, than all other offerings, for there is nothing in the world better for God than the human soul, for everything in the world will perish except the soul because it is eternal.

St. John Climacus

NEW HIEROMARTYR NICETAS OF EPIRUS. Nicetas was from eighteenth-century Epirus in northern Greece. Because of his love for Christ, he became a monk at the Skete of St. Anne on Mt. Athos, and later joined the Russian monastery of St. Panteleimon. Nicetas led a God-pleasing life and was ordained Hierodeacon and then priest. His mind haunted him because his Christian relatives pretended to be Ottomans to avoid persecution. For this reason, he resolved to openly profess his Christianity to the Ottomans at the risk of martyrdom. He departed Mt. Athos and traveled to the outskirts of the cities of Serres and Drama, where he openly declared his faith. Nicetas was imprisoned and tortured. His skin was burned, and splinters were pushed under his fingernails. A crown of thorns was then placed on his head, and he was hanged by his feet and burned. The saint would not disavow his faith. He was beaten again and then hanged. While his body remained on the gallows, a heavenly light illumined him. His relics wrought many miracles, and they continue to do so to this day.

SAINTS OF THE DAY: Apostles Philemon and Archippus of the Seventy and Martyr Apphia; Theodore of Sanaxar Monastery; Eugene and Macarius, priests and confessors at Antioch; Philothea the Athenian; Maximus, Theodotus, Hesychius, and Asclepiodote of Adrianople; Nicetas of Epirus and Mt. Athos, at Serres; Dositheus of Gaza; Rabulas of Samosata; Conon in Palestine; Mesrop the Translator of Armenia; Vladimir (Terentiev), abbot of Zosima Hermitage, Smolensk.

FEBRUARY 20

Isaiah 1:19-2:3; Genesis 1:14-23
Proverbs 1:20-33

"*Withhold not good from them to whom it is due, when it is in the power of your hand to do it*" (Proverbs 3:27). O man, give thanksgiving to God that someone seeks something good from you, be it material, or spiritual! This means that you are a man of God's trust: God has entrusted some of His goods to you because all goods belong to God. Show yourself worthy of this trust, show yourself worthy in lesser things so that you may be entrusted with greater things.

St. Nikolai Velimirovich

VENERABLE AGATHO, POPE OF ROME. Agatho was from seventh-century Italy, and his parents were devout Christians. After their death, Agatho distributed their wealth to the poor and became a monk. He was described as warmhearted, amiable, and capable. As pope, he was efficient in business matters. During his time in office, a terrible plague struck Rome. Agatho began religious processions and public litanies, asking God for mercy, and many healings followed his prayers. He became known as a worker of miracles. Whenever he embraced a leper, the disease would be cured instantly. Agatho's monumental battle during his tenure was to defeat the Monothelite heresy. He called to convene the Sixth Ecumenical Council, but before this, he ordered councils throughout the West to make sure everyone under the Roman see agreed on the subject. Agatho then sent a large delegation from Rome to Constantinople. The Monothelites were defeated, and the council proclaimed the existence of the two wills in Christ. This council also healed the schism between East and West.

SAINTS OF THE DAY: Bessarion the Great, wonderworker of Egypt; Agatho, Pope of Rome; Sadoc, Bishop of Persia, and 128 Martyrs with him; Eleutherius, bishop in Byzantium; Leo, Bishop of Catania; Cindeus, Bishop of Pisidia; Cornelius of the Pskov Caves, and his disciple Bassian of Murom; Righteous Plotinus; Agatho of the Kiev Caves; Yaroslav the Wise, Great Prince of Kiev; Macarius and 34 monks and novices of Valaam Monastery; Eucherius, Bishop of Orleans; Eleutherius, Bishop of Tournai.

FEBRUARY 21

Isaiah 2:3-11; Genesis 1:24-2:3
Proverbs 2:1-22

We should not find it strange if the passions and sicknesses war against us, but rather we should entreat God to give us patience, that great balm for the wounds of the soul as well as of the body. Patience is the one and only diamond which beautifies the Christian and makes straight the rough road of our salvation. Patience is the fortitude of the soul, the support, the deep root that holds the tree when the winds beat against it and the streams strike it.

Elder Ephraim of Arizona

VENERABLE TIMOTHY OF SYMBOLEIA IN BITHYNIA. At a very young age during the eighth century, Timothy became a monk and pursued asceticism at the monastery, called Symboleia, in Asia Minor near Mount Olympos. He remained chaste and pure his entire life and labored in fasting, prayer, and vigils. In this careful manner of watching over his soul, God granted him the gift of healing the sick and casting out evil spirits. Timothy spent many years as a hermit living in the wilderness, mountains, and forests. He died in very old age.

SAINTS OF THE DAY: Timothy of Symboleia on Mt. Olympus in Bithynia; John the Scholastic, Patriarch of Constantinople; Eustathius, Archbishop of Antioch; Zachariah, Patriarch of Jerusalem; George, Bishop of Amastris; Severian, Bishop of Scythopolis; Macarius of Glinsk Hermitage; "Cucuzelis" and "Kozelshchansk" Icons of the Mother of God.

FEBRUARY 22

Isaiah 2:11-21; Genesis 2:4-19
Proverbs 3:1-18

Let the mouth also fast from disgraceful speeches and railings. For what does it profit if we abstain from fish and fowl and yet bite and devour our brothers and sisters? The evil speaker eats the flesh of his brother and bites the body of his neighbor.

St. John Chrysostom

TELESPHORUS, BISHOP OF ROME. Telesphorus was of Greek descent born in Calabria. He was the seventh Roman bishop in succession from the Apostles, serving during the reigns of Roman Emperors Hadrian and Antoninus Pius in the second century. Before becoming a bishop, he was an anchorite. There was a great controversy at this time within the Churches throughout Asia on which day of the week Christians should celebrate the Lord's Resurrection. Some followed the custom of celebrating on other days of the week according to the calculation of the Jewish Passover. Telesphorus always celebrated Pascha on Sunday, but never abandoned the other churches that did not follow this custom. It is said that he established Lent as being seven weeks in length. St. Irenaeus writes that Telesphorus died "a glorious martyrdom."

SAINTS OF THE DAY: Thalassius, Limnaeus, and Baradates of Syria; Telesphorus, Pope of Rome; Athanasius the Confessor of Constantinople; Titus, Bishop of Bostra in Arabia; Maurice and his son Photinos, and Martyrs Theodore, Philip, and 70 soldiers; Anthusa and twelve handmaidens; Holy Nine Children of Kola; Martyr Synetus; Theoktista of Voronezh; Peter the Stylite of Mt. Athos; Babylas and Comnita of Nicosa; Leontius of Lycia; Abilius, Patriarch of Alexandria; Papius of Hieropolis; Michael Lisitsyn of Ust-Labinskaya; Herman of Stolobny Monastery; Blaise, bishop; Uncovering of the relics of the Holy Martyrs at the gate of Eugenius at Constantinople.

FRIDAY

Salutations to the Virgin Mary
Strict Fast

FEBRUARY 23

Isaiah 3:1-14; Genesis 2:20-3:20
Proverbs 3:19-34

Do not try to conceal yourself, covering your nakedness with a fig leaf and hiding in the bushes from the Lord, who comes to you in the conscience and exposes you. Blame yourself completely, and ask forgiveness without placing blame on anyone else.

St. Theophan the Recluse

HIEROMARTYR POLYCARP, BISHOP OF SMYRNA. Polycarp became an orphan at an early age. An angel directed a pious widow to raise the child. After her death, Polycarp gave away all his possessions and led a chaste life. He was ordained a deacon by St. Bucolos, Bishop of Smyrna. Polycarp met the Apostle John the Theologian and accompanied him on his missionary travels. St. Bucolos ordained Polycarp to the priesthood, and before his death expressed his wish that Polycarp become bishop of Smyrna. His ordination was accomplished, and he guided his flock with zeal. God granted him the gift of wonderworking, casting out demons and healing the sick. He had the gift of insight, and through his prayers and fasting brought forth rain. During the Christian persecutions by Emperor Marcus Aurelius, Polycarp was arrested and brought to trial. He forcefully confessed his faith in Christ, and for this was condemned to burning. When the executioners saw that the flames did not harm him, the pagans demanded that he be killed with a sword. So much blood flowed from him that the flames were extinguished. The Christians reverently gathered his relics.

SAINTS OF THE DAY: Polycarp, Bishop of Smyrna; Gorgonia, sister of Gregory the Theologian; John, Antioch, Antoninus, Zebinas, Polychronius, Moses, and Damian of Syria; Alexander of the Monastery of the Unsleeping Ones; John Theristes of Stylos in Calabria; Damian of Esphigmenou; Polycarp of Briansk; Moses of White Lake; Michael Edlinsky of Kiev; Lazarus of the Peloponnese; Seraphim (Zenobius) of Tetritskaro; Milburga of Much Wenlock; Nazarius of Valaam Monastery; Martyr Clement; Martyr Thea; Sergius Bukashkin of Novo-Alexandrovka; Antipas Kyrillov of Tatarintsevo; Philaret Pryakhin of Trubino.

SATURDAY

Commemoration of the Departed
Abstain from meat and dairy products, and fish.

FEBRUARY 24

2 Corinthians 4:6-15
Matthew 11:2-15

The soul which rejoiced in the love of God, at the hour of its departure, is lifted with the angels of peace above all the hosts of darkness. For it is given wings by spiritual love, since it ceaselessly carried within itself the love which *is the fulfilling of the law* (Rom. 13:10).

St. Diadochos of Photike

UNCOVERING OF THE RELICS OF ST. ROMANUS, PRINCE OF UGLICH. Romanus was the son of Prince Vladimir in thirteenth-century Uglich. When the Mongol hordes swept into Russia, Romanus and his father and brother traveled to Novgorod. Three years later, the Mongols left, and the family returned to Uglich. Upon the death of his father and brother, Romanus assumed leadership. He used a large portion of his inheritance to build houses of charity and reception for strangers. He built fifteen houses of worship throughout his kingdom. Romanus listened to the services, often talked with the God-fearing monks, and read the works of the Church Fathers. When his wife died, Romanus devoted himself wholly to fasting, prayer, and charity. When he died in 1285, he was buried in the Church of the Transfiguration in Uglich. Two hundred years later, his relics were uncovered and found incorrupt. One hundred twenty years later, his relics began to work wonders. Only four years after this, the Poles burned the relics of St. Romanus, and now his ashes are kept hidden in the Cathedral Temple of the Transfiguration.

SAINTS OF THE DAY: First and Second Findings of the Venerable Head of St. John the Baptist; Erasmus of the Kiev Caves; Montanus, Lucias, Julian, Victoricus, Flavian, and companions at Carthage; Cummain Ailbe, abbot of Iona; Uncovering of the relics of St. Romanus, Prince of Uglich.

FEBRUARY 25

Sunday of Orthodoxy
Abstain from meat and dairy products, and fish.
Hebrews 11:24-26, 32-40
John 1:43-51

When you perceive that God is chastising you, fly not to his enemies… but to his friends, the martyrs, the saints, and those who were pleasing to him, and who have great power.

St. John Chrysostom

TARASIOS, ARCHBISHOP OF CONSTANTINOPLE. Tarasios was a layman, senator, and chief secretary to Empress Irene, who ruled as regent for her ten-year-old son Constantine VI Porphyrigenitos. During the Iconoclast crisis, Patriarch Paul stepped down and withdrew to a monastery, but he recommended Tarasios to succeed him. For the longest time, Tarasios refused, considering himself unworthy, but he soon gave in under the condition that an Ecumenical Council be convened. Within a week, Tarasios was ordained a reader, priest, bishop, and then patriarch in eighth-century Constantinople. He summoned the Seventh Ecumenical Council, inviting over three hundred bishops from all over the empire to end the heresy of iconoclasm. He also reunited all the patriarchates with Constantinople. For twenty-two years, he wisely governed the Church. Tarasios led a strict ascetic life. He used all his money to feed and comfort the poor, impoverished, widows and orphans. When Emperor Constantine had tired of his wife, wishing to send her to a monastery and marry a relative, Tarasios refused to dissolve the emperor's marriage. He counseled, rebuked, and then excommunicated them. Empress Irene deposed Constantine. As Tarasios lay dying, he defended himself against the demons who tried to get the saint to admit to sins he had not committed. He was buried in a monastery that he built on the Bosphorus. Many miracles were worked at his grave.

SAINTS OF THE DAY: Tarasios, Archbishop of Constantinople; Reginus of Skopelos; Alexander at Drizipara; Theodore, fool-for-Christ; Erasmus and Paphnutius of Kephala; Marcellus of Apamea; Martyr Anthony; Alexander and Hypatius at Marcianopolis; Walburga of Heidenheim; Ethelbert of Kent; Venerable Polycarp; Leo of Laskov.

FEBRUARY 26

Isaiah 4:2-5:7; Genesis 3:21-4:7
Proverbs 3:34-4:22

Beware from sitting and thinking of judging your brother, for this will annihilate all your virtuous works, even if you elevated yourself to the level of perfection.

St. Isaac the Syrian

PORPHYRIOS, BISHOP OF GAZA. Porphyrios was from a noble family in late fourth-century Thessalonica. At twelve years of age, he decided to set off for Egypt, where he persued asceticism under the guidance of St. Makarios the Great. When Blessed Jerome was visiting the Egyptian monasteries, Porphyrios decided to go with him to Jerusalem to visit the holy places and to venerate the Life-Creating Cross of the Lord. He then settled in the Jordanian wilderness but soon became ill. He returned to Jerusalem for healing, and lying at the foot of Golgotha, Porphyrios beheld a vision of Jesus Christ with the words, "Take this Wood and preserve it." The Patriarch of Jerusalem soon ordained Porphyrios to the priesthood and appointed him the curator of the Venerable Wood of the Cross of the Lord. Later, Porphyrios was made the bishop of the city of Gaza. He worked many miracles by his prayers and brought more unbelievers to the knowledge of God. When he saw the injustice suffered by those in his diocese at the hands of idol-worshippers and heretics, he went for help to the patriarch, St. John Chrysostom. John led Porphyrios to Empress Eudoxia, and she approached the king. The king anticipated difficulties in unseating the heretic masters of Gaza, but the queen convinced him that it would be harder to turn down the request of this bishop. The king agreed, and the pagan temples in Gaza were destroyed, and privileges returned to Christians. A large sum of money was given to Porphyrios to build a church where the main pagan temple had stood. Porphyrios worked in this capacity for almost twenty-five years. He reposed in old age.

SAINTS OF THE DAY: Porphyrios of Gaza; Photina the Samaritan Woman, with her sisters and others; John Calphas at Constantinople.

FEBRUARY 27

Isaiah 5:7-16; Genesis 4:8-15
Proverbs 5:1-15

Don't pay any attention to dreams. Whether they are pleasant or unpleasant, you are not to pay any attention to them; because there is the danger of being deluded. Ninety five percent of dreams are deceptive. This is why the Holy Fathers say we should not pay any attention to them. Very few dreams are from God. But in order for someone to interpret even these, he must have purity and other prerequisites—much like the Righteous Joseph [the Patriarch] and the Prophet Daniel in the Bible, who both had the gift from God.

St. Paisios the Athonite

VENERABLE PROKOPIOS THE CONFESSOR OF DECAPOLIS. Prokopios was a monk from the region of Decapolis in the ninth century. During this time, Emperor Leo the Isaurian outlawed icons. He believed that these were the graven images outlawed by God through Moses. He could not understand that icons were not a form of idolatry but a veneration of the living saints portrayed. Prokopios and many other monks left their monasteries to openly speak out against this heresy. By order of Leo the Isaurian, Prokopios was imprisoned and flogged with iron flails, then exiled. After the death of the emperor, Prokopios was set free. He spent the remainder of his life in monastic deeds and guiding many to salvation. He died in old age.

SAINTS OF THE DAY: Prokopios the Confessor of Decapolis; Julian, Chroniun and Besas at Alexandria; Asclepius and James of Syria; Gelasius the Actor of Heliopolis; Stephen of Constantinople; Thalaleos of Syria; Timothy of Caesarea; Pitirim of Tambov; Martyr Nesius; Titus of the Kiev Caves, the former soldier; Elias of Trebizond; Titus of the Kiev Caves, presbyter; Raphael, Bishop of Brooklyn; Macarius, Bishop of Jerusalem; Herefrith, Bishop of Lincolnshire.

FEBRUARY 28

Isaiah 5:16-25; Genesis 4:16-26
Proverbs 5:15-6:3

I kept one right: not to have any right.

+Elder Epiphanios Theodoropoulos of Athens

HIEROMARTYR NESTOR, BISHOP OF MAGYDOS. Nestor was the bishop of third-century Magydos and was held in high esteem by both Christians and pagans. During the persecutions of Emperor Decius, Nestor sent the faithful of his diocese to safe places while he awaited his fate at home. While praying in his home, officers arrived and arrested him. He signed himself with the cross and followed them. When Nestor entered the court, everyone rose out of respect for him. The magistrate asked him to quietly defer to their gods and avoid condemnation, but Nestor was inflexible and said that he only feared the torments of God. Nestor was sent to the governor, who urged him kindly and then threatened him with torture. He was put on an instrument of torture called the "little horse, " and his sides were torn with iron hooks. All the while Nestor sang praises to God. The judge taunted him, saying that he was placing his trust in a crucified Man. When the crowd called for Nestor to be put out of his misery, the governor asked him again to sacrifice to their gods, but Nestor answered that he had always been with Christ and intended to be so forever. He was then crucified, and still, he encouraged the Christian onlookers. His final prayer was that they kneel and pray to God through Jesus Christ, and pagans and Christians alike did as he had instructed.

SAINTS OF THE DAY: Proterius, Patriarch of Alexandria, and six companions; Apostles Nymphas and Eubulus; Nestor in Pamphylia; Barsus, Bishop of Damascus; Basil the Confessor; Marana, Kyra, and Domnica of Syria; Kyranna of Thessalonica; Sergius, priest; Martyr Avrikios; Romanus of Condat in Gaul; Arsenius of Rostov; Nicholas of Pskov; Oswald, Bishop of York; Leo, Cappadocian monastic; John Cassian the Roman; John (Barsanuphius) of Nitria in Egypt; Cassian of the Kiev Caves; Theocteristos of Pelecete Monastery; Germanus of Dacia Pontica; Cassian of Mu-lake Hermitage; Meletius, Archbishop of Kharkov.

MARCH 1

Isaiah 6:1-12; Genesis 5:1-24
Proverbs 6:3-20

Strength to pray lies in the deliberate privation of food, and strength to go without food lies in not seeing or hearing about worldly things except when strictly necessary. He who is negligent in this fails to build his fasting on a firm foundation, and so he brings about the collapse of the whole edifice of prayer, which itself is based on fasting.

St. Ilias the Presbyter

VENERABLE AGAPIOS OF MT. ATHOS. Agapios was a novice monk on Mt. Athos at the monastery of Vatopedi. One day he was taken prisoner by Hagarene pirates who landed on the shores of Mt. Athos. He was taken to Magnesia and sold into slavery to an agha, where he was bound in chains and worked for twelve years. When he was not working, he was imprisoned in a dark dungeon. Agapios did not lose hope, and he fervently prayed to the Mother of God. One night while sleeping, the Theotokos appeared to Agapios, telling him to arise and go without fear to his elder. When he awoke, he found his chains unlocked. Agapios did what he was told and made his way back to his elder on Mt Athos. Testing the humility of Agapios, the elder told him to return to his master until he receives permission to be set free. Therefore, Agapios returned to captivity. Seeing the great humility and faith of Agapios, the master not only freed Agapios but he himself and his two sons departed with him to the Holy Mountain.

SAINTS OF THE DAY: Eudocia of Heliopolis; Antonina of Nicaea; Martyrs Charisius, Nikephoros, and Agapius; Agapios of Kolitsou Skete of Vatopedi, and his four companions; Domnina, ascetic of Syria; Martyrs Sylvester and Sophronius; Antonina of Kizliar; Anastasia Andreyevna, fool-for-Christ; Anthony (Korzh) of Kiziltash Monastery (Crimea); Martyrius, founder of Zelenets Monastery; David of Wales; Paraskevas of Trebizond; Leo-Luke of Corleone, Sicily; Albinus, Bishop of Angers; Swidbert (Suitbert), bishop in southern Westphalia and monastic founder on the Rhine River.

FRIDAY

Salutations to the Virgin Mary
Strict Fast

MARCH 2

Isaiah 7:1-14; Genesis 5:32-6:8
Proverbs 6:20-7:1

Humble-mindedness and humility are of great help on the road to salvation, for they wash away sins.

+Elder Paisius of Sihla

BARSANUPHIUS AND SABBAS OF TVER. Brothers by birth, Barsanuphius and Sabbas were abbots of a monastery built in 1397. After five years of serving as abbot, Barsanuphius left the monastery to live in the wilderness, and Sabbas was chosen to take over. Barsanuphius stayed in the wilderness for forty years in solitude. He prayed, sang hymns, and read books about the love of Christ. When he finished reading the books, he either returned them or took them elsewhere. He had nothing and loved poverty. He received such grace that he memorized all the Holy Scriptures by heart and communicated it upon demand. Many monks and nobles would go to him for the good of their souls or explanation from something in Scripture. One day, the devil seduced a monk to take books from Barsanuphius' cell, but he fell down dead until the saint's prayers raised him, and the culprit later pursued asceticism. In old age, Barsanuphius returned to the monastery and the fifty-year strict spiritual leadership under Sabbas. Sabbas always stood by the door of the church, making certain that the monks arrived on time, and not leave early. He could be strict or kindly as the situation dictated. There was once a terrible epidemic at the monastery, and all the other priests died. Sabbas made visits, heard confessions, communed the sick, and buried the dead. Under the guidance of Barsanuphius and Sabbas, the monastery was all decorum, quiet, and peaceful. After the death of the brothers, a new abbot made a mess of the discipline and traditions. Sabbas appeared to him in a dream, and calling him a wretch, he asked why he was neglecting the monastery. The abbot was unable to rise from his bed, and when he recovered, he soon left. Even in death, Sabbas watched over his monastery.

SAINTS OF THE DAY: Hesychius of Antioch; Nicholas Planas of Athens;Quintus of Phyrgia; Euthalia of Sicily; Theodotus of Cyrenia.

Saturday

March 3

Abstain from meat and dairy products, and fish.
Hebrews 3:12-16; Mark 1:35-44

There is nothing we can offer to God more precious than good will. But what is good will? To have good will is to experience concern for someone else's adversities as if they were our own, to give thanks for our neighbor's prosperity as for our own; to believe that another person's loss is our own, and also that another's gain is ours; to love a friend in God, and bear with an enemy out of love, to do to no one what we do not want to suffer ourselves, and to refuse to no one what we rightly want for ourselves; to choose to help a neighbor who is in need not only to the whole extent of our ability, but even beyond our means. What offering is richer, what offering is more substantial than this one? What we are offering to God on the altar of our hearts is the sacrifice of ourselves.

St. Gregory the Great

ALEXANDRA OF ALEXANDRIA. Alexandra was from a wealthy home with a good father and an evil mother. Alexandra's mother had an easy life, and upon her death, she was buried with honor. On the other hand, her father suffered greatly and had a difficult death. There was so much rain on the day of his burial that it was difficult to bury him. Alexandra was uncertain who's example she should follow until she had a vision of both parents in their afterlife. She visited her father in the kingdom of God and witnessed her mother's darkness and torments in hell. Alexandra devoted the rest of her life to God, without regard to misfortune or opposition. Following God's commandments to the end of her life, she was made worthy of the kingdom and rejoiced with her father.

SAINTS OF THE DAY: Eutropius and Cleonicus of Amasea, and Basiliscus; Alexandra of Alexandria; Zeno and Zoilos; Hemetherius of Spain; Piamon of Egypt; Theodoretus of Antioch; Caluppan of Auvergne; John IV, Catholicos of Georgia; Non, mother of David of Wales; Winwaloe of Brittany; "Volokolamsk" Icon of the Mother of God.

SUNDAY

Sunday of St. Gregory Palamas
Abstain from meat and dairy products, and fish.
Hebrews 1:10-2:3; Mark 2:1-12

MARCH 4

Today, there are more words and books and fewer living examples.
St. Paisios the Athonite

NEW HIEROMARTYR VYACHESLAV. Brought up in Orthodox piety, Vyacheslav and his brother became priests in early twentieth-century Russia. Vyacheslav was arrested several times by the Communists. The peasants of his parish helped him buy a house, but the authorities confiscated it. Fr. Vyacheslav even helped them load his belongings into the cart. He and his wife wandered from house to house for six months, until they found a one-room refuge in a warden's hut. Vyacheslav performed baptisms there, and through a wonderworking Tikhvin icon of the Mother of God, he helped many sick and demon-possessed people. He refused nobody who asked for his prayers, and he visited the homes of his parishioners and preached in each of them. The authorities continued to harass him. They demanded contributions of flax and honey, which he did not have, so the peasants supplied these for him. Towards the end of the 1920's, the authorities decided to kill Vyacheslav, but the peasants surrounded him in a solid ring. Now he never went out alone, but the authorities waited for the right moment. Vyacheslav was eventually arrested and condemned to three years in prison. Upon his release, he went back to his parish for one year. He was arrested again, but before leaving, he instructed his parishioners, "Live according to God. Now that's all. They're going to close the churches. And you will sit behind the chimney and pray. I am leaving you forever, and I bless you all." Fr. Vyacheslav was executed.

SAINTS OF THE DAY: Gregory of Constantia; Gerasimus of the Jordan; Julian of Alexandria; Gregory of Assos; Paul, Juliana, Quadratus, Acacius, and Stratonicus, at Ptolemais; John of al-Sindiyana; James the Faster of Phoenicia; Saints of Pskov martyred by the Latins: Ioasaph of Snetogorsk and Basil of Mirozh; Basil, Prince of Rostov; Dimitry Ivanov of Kiev; Vyacheslav of Nizhegorod; Daniel, Great Prince of Moscow; Gerasimus of Vologda; Basil, Prince of Rostov.

MARCH 5

Isaiah 8:13-9:7; Genesis 6:9-22
Proverbs 8:1-21

All Christians must prove what they believe in by their way of life!
+Elder Joseph the Hesychast

VIRGIL, ARCHBISHOP OF ARLES. Virgil became a monk at the monastery on the island of Saint Honorat, one of the Lerins Islands, two miles south of the French Riviera town of Cannes. According to his biographer, Virgil was walking by the shore one night when he saw a strange ship drawn up on the beach. He saw two of the sailors disembark and came to meet him. They knew him by name, saying that his reputation had spread to foreign lands, and asked him to accompany them to Jerusalem where he would attain great sanctity. Virgil was not deceived, and with an admonishment and the sign of the cross, the ship and its sailors vanished. Virgil was called from the monastic life to become archbishop of Arles by Pope St. Gregory I. Though he was vigorous and able in this capacity, Gregory admonished him for trying to convert the Jews of his diocese by force. Virgil built several churches in Arles. In one instance, stone pillars were being brought there, and suddenly it was impossible to move them. When Virgil arrived, he perceived the devil in the form of a short, powerful dark person hanging on to the stone. He spoke sternly to the demon, and it vanished, leaving the pillars free to be taken to their destination. His biographer writes that many miracles are attributed to Virgil, including raising the dead, healing the sick, and destroying a terrible serpent which had been causing considerable damage. The people of Arles believed that so long as they kept St. Virgil with them, alive or dead, he would deliver them from all their foes.

SAINTS OF THE DAY: Mark the Faster; Mark of Athens; Conon of Isauria; Conon the Gardener; Onisius of Isauria; Eulampius of Palestine; Rhais of Antinoe, with Archelaus and others; Eulogius of Palestine; Theophilus of Caesarea; Basil and Constantine of Yaroslavl; George of Rapsana; Hesychius the Faster; Nikolai Velimirovich of Ochrid; John the Bulgarian; Adrian and Leonid of Poshekhonye; Theodore of Smolensk; Kieran of Munster.

March 6

Isaiah 9:9-10:4; Genesis 7:1-5
Proverbs 8:32-9:11

Christ said it in a timely fashion: that in this life we must be warriors, even within our own family; our own people will behave as enemies, because we follow the Christian life. Real peace is to be found only in the meeting of man with God. By having this divine peace, we have everything and become fearless before every aggression and every enemy. By having the peace of God, we can then have peace with our fellow human beings.

+Blessed Moses the Athonite

THE HOLY FORTY-TWO MARTYRS OF AMMOREIA: CONSTANTINE, AETIOS, THEOPHILOS, THEODORE, CALLISTOS, BASOES, MELISSENOS, AND THE OTHERS WITH THEM. During the time of war between the Saracens and the Byzantine Emperor Theophilos in the ninth century, the city of Ammoreia fell, and 42 Byzantine military defenders were taken captive and sent off to Syria. They were imprisoned for seven years, and over the course of this time, their captors tried in vain to persuade them to renounce their Christian faith and accept Mussulmanism. Even torture did not break their spirit. The prisoners resisted many threats and seductive offers and were condemned to death. Without fear, the forty-two martyrs walked up to the executioners and were beheaded. Their bodies were thrown into the River Euphrates, whereupon they floated across the waters and were gathered up by Christians and given burial.

SAINTS OF THE DAY: The uncovering of the Precious Cross and the Precious Nails by Empress St. Helen; The 42 Martyrs of Ammoreia in Phrygia; Hesychius of Galatia; Conon and his son Conon of Iconium; Fridolin, enlightener of the Upper Rhine; Arcadius of Cyprus, with Julian and Bulius; Job (Joshua) of Anzersk Island (Solovki); Martyrs Maximus and Euphrosynus; Martyrs Julian and Eubulus; Cyriacus and 12 companions, in Augsburg; "Chenstokhov" and "Blessed Heaven" Icons of the Mother of God.

March 7

Isaiah 10:12-20; Genesis 7:6-9
Proverbs 9:12-18

Great is the power of prayer, and it brings most of all the Spirit of God, and is most easily practiced by everyone. We shall be happy indeed if the Lord God finds us watchful and filled with the gifts of His Holy Spirit.

St. Seraphim of Sarov

VENERABLE EMILIAN OF ITALY. Emilian was a Roman by birth, and until old age, he led a sinful life in Italy. At last, he repented and withdrew to a monastery, where he accepted monasticism. He spent the rest of his life humbly serving God. He fasted strictly and fulfilled his obedience without complaint. However, the monks noticed that by night Emilian secretly visited a cave not far from the monastery. One night the abbot followed and found Emilian in the cave praying with tears of remorse, with a heavenly light illuminating him. A Voice was heard from above, saying, "Emilian, your sins are forgiven." The next morning the abbot asked Emilian to tell the brethren his secret and the great mercy that God had shown him. Then the abbot explained to the brethren, "The Lord could have forgiven him his sin in quiet, but for the sake of us all He did manifest His mercy with the appearance of light and a voice, so that we all might behold His grace and mercy to sinners sincerely repenting." St. Emilian died peacefully.

SAINTS OF THE DAY: Ephraim, Patriarch of Antioch; Holy Hieromartyrs of Kherson: Basil, Ephraim, Eugene, Capiton, Elpidius, Agathorodus, and Aetherius; Emilian of Italy; Paul the Simple of Egypt; Lawrence, founder of Phanerumene Monastery on Salamis; Nestor and Arcadius, Bishops of Tremithus; Dandus and All Saints of Thrace; Nilus (Tyutyukin) of St. Joseph of Volokolamsk Monastery; Eosterwine, abbot of Wearmount; "Surety of Sinners" and "Of Czestochowa" Icons of the Mother of God.

MARCH 8

Isaiah 11:10-12:2; Genesis 7:11-8:3
Proverbs 10:1-22

Nothing is far from God.

St. Monica of Hippo

SENAN OF SCATTERY ISLAND. Senan was born to Christian parents from sixth-century Munster. When he was young, and the family was moving elsewhere, Senan was put in charge of arranging the furniture and the cooking utensils. Absorbed in prayer, he neglected to do so and was scolded by his mother. He told her to put her trust in God, and immediately the pots and pans shot up to their place on the shelves and the furniture moved into their position. Everyone present saw this miracle. After some time, Senan took himself to a holy abbot named Cassidus, who trained him in monastic discipline, and then was sent to St. Natalis of Kilmanagh. Senan was soon distinguished for his piety, docility, and miracles. One day, as he minded a herd of cows so the monastery would have enough milk, Senan tried to keep the calves away from the cows. When he laid his staff on the ground between them and went off to pray, the calves would not cross the barrier. News of Senan's wonders soon spread, and multitudes flocked to him for healing and prayers. Later he was directed by an angel to a place where he would build many cells and churches to God's glory and to promote and increase monastic discipline in Ireland. He finally settled at present-day Scattery Island. The monastery soon became famous, and many men went to live there, but women were not allowed. One day St. Cannera, who knew she was about to die, greatly desired to be buried at Scattery Island. An angel brought her across the water, but Senan met them on the shore refusing her to proceed. She said, "If Christ will receive my soul, why should you reject my body?" She died on the shore and was buried on the island. Senan died during a journey to visit the monastery of St. Cassidus and the convent of St. Scotia, his aunt.

SAINTS OF THE DAY: Theophylaktos of Nicomedia; Paul of Plousias; Martyr Dion; Dometius; Quintilian and Capatolinus at Nicomedia; Athanasius and Lazarus of Murom; Felix of Burgundy; Andronicus of Tbilisi.

Salutations to the Virgin Mary
Strict Fast

MARCH 9

Hebrews 12:1-10; Matthew 20:1-16

Our Panagia is the salvation of the whole world, she is the only mother for all Christians.

St. Anthimos of Chios

THE HOLY FORTY MARTYRS OF SEBASTE. Symbolic crowns are placed on the heads of the bride and groom during the Orthodox wedding ceremony in remembrance of the Forty Martyrs. The priest reads, "Remember them, O Lord our God, as You remembered Your holy Forty Martyrs, sending down upon them the crowns from the heavens." In the year 320, there was a garrison of forty brave Cappadocian soldiers in the Armenian city of Sebaste. They were all Christians. When they refused to offer sacrifice to the pagan gods, they were imprisoned. The military commander at the time was Agricolaus, a pagan. He tried flattery and praise, urging them to disavow Christ, but they would not. They were shackled and returned to prison. A commander ordered them stoned, but the stones turned back in midair on the throwers, one breaking the commander's teeth. In the bitter cold, the soldiers were forced into a frozen lake. Fires and warm baths were built to lure the soldiers into renouncing Christ. One of the soldiers could not hold out, and as soon as he left the lake, he fell dead. During the night as all the guards were asleep, except one by the name of Aglaios who was keeping watch, thirty-nine radiant crowns descended from heaven and were placed on the heads of the soldiers. Aglaios removed his uniform and entering the lake, said, "I too—am a Christian." The next morning, the guards were surprised to find everyone alive and Aglaios in the lake. They then broke their legs and committed them to fire. Their bones were thrown into the water so the Christians could not find them. Three days later, the martyrs appeared in a dream to Peter, bishop of Sebaste, telling him where to find their bodies for burial.

SAINTS OF THE DAY: Caesarius, brother of St. Gregory the Theologian; Philoromus of Galatia; Urpasianus of Nicomedia; Tarasius of Lycaonia; Jonah of Novgorod; Theodosius of Balta; Bosa of York.

SATURDAY

Abstain from meat and dairy products, and fish.
Hebrews 10:32-38; Mark 2:14-17

MARCH 10

Ask with tears, seek with obedience, knock with patience. For thus he who asks receives, and he who seeks finds, and to him that knocketh it shall be opened.

St. John Climacus

KESSOG, BISHOP OF LOCH LOMOND. Kessog was one of the first Christian martyrs in Scotland. The town of Luss on Loch Lomond was one of the major pilgrimage centers in Scotland. People came from afar to worship at the holy places associated with St. Kessog. He was born into a royal family in fifth-century southern Ireland. On one occasion, while still a child, Kessog was playing with neighboring princes while their fathers gathered. There was a terrible accident, and all the princes drowned except Kessog. When the kings discovered what had happened, a major war was averted by Kessog who prayed all night and brought the young men back to life. Kessog was sent to a monastery to be educated. After some time, he was sent to Lennox, a place that lay on the border of three nations, for missionary work. At the beginning of the sixth century, Kessog arrived in Luss and built a monastery in a place called "monk's island." There is a strange mystic beauty there that the writer William Wordsworth found to be most moving. Kessog was killed just south of Luss, perhaps by mercenaries or brigands. Shortly after his death, his name became the rallying cry to troops all over Scotland. St. Kessog's cozier led the victorious Scots into the battle that set Scotland free.

SAINTS OF THE DAY: Quadratus (Codratus) of Corinth, and with him, Cyprian, Dionysius, Anectus, Paul, Crescens, and Dionysius; Anastasia the Patrician of Alexandria; Martyr Marcian; George Arselaites, brother of St. John Climacus; Attalus, abbot of Bobbio; John of Khakhuli, Georgia, who was called Chrysostom; New Martyr Michael Mavroeidis of Adrianople; Paul of Taganrog; Kessog, Bishop of Loch Lomond; Alexander (Badanin) of Vologda.

SUNDAY

MARCH 11

Sunday of the Holy Cross
Abstain from meat and dairy products, and fish.
Hebrews 4:14-5:6; Mark 8:34-9:1

Knowing the will of God is one of the most delicate and complicated matter of our lives, especially for those who are trying to find it through prayer. For although His will is revealed according to Thy words: *"Ask, seek, knock, and it shall be given you"*, yet it requires patience, trials, temptations and [ascetic] experience, to extinguish man's own will and passions that cannot withstand the inexpressible tenderness and sensitivity of divine grace.

+Elder Joseph the Hesychast

HIEROMARTYR PIONIOS OF SMYRNA. Pionios was a third-century priest and hagiographer from Smyrna, having written the life of St. Polycarp, Bishop of Smyrna. During the persecutions of Emperor Decius, Pionios was condemned to crucifixion. He accepted this fate with great joy and willingly laid down, ordering the soldiers to drive the nails into his hands. Before many witnesses, the cross was driven into the ground upside down, and a fire was lit under the martyr's head. Pionios closed his eyes and silently prayed. When the flames subsided, everyone saw the saint's body unharmed, and not a hair on his head was burnt. St. Pionios' face was radiant.

SAINTS OF THE DAY: Trophimos and Thallus at Laodicea; George of Sinai; Sophronius, Patriarch of Jerusalem; Sophronius, Bishop of Vratsa; Euthymius, Bishop of Novgorod; Pionios of Smyrna, with Asclepiades, Macedonia, Linus, and Sabina; John Moschos; Sophronius of the Kiev Caves; Theodora, Queen of Arta; George the New of Constantinople; Eulogius, Metropolitan of Cordoba; Alexis of Goloseyevsky Skete, Kiev Caves; Patrick (Petrov) of Valaam Monastery; Michael (Galushko) of Svyatogorsk Monastery; Oengus (Angus) the Culdee, bishop, of Clonenagh (Ireland); Translation of the relics of St. Epimachos of Pelusium.

MARCH 12

Isaiah 14:24-32; Genesis 8:21-9:7
Proverbs 11:19-12:6

It is an insult to the intelligence to be subject to what lacks intelligence and to concern itself with shameful desires.

St. Thalassios the Libyan

ALPHEGE, BISHOP OF WINCHESTER, ENGLAND. Alphege was born in the tenth century and became a monk in Gloucester, England. After a few years, he became a hermit and settled in a small hut near Somerset, England. At the age of thirty-one, he became the abbot of the abbey of Bath that he founded together with St. Dunstan. Many of his disciples from Somerset joined him there. That same year, he became bishop of Winchester. He served for two decades and became known for his austerity and care of the poor. The king once sent him to mediate with the invading Danes, and as a result, the Danish chieftain Anlef converted to Christianity. Anlaf vowed never to invade Britain again. Alphege became the Archbishop of Canterbury and was soon after captured by the Danes. They demanded about 3,000 pounds for his release, but Alphege refused to pay, and this infuriated the Danes. He was hit with an ax and then beaten to death. When his relics were later uncovered, they were found incorrupt. St. Alphege was the first martyr of Canterbury.

SAINTS OF THE DAY: Gregory the Dialogist, Pope of Rome; Symeon the New Theologian, and his elder Symeon the Reverent, of the Studion; Theophanes the Confessor of Sigriane; Aaron the High Priest, brother of Prophet Moses; Phineas, grandson of Aaron; Demetrius the Devoted, King of Georgia; Cyrus of Alexandria; Nine martyred by fire; Dragutin (Theoctistus) of Serbia; Paul, Bishop of Leon in Brittany; Nicodemus of Mammola in Calabria; Alphege, Bishop of Winchester, England; Vladimir (Volkov) of Islavskoe (Moscow); "Not-Made-by-Hands" (on the pillar) Icon of the Mother of God at Lydda.

MARCH 13

Isaiah 25:1-9; Genesis 9:8-17
Proverbs 12:8-22

Set the name of the Lord before you always.

St. John Chrysostom

RIGHTEOUS YPOMONI OF SERBIA. Ypomoni was the daughter of Constantine Dragash, one of the Serbian leaders during the fourteenth century. Many of her ancestors were saints, including St. Symeon the Myrrh-gusher and King St. Stefan of Serbia, who founded the Hilander Monastery on Mt. Athos. Ypomoni married Emperor Manual II Palaiologos. They worked together in harmony for thirty-five years. She was meek and sweet and gained many virtues. She was the great mother who anyone could approach and be consoled by her words. Ypomoni had eight children. Two ascended the emperor's throne, and three became monks. She taught them the Orthodox faith, taking them to holy shrines and monasteries. She sought prayers for her children from holy ascetics, and with patience and persistence shaped their characters. She also received rest, strength, and courage from the monasteries. Her son once wrote about her that no one came into contact with her that did not become better. When Manuel died, Ypomoni became a humble nun for the last twenty-five years of her life. A recent miracle is told that she appeared as a nun to a taxi driver in Athens. The taxi driver had skin cancer on his hands and was feeling a great lack of faith. During the ride, Ypomoni asked, "Why are you sad?" He proceeded to confess everything to her. She asked him if he wanted her to make the sign of the cross so that he would become well, and he agreed. He soon became sleepy and pulled over to rest. When he woke, his hands were better, but Ypomoni had disappeared. He immediately went to see his doctor and told him what had happened. At that moment, he saw an icon of St. Ypomoni hanging on the wall. This miracle occurred on the day when St. Ypomoni is celebrated.

SAINTS OF THE DAY: Publius of Athens; Habib of Hermopolis; Alexander of Thessalonica; Africanus, Publius, and Terence at Carthage; Christina of Persia; Aninas of the Euphrates; Leander of Seville.

MARCH 14

Isaiah 26:21-27:9; Genesis 9:18-10:1
Proverbs 12:23-13:9

Humility is the only power that can free the human soul and the nations.

+Elder Arsenie Papacioc of Romania

ROSTISLAV-MICHAEL, GREAT PRINCE OF KIEV. Rostislav was one of the great civil and church leaders of the mid-twelfth century, and his father and brother were also saints of the Church. Rostislav was given the province of Smolensk as an inheritance, and over the forty years of his rule, he built up cities, villages, churches, and monasteries. He set up a separate Smolensk diocese and endowed it. During this time, there was a drawn-out struggle among the princes for Kiev. When his brother Izyaslav died, Rostislav became Great Prince of Kiev. He later handed over this responsibility to his uncle. This was also a complicated period in the history of the Russian Church, as it was attempting autocephaly of the Russian metropolitanate. Rostislav had unconditional obedience to Church elders and a great respect for Church hierarchy. He had a custom on the Saturdays and Sundays of Great Lent to invite the abbot and twelve monks to dine at his table, and he served them. They had a tremendous influence on him, and they urged him to think about the independence of the Russian Church, which up to that time was primarily administered by Greek metropolitans sent from the Patriarch of Constantinople. This independence did not come to pass during Rostislav's tenure. When Rostislav fell gravely ill, he gave orders to be buried at the Kiev Theodosiev Monastery that his father founded.

SAINTS OF THE DAY: Euschymon, Bishop of Lampsacus; Benedict of Nursia; Eustathius and his company at Carrhae, Mesopotamia; Theognostus, Metropolitan of Kiev and Moscow; Alexander of Pidne; Andrew of Holy Trinity Monastery in Rafailovo, Siberia; Rostislav-Michael, Great Prince of Kiev; Talmach of Lough Erc; Kostroma "Feodorovskaya" Icon of the Mother of God.

MARCH 15

Isaiah 28:14-22; Genesis 10:32-11:9
Proverbs 13:19-14:6

Patiently endure the distressing and painful things that befall you, for through them God in His providence is purifying you.
St. Thalassios the Libyan

NEW MARTYR MANUEL OF CRETE. Manuel was a Christian in eighteenth-century Sfakion, Crete. In his childhood, he was taken into captivity by the Turks, who converted him to Mahometanism. When he became an adult, he escaped to the island of Mykonos and confessed his faith in Christ. He married and had six children. When Manuel discovered that his wife had committed adultery, he took the children and left her. On one occasion, when he was bringing a boat of wood from Samos, a patrol ship pulled up alongside him with his wife's brother on board. He accused Manuel of abandoning Mahometanism, and for this, he was arrested and imprisoned. During his interrogation, Manuel was stripped of his clothing, revealing his circumcision. His sentence was death, and Manuel responded, "Glory to Thee, O God." At the place of execution, Manuel knelt, and when he bowed his head, the executioner was so overcome with fear that he fled. Another officer attempted many times to behead Manuel, but he remained unharmed. Finally, the officer slit his throat. Because many pilgrims venerated the relics of St. Manuel, they were weighted with stones and thrown into the sea.

SAINTS OF THE DAY: Apostle Aristobulus of the Seventy, Bishop of Britain; Agapius, Pauplius, Timolaus, Romulus, two named Dionysius, and two named Alexander, at Caesarea in Palestine; Alexander of Side in Pamphylia; Zachariah, Pope of Rome; Nicander of Egypt; St. Habarestes; Nicander, founder of Gorodnoezersk Monastery (Novgorod); New Martyr Manuel of Crete.

FRIDAY

Salutations to the Virgin Mary
Strict Fast

MARCH 16

Isaiah 29:13-23; Genesis 12:1-7
Proverbs 14:15-26

The humility of the Theotokos also has much to teach women today. Let us all call upon her, for we all suffer from a lack of humility. Holy humility will provide us with ease, freedom, joy, grace, sanctity, redemption and a foretaste of the delight in Paradise, which will render us without problems, graceful and truly joyful even in this life.

+Blessed Moses the Athonite

VENERABLE ANANIAS, MONK OF MESOPOTAMIA. Ananias was born into a Christian family in Chalcedon. After the death of his parents, he went to live in a monastery, receiving monastic tonsure. He was just fifteen years old. In search of solitude, he went into the wilderness to live as an ascetic under the spiritual guidance of an elder named Maium. They ate nothing during the whole forty days of Great Lent. By constant ascetical deeds, God granted Ananias the gift to heal the sick, tame wild animals, perceive the thoughts of man, and fill a dry well with water. Two lions always accompanied him. He once perceived a certain distant pillar dweller who had been beaten by a robber, resolving to report him to the authorities. Ananias wrote him a letter, advising him not to leave his pillar. The letter was brought to him by a lion. Since Ananias himself carried drinking water from afar off, a bishop twice gave him donkeys to carry the water, but he gave them away both times to the poor. This same bishop ordained Ananias presbyter, against the wishes of the humble Ananias. Before his death, St. Ananias conversed with the Prophets Moses and Aaron and then gave up his soul.

SAINTS OF THE DAY: Alexander, Pope of Rome; Julian of Anazarbus; Ananias of Mesopotamia; Sabinas of Hermopolis; John of Rufinianae; Ten Martyrs in Phoenicia; Serapion of Novgorod; Christodoulos of Patmos; Papas of Lycaonia; Pimen of Dagestan, and Anthony of Meskhi; Romanus at Parium; Ambrose (Khelaia) of Georgia; Eutropia of Kherson; Abban of Kilabban (Ireland); Malachi of Rhodes.

Abstain from meat and dairy products, and fish.
Hebrews 6:9-12; Mark 7:31-37

March 17

When the flame of love exists, it consumes whatever evil approaches.
+Elder Amphilochios Makris of Patmos

PATRICK, ENLIGHTENER OF IRELAND. A native of Britain, Patrick was the son of a deacon and grandson of a priest. The sixteen-year-old Patrick was captured with hundreds of others by marauders and taken to Ireland. He herded the chief's swine in the solitude of the mountains. He began to pray day and night and sought the Lord with all his heart. After six years of slavery, God appeared to Patrick in a dream, telling him to escape to a ship several hundred miles away, and Patrick obeyed. While in port, the crew went looking for food. When Patrick prayed, a herd of swine appeared. Afterward, he struggled in France under the guidance of Bishop Germanus. Patrick arrived home and once again in a dream he was told to go back to Ireland. Many years later, he was ordained bishop and was once again sent to Ireland to convert the Irish to Christ. The Irish king called Patrick in for questioning, accusing him of building a fire to celebrate Pascha. Using a shamrock, Patrick attempted to teach the king about the Holy Trinity. However, after much discussion, Patrick was unable to convert the king, but his daughters and other relatives accepted Christ. Therefore, Patrick was given permission to preach Christ in Ireland. Once, during a certain Lenten season, Patrick spent forty days on a mountain praying and battling demons disguised as blackbirds. His concern was that Christianity would disappear from Ireland after his death, but an angel of God was sent to reassure him that Christianity would survive there until the Second Coming. Patrick would not leave Ireland for fear of losing the Christian foothold that he had fought for and for which his very life was in danger of twelve times. Before he died, Ireland had churches and monasteries even in the most remote areas, where souls were continually being converted.

SAINTS OF THE DAY: Alexis the Man of God; Theosterictus the Confessor; Marinus the Soldier; Ambrose of Alexandria; Paul of Crete; Gertrude of Nivelles; Gabriel the Lesser; Gurias of Tauria.

SUNDAY

MARCH 18

Sunday of St. John Climacus
Abstain from meat and dairy products, and fish.
Hebrews 6:13-20; Mark 9:17-31

Even without any other passion, self-esteem can ruin a man; and in the same way, if we have formed the habit of judging, we can be utterly ruined by this alone; for indeed, the Pharisee was condemned for this very thing.

St. John Climacus

MARTYRS TROPHIMOS, EUKARPIOS OF NICOMEDIA, AND THEIR COMPANIONS. Trophimos and Eukarpios were third-century Roman soldiers during the persecutions of Emperor Maximian. They were in command of troop detachments whose objective was to find and arrest Christian men, women, and children. Even their names were feared among the Christians. The Roman generals looked upon these two as heroes. One time, the two soldiers were brought to their knees when thunder exploded, and lightning flashed around them. Like the conversion of St. Paul, they heard a Voice from a cloud asking them why they persecuted the Christians. The Lord told them to become servants of Jesus Christ and to join the Heavenly Kingdom. After this miracle, the two men were filled with the Holy Spirit, and they released all the imprisoned Christians. Having joined the Christian camps, Trophimos and Eukarpios taught the Christians the search techniques that were being used by the Roman army. It was as if the Christians had vanished from the earth, and this angered the Roman high command. Finally, a Roman spy, posing as a Christian convert, located Trophimos and Eukarpios. They were arrested together with other Christians, tortured, and then burned to death in a bonfire.

SAINTS OF THE DAY: Cyril, Archbishop of Jerusalem; Trophimos, Eukarpios, and those with them in Nicomedia; Tetricus, Bishop of Langres in Gaul; Daniel, monk of Egypt; Cyril of Astrakhan; The 10,000 Martyrs of Nicomedia; Edward, King of England; Maria (Skobtsova), nun, at Ravensbruck.

MARCH 19

Isaiah 37:33-38:6; Genesis 13:12-18
Proverbs 14:27-15:4

At the beginning of every task, call on the name of the Lord your God, and begin it with prayer, that the Lord may prosper you to begin it and complete it. And from this it is evident that a Christian ought not to begin anything that is contrary to the Law of God, but only that which is in agreement with it.

St. Tikhon of Zadonsk

MARTYR PANCHARIOS AT NICOMEDIA. Pancharios was born a Christian but forsook his faith. He left home to become a Roman soldier during the reign of Emperor Diocletian in the third century. He soon became captain of the royal guard and developed a strong friendship with the emperor. When his family heard that he had denied his faith, they sent him a letter urging him to heed the fear of God. They quoted the words of the Holy Gospel, "Whosoever shall deny Me before men, him will I also deny before My Father which is in heaven (Mt. 10:33)." Filled with compunction, Pancharios openly confessed his faith in Christ, and some soldiers overheard this. He was brought before Diocletian and was asked to deny his Christian faith. When he would not, a judge ordered torture and imprisonment. St. Pancharios was martyred.

SAINTS OF THE DAY: Chrysanthus, Daria, Claudius, Hilaria, Jason, Maurus, Diodorus, and Marianus, at Rome; Maria, wife of Vsevelod III; Innocent, founder of Komel (Vologda); Bassa, nun of Pskov Caves; Pancharios at Nicomedia; Sophia of Slutsk and Minsk; New Martyr Nicholas Karamanos of Smyrna; New Martyr Demetrios at Constantinople; Symeon (Popovic) of Dajbabe, Montenegro; Dimitri of Tornada; Alcmund, Prince of Northumbria; Commemoration of the Miracle of Kollyva wrought by St. Theodore the Tyro; Smolensk "Umileniye" (Tender Feeling) Icon of the Mother of God.

MARCH 20

Isaiah 40:18-31; Genesis 15:1-15
Proverbs 15:7-19

Where would there be opportunities for struggling for great deeds if we were not occasionally injured by our neighbors, if they did not offend us? Where would there be opportunities for patiently bearing offenses, for meekness and humility? You see, then, that we must be tried by many and various evils in order to prove our virtue and be eventually crowned.

St. John of Kronstadt

HERBERT, HERMIT OF DERWENTWATER. Herbert was an Anglo-Saxon priest and hermit in the seventh-century. He dwelled on a little island called St. Herbert's Island, in the Lake of Derwentwater. St. Bede wrote the life of St. Herbert in his book, "Ecclesiastical History of the English People." Herbert was a close friend and disciple of St. Cuthbert of Lindisfarne, who directed him to become an anchorite. He lived on fish from the lake and vegetables that he grew. Every year he visited Cuthbert to receive direction in spiritual matters. On his last visit, Cuthbert told Herbert to ask all that he needed for they would never see each other again in the world. Herbert fell weeping at Cuthbert's feet, asking that he be granted the grace to praise God in heaven at the same time. Cuthbert prayed and answered saying that the mercy of God had granted their desire. Upon his return to his hermitage, St. Herbert suffered through a long illness, and purified of his imperfections, gave up his soul on the very same day as St. Cuthbert.

SAINTS OF THE DAY: Seven Virgin-martyrs of Amisus: Alexandra, Claudia, Euphrasia, Matrona, Juliana, Euphemia, and Theodosia; Nicetas the Confessor; Holy Fathers martyred at the Monastery of St. Sabbas; Martyrs Rodion, Aquila, Longinus, and Emanuel; Euphrosynus of Blue-Jay Lake; Tadros of Edessa; Martin of Braga; Austreigiselis of Bourges; Wulfram, missionary; Cuthbert of Lindisfarne; Archil II, King of Georgia; Myron of Mega Castro on Crete; Herbert of Derwentwater; Michael the Sabbaite; Nicholas Holz of Novosiolki.

MARCH 21

Isaiah 41:4-14; Genesis 17:1-9
Proverbs 15:20-16:9

If in desiring to rebuke anyone you are yourself moved to anger, you satisfy your own passion; but in saving another do not lose yourself.

St. Macarius the Great

SERAPION THE SINDONITE, MONK OF EGYPT. Serapion was an ascetic in the fourth-century Egyptian desert when monasticism flourished. He constantly strove to perfect himself in the virtues. When he had no money for alms, he would sell himself into the service of others. During one winter journey, he gave away his coat to a poor man and his garment to another. For the sake of the gospel, he was once sold to idol-worshippers. He worked for them all day and kept vigil all night, reciting Scripture, which he knew by heart. He astonished his master with his moral excellence. He spoke the Word of God to them, washed their feet, and converted and baptized them. Serapion delivered them from paganism and the devil. Then he gave them back his purchase price, and they gave alms to the poor with this money. He said that he had three creditors—avarice, fornication, and gluttony and that he had defeated the first two, but the third demanded payment. Another time he corrected a pride-filled nun because for twenty-five years she only prayed in solitude. He instructed her to live a humble life in public. Another time, at a desert monastery, he openly confessed that he was troubled by the demon of gluttony and that by night he had stolen a loaf of bread to eat. Since he confessed this openly, he put the demon to shame and it no longer had power over him. Serapion later died peacefully.

SAINTS OF THE DAY: Thomas, Patriarch of Constantinople; Philemon and Domnina of Rome; Cyril, Bishop of Catania; Beryllus of Catania; Lupicinus of the Jura Mountains (Gaul); James the Confessor, Bishop of the Studion; Michael of Agrapha; Seraphim of Vyritsa; Serapion the Sindonite of Egypt; Enda of Aran (Ireland); Pachomius of Nerekhta; Sophronius, abbot in Palestine.

MARCH 22

Isaiah 42:5-16; Genesis 18:20-33
Proverbs 16:17-17:17

Serve God faithfully.

St. Pachomios the Great

MARTYR DROSIS OF ANTIOCH WITH FIVE VIRGIN-MARTYRS. Drosis was the daughter of Emperor Trajan of Rome, who martyred Christians and refused them burial. She was secretly a Christian. She heard about the holy virgins who secretly gathered the bodies of martyrs by night, giving them burial. She went to them one evening, asking to help. Adrian, a member of the court and fiancé of Drosis, ordered a guard set to arrest those who were burying the bodies. That very night, the six women were captured. When Trajan heard that his daughter was among the women, he put Drosis in seclusion and sentenced the others to burning in a copper-foundry furnace. They accepted their execution and received martyrs' crowns. The ashes from the furnace were mixed with copper and used to make copper steps at the public baths. For as long as they were there, every pagan that crossed them fell down dead. When the pagan priests realized why this was happening, they advised Trajan to remove them, but Adrian suggested to Trajan to melt this copper and make five statues of naked virgins that resembled the martyrs. When the statues were set up, the emperor saw in a dream five pure lambs in Paradise, and Jesus chastised him, foretelling that Drosis would also become a pure lamb in heaven. Enraged, Trajan had two large furnaces built and invited Christians to cast themselves therein, and with great faith, many did. Drosis prayed to the Lord to help her escape, and miraculously all the guards fell asleep. For seven days she hid herself, praying and fasting. On the eighth day, she gave up her spirit in the red-hot ovens.

SAINTS OF THE DAY: Drosis of Antioch, and five Virgin-martyrs; Callinica and Basilissa of Rome; Basil of Ancyra; Sophia (Grineva) of Kiev; Euthymius of Demitsana; Paul of Brittany; Basil (Zelentsov) of Priluk; "The Izborsk" Icon of the Mother of God.

FRIDAY

Akathist to the Virgin Mary
Strict Fast

MARCH 23

Isaiah 45:11-17; Genesis 22:1-18
Proverbs 17:17-18:5

If you cultivate prayer, be ready for the attacks of demons and endure them resolutely; for they will come at you like wild beasts and maltreat your whole body.

St. Nicodemus the Hagiorite

VENERABLE LUKE THE NEW OF MITYLENE. Luke was orphaned at an early age. He was entrusted to a merchant who traveled with him to Russia and Constantinople. After fighting with a Turkish boy, he was captured by the Turks and forced to become a Muslim. He fled from the Turkish home where he was staying and met with a spiritual father who told him to go the Holy Mountain. He met many elders there who strengthened him in the faith and love for Christ. A desire grew in him to confess his sin of denying Christ. He left Mt. Athos and traveled to Mytilene. He appeared before the agha and bravely confessed that he was a Christian. He was interrogated, flattered, given promises, and threatened with torture, but Luke stood firm. While in prison, Holy Communion was brought to him, and a man was sent to Luke to bolster his steadfastness. The agha asked him many times to return to Islam, but Luke responded to this saying, "I worship and believe in Christ." St. Luke was hanged. His body remained on the scaffold for three days, then was weighed down and thrown into the sea. It was later recovered and secretly buried.

SAINTS OF THE DAY: Nicon and 199 disciples in Sicily; Bassian, Archbishop of Rostov; Dometius the Persian; Nicon, abbot of the Kiev Caves; Ephraim and Theodosios of Vologda; Pachomius of Nerekhta; Basil of Mangazea in Siberia; New Martyr Luke of Adrianople and Mt. Athos, at Mytilene; Helen, nun of Florovsk Ascension Convent in Kiev; Gwinear of Cornwall; Sergius (Serebriansky) of Tver; Elijan (Vyatlin) of Vladimir; Ethilwald of Farne.

SATURDAY

MARCH 24

Forefeast of the Annunciation
Abstain from meat and dairy products, and fish.
Hebrews 9:1-7; Luke 1:39-49, 56

Let us strive to enter by the narrow gate. Just as the trees, if they have not stood before the winter's storms cannot bear fruit, so it is with us; this present age is a storm and it is only through many trials and temptations that we can obtain an inheritance in the kingdom of heaven.

+Amma Theodora of Alexandria

MARTYR PETER OF KAZAN. During the sixteenth century, Peter was a newly-baptized convert to Christianity from Mussulmanism. After leaving the Russian army, he was dragged by force from his home by the Kazan Tatars and was addressed by his former non-Christian name, hoping that he would renounce his new faith. However, Peter answered, "Father for me and mother—is God glorified in Trinity: Father and Son and Holy Spirit... If ye believe in the Father and the Son and the Holy Spirit, then ye be kin to me; in holy Baptism the name Peter was given me, and not that, by which ye address me." Seeing that he remained steadfast in the faith, his relatives turned Peter over to torture. Until the hour of his death, Peter did not cease repeating, "I am a Christian." He was martyred and buried in Kazan, on the site where a church would later be built dedicated to the Resurrection of Christ.

SAINTS OF THE DAY: Artemon, Bishop of Seleucia; Artemon, presbyter of Laodicea; Parthenios III, Patriarch of Constantinople; Zachariah the Recluse of Egypt; Zachariah the Faster of the Kiev Caves; Zachariah the Hospitable of the Kiev Caves; James, Bishop of Catania; Martin of Thebes; Eight Martyrs of Caesarea; Stephen and Peter of Kazan; Caimin of Holy Island on Lough Derg (Ireland); Thomas, abbot of St. Euthymius Monastery; Sabbas the New of Kalymnos; Dunchad, abbot of Iona; Severus of Catania; Miracle at the Monastery of the Caves in Kiev; "The Clouded Mount" Icon of the Mother of God.

SUNDAY

MARCH 25

The Annunciation of the Theotokos
Abstain from meat and dairy products, and fish.
Hebrews 2:11-18; Luke 1:24-38

Do not trust the mindset of secular people. Decide what you want most: the sympathy of the world or a return near to God.

St. Paisios the Athonite

NEW HIEROMARTYR TIKHON, PATRIARCH OF MOSCOW AND ALL RUSSIA. Tikhon was a meek and humble son of a village priest in nineteenth-century Russia. His father once had a revelation about the future of his three sons and that Tikhon would be a great man. At the seminary, Tikhon was always ready to help a classmate. He was well loved, and most of the town attended the ceremony when he took his monastic vows. He was soon elevated to the rank of archimandrite and then bishop. He was made the head of the Orthodox Church in America. He reorganized the diocese and did much to spread Orthodoxy. He was made an honorary citizen of the United States, established churches, consecrated St. Nicholas Cathedral in New York City, and established St. Tikhon's Monastery in Pennsylvania. He was made Bishop of Yaroslavl and returned to Russia. He won the affection of his people for his wisdom and kindness. He helped support charities. When WWI began, he helped a multitude of poor in war-ravaged areas. Then the Russian Revolution brought atheism, persecutions, civil war, and hunger, and Church property was confiscated. But the Church rallied around the new patriarch Tikhon. He sought not to quarrel with the Communist government and asked the clergy not to make political statements. He gave his blessing to give church valuables to the poor so they could buy food. After nearly two thousand trials around Russia, over ten thousand Orthodox Christians were shot and killed. Even Patriarch Tikhon was imprisoned for over a year. When St. Tikhon died in 1925, after serving seven and a half years as patriarch, almost a million people attended his funeral.

SAINTS OF THE DAY: Pelagia, Theodosia, and Dula of Nicomedia; Tikhon, Patriarch of Moscow and All Russia; Nicander of Pskov; Parthenius of the Kiev Caves; Justin Popovich of Chelije in Serbia; Sabbas the New; Senuphius the Wonderworker of Latomos in Thessalonica.

MONDAY

MARCH 26

Synaxis of the Archangel Gabriel
Abstain from meat and dairy products, and fish.
Isaiah 48:17-49:4; Genesis 27:1-41
Proverbs 19:16-25

Let us remember love for the poor, that this love might save us from greed, when the sin of greed shall come to meet us. Let us acquire peace with all, the humble and the great, that this might guard us against hate, when it shall come to meet us. Let us acquire patience before all and in all things, that this might guard us against carelessness, when it shall come to meet us. Let us love all of our brothers and sisters, without hating anyone or repaying anyone any ill done against us; for this shall guard us against envy, when this demon too shall come to meet us.

St. Isaac the Syrian

GOVAN, HERMIT OF PEMBROKESHIRE. Govan was once set upon by pirates in the sixth century, and a fissure opened in a cliff large enough to hide himself in until the pirates left. It is located in the Pembrokeshire Coast National Park in Wales. He decided to stay along the cliff to warn locals of any impending attacks. He lived in a small cave in that fissure that can now be reached by a long flight of stone steps. Govan caught fish and drank water from two nearby springs. There is now a vaulted limestone chapel built over his cave that was built in the fourteenth century.

SAINTS OF THE DAY: Synaxis of the Archangel Gabriel; Quadratus (Codratus), Theodosius, Manuel, and 40 other Martyrs; Stephen the Confessor and Wonderworker, abbot of Tryglia; Basil the Younger; Eusebius, Bishop of Kival, and Pullius the Reader; Irenaeus, Bishop of Sirmium; Malchus of Chalcis in Syria; Montanus the priest, and his wife Maxima, at Sirmium; George of Sofia, at Adrianople; Eutychius of Alexandria; Bathusius and Bercus, presbyters, and others in Crimea; Braulio of Saragossa in Iberia; Ludger, Bishop of Munster; Govan, hermit of Pembrokeshire.

MARCH 27

Isaiah 49:6-10; Genesis 31:3-16
Proverbs 21:3-21

Adorn the soul, care for it, so that, by means of careful attention, you may remove every defilement which results from sin, and every shameful vice, that you may embellish and make bright the soul with the ornaments of virtue.

St. Basil the Great

VENERABLE JOHN THE CLAIRVOYANT OF LYCOPOLIS. John was a carpenter from fourth-century Lycopolis, Egypt. At the age of twenty-five, he decided to become a monk. For the next five years, he lived in several different monasteries. He finally decided that he preferred complete quiet and solitude, and withdrew into the Thebaid. He lived there for thirty years in a small cell. He conversed with visitors and received food through a small window. God granted John the gift of clairvoyance. He foretold that Emperor Theodosius the Great would win a victory over his enemies Maximus and Eugenios, as well as the Gauls. He told visitors what their future held for them and gave them guidance. He anointed the sick with holy oil and healed them. John's directives included first to be humble, to imitate the saints as much as possible, and never to give yourself praise because sometimes those who reach perfection and whose prayers can cause miracles, can fall into the abyss. John instructed to love silence, divine contemplation, to have a pure mind, avoid sinful thoughts, give kindness to strangers, give alms, to help others, and to live without anger. By the example of his angelic life and soul-saving words, many people received spiritual benefit. St. John lived to the age of ninety.

SAINTS OF THE DAY: Paul, Bishop of Corinth; Matrona of Thessalonica; John the Clairvoyant of Lycopolis; Prophet Ananias; Cyricus of Thrace; Eutychius, monk; Ephraim of Rostov; Paphnutius, disciple of St. Anthony the Great; Philetos, Lydia, Macedonos, Theoprepios, Cronides, and Amphilochios in Illyria; Alexander of Voche; Anthony of Tobolsk; Rupert of Salzburg; Martyrs Baruch and John; "Sweet Kissing" (Glykophilousa) and "Of the Akathist" Icons of the Mother of God.

MARCH 28

Isaiah 58:1-11; Genesis 43:26-31, 45:1-16
Proverbs 21:23-22:4

Do not try to resolve a tangled situation with contentiousness, but rather with what the spiritual law calls for: patience and prayer and unwavering hope.

St. Mark the Ascetic

STEPHEN THE WONDERWORKER, ABBOT OF TRIGLEIA. Stephen was the ninth-century abbot of Trigleia Monastery, south of the Sea of Marmara. He accepted monastic tonsure at a young age. He was meek, serene, and filled with compunction and love. He kept all-night vigils and had many virtues. God granted him the gift of working miracles, and he healed the sick. He also helped widows and was a father of orphans. His prayers cast down demons and silenced heretics. When Emperor Leo the Armenian began the persecution against those who venerated the icons, Stephen was summoned for interrogation. Leo attempted to force him to sign a document that rejected the veneration of icons, but Stephen refused to sign it and denounced Leo's impiety. The iconoclasts tortured Stephen by various means, then imprisoned him, where he died from his weakened condition. Sweet-smelling myrrh exuded from his relics, and his reliquary proved to be the site of countless healings. He cured the demon-possessed, the blind, and paralytics.

SAINTS OF THE DAY: Apostle Herodion of the Seventy; Priscus, Malchus, and Alexander of Caesarea; Hesychius the Theologian of Jerusalem; Hilarion the New, abbot of Pelecete; Dionysius the Merciful, Bishop of Larissa; John, Bishop of Manglisi, Georgia; George, Bishop of Zagora, Parodus and Peter, priests, and Prince Enravota-Boyan, of Bulgaria; Eustratius of the Kiev Caves; Hilarion, founder of Pskovoezersk Monastery; Jonah, founder of Klimets Monastery (Olonets); Peter Ochryzko of Chartoviec; The miraculous occurrence of Taxiotis; "Of the Sign" Icon of the Mother of God.

MARCH 29

Isaiah 65:8-16; Genesis 46:1-7
Proverbs 23:15-24:5

My brother, is it—by any chance—possible for an island located in the middle of the sea to hinder the waves from hitting up against it? The only thing the island can manage is to drive back the waves. So it is with us. We are not able to cut off the waves of thoughts, so that they do not hit up against us—especially since we are filled with passions. We are, however, capable of driving back the thoughts and hindering them from entering our souls. Otherwise, if we allow them entry into our soul, they will dominate it and quickly destroy it.

St. Ephraim the Syrian

GUNDLEUS AND GWLADYS, PARENTS OF ST. CADOC. Gundleus was a chieftain of southeast Wales. He desired to marry Gwladys, who the biographer says was one of many children, the daughter of Brychan of Brecknock. Brychan refused the marriage, so Gundleus rode with an army of 300 men and carried off his bride. Their first born was the great St. Cadoc, but these parents lived much of their lives given over to violence and brigandage. After some time, Cadoc decided to reform his parents and succeeded. The two left the world and lived close to one another. They lived austerely on the fruits of their labor. Cadoc insisted that his parents should separate altogether. Both passed the rest of their days in devout retirement. Their memory is preserved in several church dedications and place-names.

SAINTS OF THE DAY: Mark the Confessor, Bishop of Arethusa, with Cyril of Heliopolis, and others who suffered under Julian the Apostate; Diadochus, Bishop of Photike; Martyrs Jonah and Barachisius and those with them in Persia: Zanithas, Lazarus, Maruthas, Narses, Elias, Mares, Habib, Sivsithina, and Sabbas; Paul Voinarsky, and brothers Paul and Alexis Kiryan, of Crimea; Eustathius the Confessor, Bishop of Kios in Bithynia; Jonah and Mark of the Pskov Caves Monastery; Eustasius, abbot of Luxeuil; Gundleus and Gwladys, parents of St. Cadoc.

MARCH 30

Isaiah 66:10-24; Genesis 49:33-50:26
Proverbs 31:8-31

When you want to resolve a complicated matter, look for what will please God in the situation, and you will find His solution to be to your benefit.

St. Mark the Ascetic

VENERABLE JOHN CLIMACUS OF SINAI. At the age of sixteen, John went to Mt. Sinai. Two holy men foresaw that one day John would be abbot of Sinai. For nineteen years, his spiritual instructor was Abba Martyrios, and when he died, John chose to live as a hermit in a wild place called Tholos. For forty years, he fasted, prayed, and shed tears of penitence. He shunned contact with society to diminish his carnal desires. He only slept as much as was necessary to keep up his strength. Most importantly, he received humility. There came to him many visitors, wanting to receive spiritual guidance and salvation. He did not deprive anyone. At the age of 75, John became abbot of Sinai. He is best known for his book titled, *The Ladder of Divine Ascent*, which was written at the request of the abbot of the nearby monastery of Raithu. The book describes the virtues one must master to rise to spiritual perfection. The pope of Rome asked for John's prayers and sent him money and beds for the many pilgrims that visited the monastery. After only four years as abbot, John appointed his brother George to succeed him. As John lay dying, George lamented their separation; therefore, John said that he would ask God to reunite them soon. George died ten months later.

SAINTS OF THE DAY: John Climacus of Sinai, author of *The Ladder*; John the Hermit of Cilicia; Prophet Joel (Joad), who dwelled in Bethel; Zachariah, Metropolitan of Corinth; Eubula, mother of St. Panteleimon; John II, Patriarch of Jerusalem; Matrona the Barefoot of St. Petersburg; Sophronius, Bishop of Irkutsk; Osburga of Coventry; Translation of the relics of Martyr-King St. Edmund of East Anglia.

SATURDAY

Lazarus Saturday
Abstain from meat and dairy products, and fish.

MARCH 31

Hebrews 12:28-29, 13:1-8; John 11:1-45

Lord God, we can hope for others nothing better than the happiness we desire for ourselves. Therefore, I pray Thee, do not separate me after death from those I tenderly loved on earth. Grant that when I am, they may be with me, and that I may enjoy their presence in heaven, after being so often deprived of it on earth. Lord God, I ask Thee to receive Thy beloved children immediately into Thy life-giving heart. After this brief life on earth, give them eternal happiness.

St. Ambrose of Milan

AKAKIOS THE CONFESSOR, BISHOP OF MELITENE. At the time of the persecutions of Emperor Decius, Akakios was imprisoned under the authority of the governor of Cappadocia. Over a six-month period, he was tortured. During this time, he gave a discourse on the Christian faith. When he was finally brought before the governor, he was mysteriously set free by order of Emperor Decius. He returned to Melitene as bishop and died peacefully.

SAINTS OF THE DAY: Blaise of Amorium and Mt. Athos; Akakios the Confessor, Bishop of Melitene in Pisidia; Hypatios the Wonderworker, Bishop of Gangra; Innocent, Metropolitan of Moscow and enlightener of Alaska and Siberia; Jonah, Metropolitan of Kiev, Moscow, and All Russia; Joseph the Fair, son of Jacob; Abdas, Bishop of Hormizd-Ardashir, the deacon Benjamin, of Persia, and Ormisdes the Confessor; Martyr Menander; Stephen the Wonderworker; Hypatius, abbot of Rufinus in Chalcedon; Philaret of Glinsk Hermitage; Hypatius the Healer of the Kiev Caves; Apollo, ascetic of the Thebaid; Appearance of the Iveron Icon of the Mother of God (Mt. Athos).

It behooves us to live according to the traditions of the saints and fulfill the commands of God and observe the traditions of the holy Fathers and not to excuse ourselves by ignoring the blame of sins saying that nowadays it is impossible to live according to the Scriptures and follow the writings of the holy Fathers.

St. Nilus of Sora

SUNDAY

Palm Sunday
Abstain from meat and dairy products.
Philippians 4:4-9; John 12:1-18

APRIL 1

Prayer is a remedy against grief and depression.

St. Nilus of Sinai

HIEROMARTYR JOACHIM, ARCHBISHOP OF NIZHNI-NOVGOROD. Joachim was the son of a junior deacon in nineteenth-century Kiev. He attended the Kiev Theological Seminary, and was married and ordained to the priesthood at the Riga Cathedral. He had two sons, but when his wife died, Joachim was tonsured archimandrite and made editor of the diocesan journal. He was later consecrated bishop of several areas. He was a fiery preacher with a warm heart. His missionary work converted a huge number to Orthodoxy. He employed and found a good salary for four missionaries and 50 parishes were founded, each with their own clergy. In 1903, resettlement to the Turgai region began, and the settlers had to cope for themselves, and there was no one to carry out the rites. The whole area was in captivity to the Sectarians. Joachim sent a report to the Holy Synod, and he received an additional 50,000 rubles to build churches and schools. They trained teachers, readers, deacons, and priests, and soon the region was covered with well-organized parishes, and an end was put to Sectarian propaganda. Joachim traveled tirelessly on a cart around his huge diocese. Church schools flourished, he clothed the poor seminarians and provided them with money to live. He was a true benefactor. He was imprisoned for a time when the Russian Revolution began. While visiting his son and family in the Crimea, Joachim was martyred by the Bolsheviks. He was hanged with his head down, on the royal doors of the Sebastopol cathedral.

SAINTS OF THE DAY: Mary of Egypt; Macarius of Pelecete; Meliton of Sardis; Achaz, King of Judah; Abraham of Bulgaria; Martyrs Gerontius and Basilides; Gerontius of the Kiev Caves; Euthymius of Suzdal; Barsanuphius of Optina; Macarius (Vasiliev), at the Pskov Caves; Pachomius of Moldavia; John of Shavta, and Eulogius the Prophet, fool-for-Christ; Joachim of Nizhni-Novgorod; Tewdrig of Tintern.

Holy Monday
Strict Fast
Matthew 21:18-43; Matthew 24:3-35

APRIL 2

From the sacrament of the cross you receive both food and drink; let the wood, which availed at Mara in a figure for sweetening the taste, avail you in truth for soothing the softened breast, and you will not labor for the remedy for increasing the health. Cure yourself at the source from which you had been wounded. Love those whom you hated before; esteem those whom you envied with unjust disparagements. Imitate the good, if you can follow them; if you cannot follow them, surely rejoice with them and congratulate your betters. Your debts will be forgiven you, when you yourself shall forgive. Your sacrifices will be accepted, when you shall come to God as a peacemaker.

St. Cyprian of Carthage

GEORGE OF MATSKVERI MONASTERY. George lived during the end of the ninth and beginning of the tenth centuries and was raised in an aristocratic and pious family. He succeeded the great feudal lord George Chorchaneli as ruler of the Samtskhe region in southern Georgia. He served for many years as their chief political leader and spiritual leader of the Atsquri diocese. According to tradition, Apostle Andrew the First-called founded this diocese, and he left there the "Not-Made-By-Hands" icon of the Most Holy Mother of God. George was also known as a great writer of the Church. He left biographical accounts of several saints, including St. Serapion of Zarzma and St. Grigol of Khandzta.

SAINTS OF THE DAY: Gregory of Nicomedia; Titus the Wonder-worker; Theodora (Theodosia) of Tyre; Polycarp of Alexandria; George of Matskveri; Amphianus and Aedesius of Patara, Lycia; Nicetius of Lyons; Sabbas, Archbishop of Sourozh.

Tuesday

Holy Tuesday
Strict Fast

April 3

Matthew 22:15-23:39, Matthew 24:36-26:2

I counsel my penitents that before they express their anger, be it in speech or gestures, be it only mentally, to utter three or five times, *"Lord Jesus Christ, Son of God, have mercy on me, a sinner."* And if they say the prayer quickly and inattentively under the oppression of anger, then they should concentrate with humility upon the word *"sinner,"* and their anger will abate. Many of them have succeeded in making their life, their family relationships, their relations with other people, and even their interior life change for the better.

+*Elder George Calciu of Romania*

FARA (BURGUNDOFARA) OF FAREMOUTIERS. Fara's father, Count Agneric, was a courtier to King Theodebert II. Three of his children became saints of the Church: St. Cagnoald of Laon, St. Faro of Meaux, and St. Fara. As a child, Fara received a blessing from St. Columban when he was a guest at their home. Fara resolved to lead a religious life, but she faced opposition and persecution from her father, who wanted to bestow her in marriage. This struggle caused Fara to fall into a prolonged illness, which was later cured by St. Eustace. Eventually, her father was so reconciled to Fara's wishes that he built her a convent which he richly endowed. At her young age, she became the abbess and capably continued there for thirty-seven years. For a time the convent kept the Rule of St. Columban. After St. Fara's death, the monastery was renamed in her honor and developed into the celebrated Benedictine abbey of Faremoutiers.

SAINTS OF THE DAY: Joseph the Hymnographer of Sicily; Nicetas the Confessor, of Medikion; Cassius, Philip, and Eutychius of Thessalonica; Paul the Russian at Constantinople; Evagrius, Benignus, Christos, Arestus, Kinnudius, Rufus, Patricius, and Zosima, at Tomis; Illyricus of Mt. Myrsinon; Elpidephorus, Dius, Bithonius, and Galycus; Nectarius of Bezhetsk Monastery (Tver); Ulphianus of Tyre; Fara of Faremoutiers; "The Unfading Flower" Icon of the Mother of God.

WEDNESDAY

Holy Wednesday
Strict Fast

APRIL 4

John 12:17-50; Matthew 26:6-16

A good man does not sell his inner freedom for money, even if he happens to be offered a huge sum. For things belonging to this life are like a dream, and the fantasies of wealth are uncertain and short-lived.

St. Anthony the Great

VIRGIN-MARTYR FERFOUTHA OF PERSIA, ALONG WITH HER SISTER AND SERVANTS. Ferfoutha lived during the fourth-century reign of Persian emperor Sapor. Ferfoutha and her sister were servants to the empress. Ferfoutha was extraordinarily beautiful, and the empress suggested to her to enter marriage to gain a high position, but she refused since she had given a vow of virginity to God. When one of the king's sorcerers saw her beauty, he asked Ferfoutha to become his wife, and again she refused, saying that she was a Christian and a bride of Christ. When Shapur's wife fell ill, the offended sorcerer accused Ferfoutha, her sister, and the other servants of giving the empress poison. The women were all taken to trial. They fearlessly defended themselves, saying that as Christians they would not do such wickedness as they were accused, and they were prepared to accept death for Christ. The chief judge secretly sent his servant to the prison, offering Ferfoutha and the others freedom if she consented to marry him. Two other judges also made the same proposal, but Ferfoutha refused them all. After this, they were all condemned to death for sorcery and for being Christians. They were each tied to two pillars and sawn in two. Their bodies were thrown into a ditch, and Christians secretly gathered them, giving them burial.

SAINTS OF THE DAY: Publius of Egypt; Theodulus and Agathopous of Thessalonica; Plato the Studite; Isidore of Seville; Theonas of Thessalonica; Ferfoutha of Persia, with others; George of Mt. Maleon; Zosimas of Palestine; Joseph the Much-ailing; James of Old Torzhok; Basil of Mangazea; Zosimas, at Lake Vorbozoma; Nicetas the Albanian; Theonas, Symeon, and Phorbinos of Egypt; Benjamin and Nichephorus of Solovki.

Holy Thursday
Strict Fast

APRIL 5

1 Corinthians 11:23-32; Matthew 26:1-20
John 13:3-17; Matthew 26:21-39
Luke 22:43-45; Matthew 26:40-27:2

Of all approaches to God, prayer is the best and in the last analysis the only means. In the act of prayer the human mind finds its noblest expression. The mental state of the scientist engaged in research, of the artist creating a work of art, of the thinker wrapped up in philosophy—even of professional theologians propounding their doctrines—cannot be compared to that of the man of prayer brought face to Face with the living God. Each and every kind of mental activity presents less of a strain than prayer. We may be capable of working for ten or twelve hours on end but a few moments of prayer and we are exhausted.

+Archimandrite Sophrony of England

TRANSLATION OF THE RELICS OF ST. JOB, PATRIARCH OF MOSCOW. After St. Job's death in the early seventeenth century, his relics were buried by the doors of the Dormition Church of the monastery in Staritsa. Many miracles took place at his grave. Forty-five years later, Metropolitan Nikon of Novgorod directed that the relics of St. Job be transferred to Moscow. Under the direction of the Metropolitan Barlaam of Rostov, the relics were uncovered and found incorrupt and fragrant, and they healed many from mental and physical illnesses. The relics were taken in procession to the Kremlin and placed in the Dormition cathedral. The altar crosses at the Staritsa monastery and the Tver cathedral contain parts of St. Job's miracle-working relics.

SAINTS OF THE DAY: Mark the Anchorite; Theodora and Didymus of Alexandria; Philip I of Moscow; Theodora of Thessalonica; Publius of Egypt; Martyrs Claudius, Diodorus, Victor, Victorinus, Pappia, Serapion, and Nicephorus; Martyrs Maximos and Terence; Theonas, Symeon, and Phorbinus of Egypt; Plato of the Studion; Martyrs Thermus, Zenon, and Pompey; George of New Ephesus; Mark the Ascetic; Five girls martyred at Neanidor; Panagiotis, at Jerusalem; Constantine of Russia with others; Derfel of Lianderfel; Ethelburga of Kent.

Holy Friday
Strict Fast

APRIL 6

1 Corinthians 5:6-8; Matthew 27:62-66

What then did the Lord, the Truth and the Light, accomplish on coming down to the world? He preserved His flesh incorrupt in virginity with which he had adorned it. And so let us too, if we are to come to the likeness of God, endeavor to aspire to the virginity of Christ.

St. Methodius of Olympus

SEBASTIAN, ELDER OF OPTINA. Sebastian had a great thirst for reading and a fondness for animals. He was meek, discerning, clairvoyant, and merciful. He was ordained to the priesthood and served five years in the Tambov province. He was arrested by the authorities in 1933. He said that the Soviet closing of churches and monasteries was destroying the Orthodox faith. Sebastian was placed in a forced labor camp, enduring beatings and torture for five years. When he was released, the nuns who helped him during that time formed a community of spiritual children, and Sebastian would conduct services secretly. People who heard about him would travel from afar to see him. Finally, in 1955, Sebastian obtained permission to create a makeshift church where he and the nuns celebrated the Divine Liturgy. Commemoration of the dead played an enormous role in Sebastian's ministry. There was a cemetery with common graves, where two hundred reposed peasants were buried each day that had died from hunger and sickness. They were buried without funerals, mounds, and crosses. Sebastian was an intercessor for them all. Also, to him all the sins of people were visible. His spiritual daughter said that if you would only run to him, he would right every wrong. He would even prolong one's life. In 1966, Sebastian's health declined rapidly, and he died peacefully.

SAINTS OF THE DAY: Eutychius of Constantinople; Methodios, Equal-to-the-Apostles; Platonida of Nisibis; 120 Martyrs of Persia; Jeremiah and Archilias of Rome; Gregory the Sinaite; Gregory of the Great Lavra; Manuel, Theodore, George, Michael, and George; Gennadios of Dionysiou; Martyrius of Glinsk; 2 Martyrs from Ascalon; Sebastian of Optina.

Holy Saturday
Strict Fast
Romans 6:3-11; Matthew 28:1-20

APRIL 7

We have one sword, the Prayer of Jesus. It is said, "Strike the unseen enemies with this sword, for there is no more powerful weapon, either in Heaven or on earth.

St. Barsanuphius of Optina

MARTYR CALLIOPIOS AT POMPEIOPOLIS. In late third-century Pamphylia, a Christian senator and his wife Theoclea implored God with tears to send them a child, vowing to dedicate him to God. Calliopios was born, and at a young age, his mother taught him the purity of life and veneration of God. When Emperor Maximian began a Christian persecution, Theoclea put the young Calliopios on a ship sailing to the Cilician city of Pompeiopolis, hoping to remove him from danger. When he arrived, the city was celebrating the pagan gods, and he was invited to take part in the celebration. When he refused, he was taken to the governor Maximus. First, the governor attempted to persuade him to worship the gods, promising him his daughter, but Calliopios refused and confessed that he was a Christian. Maximus gave orders to beat him with iron rods, and to tie him to an iron wheel, burning him over a slow fire. Then he was imprisoned. When Theoclea heard this, she went to her son. She bribed one of the guards to let her enter the prison, where she bound her son's wounds and encouraged him to endure suffering for Christ. The next day when Calliopios refused to renounce Christ, he was sentenced to crucifixion. The day of execution was Great Thursday. Out of humility toward Jesus Christ, Theoclea asked the executioner to crucify Calliopios upside down, since she thought it unworthy for him to be crucified like the Lord. St. Calliopios hung on the cross until Great Friday and died. When he was taken down, Theoclea embraced her son and gave up her spirit to God.

SAINTS OF THE DAY: George the Confessor; Rufinus, Aquilina, and 200 soldiers at Sinope; Leucius of Volokolamsk; Sabbas the New of Kalymnos; Daniel of Pereyaslavl; Gerasimus of Patmos; George of Jerusalem; Hegesippus the Chronicler; Gabriel of Ryazan; Calliopios, in Cilicia.

SUNDAY

Great & Holy Pascha
Fast-free Week

APRIL 8

Acts 1:1-8; John 1:1-17

Indeed, brethren, Christ is better than the world. The world gives little and takes all. The world offers decay and takes away life. Christ, however, seeks little and gives all. Brethren, Christ is our one and only true friend. O resurrected Lord Christ, help us to renounce rubbish, to renounce decay, and grant us eternal life.

St. Nikolai Velimirovich

CELESTINE, POPE OF ROME. Celestine was a great apologist of Orthodoxy during the reign of Emperor Theodosius the Younger in the fifth century. Celestine had an excellent education and knew philosophy well, but he was mostly a student of Holy Scripture and theological questions. His reputation as a theologian won him the esteem and love of the clergy and people. Celestine succeeded St. Boniface as pope of Rome. He successfully fought the heresy of Nestorius, which claimed that Christ existed as two persons, the man Jesus and the divine Son of God, rather than a unified person. Nestorius also rejected calling Mary the Theotokos, as the Church was beginning to do. He said that Mary was the mother of Christ only in respect to His humanity. Celestine denounced the heresy at a council in Rome and condemned Nestorius as a heretic. He sent letters to the Churches in Antioch, Alexandria, and Constantinople, asking that Nestorius be deposed and excommunicated. Nestorius was banished to Egypt where he later died. After the Council, St. Celestine preached the true teaching about Christ the God-Man. He died peacefully.

SAINTS OF THE DAY: Apostles Hermes, Herodion, Agabus, Rufus, Asyncritus, and Phlegon, of the Seventy, and those with them; Celestine, Pope of Rome; Niphont, Bishop of Novgorod; Pausilippus of Thrace; Rufus the Obedient, recluse of the Kiev Caves; New Martyr John Koulikas of Aegina; New Martyr John Naukliros the Navigator, on Kos; Philaret of Seminara, Calabria; Josiah and Joseph of Mt. Kharasam, Persia; Spanish Icon of the Mother of God.

Bright Monday
Fast-free
Acts 1:12-17, 21-26; John 1:18-28

April 9

The greatest balm that Christ's sacrifice on the Cross gave us is the crushing of the devil. After the Crucifixion of Christ, the devil is like a snake with no fangs—with no poison; he is like a wild dog without teeth. All poison was removed from the devil; all teeth were removed from the wild dogs that are the demons. So, they are now disarmed; while we are armed with the Cross.

St. Paisios the Athonite

MARTYR EUPSYCHIOS OF CAESAREA IN CAPPADOCIA. Eupsychios became a martyr in the fourth century, a period that produced more saints than any other. This was during the reign of Emperor Julian the Apostate. In a time when Christianity needed strong voices, Eupsychios came forward. He incited a riot at the construction site of a nearly completed pagan temple. The crowd succeeded in tearing the temple down. The enraged Julian ordered some to be exiled, sent Christian clergy into military service, and looted the churches of their valuables. He threatened the people to build him a new pagan temple or be executed. He gave orders to force Eupsychios to offer sacrifice to idols or be tortured. Over the course of many days, he was stretched on a rack and scraped with iron claws, but his faith was firm. The judge sentenced him to beheading. After the death of Julian, a church was built over the grave of St. Eupsychios, and many received help and healing from his relics.

SAINTS OF THE DAY: Heliodorus, Desan, Mariabus, Abdiesus, and 270 others in Persia; Newly Revealed Martyrs Raphael, Nicholas, and Irene of Lesbos; Eupsychios of Caesarea; Bademus (Vadim) of Persia; Acacius, Bishop of Amida in Mesopotamia; Woutruide, monastic foundress at Bergen (Netherlands); Martyr Patience; Fortunatus, Donatus, twelve virgins, and six laymen at Sirmium; Casilda of Toledo, Spain.

TUESDAY

Bright Tuesday
Fast-free

Acts 2:14-21; Luke 24:12-35

APRIL 10

Be mindful of God, so that in every moment he may be mindful of you. If he is mindful of you, he will give you salvation. Do not forget him, letting yourselves be seduced by vain distractions. Do you want him to forget you in your times of temptation? Stay near him and obey him in the days of your prosperity. You will be able to rely on his word in difficult days, because prayer will keep you safe in his continual presence. Remain constantly before his face, think of him, remember him in your heart. Otherwise, if you only meet him from time to time, you risk losing your close friendship with him.

St. Isaac the Syrian

THE MARTYRS UNDER THE DANES. In ninth-century England, the Danes descended upon the Anglo-Saxons in different parts of England. At the abbey of Chertsey, they massacred the abbot Beocca, the priest Hethor, and many monks. There were as many as ninety victims. The Danes showed special ferocity towards the representatives of Christianity. Eighty-four were slain along with Abbot Hedda at modern-day Peterborough. Raids were also made at Bardney, Ely, and into the Fen country. The very lack of details is probably due to the desolation almost everywhere.

SAINTS OF THE DAY: Gregory V, Patriarch of Constantinople; Terence, Africanus, Maximus, Pompeius, Zeno, Alexander, Theodore, and 36 others, including Zeno, Alexander, and Theodore, at Carthage; Prophetess Huldah (Olda); Chrysanthos of Xenophontos, Mt. Athos; James, Azas, and Abdicius of Persia; Martyrs of Kvabtakhevi Monastery; George of Cyprus, at Acre (Palestine); Misael, Archbishop of Ryazan; New Martyr Demos at Smyrna; Anastasia, abbess of Uglich and 34 nuns with her; Martyrs Beocca, Hethor, and companions, at Chertsey Abbey; The Martyrs under the Danes.

Bright Wednesday
Fast-free
Acts 2:22-38; John 1:35-51

April 11

When one gives his heart to God, he loves everything. He not only loves all people, he also loves the birds and the trees — even the snakes. He reveres, with devotion, not only God and the Saints, but also all human beings: the images of God.

St. Paisios the Athonite

JAKOV OF ZHELEZNOBOROVSK. Jakov was born into wealthy and noble lineage in fourteenth-century Kostroma Galich. The Monk Sergei of Radonezh at the Trinity Monastery tonsured him into monasticism at a young age. After several years, he sought greater solitude and settled in a dense forest, which was called Iron Pines. Everyone already knew about his holy life. At one time, the wife of Great Prince Vasily Dmitrievich was close to death shortly before delivering her son. Vasily sent a message to Jakov beseeching him to pray for his wife Sophia and asking whether she would live. Jakov told the prince to pray to St. Longinus and foretold the happy birth of a son. Thirty-five years later this son traveled to the monk Jakov following a military victory and prayed together with him. Out of gratitude, the great-prince gave Jakov the means to build a monastery with a church. The monastery followed a strict common-life rule. Much later the Kazan Tatars destroyed the homes around Galich and the monastery. Jakov rebuilt, and they fed the downtrodden people who had been defeated in these attacks. After many years, Jakov became abbot. He died peacefully and was buried at the monastery founded by him.

SAINTS OF THE DAY: Antipas, Bishop of Pergamus; Processus and Martinian of Rome; Barsanuphius, Bishop of Tver; Pharmuthius of Egypt; Euthymius and Chariton of Syandema; Callinicus of Cernica; Tryphaina and Matrona of Cyzicus; Jakov (James), founder of Zheleznoborovsk Monastery, and his fellow-ascetic St. James; Guthlac of Crowland; Philip of Gortyna; Domninus, Bishop of Salona in Dalmatia, and 8 soldiers with him; Appearance of the Mother of God "The Footprint" at Pochaev.

THURSDAY

Bright Thursday
Fast-free
Acts 2:38-43; John 3:1-15

APRIL 12

Forgive and pray, in order to live your life serenely. And do not do to others that which you do not want them to do to you, or return the evil which they have done to you.

St. Raphael of Lesvos

COMMEMORATION OF THE MIRACLE WROUGHT BY THE CINCTURE OF THE MOST HOLY THEOTOKOS. The holy cincture of the Theotokos, sometimes translated as sash, girdle, or belt, has been left to us as a symbol of her protection. According to Sacred Tradition, after the Most Holy Theotokos fell asleep, during Her ascension, she gave her Holy Belt to the Apostle Thomas. This sash was made by the Blessed Mother of God herself with camel hair. Originally it was kept in Jerusalem and then in Constantinople. The holy Cincture is currently housed in a chapel at Vatopedi Monastery on Mt. Athos. The miracle that is celebrated today happened in 886 AD. During the reign of Emperor Leo the Wise, his wife Zoe was afflicted with an unclean spirit. The Empress had a vision that she would be healed if the Cincture of the Mother of God were placed upon her. The emperor asked the patriarch to open the coffer containing the Holy Sash, and placing it upon the Empress, she was immediately healed. Out of gratitude, the empress embroidered the whole sash with gold thread, giving it the appearance which is bears today.

SAINTS OF THE DAY: Deposition of the Sash of the Most Holy Theotokos from Zela to Constantinople; Basil the Confessor, Bishop of Parium; Hieromartyr Artemon; Virgin Anthusa of Constantinople; Isaac the Syrian of Spoleto, Italy; Zeno, Bishop of Verona; Menas, David, and John of Palestine; Sergius II, Patriarch of Constantinople; Basil, Bishop of Ryazan; Acacius the New of Kapsokalyvia Skete, Mt. Athos; Martyrs Demes, Protion, and those with them; "Murom" and "Belynich" Icons of the Mother of God.

FRIDAY

Bright Friday
Life-Giving Spring of the Theotokos
Fast-free
Acts 3:1-8; John 2:12-22

APRIL 13

In order for God to help us, we must help God with our humble thought. We should say, *'Oh my God, I am such a useless person, please forgive me and help me."* Then God helps, because the soul—entrusted into the hands of God with a good and humble disposition—is entitled to divine help. We must believe that Christ and our Panaghia always protect us and help us, as long as we are of a humble mentality.

St. Paisios the Athonite

MARTIUS, ABBOT OF CLERMONT. St. Gregory of Tours recorded the life of St. Martius. Even as a young man, Martius resolved to give himself to God, and upon attaining manhood, he left the world to lead a solitary life. He hewed a cave in a mountainside and carved a bed of stone to sleep on. His way of life and spiritual gifts attracted disciples, and gradually they formed a community, dividing their time between prayer and cultivating the soil. They converted the desert ground into a flourishing garden. Once, a thief broke into the monastery, taking apples, onions, and garlic. But because of the darkness, he was unable to find his way out. At dawn, Martius summoned the prior, telling him to release a bull which had found its way inside. He said, "Do not hurt him and let him have all he wants." When the thief saw the prior, he threw down his booty and tried to escape. But the prior reassured him, and packing up his goods, he laid the sack upon the man's shoulders, telling him to go in peace and give up his evil ways. Martius died peacefully at the age of ninety. Many miracles happened at his tomb.

SAINTS OF THE DAY: Martin the Confessor, Pope of Rome; Quintilian, Maximus, and Dada of Dorostolum; Eleutherius of Persia; Zoilus of Rome; Herman of Svyatogorsk Monastery; Martyrius, Patriarch of Jerusalem; Martius, abbot of Clermont; Stephen of Izhevsk; Anastasia, foundress of Protection Convent in Kiev; Martyr Theodosius; Guinoch of Buchan; Barnabas, Archbishop of Archangelsk.

Bright Saturday
Fast-free

Acts 3:11-16; John 3:22-33

April 14

When the matter relates to God's Mysteries, do not inwardly ask: how can this be? You do not know how God created the world from nothing; you cannot and may not know here either how God mysteriously works. God's mystery must remain a mystery for you, because you are not God, and cannot know all that is known to the eternally Wise, Almighty God.

St. John of Kronstadt

MARTYR ARDALION THE ACTOR. Ardalion performed in theaters and was a talented mimic actor. In the way of all thespians, he acted out the passions and dramas of other people's lives. One time at the circus, he played the role of a Christian who refused to offer sacrifice to idols, but later consented to renounce Christ. During the play, Ardalion was suspended upon a wooden torture device, and they tore him with iron hooks. Ardalion's performance was depicted naturally, and the spectators praised him. Suddenly, with a loud voice, Ardalion told the people to be quiet and declared that he was truly a Christian and did not renounce Christ. The governor who was present admonished him to change his mind, but Ardalion stood firm. Orders were given to throw him onto a red-hot iron pan, and there St. Ardalion gave up his soul.

SAINTS OF THE DAY: Apostles Aristarchus, Pudens, and Trophimos of the Seventy; Thomais of Alexandria; Ardalion the Actor; Euthymius the Wonderworker; Azat the Eunuch and 1,000 Martyrs in Persia; Christopher of St. Sabbas Monastery; Anthony, John, and Eustathius of Vilnius (Lithuania); New Martyr Demetrius of the Peloponnese, at Tripoli; Tassach, Bishop of Raholp (Ireland); New Martyr Sergius Trofimov of Nizhni-Novgorod and companion; Pahomie of Gledin, Bishop of Rome; Commemoration of Sts. Raphael, Nicholas, Irene, and the other Newly-revealed Martyrs of Lesbos; "Vilna" Icon of the Mother of God.

Thomas Sunday
Fast-free
Acts 5:12-20; John 20:19-31

APRIL 15

It would be a great lie to tell searching souls: 'Go to church, because there you will find peace.' The opposite is true. The Church tells those who are at peace and asleep: 'Go to church, because there you will feel real anguish for your sins, for your perdition, for the world's sins and perdition. There you will feel an unappeasable hunger for Christ's truth. There, instead of becoming lukewarm, you will be set on fire; instead of pacified, you will become alarmed; instead of learning the wisdom of this world you will become fools for Christ.

St. Maria of Paris

MARTYRS ANASTASIA AND BASILISSA OF ROME. These two noble Roman women were converted to the faith by the holy Apostles Peter and Paul. Emperor Nero had Peter and Paul condemned to death for converting imperial concubines and for the demise of Nero's friend, Simon Magus. Emperor Nero arrested and executed a large number of Christians. Anastasia and Basilissa gathered the relics of these martyrs and buried them honorably. When this news reached Nero, Anastasia and Basilissa were imprisoned. They were subjected to cruel torture, but would not renounce Christ. They were beaten with whips, tore at their skin with hooks, and burned them with fire. Nero ordered their beheading with the sword.

SAINTS OF THE DAY: Leonidas, Bishop of Athens; Suchias of Iberia and 16 companions; Crescens of Myra; Anastasia and Basilissa of Rome; Daniel of Achinsk, Siberia; Mstislav-Theodore, Prince of Kiev; Pausilipus of Thrace; Ruadhan, founder and abbot of Lothra, Ireland; Paternus (Padarn), Bishop of Llandbadam Fawr.

APRIL 16

Acts 3:19-26; John 2:1-11

The husband and wife should be like the hand and eye. When the hand hurts, the eyes should be crying, and when the eyes cry, the hand should wipe away the tears.

St. John Chrysostom

PANAGIA CHRYSAFITISSA OF MONEMVASIA. This Byzantine style icon miraculously came to reside in the seventh-century church of Monemvasia. The icon seems to date from the fifteenth or sixteenth century. Originally it was discovered in the village of Chrysafa in Sparta, Greece, on the spot where today there is a spring of holy water. Various diseases are cured through this spring, and it plays a special role in helping the barren bear children, especially males. One day merchants from Chrysafa traveled to Monemvasia to celebrate a Feast to the Theotokos. When they entered the church, they saw their icon from Chrysafa, and they thought that it had been stolen. They took the case to trial, and the judge awarded the icon back to Chrysafa. The merchants took the icon back to Chrysafa and placed it in one of their churches. They celebrated a service in honor of the icon, locked up the church, and left. But that night in a miraculous manner the icon left the church and was found back in Monemvasia, where it remains today. The Theotokos continues to work miracles there for the faithful, especially for those suffering from lunacy and the demon-possessed. Thus we see whoever glorifies and honors the Mother of God becomes a partaker of the grace given to her by God.

SAINTS OF THE DAY: Virgin-martyrs Agape, Irene, and Chionia in Illyria; Irene of Thessalonica; Leonidas, Chariessa, Nice, Galina, Calisa, Nunechia, Basilissa, Theodora, and Irene of Corinth; John, fool-for-Christ of Verkhoturye; Christopher of Dionysiou, Mt. Athos; New Martyr Michael of Smyrna; New Martyr Nicholas the Deacon of Mytilene; Fructuosis of Braga in Iberia; Theodora-Bassa, Princess of Novgorod; Felix, Januarius, Fortunatus, and Septimus of Lycaonia; "Ilyin Chernigov" Icon of the Mother of God; "Panagia Chrysafitissa" of Monemvasia.

APRIL 17

Acts 4:1-10; John 3:16-21

Struggle with all your power to gain Paradise. And do not listen to those who say that everyone will be saved. This is a trap of Satan so that we won't struggle.

St. Paisios the Athonite

ELIAS OF MAKEEVKA, UKRAINE. As a young monk, Elias lived for a short time on Mt. Athos and then at the Kiev Caves Monastery, from which he was forced to leave by the communists. He had no shelter and lived in the homes of the faithful who considered it a blessing to give him hospitality because of his gifts of wonderworking and foresight. The communists were never able to capture Elias because he would know beforehand when they were coming, which also happened to St. Matrona of Moscow. From 1937 to 1946, during the years of World War II, he stayed in Makeevka because he foresaw that the city would escape the sufferings of war. When churches were closed by the atheists, he would host priests from Kiev and Moscow. Elias comforted people from morning to night. He read the gospels, Psalms, and Akathists every day. He told the faithful, "On Sundays and holy days, do not sit at home. Go to church, and all will be well with you." He also said, "If pride lives in you, then it is better to keep quiet." He once told a woman who was informed that her husband had been killed in battle to go and pray in church and take Communion every Sunday, and her husband will return. The woman did as she was told, and her husband was found alive by some local residents. He had been unconscious for a long time. Elias also foretold that Makeevka would flourish spiritually after the war. Fifty years later, a cathedral and twenty-four other churches had been built. St. Elias died peacefully.

SAINTS OF THE DAY: Agapitus, Pope of Rome; Macarius of Corinth; Symeon, in Persia, with Abdechalas, Ananias, Usthazanes, Fusicus, Ascitrea, and Azat; Acacius of Melitene; Adrian of Corinthus; Ephraim the Great of Matskveri; Paisius, fool-for-Christ of Kiev; Zosimas of Solovki; Elias of Makeevka; Donnan of Eigg and others (Scotland).

Wednesday

April 18

Abstain from meat and dairy products, and fish.
Acts 4:13-22; John 5:17-24

As God illumines all people equally with the light of the sun, so do those who desire to imitate God let shine an equal ray of love on all people. For wherever love disappears, hatred immediately appears in its place. And if God is love, then hatred is the devil. Therefore, as one who has love has God within himself, so he who has hatred within himself nurtures the devil within himself.

St. Basil the Great

BASIL RATISHVILI OF THE HOLY MOUNTAIN. Basil lived with other Georgian fathers at the Iveron Monastery on Mt. Athos. He was one of the most prominent of the thirteenth-century Church Fathers. Basil was granted the gift of prophecy, and he once beheld a vision of the Most Holy Mother of God telling him to go and censure King Dimitri for his impious rule and for not receiving a Church blessing for his marriage. Basil traveled to the king and denounced both him and his apostate feudal lords. He also promised the king that if he abandoned his way of life, he would find happiness and success. But if he refused, a terrible enemy would kill him, his children would be scattered, his kingdom defeated, and his wealth seized. The king and his court did not listen to Basil's admonitions, and everything he said came to pass. St. Basil returned to Mt. Athos and died peacefully.

SAINTS OF THE DAY: Sabbas the Commander, the Goth; John, disciple of St. Gregory of Decapolis; Acacius II, Bishop of Melitene; Cosmas, Bishop of Chalcedon, and his fellow-ascetic Auxentius; Publius of Egypt; Euthymius the Enlightener of Karelia, and Anthony and Felix of Karelia; Athanasia the Wonderworker of Aegina; John the Tailor of Ioannina; Basil Ratishvili the Georgian of Iveron; Tamara (Satsi) of Cheboksara; Alexis Krontenkov of Ekaterinburg; Nicholas and Basil Derzhavin, and the lay people of Gorodets, Nizhni-Novgorod; Miracle of the pillar at the Holy Sepulcher; Tunom, Arab emir who confessed Christ on seeing the Holy Fire in Jerusalem; "Maximov" Icon of the Mother of God.

APRIL 19

Acts 4:23-31; John 5:24-30

The man who lives daily with the thought of death is to be admired, and the man who gives himself to it by the hour is surely a saint. And yet not every desire for death is good. A habitual sinner prays humbly for death, but the man who does not want to change his ways may, in sheer despair, actually long for death.

St. John Climacus

TRYPHON, PATRIARCH OF CONSTANTINOPLE. From his youth, Tryphon was a monk. He was known for his meekness, firm faith, and love for the Church. At this time, Emperor Romanos ruled tenth-century Byzantium, and he wanted his son Theophylaktos to take the patriarchal throne. When Patriarch Stephanos died, the emperor's son was only sixteen years old, so Tryphon was chosen to take the throne until Theophylaktos came of age. For four years Tryphon governed the Church. When Theophylaktos turned twenty, the emperor asked Tryphon to resign, but he would not, considering it scandalous for such a young and inexperienced person to be given the great responsibility of the office. The emperor had the bishop of Caesarea trick Tryphon into signing a clean sheet of paper with his full name and title. Tryphon did not perceive the fraud. When the paper was given over to the emperor, he ordered to write above Tryphon's signature his resignation from the position of patriarch. The emperor relegated Tryphon to a monastery, and as a result, a period of unrest began in the Church. St. Tryphon lived only one year until his death.

SAINTS OF THE DAY: Tryphon, Patriarch of Constantinople; George the Confessor, Bishop of Antioch; Theodore of Perga in Pamphylia, and his mother Philippa, and Dioscorus, Socrates, and Dionysius; Symeon the Barefoot of Philotheou Monastery; Agathangelos of Esphigmenou Monastery; Matrona the Blind of Moscow; Victor (Ostrovidov), Bishop of Glazov; Nicephorus, abbot of Katabad; Paphnutius of Jerusalem; Ioasaph (Bolotov), enlightener of Alaska; Alphege, Archbishop of Canterbury; Uncovering of the relics of St. Joachim, founder of Opochka Monastery.

Friday

Abstain from meat and dairy products, and fish.
Acts 5:1-11; John 5:30-6:2

April 20

He that endureth to the end shall be saved (Matt. 10:22). Do we have anything to endure? In this no one is lacking. Everyone's arena of endurance is vast, and therefore our salvation is at hand. Endure everything to the end and you will be saved. However, you must endure skillfully—otherwise, you may not gain anything by your endurance.

St. Theophan the Recluse

VENERABLE JOHN OF THE OLD LAVRA. John left riches, earthly splendor, relatives, and homeland to become a monk for the love of Christ. He restrained the passions through abstinence and all-night vigil. He once went to Jerusalem to worship at the holy places and to seek counsel and instruction of holy men. He then went to live in the desert in the Monastery of St. Chariton, also known as Old Lavra at Souka. In addition to the spiritual struggles of fasting, prayer, vigil, and inner stillness, John contemplated the remembrance of death and humility. He was ordained to the priesthood and was found worthy of mystic visions. After struggling many years, he gave up his soul to the Lord.

SAINTS OF THE DAY: Apostle Zacchaeus, Bishop of Caesarea; Theodore Trichinas of Constantinople; Gregory and Anastasius I, Patriarchs of Antioch; Anastasius II, Patriarch of Antioch; Victor, Zoticus, Zeno, Acindynus, Christopher, Theonas, Caesarius, Antoninus, and Severian of Nicomedia; John the Ancient of Old Lavra; Ioasaph and Athanasius of Meteora; Alexander, abbot, of Oshevensk; Child-martyr Gabriel of Slutsk (Poland); Theodosius (Ganitsky), Bishop of Kolomna; Betran and Theotimus I, Bishops in Scythia Minor; Caedwalla, King of the West Saxons; Translation of the relics of St. Nikolai Velimirovich, Bishop of Ochrid and Zhicha; "Cyprus" and "Keepiazh" Icons of the Mother of God.

APRIL 21

Acts 5:21-32; John 6:14-27

Keep in your thoughts that when misfortune comes, you cannot throw it off like a tight-fitting garment; you must bear it. Whether in a Christian way or in a non-Christian way, you cannot avoid bearing it; so it is better to bear it in a Christian way. Complaining will not deliver you from misfortune, but only make it heavier; whereas humble submission to God's Providence and a good attitude relieve the burden of misfortunes.

St. Theophan the Recluse

VENERABLE BEUNO, ABBOT OF CLYNNOG, ENGLAND. The example and energetic preaching of Beuno made a deep impression upon his countrymen in seventh-century North Wales. Legend says that an angel announced to his long-barren parents that they would have a son. Beuno was educated in a monastery. He later moved about and obtained grants of land upon which he built churches and founded monasteries. Legend also says that he restored St. Winifred to life after she was beheaded. There are two other occasions that the dead were brought back to life by Beuno's prayers. It is believed that Beuno was buried in the monastery of Clynnog Fawr, which he had founded. After his death, sick children were brought to lay on St. Beuno's tomb until morning, to be made well.

SAINTS OF THE DAY: Januarius, Bishop of Benevento, with Proclus, Sosius, Festus, Desiderius, Gantiol, Eutychius, and Acutius, at Pozzuoli; Maximium, Archbishop of Constantinople; Anastasius of St. Catherine's on Mt. Sinai; James of Stromynsk; Alexandra the Empress, wife of Diocletian; Isaacius, Apollo, and Codratus of Nicomedia; Niphon, Bishop of Novgorod; Maelruba of Apur Crossan, Ireland; Beuno, abbot of Clynnog Fawr, Wales; Basil Martysz of Teratyn (Poland); Alexis of Bortsumany, Nizhni-Novgorod; Uncovering of the relics of St. Theodore of Sanaxar Monastery; "Mozdok" Icon of the Mother of God.

SUNDAY

Sunday of the Myrrh-bearing Women
Fast-free

APRIL 22

Acts 6:1-7; Mark 15:43-16:8

Give sincere thanks to God for everything, believing that everything which proceeds from the Lord is sent by Him for the good of our souls. Thank Him for sorrows and for consolations.

St. Theophan the Recluse

HIEROMARTYR PLATON OF BANJA LUKA. Platon was born in Belgrade, Serbia. He was educated in the nineteenth-century Belgrade Seminary and Moscow Theological Academy. He was ordained to the priesthood and later was appointed abbot of the Rakovica Monastery in Belgrade. During the war, in 1912, Platon was assigned as a brigade priest, and in World War I, was again assigned as a military priest. With the help of his friends, he managed to help all those who suffered afflictions, especially orphans and widows. In 1936, he was elected bishop of Moravice, and later Bishop of Banja Luka, which was in Bosnia. When World War II came to Yugoslavia, Platon was told to leave Banja Luka because he was Serbian, but he responded, "I took the obligation before God, Church, and people, that inseparably binding my life and my destiny with the life and destiny of my spiritual flock." The Ustase arrested Bishop Platon and took him out of Banja Luka, where he was killed. His body was cast into the Vrbanja River. Eighteen days later, it was found and buried in a military graveyard in Banja Luka.

SAINTS OF THE DAY: Apostle Nathaniel of the Twelve; Apostles Apelles, Luke, and Clement, of the Seventy; Theodore the Sykeote, Bishop of Anastasiopolis; Leonidas of Alexandria; Platon, Bishop of Banja Luka; Vitalis of the monastery of Abba Seridus at Gaza; Epipodius of Lyons; Martyr Nearchus; Ananias of Malles (Crete); Translation of the relics of St. Vsevolod (Gabriel), Prince and Wonderworker of Rostov.

April 23

Acts 12:1-11; John 15:17-16:2

Keep the holy Faith and lead an irreproachable life according to the Faith. Immediately cleanse with repentance every sin that occurs.
St. Theophan the Recluse

NEW MARTYR GEORGE OF PTOLOMAIS. George was a Christian from Cyprus. He was hired as an attendant to one of the members of the consulate. He often purchased eggs for his employer's household from a certain poor Turkish woman, who had a daughter that anxiously awaited his arrival. When the local egg sellers noticed that he only bought eggs from this girl, they became envious and resentful. One day when the mother was not home, it was observed that George entered the house, so the neighbors seized him, accusing him of wanting to become a Muslim. George was taken to the judge, who asked him if the charges were true, but he denied that he had uttered such a word. He declared that he was born a Christian and would die a Christian. They promised him gifts, glory, and rank, but George remained firm. When torments were unsuccessful, the judge issued a death sentence. At the place of execution, George stood in the midst of an entire assembly of Ottomans. He raised his chained hands to heaven, saying, "Lord Jesus Christ, receive my spirit and make me worthy of Thy kingdom." Immediately, the Moslems emptied their pistols into George, and as he fell to the ground, they began stabbing his body. God immediately caused the ocean to overflow its natural bounds, by the distance of a rifle shot, and the water washed George's relics, turning the foam red. In great fear, the Ottomans asked the Christians to remove the body, and they took him to a church for burial, and the waters subsided. For three whole nights, a fiery column appeared from heaven illuminating the grave. Every Friday evening to this day, Christians, especially the infirm, gather at the tomb, and many miracles have occurred.

SAINTS OF THE DAY: Great Martyr George; Anatolius and Protoleon, soldiers; Glycerius and others at Nicomedia; George of Cyprus; George of Shenkursk; Egor of Russia; Lazarus of Bulgaria.

APRIL 24

Acts 8:5-17; John 6:27-33

Accept everything that you must endure as from the hands of God, remembering firmly that nothing happens without God's will.

St. Theophan the Recluse

UNCOVERING OF THE RELICS OF ST. YVO, BISHOP. According to medieval records, Yvo was a Persian bishop who enjoyed great honor and luxury, but he aspired to a more disciplined and arduous life. Yvo and three companions traveled to England and settled as hermits in the wild fenlands in Huntingdonshire. They died in the seventh century, but at the beginning of the eleventh century, relics with a bishop's insignia were found in Slepe, near the Ramsey Abbey. These relics were identified as those of St. Yvo, following a peasant's revelation in a dream. Yvo's relics along with those of his three companions were taken to the Ramsey Abbey where a holy well sprung up, and at which many miracles occurred. According to the abbot Whitman, about a century later, a light appeared at night reaching from the Ramsey to Slepe. This was interpreted to mean that the relics of the four saints should be taken back to Slepe. St. Yvo is portrayed as a Persian hermit with the attributes of a bishop.

SAINTS OF THE DAY: Sabbas Stratelates of Rome, and 70 soldiers with him; Sabbas the Commander, the Goth, at Buzau in Wallachia; Elizabeth the Wonderworker of Constantinople; Thomas, fool-for-Christ of Syria; Pasicrates, Valentine, and Julius, at Dorostolum; Eusebius, Neon, Leontius, Longinus, and others at Nicomedia; Xenophon, founder of Xenophontos Monastery, Mt. Athos; Alexander of Lyons; Innocent, on the Mount of Olives; Sabbas and Alexis the Hermit of the Kiev Caves; Nicholas of Magnesia; George in Anatolia; Joseph the Confessor, Bishop of Maramures; Symeon, Elias, and Sava, Metropolitans of Ardeal; Doukas of Mytilene; Branko of Veljusa, Serbia; Wilfrid, Bishop of York; Egbert, Bishop of Iona; Mellitus, Archbishop of Canterbury; Uncovering of the relics of St. Yvo, bishop; "Molchensk" Icon of the Mother of God.

Wednesday

Abstain from meat and dairy products, and fish.

1 Peter 5:6-14; Luke 10:16-21

April 25

Love sorrow for the sake of its great salvific power and cultivate within yourself a thirst for it as for a drink which, although bitter, is healing.

St. Theophan the Recluse

VENERABLE SYLVESTER, ABBOT OF OBNORA. Sylvester was a disciple under St. Sergius of Radonezh at the Trinity Lavra in the fifteenth century. Desiring to live as a hermit, and with the blessing of his elder, Sylvester went into the deep forest at the Obnora River and began his ascetic labors. As time passed, people of that area saw a cloud in the shape of a pillar and bright rays of light above his hermitage. A man once visited Sylvester and asked him about his way of life. Sylvester confessed that he had been living there many years, eating tree bark and roots. Once, when he was in complete weakness, an angel of God appeared to him and touched his hand. From that time on, he experienced no further distress. Soon peasants began to arrive, and they built cells close to Sylvester. Sylvester went to Moscow and received a blessing from St. Alexei to build a church, and he gave Sylvester relics of saints, which are necessary to celebrate the Divine Liturgy. More monks came, and the monastery grew. Still, Sylvester retreated to a solitary place to pray. As death approached, he reminded his community that everything is according to the will of God. He instructed them not to fear misfortune in this life in order to receive a reward in heaven, to keep the commandments of God, and to pray to God and His All-Pure Mother to be delivered from temptation. Miracles have been attributed to St. Sylvester in healing demonic possession, delirium, and eye afflictions.

SAINTS OF THE DAY: Holy Apostle and Evangelist Mark; Stephen, Patriarch of Antioch; Macedonius, Patriarch of Constantinople; Basil of Poiana Marului; Aninanus, Bishop of Alexandria; Sylvester of Obnora Monastery; Martyr Nike, who believed in Christ through St. George; Eight martyred anchorites; "Constantinople" Icon of the Mother of God.

APRIL 26

Acts 8:26-39; John 6:40-44

Above all, pray, and the merciful Lord will give you strength of spirit. With such strength, when others marvel at your misfortunes, they will seem like nothing to you.

St. Theophan the Recluse

RICHARIUS, ABBOT IN PICARDY. Richarius was born in seventh-century France, at Cellas. During this time, the population there was mostly pagan. Once when two Irish priests landed on the coast trying to cross the country, they would have been seriously mistreated had Richarius not protected them. In gratitude, they instructed him in the Christian faith, after which Richarius was inspired to become a priest. After rigorous preparation, he was ordained to the priesthood and lived for some time in England. When he returned to France, he began to preach with extraordinary zeal and great success. He warned King Dagobert on the dangers and vanities of this world, and his responsibilities as king. He said, "He who has to obey will only have to render account to God of himself, but he who commands will also have to answer for all his subjects." As Richarius grew older, he gave up his responsibilities as abbot of the Celles monastery he had founded. He lived as a hermit for the rest of his life with a disciple named Sigobard. Afterward, the monastery of Forest-Montiers was built over his cell.

SAINTS OF THE DAY: Stephen, Bishop of Perm; Glaphyra of Nicomedia; Basil, Bishop of Amasea; Andrew and Anatole, disciples of St. Euthymius the Great; George of Cyprus; Ioannicius of Devic (Serbia); Nestor the Silent; Cyril, Cindeus, and Tasie of Axiopolis; Righteous Justa; Richarius, abbot in Picardy; Calantius of Tamassos on Cyprus; New Martyrs of Novo Selo, Bulgaria.

Friday

Abstain from meat and dairy products, and fish.
Acts 8:40-9:19; John 6:48-54

April 27

It is God, Who is merciful and grants everyone what he needs, Who is building him up when He gives him more than he needs; in doing so He shows the abundance of His love for me and teaches him to give thanks. When He does not grant him what he needs, He makes him compensate for the thing he needs through the working of the mind and teaches him patience.

St. Dorotheos of Gaza

HIEROMARTYR SYMEON, KINSMAN OF THE LORD. Symeon was the son of Cleopas, younger brother of St. Joseph the Betrothed. He believed in Jesus Christ and was one of the Seventy disciples, preaching in Judea. James, the Lord's brother and first bishop of Jerusalem, was martyred when he was thrown from the top of the temple. Symeon succeeded him as bishop and preached in Antioch, Alexandria, and Constantinople. He denounced idol-worship and preached the teachings of Christ. During the reign of Emperor Trajan, it was reported to the governor Atticus that Symeon was descended from the lineage of King David and was confessing the Christian faith. The Romans had exterminated all the descendants of King David. Symeon was asked to deny Jesus Christ or be condemned to death on a cross. Symeon expressed appreciation for being crucified like Jesus. He was one hundred twenty years of age.

SAINTS OF THE DAY: Eulogius the Hospitable of Constantinople; Symeon the Kinsman of the Lord, Bishop of Jerusalem; Floribert, Bishop of Luik; John the Confessor of Cathares Monastery at Constantinople; Elias (Ardunis) of Mt. Athos; Seraphim, Bishop of Phanar; Stephen, abbot of the Kiev Caves; Lollion the Younger; Pollion the Reader of Cibalis in Pannonia; Nicon, abbot of the monastery of St. Gerasimus; Machalus of the Isle of Man; Burning of the relics of St. Sava I of Siberia by the Turks; Glorification of New Hieromartyr Hilarion (Troitsky), Archbishop of Verey.

APRIL 28

Acts 9:19-31; John 15:17-27, 16:1-2

Sin, to one who loves God, is nothing other than an arrow from the enemy in battle. The true Christian is a warrior fighting his way through the regiments of the unseen enemy to his heavenly homeland. According to the word of the Apostles, our homeland is in heaven; and about the warrior he says: "our warfare is not against flesh and blood, but against principalities and powers of wickedness under heaven" (Ephesians 6:12).

St. Herman of Alaska

VENERABLE MEMNON THE WONDERWORKER. From his youth in the second century, Memnon sought to purify himself by prayer and fasting in the Egyptian desert. The Holy Spirit dwelled within him, and he was granted the gift of working miracles, healing the sick, and purging the passions. Many times, he was voted to become the monastery abbot, but he accounted himself unworthy. Once, his prayers caused a spring of water to come forth to relieve the parched lands. Another time, his prayer stopped a swarm of locusts from destroying the monastery. When sailors invoked his name during a great storm, he appeared to them and spoke words of encouragement, steering the ship to safety. St. Memnon died peacefully. According to St. Joseph the Hymnographer, streams of healing poured from St. Memnon's tomb.

SAINTS OF THE DAY: Memnon the Wonderworker; Nine Martyrs at Cyzicus—Theognes, Rufus, Antipater, Theostichus, Artemas, Magnus, Theodotus, Thaumasius, and Philemon; Dada, Maximus, and Quintilian at Dorostolum; Auxibius II, Bishop of Soli on Cyprus; Cyril, Bishop of Turov; Basil Kishkin of Glinsk; Cyril, founder of Syrinsk Monastery (Karelia); Cronan, abbot of Roscrea Monastery, Ireland; Cyriacus, abbot of Kargopol; Tibald of Pannonia; Commemoration of the Miracle at Carthage.

Sunday of the Paralytic
Fast-free
Acts 9:32-42; John 5:1-15

APRIL 29

The greatest act of love is to take care of a sick person. If you take care of him with love and patience, he's saved through you, and you're saved through him.

+Elder Paisius of Sihla

ENDELIENTA (ENDELLION), NUN-RECLUSE OF CORNWALL. According to tradition, Endelienta was the daughter of King Brychan in fifth- and sixth-century South Wales. It is said that she evangelized the local population. She later crossed the Bristol Channel to aid her siblings in converting the people of North Cornwall. She eventually settled in Trentinney and lived as a hermitess, subsisting only on the milk of a cow and water from nearby wells. This cow was killed by the Lord of Trentinney when it strayed onto his land, but King Arthur, Endelienta's godfather, was angered by this and sent men to kill that lord. Endelienta was unhappy about his revenge, and she restored the lord back to life. She had a vision of her death and asked to be placed on a cart drawn by bullocks, and that she should be buried wherever they stopped, which was at the top of a hill. A church was built over her grave, and this shrine was the site of pilgrimage through the Middle Ages.

SAINTS OF THE DAY: Jason and Sosipater of the Seventy, and their companions: Saturninus, Jakischolus, Faustianus, Januarius, Marsalius, Euphrasius, Mammius, Virgin Cercyra, and Christodolus the Ethiopian; Zeno, Eusebius, Neon, and Vitalis; John Kaloktenes of Thebes; Basil of Ostrog; Martyrs Quintian and Atticus; Secundellus in Gaul; Diodorus and Rhodopianus in Anatolia; John Tolaius of Alexandria; Arsenius of Suzdal; Nicetas of Synnada; John of Romania; Nectarius of Optina; Holy Martyrs of Lazeti (Georgia); Martyrs Quintian and Atticus; Stanko of Montenegro; Endellion of Cornwall; Glorification of St. Amphilochius of Pochaev.

MONDAY **Fast-free**

APRIL 30

Acts 12:1-11; Luke 9:1-6

A man in this world must solve a problem: to be with Christ, or to be against Him. And every man decides this, whether he wants to or not. He will either be a lover of Christ or a fighter of Christ. There is no third option.

St. Justin Popovich

HOLY APOSTLE JAMES, BROTHER OF ST. JOHN THE THEOLOGIAN. Apostle James was called 'James the Greater' to distinguish him from the other Apostle James who was called 'James the Lesser.' James was one of the two apostolic sons of Zebedee. He witnessed three important events: Jesus raising the daughter of Jairus from the dead, the Transfiguration of Christ with his brother and Peter, and the agony in Gethsemane. James and John were great preachers and teachers of theology, and for this Jesus called them 'Sons of Thunder.' James preached in Spain and other lands. He later returned to Jerusalem, where he boldly preached Jesus Christ. The sorcerer Hermogenes argued with James and attempted to refute that Christ was the Messiah, but James converted him and his pupil Philip to belief in Christ. Because of this, he was arrested by Herod Agrippa and martyred by the sword in Jerusalem in the year 44 A.D. He was the first apostle to be martyred. When Apostle James was sentenced to death, a false witness named Josiah saw the courage and cheerfulness in Apostle James, and he became convinced that Jesus must be the true God. He confessed his faith before the onlookers and was beheaded together with James. The relics of St. James are in Spain, in the Cathedral of Compostela.

SAINTS OF THE DAY: Apostle James, the brother of St. John the Theologian; Maximus of Ephesus; Clement the Hymnographer; Ignatius (Brianchaninov) of Stavropol; Maximus of Ephesus; Argyra of Prousa; James, his wife, and son Alexis of Plotava; Donatus of Euroea; Eutropius and Estelle of Saintes; Erconwald of London; Translation of the relics of St. Sabbas of Zvenigorod; "Of the Passion" Icon of the Mother of God.

May 1

Acts 10:21-33; John 7:1-13

Before the war begins, seek after your ally; before you fall ill, seek out your physician; and before grievous things come upon you, pray, and in the time of your tribulations you will find Him, and He will listen to you.

St. Isaac the Syrian

MARTYR BATAS OF PERSIA. Batas was a Christian from birth, living in fourth-century Persia. When he turned thirty years old, he heard the Lord's words from the gospel, "If anyone come to Me, and hate not his own father, and mother, and wife, and children, and brothers, and sisters, and still, his own life also, he cannot be My disciple (Luke 14:26)." Filled with the Holy Spirit, Batas followed Christ. He forsook all earthly things and departed to a monastery to become a monk. He surpassed all the brothers in vigilance, continence, and fasting, and kept watch over his heart and senses. In time, he began to yearn for a martyr's end. After Batas had spent thirty years in the monastery, the Persians instigated a Christian persecution. All the monastics decided to leave, except Batas, who was captured. He was taken to the ruler of an area called Vitzios and was commanded to offer homage to the sun. Batas declared that he was a Christian, and refused the command; therefore, he was subjected to horrible tortures. He was stretched on a rack by ten men until his shoulders dislocated. He was beaten with wood poles, then bound by the genitals and dragged by twenty men. Heavy rocks were stacked on his abdomen, and then they cut away parts of his upper body. Finally, he was beheaded.

SAINTS OF THE DAY: Prophet Jeremiah; Panaretus of Paphos; Philosophos of Alexandria; Maria of Merambelos; Tamara, Empress of Georgia; Nicephorus of Chios; Ultan of Fosse; Macarius of Kiev; Batas of Nisibis; Zosimas of Kumurdo; Michael of Chalcedon; Euthymius, Ignatius, and Acacius of Serres; Paphnutius of Borovsk; Gerasimus of Boldino Monastery; Luke Shvets of Glinsk; Brieuc, in Brittany; Romanus of Raqqa; Asaph of Wales; "Unexpected Joy" Icon of the Mother of God.

WEDNESDAY

Mid-Pentecost
Abstain from meat and dairy products.
Hebrews 13:7-16; Matthew 5:14-19

MAY 2

Do not fear God because of the greatness of His majesty, but fear Him because of the greatness of His love.

St. Isaac the Syrian

ATHANASIUS III, PATRIARCH OF CONSTANTINOPLE AND WONDERWORKER OF LUBNY. Athanasius was a well-educated young man from a prominent and pious family in sixteenth-century Crete. When his father died, he joined a monastery in Thessalonica and later went to the monastery of Esphigmenou on Mt. Athos. He visited the Palestinian monasteries, where he took monastic tonsure and returned to Thessalonica. He was ordained to the priesthood and spread the teaching of Christ to the Moldavians and Vlachs. He also translated the Psalter from Greek into their own languages. His holiness attracted many Christians, and his fame spread. Patriarch Cyril I of Constantinople sent for Athanasius and appointed him priest at the Patriarchate, and he was soon elevated to bishop and Metropolitan of the Church of Soluneia. When enemies of the Church imprisoned Patriarch Cyril, Athanasius was chosen, but he only served for forty days until the political intrigue of the heretics had him deposed and Cyril returned. Ultimately, he was deposed as patriarch three times. He traveled to Moscow seeking funds for his monastery in Moldavia and was greatly received by the tsar and the patriarch. Having been greatly weakened by his travails, he died. His relics have wrought many miracles.

SAINTS OF THE DAY: Athanasius the Great, Archbishop of Alexandria; Hesperus, Zoe, and their sons Cyriacus and Theodulus, at Attalia; Athanasius III, Patriarch of Constantinople; Boris-Michael, Prince of Bulgaria; Athanasius of Syandem and Valaam; Jordan the Wonderworker; Basil of Kadom, fool-for-Christ; Translation of the relics of Holy Passion-bearers Sts. Boris and Gleb of Russia; "Putivilsk" Icon of the Mother of God.

MAY 3

Acts 10:34-43; John 8:12-20

My dearest friends, a pure life and fearless faith in God are powerful weapons against the demons. Believe me, for I have experience with this. Night-time devotions and the prayers, fasting and gentleness of those who live rightly, terrify satan. He is afraid of these devoted ones because of their voluntary poverty, their lack of vanity, their humility, their compassion, their control over anger, and particularly because of their pure love for Christ. That foulest serpent knows that it is at God's command that he lies beneath the footsteps of the just.

St. Anthony the Great

DIODOROS AND RODOPIANOS THE DEACON. These two saints lived in the Asia Minor city of Aphrodisia, during the early fourth-century reign of Emperor Diocletian. The city was dedicated to the pagan goddess of fertility and love. With the arrival of Christianity, the name of the city would later change to Stavropolis. Soldiers arrested Diodoros and Rodopianos during the Christian persecution. They bravely endured scourges, insults, and other tortures before being stoned to death.

SAINTS OF THE DAY: Timothy the Reader and his wife Maura of Antinoe in Egypt; Peter, Bishop of Argos; Ecumenius, Bishop of Tricca; Diodoros and Rodopianos the Deacon of Aphrodisia; Ansfried, Bishop of Utrecht; Mamai, Catholicos of Georgia; Xenia of Peloponnesus; Paul of Vilnius, Lithuania; Eupraxia and Juliana of Conception Monastery in Moscow; Gregory, Bishop of Rostov; Irodion of Lainici Monastery (Romania); Theophanes of Vatopedi, Metropolitan of Peritheorion; Theodosius, abbot of the Kiev Caves Monastery; Ahmet the Calligrapher of Constantinople; Michael and Arsenius the Georgians; Paul of Vilnius, Lithuania; Glywys of Cornwall; Finding of the relics of St. Luke of Mt. Steirion; "Svensk" Icon of the Mother of God.

FRIDAY

Abstain from meat and dairy products, and fish.
Acts 10:44-11:10; John 8:21-30

MAY 4

Conceit—that subtle arrow of the devil—secretly wounds the heart, and its seed is subtly planted; so that—little by little—it grows into a Pharisee.

St. Macarius of Optina

MARTYR FLORIAN AND 40 COMPANIONS, AT LORSCH, AUSTRIA. Florian was born near the modern-day city of Vienna. He joined the Roman army and later became a commander in a town now called Lorsch. He secretly practiced his Christian faith in the early fourth century, until Emperor Diocletian started what became the largest persecution of Christians since Nero. Florian remained silent until he heard that forty Christians, including soldiers, were awaiting execution in the Lorsch prison. Some accounts say that when he tried to free them, he was captured and given the opportunity to abandon his faith. When he refused, he was scourged and flayed. Rather than give him a soldier's death, by the sword, Florian was given a martyr's death. He was drowned in the River Enns with a millstone around his neck. A pious woman received his body and buried it. A chapel was built over his grave and became St. Florian Priory. The relics were later moved several times, including Rome and Poland. A legend says that the ox carrying the relics suddenly stopped and would not move and no one could lift them. This is where they built the Collegiate Church of St. Florian. St. Florian is invoked for protection from fire, water damage, storms, drought, and burns. He is portrayed as a young man, sometimes in armor, pouring water onto a burning church.

SAINTS OF THE DAY: Silvanus of Gaza and 40 martyrs; Nicephorus the Hesychast; Pelagia of Tarsus; Hilary the Wonderworker; Olbian of Anaea, and his disciples; Erasmus of Formia; Aphrodisius and others, at Scythopolis; Athanasius of Corinth; Nicephorus of Medicium; Dimitry of Gdov; The Alphanov Brothers; Monica of Tagaste; Florian and 40 companions at Lorsch; Ethelred of Mercia; Synaxis of the Venerable Fathers of Mt. Sinai; Translation of the relics of Righteous Lazarus and St. Mary Magdalene.

MAY 5

Acts 12:1-11; John 8:31-42

If you do good, you must do it only for God. For this reason you must pay no attention to the ingratitude of people. Expect a reward not here, but from the Lord in heaven. If you expect it here—it will be in vain and you will endure deprivation.

St. Ambrose of Optina

VENERABLE EFTHYMIOS THE WONDERWORKER. Efthymios was from a pious and prosperous farming family in tenth-century Thrace. When he was very young, his father died, and his mother took him to live in a monastery in Constantinople. Efthymios lived there for thirty years, and through his exemplary ascetic struggles, he was compared to the Holy Fathers of old. As time passed, he developed a longing to live completely alone, so he lived four years in that manner. Hearing of these struggles, the bishop of Perinthos ordained him deacon, and later another bishop ordained him to the priesthood. He eventually was elevated to bishop of Madytos. Over the next forty years, Efthymios continued to attain the virtues and was an exceptional priest. God imbued him with the gift of working miracles through his prayers. He rescued various people from demonic possession, including a nun. He helped many women through difficult childbirth and fever. He healed a leper, and during a great famine, he collected and distributed food. Hearing all this, the Emperor Basil II came to Madytos to visit Efthymios, who foretold the emperor's famous victory against Bardas Phokas. Many miracles occurred after St. Efthymios' death, and his holy relics produce myrrh that flows from his tomb.

SAINTS OF THE DAY: Great Martyr Irene of Thessalonica; Martyrs Neophytos, Gaius, and Gaianus; Barlaam of Serpukhov; Martin and Heraclius of Illyria; Eulogius the Confessor, of Edessa; Adrian of Monza; Ephraim of Nea Makri; Efthymios, Bishop of Madytos; Eleni of Lesbos; Hydrock of Cornwall; Translation of the relics of St. Aldhelm, Bishop of Sherborne; Uncovering of the relics of St. James of Zhelezny Borok Monastery; "Inexhaustible Chalice" Icon of the Mother of God.

SUNDAY

Sunday of the Samaritan Woman
Fast-free

MAY 6

Acts 11:19-30; John 4:5-42

Let us also imitate the woman of Samaria, and in the face of our own sins not be ashamed because of what men might think. Rather, it is proper to fear God Who sees now what we have done and Who punishes later for what we do not repent of.

St. John Chrysostom

VENERABLE MICAH OF RADONEZH. Micah was a monk and one of the first disciples of St. Sergei of Radonezh. They lived in the same cell, and under Sergei's guidance, he attained to high spiritual perfection. Micah became known for his pure heart and meekness. One day, after they had completed their morning prayers, Sergei told Micah that they were about to receive a visit from the Most Holy Mother of God. Suddenly, an extremely bright light filled their cell, and Micah fell upon the ground, and out of fear lay there as though dead. The Mother of Good appeared together with the Holy Apostles Peter and John the Theologian. Micah later died peacefully, and his relics were buried at the Trinity-Sergiev Lavra. About three hundred fifty years later, a church commemorating the appearance was built over St. Micah's tomb.

SAINTS OF THE DAY: Barbarus the Soldier, Bacchus, Callimachus, and Dionysius, in Morea; Barbarus the former robber, in Epirus; Mamas, Pachomius, and Hilarion, monks; Martyrs Danax, Mesiurs, Therin, and Donatus; Job the Long-suffering; Job of Pochaev; Micah of Radonezh; New Martyr Demetrios of Peloponnesus; Seraphim of Mt. Dombos; Sophia of Pontus and Kastoria; Edbert, Bishop of Lindisfarne; The Sinaites of Serbia: Romilus of Ravanica, Romanus of Djjunisa, Sisoes of Sinai, Martyrius of Rukumije, Gregory of Gornjak, Zosimas of Tuman, and Gregory of Sinai; Translation of the relics of St. Sava I of Serbia and Pachomius of Nerekhta.

MAY 7

Acts 12:12-17; John 8:42-51

People are generally called intelligent through a wrong use of this word. The intelligent are not those who have studied the sayings and writings of the wise men of old, but those whose soul is intelligent, who can judge what is good and what is evil; they avoid what is evil and harms the soul and intelligently care for and practice what is good and profits the world, greatly thanking God.

St. Anthony the Great

JOHN PSYCHAITES THE CONFESSOR. John was from eighth-century Constantinople. At an early age, he desired to imitate the life of St. John the Baptist and Prophet Elias, so he pursued strict asceticism. He fought the demons, cleansed his soul with tears, and offered all-night vigils in prayer. God bestowed upon him the working of miracles, healing both souls and bodies. He fought the iconoclasts and denounced the heretics' teachings. John became the abbot of the Psycha Monastery at Constantinople. He suffered persecution for his defense of the veneration of icons and was exiled by Emperor Leo V. He was eventually recalled and sent to his monastery, where he gave up his soul.

SAINTS OF THE DAY: Commemoration of the Apparition of the Sign of the Precious Cross over Jerusalem; Nilus, abbot of Sora; Domitianus, Bishop of Maastricht; Quadratus (Codratus), Rufinus, and Saturninus of Nicomedia; Acacius the Centurion at Byzantium; Nilus, founder of Sora Skete; John of Zedazeni in Georgia and 12 disciples; Pachomius the Russian of Usaki; John Psychaites the Confessor; John of Beverley, Bishop of York; Repose of St. Alexis Toth in America; Uncovering of the relics of St. Euthymius the Great and St. Nilus the Myrrh-gusher of Mt. Athos; "Zhirovits" and "Lubech" Icons of the Mother of God.

May 8

1 John 1:1-7; John 19:25-28, 21:24-25

The egotistical and carnal man is easily deceived by the cunning devil... If a person does not have his guard up, the evil one can readily enter his mind with fantasies and false lights—none of which can raise us to Paradise. Instead, they will hurl us into chaos. This is why a person must seek repentance, not lights and divine gifts. It is repentance that leads to humility, and then the Benevolent God provides for us all that is necessary.

St. Paisios the Athonite

WIRO, BISHOP OF UTRECHT. It is believed that Wiro was from mid-eighth-century Northumbria, but it's unclear. The Roman Martyrology calls him Wiro, Bishop of Scotiae, now Scotland. His biographer tells us that he was ordained to the priesthood, and together with a fellow Northumbrian Plechelm were later consecrated as regionary bishops in Rome. After doing missionary work in Northumbria, the two went to Friesland in the Netherlands, where they evangelized the inhabitants. They built a small church and monastery at Peterkloster. Later they were martyred by the Frieslanders while preaching the gospel. Their relics were transferred to the church they built. St. Wiro is portrayed as hearing the confession of the king.

SAINTS OF THE DAY: Holy Apostle and Evangelist John the Theologian; Arsenius the Great of Scetis; Emilia, mother of St. Basil the Great; Pimen the Faster of the Far Caves; Macarius of Ghent; Milles the Hymnographer; Arsenius the Lover of Labor of the Kiev Caves; Iduberga, foundress of Nivelles; Zosima and Adrian of Volokolamsk; Hierax of Egypt; Wiro, Bishop of Utrecht; Plechelm, missionary bishop, and Otger of Odilienberg; Soldier martyrs slain by the sword; Translation of the relics of St. Arsenius of Novgorod, fool-for-Christ; Miracle wrought by the icon of the Mother of God of Cassiope.

WEDNESDAY

Abstain from meat and dairy products, and fish.
Acts 13:13-24; John 6:5-14

MAY 9

If it is a mark of extreme meekness, even in the presence of one's offender, to be peacefully and lovingly disposed towards him in one's heart, then it is certainly a mark of hot temper when a person continues to quarrel and rage against his offender, both by words and gestures, even when by himself.

St. John Climacus

"ZARAZSK" ICON OF ST. NICHOLAS THE WONDERWORKER. This icon is one of the most well-known icons in Russia. It was from the ancient Byzantine colony of Korsun, in the Crimea, and was situated in the church in which Vladimir the Great was baptized in the tenth century. In 1225 AD the icon was escorted by the priest Eustathius from Korsun to Ryazan. It safely passed through the dangerous land of the Tartars and delivered to Prince Theodore of Ryazan. Fr. Eustathius was guided miraculously by St. Nicholas. The prince built a church in honor of St. Nicholas and placed the miraculous icon within it. However, catastrophe later came upon Ryazan from Tatar forces led by Batu. Theodore was captured and later died. His wife Eupraxia threw herself and her baby son from a bell tower rather than face Tatar captivity. The town name of Ryazan was later changed to Zarazsk, as was the name of the icon, which means "to fall to death." When the image was transferred to Kolomna in the sixteenth century, it gained a wider devotion. Copies spread widely throughout Russia showing St. Nicholas blessing with his right arm and holding a gospel aloft in his left hand. Some of these copies have also been considered wonderworking.

SAINTS OF THE DAY: Isaiah the Prophet; Christopher of Lycia, with Callinica, Aquilina, and 200 soldiers; Epimachus of Pelusium; Gordion at Rome; Maximus III, Bishop of Jerusalem; Nicholas of Vuneni; Joseph of Optina; Shio of Mgvime, Georgia; Translation of the relics of St. Nicholas the Wonderworker from Myra to Bari; Translation of the relics of Child-martyr St. Gabriel of Slutsk; "Zarazsk" Icon of St. Nicholas.

May 10

1 Corinthians 4:9-16; Luke 6:12-19

Is our entire body suffering from illness? This is how our inner man gains perfect health. Let us, therefore, not be dismayed when we fall ill, but let us give thanks to God, Who arranges all things for our benefit; and Who oftentimes, through the temporary sickness of our perishable body, bestows eternal health and salvation upon our immortal soul.

St. Syncletica of Alexandria

CONLETH, HERMIT AND BISHOP OF KILDARE. Conleth was an Irish hermit and metal worker in the fifth and sixth centuries. He was also a copyist and skilled illuminator of manuscripts. St. Brigid persuaded Conleth to make sacred vessels for her convent. Conleth was one of three chief artisans of Ireland during that time. A community of monks grew up under his guidance, and they excelled in the making of beautiful chalices and other metal objects needed in the church. They also wrote missals, gospels, and Psalters. Conleth later acted as a priest for St. Brigid's monastic community in Kildare. He and Bridget also presided over the monastery and built a cathedral, where he became the first bishop and abbot of the monks of Kildare. Conleth died when he was attacked by wolves while on a pilgrimage to Rome and was buried nearby. His relics were finally laid to rest in Connell to protect the inhabitants from invading Danes.

SAINTS OF THE DAY: Cyril and Methodius, Equal-to-the-Apostles; Mocius of Amphipolis; Nicodemus of Pech; Dioscorus the New and Argyrus; Sophronius of the Kiev Caves; Rostislav of Greater Moravia; Cathan of Bute; Joseph of Astrakhan; Olympia of Mytilene; Mayeul of Cluny; Asaph of Llanelwy, North Wales; Acacius of Lower Moesia; Theophylactus of Stavropol; Christesia (Christopher) of Gareji; Bassus of Persia; Commemoration of the founding of Constantinople.

Abstain from meat and dairy products, and fish.
Acts 15:5-12; John 10:17-28

May 11

You have heard an insult, like the wind. You are angry, like a wave. When the wind blows, and the wave swells, the ship is then endangered, the heart is in jeopardy, and the heart is tossed back and forth. When you were insulted, you longed for revenge. But if you have been avenged and so rejoice in the person's pain, you have suffered shipwreck. Why is this? Because Christ is asleep in you. What does it mean that Christ is asleep in you? That you have forgotten Christ. Rouse Him then. Call Christ to mind and let Him wake up in you. Pay attention to Him.

St. Augustine of Hippo

NICODEMUS OF PECH, ARCHBISHOP OF SERBIA. Nicodemus was a Serbian monk on Mt. Athos toward the end of the thirteenth century. He loved the ascetical life and attempted to help strengthen it throughout Serbia. He was chosen abbot of Hilander Monastery on Mt. Athos and was elected archbishop of all-Serbia and the coastal lands in Pech. He translated the Jerusalem Typikon into the Slavonic language. The Typikon is a book of directives and rubrics that establishes for the Orthodox Church the order of divine services for each day of the year. In this book, Nicodemus wrote that God knows our weaknesses and gives us spiritual strength, but first, we must show Him that we are making an effort. He continuously worked to weed out heresies and to strengthen the faith. St. Nicodemus died peacefully, and his wonderworking relics are buried in the monastery of the Patriarchate of Pech.

SAINTS OF THE DAY: Cyril and Methodius, Equal-to-the-Apostles; Mocius of Amphipolis; Nicodemus of Pech; Dioscorus the New and Argyrus; Sophronius of the Kiev Caves; Rostislav of Greater Moravia; Cathan of Bute; Joseph of Astrakhan; Olympia of Mytilene; Mayeul of Cluny; Asaph of Llanelwy, North Wales; Acacius of Lower Moesia; Theophylactus of Stavropol; Christesia (Christopher) of Gareji; Bassus of Persia; Commemoration of the founding of Constantinople.

MAY 12

Acts 15:35-41; John 10:27-38

To do good to your neighbor is the fruit of love. Apparently, the person who has the fear of God and prays to God helps only himself; and since every virtue is fulfilled through love of neighbor, this is why the Elder said to do good to your neighbor. Even if one fears God and prays to Him, he is also obliged to be useful to his neighbor and to be good to him. This, as I have said, is the fruit of love—which is the fulfillment of all virtues.

St. Poemen the Great

MARTYR JOHN OF WALLACHIA, AT CONSTANTINOPLE. John was a handsome Christian of noble birth from seventeenth-century Wallachia, which was ruled by the Turks. When the people revolted over an unfair tax, they attacked the Turks, killing, burning, and imprisoning great numbers. The Turks mounted an overwhelming army in retaliation, massacring and imprisoning vast numbers of women and men. The fifteen-year-old John was taken into captivity and was purchased by a Turkish soldier, wanting to seduce him. Fearing the worst, John killed the soldier. He was bound and taken to Constantinople, to the wife of the man he had slain. Seeing that he was so handsome, she promised to marry him and make him wealthy, if he became a Muslim. John made the sign of the cross and asked God to protect and strengthen him. When she saw his resolve, she sent him to the prefect, where he was then imprisoned and tortured. However, the woman persisted in her attempts to seduce John and to turn him away from his Christian faith. John refused to violate Christianity, so he was hanged.

SAINTS OF THE DAY: Germanus, Patriarch of Constantinople; Sabinus, Archbishop of Cyprus; Pancratius of Rome; Epiphanius, Bishop of Cyprus; Polybius of Cyprus, Bishop of Rinocyria; Athanasia of Smolensk; Philip of Sicily; Theodore of Cythera; John of Serres; John of Wallachia; Dionysius and Anthony of St. Sergius Lavra; Glorification of St. Hermogenes, Patriarch of Moscow and all-Russia.

SUNDAY

Sunday of the Blind Man
Fast-free
Acts 16:16-34; John 9:1-38

MAY 13

Love separates the visible world, and causes one to forget all distressing things in life. And love makes things grow, and heals thirst and freely gives strength to those who toil virtuously. Love puts out rage, and the seething heart and it does not allow one to get angry or upset. When love flees, it is pursued by those who are wounded, and it is sought with much love from the heart. But it returns and appears, and shines benevolently... Oh gift beyond telling! For what has love not accomplished, and what is it not?

St. Symeon the New Theologian

SERGIOS THE CONFESSOR OF CONSTANTINOPLE. Sergios was a wealthy and distinguished Christian from ninth-century Constantinople. He lived during the iconoclast persecution. It is said that Sergios was great in spirit. He was married and had children. Sergios was arrested for venerating the holy icons and was brought before the emperor. A rope was placed around his neck, and he was paraded through the streets where he endured ridicule and insults. All of his wealth was confiscated by the state, and he was cast into prison. He was later sent into exile with his family, where they suffered afflictions and tribulations. Sergios gave up his spirit to God.

SAINTS OF THE DAY: Glyceria at Heraclea, and Laodicius, her jailer; Sergios the Confessor, his wife Irene and children; Pausicacius of Synnada; Alexander of Rome; Nicephorus of Ephapsios Monastery; Martyrs killed by the Latins at the Iveron Monastery; John, Euthymius, George, and Gabriel of Iveron; Servatius of Maastricht; Alexander of Tiverias; Leander of Seville; Macarius, Amphilochius, and Tarasius of Glushitsa; Glyceria of Novgorod; Basil Sokolov, Christopher Nadezhdin, Alexander Zaozersky, Macarius Telegin, and Sergius Tikhomirov of Moscow; Translation of the relics of St. Macarius of Kanev; Synaxis of the 103 New Martyrs of Cherkassy; Commemoration of the monks of Iveron Monastery martyred in the thirteenth century; Consecration of the Church of Theotokos Pantanassa.

MAY 14

Acts 17:1-9; John 11:47-54

Humble-mindedness will bring all the virtues.

St. Anthimos of Chios

MARTYR ALEXANDER OF KENTOUKELLAI. Alexander was a Roman soldier in the third- and fourth-century. When Tiberius decided that his army should worship the idols, Alexander mocked them all, calling them madmen, since they forsook the Creator and worshiped demons. Maximian tried to convert Alexander, but while this was happening, the heavens opened, and Alexander saw Jesus sitting at the right hand of the Father. Alexander appeared angelic, and Maximian lost all hope of converting him. He, therefore, sent Alexander to Tiberius who was entrusted with the persecution of Christians. Alexander was scourged, and his sides burned with torches. He was thrown upon prickly plants and beaten with rods. While this was being carried out, an angel of the Lord appeared to Alexander and strengthened him. All the Christians came out to greet Alexander, and they kissed his chains. They continued to Veroe, and seeing that there was no water in that area, Alexander prayed, and he caused water to spring forth from the ground. When they tried to pour boiling oil over his back, the cauldron overturned, burning many of the prefect's servants. The executioner was given the order to behead Alexander, but he could not raise his sword because he saw angels guarding Alexander. At last, Alexander asked them to stand off a little so that the executioner could finish his job.

SAINTS OF THE DAY: Isidore of Chios; Serapion the Sindonite; Leontios of Jerusalem; Aprunculus of Clermont; Maximus, under Decius; Nicetas of Novgorod; Alexander, Barbarus, and Acolythus in Constantinople; Alexander of Kentoukellai; Isidore, fool-for-Christ of Rostov; Mark of Crete; Nicetas of the Kiev Caves; John-Raiko of Bulgaria; Anthony, with 40 monks, 1,000 laymen, and Daniel, with 30 monks and 200 laymen, martyred in Russia by the Latins; Andrew, in Tyumen; Matthew of Yaransk; Therapontus of Cyprus; Uncovering of the relics of St. Tikhon, Bishop of Voronezh; "Yaroslavl" (Pechersk) Icon of the Mother of God.

MAY 15

Acts 17:19-28; John 12:19-36

Whoever slanders us—showers us with gifts, and whoever praises us—robs us.

St. Ambrose of Optina

VENERABLE ACHILLES, BISHOP OF LARISSA. Achilles was born in Cappadocia. From a young age, he imitated his parents' virtues. When his parents died, he gave away their wealth to the poor and remained penniless. He went to Jerusalem to visit the holy shrines and then to Rome to reverence at the tombs of the holy Apostles Peter and Paul. In Rome, he guided many idolaters to the Christian faith, and God granted him the gift of working miracles. He healed the sick, expelled demons, and cleansed lepers. His fame had spread, and a multitude of people thronged to him to hear his angelic discourses. He spoke publicly in Larissa and was known as the greatest orator to visit Greece since the Apostle Paul. He was chosen archbishop of Larissa. The holy Emperor Constantine the Great invited Achilles to the First Ecumenical Synod at Nicaea in 325. It is said that Achilles put the heretics to shame because of his purity and knowledge. Holding up a rock he said, "O Arius… if what you speak is consistent with truth, that the Son of God is a creature and creation of God, command this rock which is before all to gush forth oil." The Arians fell silent, then asked Achilles to extract oil. Achilles prayed, "… let oil flow forth from this rock that the factious might believe and be given assurance." Then immediately oil gushed down from the rock, soaking the ground. The Synod banished the Arians. Emperor Constantine invited Achilles to Constantinople, and when he departed there, the emperor gave him gold and silver to be used for the construction of churches in Larissa. He served his flock for thirty-five years. He foreknew the day of his death.

SAINTS OF THE DAY: Pachomios the Great; Euphrosynus of Pskov and Serapion; Barbarus the Myrrh-gusher; Isaiah of Rostov; Isaiah of the Kiev Caves; Andrew the Hermit; Silvanus and Pachomius of Nerekhta; Dymphna of Geel; Arethas of Valaam; Pachomius of Chernigov.

WEDNESDAY

Leave-taking of Pascha
Abstain from meat and dairy products.
Acts 18:22-28; John 12:36-47

MAY 16

Desire and effort must come from you. God will provide the power and the result.

St. Paisios the Athonite

MARTYR VUKASIN OF SERBIA. Vukasin was born a Serbian Orthodox Christian in the late nineteenth-century village of Klepci, in Herzegovina. He served in the church as a reader. The family moved from Klepci to Sarajevo, and at the beginning of World War II, Vukasin fled Sarajevo back to Klepci to hide from the fascists. But the Croatian fascist Ustasas arrested him and other Serbs of the region and transported them to the notorious Jasenovac concentration camp, where at least 700,000 were killed. One night, four Ustashe's soldiers decided to see who could kill the most in one night. The soldier Zhila had already killed 1,100 in several hours, but when he saw Vukasin, he was struck by his calmness, and Zhila found himself temporarily unable to move. Zhila approached Vukasin and told him that he would spare his life if he cried loudly, "Long live Pavelic," who was the leader of the Ustashe movement. Vukasin calmly replied, "My child, you do what you must." Zhila repeated his request, but Vukasin refused to obey. He proceeded to cut off Vukasin's ears, then his nose, and scarred his face. Then he cut his tongue, repeating his request at each assault. But Vukasin again calmly repeated his reply. Zhila eventually killed Vukasin, but he lost his senses and found that he could no longer kill. He started to see a vision of Vukasin repeating those same words, and this became so unbearable because the voice would not stop. He began running around attacking random people, trying to suppress his memory, and then he was hospitalized.

SAINTS OF THE DAY: Theodore the Sanctified; Nicholas I Mystikos; Abdas and Abdiesus, with 38 martyrs; Peter of Blachernae; George II, of Mytilene; Nicholas of Metsovo; Isaacius, Symeon and Bachthisoes of Persia; Martyr Papylinos; Alexander of Jerusalem; Euphemia near Neaorion; Cassian and Laurence of Komel; Ephraim of Novgorod; Musa of Rome; Bardas of Petra.

THURSDAY

MAY 17

The Ascension of our Lord
Fast-free
Acts 1:1-12; Luke 24:36-53

God asks little, but He gives much.

St. John Chrysostom

GREAT MARTYR NICHOLAS OF SOFIA. Nicholas lived during the seventeenth-century rule of Bulgaria by the Ottomans. From a young age, he read the divine words and visited the temples of God. Nicholas became a quality shoemaker and helped those in need. He would stand throughout the night praying, and God granted him the gift of weeping. Because he lived his faith, people noticed his decency and meekness, and they developed a love for him. They convinced him to marry, even though he confessed to preferring the life of a wanderer. He led a simple life, giving alms, visiting prisoners, the sick, widows, and orphans. After many years, he secretly boarded a ship and freed himself from the burdens of the world. Nicholas settled in Ungro-Wallachia, where even the king valued his workmanship and wisdom. After three years, some people from Sofia were visiting that area, and they saw Nicholas, and he agreed to return to Sofia. However, the Ottomans wanted to convert him to their faith. Not suspecting their plot against him, Nicholas accompanied them to an event where they put something in his drink, and he did not know what he was doing. The men removed his clothes and circumcised him. When he had woken, and realized how he had been wounded, he offered long prayers to God. One year later, a confrontation was staged against Nicholas, and an angry mob took him to a judge. Nicholas calmly defended himself. The judge sympathized with him, telling him to acquiesce publicly, and then secretly leave Sofia to practice his faith. The judge told the mob, "I have found no blame in this man." The mob took hold of Nicholas, stoning and murdering him. They trampled his skull and burned him to ashes. At midnight, a light, like a pillar of fire, illumined the area.

SAINTS OF THE DAY: Andronicus of the Seventy, and Junia; Solochon, Pamphamer, and Pamphalon; Nectarios and Theophanes of Varlaam; Athanasios the New; Nicholas of Sofia.

FRIDAY

Abstain from meat and dairy products, and fish.
Acts 19:1-8; John 14:1-11

MAY 18

"The first and great commandment is 'You shall love the Lord your God,'" he added "and the second … is like it. 'You shall love your neighbor as yourself.'" And see how with nearly the same excellence he also requires this. For as concerning God, he said "With all your heart": so concerning your neighbor, 'as yourself' is the same as 'with all your heart." If this commandment were duly observed there would be neither slave nor free, neither ruler nor ruled.... There would be no poverty, no unbounded wealth if there were love, but only the good parts that come from each. From the one we should reap its abundance, and from the other its freedom from care and should neither have to undergo the anxieties of riches nor the dread of poverty.

St. John Chrysostom

MARTYRS SYMEON, ISAAC, AND BACHTISIUS OF PERSIA. Symeon, Isaac, and Bachtisius were Christians living in third-century Persia under the emperor Sapor, who fiercely persecuted Christians. The saints were arrested and ordered to worship fire. But they refused to deny the Creator, answering, "We will not recant from the Creator of all and we will not worship fire nor the sun." They were cruelly tortured and thrown into prison, and for seven days were not given any food. Finally, they were beheaded.

SAINTS OF THE DAY: Peter of Lampsacus with Dionysia, Andrew, Paul, Christina, Heraclios, Paulinus, and Benedimus; Tecusa with Alexandra, Claudia, Phaine, Euphrasia, Matrona, Julia, and Theodotus of Ancyra; Stephen the New, Patriarch of Constantinople; Theodore, Pope of Rome; Christina of Athens; Euphrasia of Nicaea; Symeon, Isaac, and Bachtisius of Persia; Potamon, Bishop of Heraclea; Anastaso of Lukada; Martinian of Areovinthus; Martyr Julian; Theodore in Orenburg; Davit and Tarichan of Georgia; Elgiva, Queen of England; Macarius, Apostle to the Altai; Damian Strbac of Serbia; John Gashkevich of Korma.

MAY 19

Acts 20:7-12; John 14:10-21

Sobriety if the path to every virtue.

St. Nikon of Optina

NEW HIEROMARTYR JOHN KARASTAMATIS OF SANTA CRUZ. At the age of twenty, John moved to America from the island of Andros, started a family, and was ordained to the priesthood. In 1981, he came to the Church of Prophet Elijah in Santa Cruz, California, which he restored. The church soon became the center of Orthodoxy. He would go to parks and public streets to talk to young people who didn't know Christ. On the island of Andros, a miracle occurred each year. When the lilies bloomed, they were cut and placed before the miraculous icon of the Mother of God. After they had withered, they sprouted and bloomed again at the Feast of the Dormition. Father John brought some of these dried lily stalks with him to Santa Cruz, and they also blossomed before the icon of the Virgin Mary during the Feast of Assumption. This miracle strengthened the faith of many. Father John would talk about the miracles of the Virgin Mary, and many became Orthodox. But his preaching angered some, and he was murdered in his church. His head was hit with a hammer, his body butchered with a knife, and the murderers hanged him with a chain. They used the saint's blood to write slogans on the walls. The police found three of the killers. They were priests and worshipers of Satan. Two of them died when they drank cobra venom, and one lost his mind. Father John's vestments were taken to the monastery in Andros, where the church bells began to ring of their own accord.

SAINTS OF THE DAY: Patrick of Prousa, and Acacius, Menander, and Polyenus; John, Conon, Jeremias, Cyril, Theoctistus, Barnabas, Maximus, Theognostus, Joseph, Gennadius, Gerasimus, Mark, and Herman of Cyprus; John, of the Goths; Kyriake and Theotima of Nicomedia; Demetrius Donskoy of Moscow; Acoluthus of the Thebaid; Memnon, wonderworker; Cornelius of Komel; Onuphrius of Kursk; Cornelius of Paleostrov; John of Uglich; Ivan of Vologda; Sergius of Shukhtom.

SUNDAY

Fathers of the First Ecumenical Council
Fast-free

MAY 20

Acts 20:16-18, 28-36; John 17:1-13

If one feels contrition for the sins of his youth, and has already confessed them, there is no reason to be troubled over them, since God has forgiven him from the moment he confessed. Henceforth, one should not dig up and dwell upon old things, particularly carnal sins, because one can thus be greatly harmed. During a war, for example, a hand grenade falls next to a soldier, but God protects him and it doesn't explode. After the war, the soldier finds the hand grenade—which didn't explode—and begins to scrutinize it; and finally is blown to smithereens during peacetime.

St. Paisios the Athonite

VENERABLE STEPHEN, ABBOT OF PIPER IN SERBIA. Stephen was a Christian from a poor and devout family in the seventeenth-century village of Zupa. In order to learn the ascetic life, he became a monk at the Monastery of Moraa, where he later became abbot. During this time of Turkish occupation, Stephen and the other monks were driven out of their monastery. Stephen settled in Rovaki Turmanj, now called Celiste. He eventually settled in a small monastic cell in Piper, where he remained until his peaceful death. St. Stephen's wonderworking relics are still preserved there to this day, continuing to work many miracles.

SAINTS OF THE DAY: Martyr Thalelaeus with Alexander and Asterius, at Aegae in Cilicia; Lydia of Philippi; Thalassios the Myrrh-gusher of Libya; Zabulon and Susanna, parents of St. Nino; Stephen of Piper; Asclas of Egypt; Dovmont-Timothy, Prince of Pskov; Nicetas, John, and Joseph, monks on Chios; Ethelbert, King of East Anglia; Austregiselus, Bishop of Bourges; Dodo of St. Davit-Garesja Monastery, Georgia; Recovery of the relics of St. Alexis, Metropolitan of Moscow.

MAY 21

Acts 26:1, 12-20; John 10:1-9

Blessed, indeed, is he against whom the leaders of darkness can find nothing. He will find joy, honor and rest beyond all measure. Therefore, let us weep before God with the whole power of our soul; so that, in His goodness, He will take pity on us and send us aid from on high.

St. Isaiah the Anchorite

"KRASNOGORSK" VLADIMIR ICON OF THE MOTHER OF GOD. The Krasnogorsk icon of the Mother of God dates to 1601. The abbot Varlaam of the church of the Resurrection of Christ at Keurola had it in his possession. In 1603, he heard a gentle feminine voice in a dream, telling him to give the icon to the priest Miron. After some time, Miron visited the abbot on other business. Varlaam told him about his dream, and Miron told him about a desolate mountain, called Black Mountain, near the Urals that was suitable for forming a monastery. The abbot gave Miron the icon, who put it in a local church, and it brought healing to a woman named Martha, who in turn had a dream of the Mother of God, telling her where Miron should place Her icon. Miron, with the help of a monk Jona, built a church and founded a monastery at Black Mountain. The Vladimir icon was installed in the church, and the monastery was named Krasnogorsk.

SAINTS OF THE DAY: Emperor Constantine and Helen, his mother; Basil, Bishop of Ryazan; Constantine, Michael, and Theodore, of Murom; Cassian the Greek of Uglich; Secundus and others, in Alexandria; Cyril of Rostov; Pachomios of Patmos; Hospicius of Trier; Helen of Dechani; Agapitus of Markushev; Synaxis of the Saints of Simbirsk and Karelia; Synaxis of the Hieromartyrs of Ufa; Meeting of the Vladimir Icon of the Mother of God; Pskov-Pechersk "Virgin of Tenderness," "Zaonikievsky," "Oransk," and "Krasnogorsk" Icons of the Mother of God.

MAY 22

Acts 21:26-32; John 16:2-13

When your life is according to God, do not be saddened over afflictions or your passions, for God will lift them from you one day. Fear not death, my child for God has prepared greater things in order to raise us above death.

+Elder Justin Parvu of Romania

HIEROMARTYR BASILISKOS OF COMANA. The blood of St. Basiliskos caused the idol-worshipping governor Agrippa to come to his senses and receive Holy Baptism. Basiliskos was spared martyrdom when Sts. Kleonikos and Eutropios were crucified on crosses under the fourth-century emperor Galerius. However, Basiliskos languished in prison in the city of Comana, awaiting his impending death. Jesus appeared to him in a dream, promising His help and foretold his martyr's end. Basiliskos requested release to travel to his kinsfolk to bid them farewell, and this was granted out of respect for his holy life. When the new governor Agrippa learned that the saint was released, he sent soldiers after him. Already on his way back to Comana, the soldiers found him. Chained and shod in metal sandals, Basiliskos performed miracles and converted many along the way. Agrippa commanded Basiliskos to offer sacrifice to the pagan gods, and he was led into a pagan temple. Instantly, a flash of fire from heaven burned the temple, and the idol turned to dust. Calling it magic, the governor ordered the saint's beheading, but he immediately became insane. He went to the place of the execution and found some of the martyr's blood in the dust and smeared it on himself, and he was restored to health. A Christian gathered the relics for burial. Later he built a church in Comana where the relics were laid to rest, and a multitude of miracles took place.

SAINTS OF THE DAY: Commemoration of the Second Ecumenical Council; Melchisedec, King of Salem; John-Vladimir of Serbia; Basiliskos of Comana; Donatus of Thmuis, with Macarius and Theodore; James of Borovichi; Markella and Codratus; Sophia the Healer.

Wednesday

Abstain from meat and dairy products, and fish.
Acts 23:1-11; John 16:15-23

May 23

No matter what kind of language is used, it will be unable to speak of God as He is and what He is. The perfection of learning is to know God in such a manner that, although you realize He is not unknown, you perceive that He cannot be described.

St. Hilary of Poitiers

DESIDERIUS, BISHOP OF VIENNE. At the time when Queen Brunhildis was exercising her woeful influence over the courts of her grandsons in Austrasia and Burgundy, Bishop Desiderius administered the diocese of Vienne. He was one of the prelates that St. Gregory the Great commended St. Augustine and his companion missionaries on their way to evangelize England. The zeal of Desiderius in enforcing clerical discipline, repressing simony, which is the sin of making a profit from sacred things, and profligacy or reckless extravagance, made him enemies in the court, including the queen herself. Attempts were made to discredit Desiderius with Pope Gregory, accusing Desiderius of paganism because he read the great Latin classics, but the pope exonerated him. The queen had Desiderius banished for four years, but upon his return, both the governor of Vienne and other old opponents hampered Desiderius in his duties. Even this did not dissuade him to boldly rebuke the king for his shameless wickedness. On his way home from the court, three men murdered St. Desiderius.

SAINTS OF THE DAY: Michael the Confessor, Bishop of Synnada; Mary Cleopa the Myrrh-bearer; Michael the Black-robed of St. Sabbas Monastery; Salonas the Roman; Paisius, abbot of Galich; Martyr Seleucus; Damian of Georgia; Euphrosyne, Princess of Polotsk; Ioannicius I, Archbishop of Serbia; Desiderius, Bishop of Vienne; Uncovering of the relics of St. Leontios, Bishop of Rostov; Uncovering of the relics of St. Abramius of Rostov; Synaxis of All Saints of Rostov and Yaroslavl; "Thou Art the Vineyard" Icon of the Mother of God.

MAY 24

Acts 25:13-19; John 16:23-33

When the mind begins to make progress in the love of God, then the demon of blasphemy starts to tempt it. He suggests such thoughts to it as no man—but only their father, the Devil—could devise. He does this out of envy for the God-loving man, in order that—coming into despair at having conceived such thoughts—he might no longer dare to soar up to God in his customary prayer. The pernicious demon receives no aid from this trickery in attaining his purpose, but—in fact—renders us more steadfast; for, in being attacked and fighting back, we become more proven and more genuine in our love for God. *'Let their sword enter into their own hearts, and let their bows be broken' (Psalm 36(37):15).*

St. Maximos the Confessor

VENERABLE VINCENT OF LERINS. Vincent was a distinguished military officer from a wealthy family in fifth-century northern Gaul. He was the brother of St. Lupus, Bishop of Troyes. Vincent decided to become a monk at the monastery of Lerins and was later ordained to the priesthood. He became well known for his study of Holy Scripture and the writings of the Holy Fathers. He wrote his *Commonitorium*, a well-written and clear thesis, which was widely accepted in the West, about the rules one should follow to distinguish himself and his Christian faith from the heresies that abounded. He stated, "Every care should be taken to hold fast to what has been believed everywhere, always, and by all." Vincent died peacefully at his monastery.

SAINTS OF THE DAY: Meletios Stratelates with Stephen, John and 1,218 soldiers with women and children, including Serapion of Egypt, Callinicus the Magician, Theodore, Faustus, Marciana, Susanna, Palladia, Cyriacus and Christian, and 12 tribunes, in Galatia; Gregory, Archbishop of Novgorod; Symeon Stylites (the Younger) of Wonderful Mountain; Vincent of Lerins; Nicetas the Stylite, wonderworker of Pereyaslavl-Zalesski; Martha of Monemvasia; Sava Brancovic.

FRIDAY

Abstain from meat and dairy products, and fish.

2 Corinthians 4:6-15; Matthew 11:2-15

MAY 25

Our prayer is often performed at the expense of inward prayer, and inward at the expense of outward; that is, when I pray with my lips or read, if many words do not penetrate into the heart, I become double-minded and hypocritical; with my lips I say one thing, whilst in my heart I feel another. The lips speak truth, whilst the disposition of the heart does not agree with the words of the prayer. But if I pray inwardly, heartily, then, without paying attention to the pronunciation of the words, I concentrate upon their contents, their power, gradually accustoming my heart to the truth, and thus entering into the same disposition of spirit in which the words of the prayer were written.

St. John of Kronstadt

ALDHELM, BISHOP OF SHERBORNE. Aldhelm is known as the first Englishman to attain distinction as a scholar. His Latin writings are preserved in prose and verse. In the seventh century, he found his way to Canterbury, which had become a great center of religious and secular learning. He received tonsure and took charge of the school he had attended and was appointed abbot. He became a counselor to the king and did much to foster religion and education in Wessex. He primarily worked for the spiritual needs and instruction of the poor. He founded monasteries and built several churches. He also became the bishop of West Wessex. Four years later, he died on a trip to Doulting, near Westbury. His body was conveyed back to his monastery, crosses being set up at places where the body had rested on the way. St. Aldhelm's best-known writing is a treatise on virginity dedicated to the nuns of Barking.

SAINTS OF THE DAY: Third Finding of the Precious Head of St. John the Baptist; Martyr Celestine; Olbian, monk; Mary of Ustiug; Therapontus of Cyprus; Innocent of Kherson; Aldhelm of Sherborne; Thaddeus of Svyatogorsk; Synaxis of Saints of Volhynia.

Saturday of the Souls
Fast-free

MAY 26

1 Thessalonians 4:13-17; John 21:14-25

All the programs I made—all failed. For this reason, I let God make the program of my life.

+Elder Epiphanios Theodoropoulos of Patmos

TRANSLATION OF THE RELICS OF NEW MARTYR GEORGE OF KRATOVO. George was born in Bulgaria to wealthy but aged parents, who fervently prayed that God might one day send them a child. George received a fine upbringing and was pious and chaste. He attentively studied the Holy Scriptures. During this time in sixteenth-century Bulgaria, Christians were being forced to convert to Mahometanism. One day, several Mussulmans put a fez (prayer hat) on George's head, but he knocked it to the ground. The Turks beat him and took him to the governor. The governor was impressed with George and tried to persuade him to accept their faith, with promises of wealth and honors. But George was steadfast, confessing his faith in Jesus Christ. The governor gave orders to flog George with canes, but he remained constant, and the tortures worsened. George called upon Jesus Christ for help. Then he was marched through the city streets to the beat of a drum and shouts. A bonfire was set up, and while still alive, George was thrown into the fire. Dead dogs were thrown in with him so that Christians would not be able to find the remains of the saint. Suddenly, a torrential rain started pouring and extinguished the flames. When night fell, a heavenly light illumined St. George's relics. Metropolitan Jeremiah and his clergy retrieved the holy relics and buried them in the church dedicated to St. George the Great Martyr in the city of Sredets.

SAINTS OF THE DAY: Apostles Carpus and Alphaeus, of the Seventy; Abercius and Helen, children of Apostle Alphaeus; Alexander of Thessalonica; Synesius of Carpasia; Augustine of Canterbury; Milan Banjac and Milan Golubovic of Serbia; Translation of the relics of St. George of Kratovo and Sofia; Uncovering of the relics of St. Macarius of Kolyazin; "Tabynsk" Icon of the Mother of God.

Holy Pentecost
Fast-free Week
Acts 2:1-11; John 7:37-52, 8:12

MAY 27

On the day of Pentecost, He triumphantly sent down on them (the Apostles) the Holy Spirit in the rush of a mighty wind like tongues of fire, which sat upon each one of them and entered in and filled them with the strength of Divine flame-like grace; whose breath is laden with dew, and it creates joy in the souls partaking of its power and influence.

St. Seraphim of Sarov

VENERABLE MICHAEL OF PAREKHI. Michael was from eighth-century Georgia. He was tonsured a monk in the Midznadzori Wilderness. He traveled to the Khandzta Monastery and built a chapel and cells for the monks, in a difficult location on the side of a cliff. The monastery was called "Parekhi" or "cave." God granted Michael the gift of wonderworking, and in a divine revelation, he was instructed to send two of his disciples to build a beautiful monastery in the village of Zarzma. After some time, Michael went to live at the top of a huge boulder. Once the devil caused him to fall from it, but the Lord kept him unharmed. Shaken by this experience, Michael sent for St. Grigol of Khandzta and told him all that had happened. St. Grigol built two crosses on either side of Michael's cell, saying, "These two crosses of Christ will protect you, and the mercy of the Most Holy Trinity and the Precious Cross will be upon you." Michael lived into old age and was buried at Parekhi Monastery, where many of the faithful have been healed.

SAINTS OF THE DAY: Helladius, bishop in the East; John the Russian; Therapontus of Sardis; Venerable Bede; Therapontes of White Lake; Martyrs Alypius and Eusebiotus; Michael of Parekhi; Basil of Georgia; Julius the Veteran; Therapontus of Monza; Lazarus the Clairvoyant; Translation of the relics of St. Nilus of Stolben Island; Translation of the relics of Sts. Cyprian, Photius, and Jonah of Kiev.

MONDAY

MAY 28

Feast of the Holy Spirit
Fast-free

Ephesians 5:8-19; Matthew 18:10-20

The grace of the Holy Spirit is the light which lighteneth man.

St. Seraphim of Sarov

GERMANUS, BISHOP OF PARIS. Germanus was born in Autun, France in the late fifth century. From his youth, he was exceedingly pious, never missing midnight vespers at a church a mile from his home, regardless of the weather. He was trained for the priesthood and ordained by St. Agrippinus, the bishop of Autun. Germanus was made abbot of the monastery of St. Symphorian on the outskirts of town. At that time, he already had the gifts of prophecy and miracles. When the bishop of the capital died, Germanus tearfully tried to refuse to become the next bishop. But even as the bishop, Germanus continued to lead a life of austerity, prayer, receiving the poor at his residence, and dining with them at his table. He nourished both their bodies and souls. Even King Childebert, until then a worldly prince, converted to a life of piety, building churches, and placing his wealth in the hands of Germanus for the aid of the poor. During his time as bishop, he strove to reprove the behavior of wayward nobles and even excommunicated King Charibert for his wicked, immoral life. St. Germanus died peacefully at the age of eighty.

SAINTS OF THE DAY: Nicetas the Confessor, Bishop of Chalcedon; Eutychius, Bishop of Melitene; Crescens, Paul, and Dioscorides of Rome; Germanus, Bishop of Paris; Ignatius, Bishop of Rostov; Heliconis and Dapni of Thessalonica; Gerontius, Metropolitan of Moscow; Demetrios (Mitros) of Tripoli; Helen of Diveyevo; Macarius, Dionysius, Nicholas, Ignatius, and Peter; Zacharias of Prousa; Heraclius of Turkistan; Rodion (Fyodorov) of St. Sergius Lavra; Domnica of Kherson; Andrew, fool-for-Christ of Constantinople; Sophronius of Bulgaria; William of Languedoc (Gaul); “The Consoler of Angry Hearts” and “Unbreakable Wall” Icons of the Mother of God.

May 29

Romans 1:1-7, 13-17; Matthew 4:23-25, 5:1-13

The Lord abides in simple hearts. Gold is everywhere and everywhere it shines through, no matter from what angle; but something else, no matter how much you work with it, it still is not gold.

St. Ambrose of Optina

BLESSED JOHN OF USTIUG, FOOL-FOR-CHRIST. John was born to pious parents near fifteenth-century Old Ustiug. During his youthful years, he strictly fasted. On Wednesdays and Fridays, he ate nothing, and the remainder of the days, he ate only bread and water. When John's father died, his mother became a nun. John chose the discipline of remaining silent, then decided to become a fool for the sake of Christ. This is a separate category of saints who follow this course to hide their holiness. John lived in a hut in Ustiug, and he prayed all night. During the day, he walked about barefoot and dressed in rags, suffering the elements throughout the year. Sometimes he threw himself on a dung heap, and the citizens of the city abused and chastised him. But God granted him the gift of working miracles, healing those afflicted with various diseases. John died at a young age and was buried near the Uspensky cathedral in Ustiug. A church was later built over his relics in his name. St. John was famed as an intercessor during the invasion of enemies, and by healings of various illnesses.

SAINTS OF THE DAY: Commemoration of the First Ecumenical Council; Alexander, Patriarch of Alexandria; Theodosia of Constantinople; Theodosia of Tyre; John of Thessalonica, at Smyrna; Luke, hierarch-surgeon of Simferopol; Constantine XI, last Byzantine emperor; Olbian, Bishop of Aneus, and his disciples; New Martyr Andrew Argentes of Chios; John of Ustiug, fool-for-Christ; Cyril, Carellus, Primolus, Phinodus, Venustus, Gissinus, Alexander, Tredentius, and Jocunda, at Caesarea; "Surety of Sinners" Icon of the Mother of God in Moscow.

MAY 30

Romans 1:18-27; Matthew 5:20-26

Follow the saints, because those who follow them will become saints.

St. Clement of Alexandria

HUBERT OF MAASTRICHT. Hubert's father was the Duke of Aquitaine in seventh-century France, and Hubert was the heir apparent. He was sent to the Neustrian court, where his charm led him to the appointment of "count of the palace." He moved to the court of Austrasia at Metz, where he was made the grand master of the household. He married the daughter of a count, and they had a son named Floribert, who would later become a bishop. But his wife died in childbirth, and Hubert gave himself up entirely to hunting. Once, on Good Friday morning, he was chasing a magnificent stag. A legend says that when the animal turned, Hubert perceived a crucifix standing between its antlers, and he heard a voice saying, "Unless thou turnest to the Lord, and leadest a holy life, thou shalt quickly go down into hell." Hubert asked what he should do, and the Lord said, "Go and seek Lambert, and he will instruct you." He was also commanded to hold animals in a higher regard, for they are God's creatures with a value of their own. Hubert distributed his wealth to the poor and made his brother Odo guardian of his infant son. He then went to Maastricht and found St. Lambert, who became his spiritual guide. He studied for the priesthood, was ordained, and became one of the chief administrators of the diocese. When Lambert was assassinated, Hubert was appointed the bishop of Maastricht. He gave his episcopal pay to the poor, fasted and prayed, and taught the pagans in the Ardennes forests. He became renowned for his eloquence in the pulpit. St. Hubert is known as the Apostle of the Ardennes, and his relics became a focus for pilgrimages until the coffin disappeared during the Reformation.

SAINTS OF THE DAY: Isaac the Confessor; James of Starotorzhok; Martyr Natalius; Barlaam of Caesarea; Martyrs Romanus, Meletius, and Euplius; Macrina, grandmother of St. Basil the Great; Hubert of Liege.

MAY 31

Romans 1:28-2:9; Matthew 5:27-32

Blessed is the one who is always full of spiritual joy and has not grown slack in bearing the Lord's good yoke, for he will be crowned with glory.

St. Ephraim the Syrian

MARTYR HERMEIAS AT COMANA. Hermeias, an old Roman soldier, suffered horrible tortures during the second-century persecution of Emperor Antoninus Pius. He responded by healing his tormentors. Hermeias was a religious leader throughout his life. When governor Sebastian arrived in Cappadocia, he singled out Hermeias and publicly degraded him. He urged the saint to offer sacrifice to the pagan gods, but Hermeias bravely confessed his faith in Christ. The governor gave orders to torture him. His teeth were broken and his face skinned, and they threw him into a red-hot oven. When the oven was opened after three days, Hermeias emerged unharmed. A sorcerer gave Hermeias a strong poison, but it had no effect, and he was given an even stronger potion, and it failed to kill him. The sorcerer believed in Christ and was immediately beheaded. Hermeias was subjected to even more tortures. His eyes were dug out and his sinews torn, but Hermeias gave thanks to God. For three days, he remained suspended upside down. When the governor sent people out to verify that Hermeias was dead, they found him alive and immediately they were blinded from fright. Hermeias laid his hands on them, and they were healed. The angry governor beheaded Hermeias by his own hand. Christians secretly buried St. Hermeias, and his holy relics wrought many miracles.

SAINTS OF THE DAY: Hermeias at Comana; Marus the Magician; Hierotheus of Nikolsk, and Seraphim Nikolsky; Five Martyrs of Ascalon; Eustathius of Constantinople; Martyrs Eusebius and Charalampus; Philosophus of Alexandria; Philotheus of Tobolsk; Philosophus Ornatsky, with Nicholas and Boris; Winnow, Mancus, and Myrbad of Cornwall; First translation of the relics of St. Philip, Metropolitan of Moscow.

What I see around me would drive me insane, if I did not know that no matter what happens, God will have the last word.

St. Paisios the Athonite

JUNE 1

Romans 2:14-28; Matthew 5:33-41

Familiarity between people comes about through physical presence. Familiarity with God, by contrast, is built on meditation and self-abandonment to Him during prayer.

St. Isaac the Syrian

WISTAN OF MERCIA, THE PASSION-BEARER. A passion-bearer is one who in most cases was not killed explicitly for Christ, but rather for truth and righteousness. Someone usually murdered them because of spite or involvement in plots, or those wishing to seize power. Wistan was from ninth-century Mercia, the largest early English kingdom. From his childhood, he decided to devote his life to the service of God in prayer and seclusion. Later, as a young man, he was proclaimed king. At some point, he abdicated and temporarily appointed his mother Aelflaed as regent. But Wistan's godfather, Beorhtric, soon wished to marry Aelflaed, being seized by a thirst for power. Wistan told him that such a marriage would contradict the Canons of the Church. Beorhtric beheaded Wistan while he was standing in prayer, in the mid-ninth century. For thirty days after the tragedy people saw a column of unearthly light at the scene of the murder, and at once the faithful began to venerate the young prince. Countless miracles occurred for centuries afterward. His relics were transferred to Repton Monastery in Mercia, the burial place of the kings of Mercia. Also, a church was built on the scene of the murder. The Norman Abbot Walter often doubted the sainthood of many local saints of Britain, so he tested the relics to "ordeal by fire." When he checked St. Wistan's relics, the fire would not even touch them.

SAINTS OF THE DAY: Justin the Philosopher, with Justin, Chariton, Charita, Euelepistus, Hierax, Peon, Valerian, and Justus; Thespesius of Cappadocia; Mertius the Farmer of Myra; Dionysius of Glushitsa; Onuphrius of Kharkov; Firmus of Magus; Shio the New, David, Gabriel, and Paul of Gareji, Georgia; Justin Popovich of Chelije in Serbia; Agapitus of the Kiev Caves; Martyr Neon; Pyrrhus the Virgin; Wistan of Mercia.

SATURDAY

Leave-taking of Pentecost
Fast-free

Romans 1:7-12; Matthew 5:42-48

JUNE 2

Stay near Him and obey Him in the days of your prosperity. You will be able to rely on His word in difficult days, because prayer will keep you safe in His continual presence.

St. Isaac the Syrian

NICEPHOROS THE CONFESSOR OF CONSTANTINOPLE. Nicephoros was born in eighth-century Constantinople and was given a Christian upbringing. He received a secular education, but studied the Holy Scriptures and read spiritual books. Nicephoros followed his father as the imperial counselor in the emperor's court. He preserved the purity of the Orthodox faith and defended the veneration of icons. At the request of the emperor and patriarch, he took part in the Seventh Ecumenical Council, which condemned the Iconoclast heresy. After several years, he left the court to seek solitude, settling near the Bosphorus. He spent his life in fasting and prayer. He built a church, founded a monastery, and took monastic tonsure. After the death of Patriarch Tarasios, Nicephoros was elevated to the patriarchal throne. Several emperors, favorable towards the Church, died in short order. The adversary, Emperor Leo the Armenian, convened a heretical council and demanded Nicephoros to argue the faith with heretics. Nicephoros tried to reason with them, explaining the teaching about the veneration of holy icons. The Council excommunicated Nicephoros, and exiled him for the remaining thirteen years of his life. His relics remained there another nineteen years. When the Iconophiles, those who favored icons, finally emerged victorious, Emperor Michael and Empress Theodora transferred the remains of St. Nicephoros to the cathedral church of St. Sophia in Constantinople in the ninth century.

SAINTS OF THE DAY: Nicephoros the Confessor; John the New of Suceava; Pothinus of Lyons; Marinus of Constantinople; Constantine the Hagarene; Nicephorus of Milet; Demetrius of Philadelphia; Andrew of Nizhegorod; New Martyr Asprocastron; Erasmus of Formia in Campania, and 20,000 with him; Odo of Canterbury; "Kiev-Bratsk" Icon of the Mother of God.

All Saints Sunday
Fast-free

Hebrews 11:33-12:2
Matthew 10:32-33, 37-38, 19:27-30

JUNE 3

If you are in any sort of temptation, the Lives of the Saints will help you overcome it both now and forever.

St. Justin Popovich

MARTYR LUCILLIAN AND THOSE WHO SUFFERED WITH HIM—MARTYRS HYPATIOS, PAUL, CLAUDIUS, DIONYSIOS, AND PAULA THE VIRGIN. Lucillian was a high priest of the pagan temple in Nicomedia during the third-century reign of Roman Emperor Aurelian. When he had reached old age, he learned about Christianity and was baptized. He spread the faith among the pagans and converted many to Christianity. He was reported to the governor Sylvanus, who urged Lucillian to return to idol-worship. When he refused, he was tried, whipped, and imprisoned. In prison, he met four young men who were confessors of Christianity. They spent their time spiritually edifying and encouraging one another with psalms and prayers. Refusing to deny Jesus Christ, Lucillian and the four men were thrown into a red-hot furnace, but rain poured down, extinguishing the flames. The governor gave orders to take them to Byzantium for execution. The young men were beheaded by the sword, and Lucillian was crucified. In the tradition of defilement after death, the bodies were denied burial and were thrown into an open ditch. The holy Virgin Paula had dedicated herself to those suffering for the faith. She gave food to the Christian prisoners, washed their wounds, and buried the martyrs. After the death of Lucillian and the four lads, she was arrested and thrown into a furnace, but God kept her unharmed. Likewise, she was sent to Byzantium and was beheaded by the sword.

SAINTS OF THE DAY: Lucillian, with Hypatios, Paul, Claudius, Dionysios, and Virgin Paula, at Byzantium; Athanasius the Wonderworker; Lucian, Maxianus, Julian, Marcellinus, and Saturninus, at Beauvais; Achilles of Alexandria; Barsabus of Ishtar, and 10 companions; Hieria of Mesopotamia; Chlotilda of France; Joseph of Thessalonica; Cyprian of Moscow; Kevin of Glendalough; Pappus, monk; "Yugsk" Icon of the Mother of God.

MONDAY

Fast of the Holy Apostles Begins
Abstain from meat and dairy products.

Hebrews 7:26-8:2; John 10:1-9

JUNE 4

Truth is not a thought, not a word, not a relationship between things, not a law. Truth is a Person. It is a Being which exceeds all beings and gives life to all. If you seek truth with love and for the sake of love, she will reveal the light of His face to you in as much as you are able to bear it without being burned.

St. Nikolai of Serbia

NEW MARTYRS ARCHBISHOP ANDRONICUS OF PERM AND ARCHBISHOP BASIL OF CHERNIGOV. During the communist takeover of Russia, Andronicus publicly criticized the separation of Church and State and the Communist decree. When he instructed his archdeacon to anathematize the Communists, Andronicus was arrested, shot, and buried on the road from Perm to Motoviliha. His assistant Bishop Theophanes was also arrested and drowned in the Kama River. When the bishops of the Moscow Church Assembly learned of the executions, they sent a special commission to investigate, led by Bishop Basil of Chernigov. The Communists, however, concealed the facts from the investigators. When Bishop Basil and the other members of the commission boarded a train to return to Moscow, Red soldiers attacked, killing them all and throwing their bodies from the train. Peasants buried the bodies, and pilgrims began to flock to the graves. Upon hearing this, the Communists dug up the bodies and burned them.

SAINTS OF THE DAY: Metrophanes, first Patriarch of Constantinople; Andronicus, Archbishop of Perm; Basil, Archbishop of Chernigov; Mary and Martha, sisters of St. Lazarus; Concordios of Spoleto; Alonius of Scete in Egypt; Frontasius, Severinus, Severian, and Silanus of Gaul; Astius of Dyrrachium; Zosimas of Cilicia, Bishop of New Babylon; Sophia of Thrace; Optatus, Bishop of Milevum; Methodius of Peshnosha; Eleazar and Nazarius of Olonets; Titus, Bishop of Byzantium; John of Monagria; Ioannicus of Montenegro; Petroc of Cornwall; Martyrs of Niculitsel: Zoticus, Attalus, Camisius, and Philip.

 Abstain from meat and dairy products.

JUNE 5

Romans 4:4-12; Matthew 7:15-21

Patience is a sweet word. Patience is a sweet breath. Patience is an invincible weapon. Patience is a priceless adornment of man. Patience is a blessing of God. When our Lord Jesus Christ was in His earthly life and taught the crowds, if He did not have patience within Himself what would have happened? He came to earth in order to save the lost sheep and to uplift us through His patience, and then to go up to Golgotha for us who are unworthy and careless. Patience reigns quietly and fruitfully in the life of the man who does not harm or endanger anyone, who is content with little and is obedient to the commandments of the Heavenly Father.

St. Raphael of Lesvos

VENERABLE THEODORE THE WONDERWORKER, HERMIT OF THE JORDAN. Theodore was a sixth-century monk, living in the Jordanian wilderness. Because of his long ascetic labors, God granted him the gift of working miracles. Once while traveling by ship to Constantinople, the vessel went astray, and everyone aboard was in danger of dying from thirst. Theodore raised his arms towards heaven and prayed to God to make fresh the water drawn from the sea. When they began to thank Theodore for this miracle, he directed them to thank God who has compassion, rather than his unworthy prayer. St. Theodore died peacefully.

SAINTS OF THE DAY: Dorotheos, Bishop of Tyre; Dorotheos of Palestine; Marcian, Nicander, Hyperechius, Apollonius, Leonides, Arius, Gorgias, Selenias, Irene and Pambo of Egypt; Christopher of Rome; Conon of Rome; Constantine, Metropolitan of Kiev; Illidius of Gaul; Dorotheus, abbot at Chiliokama; Agapius and Nicodemus of Vatopedi; Dorotheus, abbot at Chiliokama; Theodore of the Jordan; Theodore Yaroslavich, brother of St. Alexander Nevsky; Peter of Korisha, Serbia; Boniface, Archbishop of Mainz; Mark of Smyrna; Uncovering of the relics of Sts. Jonah and Bassian of Solovki; "Igor" Icon of the Mother of God.

JUNE 6

Romans 4:13-25; Matthew 7:21-23

What is more beautiful than prayer! Whoever prays is enlightened and comes to know the will of God. And how does he know it? When he prays well, of course. And when does he pray well? When he sends his prayers to God with all the right ingredients. And what are the ingredients that make the prayer savory? Humility, tears, self-reproach, simplicity, and especially obedience with love. Prayer sheds light, and this light shows the right path which God wills.

Elder Ephraim of Arizona

JARLATH OF CLUAINFOIS. Jarlath was educated by the Archbishop Benignus of Armagh. After some time, Jarlath went to live in seclusion near Tuam, at a placed called Cluainfois. He founded a monastery, and it is now a chapel within the parish of Tuam. He also opened a famous school, to which numbers flocked for education in piety and learning, among whom were St. Brendan, abbot of Clonfert and St. Coman, first bishop of Cloyne. Jarlath was called from there to be consecrated the first bishop of Tuam. He died of old age in the mid sixth century. His relics were placed in a shrine in a church in Tuam.

SAINTS OF THE DAY: Bessarion the Great of Egypt; Five Virgin-martyrs of Caesarea in Palestine: Martha, Mary, Cyria, Valeria, and Marcia; Virgin-martyrs Archelais, Thecla, and Susanna, at Salerno; Attalus the Wonderworker; Hilarion the New; Justus, Patriarch of Alexandria; Anoub of Egypt, the Worker of Signs; Martyr Gelasius; Amandus, Amantius, Alexander, Lucius, Alexander, Alexandria, Donatus, and Peregrius in Scythia Minor; Claudius of Besancon, Gaul; Raphael of Optina Monastery; Jonah of Klimetsk; Paisius of Uglich; Jonah, Bishop of Perm; Jarlath of Cluainfois (Ireland); "Pimen" Icon of the Mother of God.

 Abstain from meat and dairy products.

JUNE 7

Romans 5:10-16; Matthew 8:23-27

Don't exchange your love toward your neighbor for some type of object, because in having love toward your neighbor, you acquire within yourself Him, Who is most precious in the whole world. Forsake the petty so as to acquire the great; spurn the excessive and everything meaningless so as to acquire the valuable.

St. Isaac the Syrian

PRINCESS ARTEMIA OF ROME. Artemia was the demon-possessed daughter of the Christian-persecuting emperor Diocletian. When Diocletian learned that St. Cyriacus, who was imprisoned at the time, could cast out demons, he summoned him. Cyriacus healed Artemia with his prayers, and Diocletian freed him. Shortly after that, he was sent to the Persian emperor to heal his daughter. When Cyriacus returned to Rome, Diocletian was no longer emperor, and his son-in-law Galerius held the throne. Cyriacus was arrested because Artemia converted to Christianity. Galerius had Cyriacus stripped, placed in chains, and dragged behind his chariot, while the crowds ridiculed the saint. St. Marcellus, bishop of Rome, openly denounced Galerius for his cruel treatment of innocent Christians, and he was also beaten. In the end, Cyriacus and three others were tortured to death. Galerius also murdered Artemia and twenty-one others.

SAINTS OF THE DAY: Marcellus, Bishop of Rome, and those with him: Sisinius and Cyriacus, deacons, Aproniun, Saturninus, Smaragdus, Largus, Pappias, Maurus, Crescentian, Priscilla, Lucina, and Princess Artemia; Cyria, Valeria, and Marcia, of Caesarea; Theodotus of Ancyra; Lycarion of Hermopolis; Daniel of Scetis in Egypt; Potamiane of Alexandria; Aesia and Susanna of Taormina; Panagis of Cephalonia; Anthony of Kozha Lake; Zenais of Caesarea; Stephen and Anthimus, of the Fervent Ones; Martyrs Tarasius and John; Colman, Bishop of Dromore, Ireland; Andronicus, Archbishop of Perm; Synaxis of All Saints of Ivanovo.

FRIDAY

JUNE 8

Abstain from meat and dairy products, and fish.

Ephesians 2:4-10; Matthew 10:16-22

If a person remembers the words of Scripture: By your words you shall be justified, and by your words you shall be condemned (Mt. 12:37), then he will choose to remain silent.

St. Sarah of Egypt

VENERABLE NAUCRATIOS. Naucratios was the brother of St. Basil the Great, St. Gregory of Nyssa, St. Peter of Sebaste, and St. Macrina the Younger. Their parents, St. Basil the Elder and St. Emelia, suffered persecution under the reign of Maximinus. Naucratios had achieved fame for his public speaking and industry, but he despised worldly wealth and was influenced by his sister Macrina to have a love for God and a desire to live the life of an ascetic, so he went into the wilderness to live. One of their household, Chrysaphios, also had a love for the monastic life and he journeyed with Naucratios. They found a thickly wooded spot at the foot of a mountain, next to the Iris River, and lived there for five years. Naucratios cared for some old men who lived in poverty nearby. Since he was an accomplished fisherman, he would also provide food for them. Naucratios would also obey his mother whenever she asked him to do something. These two ascetic disciplines helped him to progress spiritually. Tragically, Naucratios and Chrysaphios drowned while on a fishing expedition for the old men. When his mother Emelia heard the news, she became overwhelmed, breathless, and speechless. It was then that Macrina brought her mother up from the depths of her sorrow, asking her to be brave and to maintain her composure and solemnity.

SAINTS OF THE DAY: Ephraim, Patriarch of Antioch; Nicander and Marcian at Dorostolum; Atre of Nitria; Naucratios of the Studion; Kalliope, at Rome; Theophanes at Constantinople; Medardus of Noyon; Theodore of Rostov; Zosimas of Phoenicia; Theophilus of Luga; Melania the Elder; Barlaam and Herman of Russia; Theodore of Kvelta; Paul the Confessor of Kaiuma; Martyr Mark; Uncovering of the relics of Sts. Basil and Constantine of Yaroslavl.

Abstain from meat and dairy products.

JUNE 9

Romans 3:19-24; Matthew 7:1-8

The worst thing is not forgiving and not loving, and to have enmity in your heart.

+*Elder Sampson the Russian*

VENERABLE CYRIL OF BELOZERSK. Cyril was born to pious Christian parents in Moscow. Bored by secular life, Cyril became a monk at the Simonov monastery. He was strict with himself, asking permission to eat only every second or third day. But his elder told him to eat with the brethren, only not to the extent of being full. He worked in the kitchen for nine years, carrying water, chopping wood, and distributing bread. He achieved such tender emotion that he could not eat bread without tears. To hide his spirituality, he began to act as a fool-for-Christ, but he was punished for this. Against his will, he was made a priest and later abbot of the monastery. Bothered by many seeking spiritual advice, Cyril was enlightened by the Mother of God to go to Belozersk. After he had spent almost a year in solitude, monks from the Simonov monastery asked to live with him. He set a rule for them that mirrored his own life. No one spoke in church or at meals, none could receive or write letters without a blessing, and no one possessed anything other than icons and Christian books. Cyril was granted the gift to work miracles. He tamed a storm on a lake to save fishermen. He caused an empty vessel to be filled with wine for the Divine Liturgy. He continuously distributed bread to the needy from a near-empty storeroom. Cyril said that none of the brethren would die until after his death. Within a year of Cyril's death, thirty of the fifty-three brethren died. Cyril appeared to the remaining brothers with spiritual advice and guidance. St. Cyril loved books on spiritual enlightenment. There were more than two thousand books at the monastery for their edification.

SAINTS OF THE DAY: Cyril of Alexandria; Thecla, Mariamne, Martha, Mary, and Enmatha in Persia; Alexander of Prousa; 3 Virgin-martyrs of Chios; Righteous Cyrus; Cyril of Belozersk; Alexander of Kushta; Cyril of Vologda.

Second Sunday of Matthew
Abstain from meat and dairy products.
Romans 2:10-16; Matthew 4:18-23

JUNE 10

The best guide for you will be the reading of the Lives of the Saints.
St. Barsanuphius of Optina

OLGA OF KWETHLUK. Olga was the wife of Archpriest Nikolai from the village of Kwethlum in Alaska. She raised eight children, giving birth to several without a midwife; several others died. Olga not only kept busy raising their children and doing many things for other people, but she also sewed her husband's vestments and made parkas, boots, and mittens for her children. She was also always making socks and fur outerwear for others. She not only made things for friends and neighbors but also for parishes hundreds of miles away, including gloves and socks for all the clergy. She knew the hymns of many feasts by heart. She eventually died from cancer in 1979, but the normal snow and ice in November thawed for one day to allow people to travel to her funeral and burial. A flock of birds that should have long since gone south circled overhead and accompanied her coffin to the grave. Afterward, it was the encounters with Olga's caring presence that is remarkable. For example, one woman from Arizona dreamed of Olga who assured her that her mother would be joining her in a bright and cheerful place after her life. The woman didn't even know that her mother who lived in Alaska was sick. But the next day she received news that her mother was in a hospital, and she rushed to Alaska. When the mother heard Olga's words, she died in peace. Another Orthodox woman who suffered for many years from the consequences of severe sexual abuse experienced as a child was visited by Olga in a vision, who helped her rid the burden she had carried with her all those years.

SAINTS OF THE DAY: Theophanes and Pansemne of Antioch; Timothy of Prousa; Asterius of Petra; Alexander and Antonina at Constantinople; Canides of Cappadocia; Metrophanes and the Chinese Martyrs of the Boxer Uprising; Basil of Ryazan; Alexis of Bithynia; Silouan of the Far Caves; John Maximovitch of Tobolsk; 2nd Sunday after Pentecost: Olga of Kwethluk ; Synaxis of the Saints of North America.

 Abstain from meat and dairy products.

JUNE 11

1 Corinthians 4:9-16; Luke 10:16-21

During prayer there sometimes occur moments of deadly darkness and spiritual anguish arising from unbelief of the heart (for unbelief is darkness). Do not let your heart fail you at such moments, but remember that if the Divine light has been cut off from you, it always shines in all its splendor and greatness in God Himself, in God's Church, in heaven and on earth, and in the material world in which "His eternal power also and divinity" are visible.

St. John of Kronstadt

HOLY APOSTLE BARNABAS. For hundreds of years, the unknown and unmarked grave of the Apostle Barnabas on Cyprus was known only as the healing place. Many who came to this area were healed without knowing why. Barnabas was one of the Seventy Apostles. Born into wealth, he received his initial religious training under Gamaliel, even before the Apostle Paul. Barnabas was present at the first Pentecost, and he gave the money from the sale of his considerable lands to the apostles, as was the custom with the early Christians. He preached with Apostle Paul and his cousin Apostle Mark throughout Syria, Asia Minor, Cyprus, Greece, Egypt, Jerusalem, and Rome. He was burned to death by the Jews on Cyprus, and was buried by his cousin Mark holding the Holy Gospel. Five centuries after his death, he appeared to the archbishop of Cyprus on three successive nights to make known the place of his relics and to ensure that the Church of Cyprus remains independent.

SAINTS OF THE DAY: Holy Apostles Bartholomew and Barnabas; Niphon, Patriarch of Constantinople (Romania); Barnabas, abbot of Vetluga; Barnabas of Basa in Cyprus; Martyr Theopemptus and 4 others; Arcadius, monk of Vyazma; Uncovering of the relics of St. Ephraim of New Torzhok; Commemoration of the appearance of Archangel Gabriel to a monk on Mt. Athos and the revelation of the hymn "It is Truly Meet" (Axion Esti); "It is Truly Meet" Icon of the Mother of God.

 Abstain from meat and dairy products.

JUNE 12

Romans 7:14-8:2; Matthew 10:9-15

More than a well-lighted window, a man must seek after the company of holy men; so that he can see his heart, as if reading a clearly written book, and thus perceive the idleness in his way of life by contrast with their lives. For many are the traits of virtuous men, which bear witness to the purity of their souls, such as: the subtle look that the Godly way of life imprints on a face; the style of dress; the simplicity of character; humility in conversation; the absence of an inquisitive tone in their words; the prudence of their expressions; the piety of their manner. All of these things greatly benefit those who attend to them, and engrave on their souls the immutable archetypes of virtue.

St. Palladios the Anchorite

ANTONINA OF NICAEA. Antonina lived in early fourth-century Asia Minor, in the city of Nicaea during the persecutions of joint Emperors Diocletian and Maximian. When she confessed her Christian faith, she was arrested and taken before the Magistrate Priscillianos. He had Antonina delivered to the executioners who beat her cruelly and then imprisoned her. When she was brought before the magistrate again, he had her suspended on a wooden pole over a fire. Her hands were pierced with red-hot skewers, and a myrrh-like fragrance poured from them. Later her ankles were also pierced with these skewers. She endured the hardship of prison again, this time for two years. Finally, St. Antonina was drowned at sea.

SAINTS OF THE DAY: Onuphrius the Great; Onuphrius of Malsk; Onuphrius and Auxentius of Vologda; Antonina of Nicaea; Amphianos in Cilicia; Olympius in Thrace; Julian of Dagouta Church in Constantinople; John the Soldier; Peter of Mt. Athos; Triphyllius of Nicosia; John Tornike of Mt. Athos; Stephen of Komel; Timothy of Egypt; Arsenius of Konevits; Bassian and Jonah of Solovki; Cunera of Rhenen; Synaxis of All Saints of St. Onuphrius Monastery at Jablechna (Poland); Miracleworking icons of the Theotokos and St. Onuphrius at St. Onuphrius Monastery.

JUNE 13

Romans 8:2-13; Matthew 10:16-22

And what is the specious plea of the many [for loving wealth]? I have children, one says, and I am afraid lest I myself be reduced to the extremity of hunger and want, lest I should stand in need of others. I am ashamed to beg. For that reason therefore do you cause others to beg? I cannot, you say, endure hunger. For that reason do you expose others to hunger? Do you know what a dreadful thing it is to beg, how dreadful to be perishing by hunger? Spare also your brethren! Are you ashamed, tell me, to be hungry, and are you not ashamed to rob? Are you afraid to perish by hunger, and not afraid to destroy others? And yet to be hungry is neither a disgrace nor a crime; but to cast others into such a state brings not only disgrace, but extreme punishment.

St. John Chrysostom

ANTIPATER, BISHOP OF BOSTRA IN ARABIA. Antipater was a fifth-century bishop of Bostra in Arabia. He flourished during the time of the Fourth Ecumenical Synod in 451. He was held in high esteem by his contemporaries, both civil and ecclesiastical. He was a pronounced opponent of the heresy of Origenism and its author Origen of Alexandria. Origen authored and professed that all created beings including Satan would be saved. Out of zeal for purity, he also castrated himself. Antipater's excellent composition against Origen was ordered to be read in the churches of the East. He also wrote against the Apollinarists, who said that Christ could not be perfect God and perfect man. They said that this was not unlike the monsters of mythology.

SAINTS OF THE DAY: Aquilina of Byblos in Lebanon; Eulogius, Patriarch of Antioch; Anna and her son John of Constantinople; Antonina of Nicaea; Diodorus of Emesus; Antipater, Bishop of Bostra in Arabia; Sabbas and Andronicus, abbots of Moscow; Anthimus the Georgian, Metropolitan of Wallachia; Alexandra, foundress of Diveyevo Convent; Synaxis of New Martyrs and Confessors of Zaporozhie (Ukraine).

 Abstain from meat and dairy products.

JUNE 14

Romans 8:22-27; Luke 4:22-30

Let yourself die in striving rather than living in laziness. For those who die trying to keep the commandments are martyrs just as much as those who died for Christ's faith.

St. Isaac the Syrian

METHODIUS, PATRIARCH OF CONSTANTINOPLE. Methodius was tormented and humiliated because of his support of the icons, yet he endured and prevailed. Born in ninth-century Sicily, he was well educated before he became a monk. In a short time, he became the abbot of the monastery in Chenolakkos near Byzantium, then was appointed archbishop of Cyzicus by Patriarch Nicephorus. Methodius was known for his effort to spiritually elevate his people, as well as his staunch defense of the icons. For the latter, the Emperor Theophilos had him tortured and exiled to a deep cave where the light of day did not penetrate. He languished there for seven years until the death of the Emperor. Empress Theodora released the imprisoned confessors and banished the heretic Annios who occupied the patriarchal throne. She chose Methodios to replace him, and he convened a Local Council that restored icon veneration. But the heretics still pursued him. They slandered him with the accusation of having transgressed chastity. His defense before the court put the heretics to shame. Methodius wisely guided the Church and his flock. He renovated churches, gathered the relics of saints scattered by the heretics, and transferred the relics of Patriarch Nicephoros from the place of his imprisonment back to Constantinople. St. Methodius died peacefully.

SAINTS OF THE DAY: Elisha the Prophet; Methodius, Patriarch of Constantinople; Niphon of Kapsokalyvia, Mt. Athos; Julitta of Tabennisi in Egypt; John, Metropolitan of Euchaita; Cyril, Bishop of Gortyna in Crete; Methodius, abbot of Peshnosha; Sabbas, fool-for-Christ of Vatopedi, Mt. Athos; Elisha of Solovki; Joseph, Bishop of Thessalonica; Mstislav-George, Prince of Novgorod.

JUNE 15

Romans 9:6-19; Matthew 10:32-26, 11:1

Another person's evil does not add to our own sins unless we welcome it by means of our own evil thoughts.

St. Mark the Ascetic

VENERABLE DOULAS THE PASSION-BEARER OF EGYPT. Doulas was a monk in an Egyptian monastery. For twenty years, he humbly endured abuse and contempt from some of the other monks. Finally, he reached such a degree of passivity, that he pitied and prayed for those who continually insulted him. Toward the end of his life, a certain monk stole some of the precious church vessels, and Doulas was accused of the theft. In fact, some monks said they had witnessed the deed. When the elders refused to believe him, Doulas did not argue but finally just asked for forgiveness. He was stripped of his monastic garb, placed in chains, and turned over to the civil authorities. When asked where the church vessels were hidden, he answered, "Forgive me, I have sinned." He was then turned over for torture and sentenced to have his hands cut off. The thief had remorse and confessed to the abbot to stop the execution. Doulas was permitted to return to the monastery, and he bore no malice as the other monks asked his forgiveness. He also asked the Lord to pardon those who had accused him. Doulas died three days after his return while kneeling in prayer. When all the monks gathered for his funeral in the cathedral, the body of St. Doulas had disappeared, only his clothes and shoes remained.

SAINTS OF THE DAY: Prophet Amos; Apostles Stephanas, Achaicus, and Fortunatus, of the Seventy; Augustine, Bishop of Hippo, and his mother Monica; Dulas of Cilicia; Cedronus, Patriarch of Alexandria; Ephraim II, Patriarch of Serbia; Jonah of Moscow; Modestus, Vitus, and Crescentia at Lucania; Doulas the Passion-bearer; Hesychius of Dorostolum; Lazar of Serbia; Gregory and Cassian of Avnezh; Orsiesius of Tabennisi; Michael of Kiev; Symeon of Novgorod; Spyridon of Serbia; Abraham of Auvergne; Sergius and Barbara of Oyatsk; Jerome of Stridonium.

SATURDAY **Abstain from meat and dairy products.**

JUNE 16

Romans 3:28-4:3; Matthew 7:24-8:4

Look for and find the poor and gather them and help them. This is what God wants, and not to go to church as if to pray.

St. Sophia of Kleisoura

NEW MARTYR HERMOGENES, BISHOP OF TOBOLSK. Educated at the St. Petersburg Theological Academy, Hermogenes was tonsured and ordained to the priesthood in nineteenth-century Russia. He founded church schools and assisted in the spread of missionary work. He was consecrated Bishop of Saratov and built many churches, sketes, and chapels in his diocese. Monks from Mt. Athos and other places came to his monasteries. Hermogenes took an active part in the struggle against the growing revolutionary fervor. He told his flock, "Always remember also that it is not joys and satisfactions that lead to the blessed life, but sorrows." Bishop Hermogenes had the gift of clairvoyance. When the atheists continued closing churches, Hermogenes said, "the Orthodox Church cannot teach and save believers without churches, and that the faith of the Russian people is closely bound up with the veneration of the holy things of the Church." Hermogenes began receiving threats against him, but he foreknew that they would kill him. Still, he did not sorrow for himself, but for the city. He was imprisoned, then drowned with an eighty-pound weight tied to his bound hands. His relics washed ashore a few weeks later and were buried by the peasants of the village of Usolsk at the place where his remains were found. Later the bishop was disinterred and clothed in his hierarchical vestments. His coffin was carried in a procession accompanied by many thousands of people.

SAINTS OF THE DAY: Tychon the Wonderworker, Bishop of Amathus; Tigrius and Eutropius of Constantinople; Mark the Just of Apollonias; Five Martyrs of Nicomedia; Forty Martyrs of Rome; Kaikhosro the Georgian; Tikhon of Krestogorsk; Hermogenes of Tobolsk, and Euphremius, Michael, Peter, and Constantine; Tikhon of Lukh; Tikhon of Kaluga and Medin; Moses of Optina; Translation of the relics of St. Theophan the Recluse.

SUNDAY

Third Sunday of Matthew
Abstain from meat and dairy products.
Romans 5:1-10; Matthew 6:22-33

JUNE 17

The soul of Adam fell sick when he was exiled from Paradise, and many were the tears he shed in his distress. Likewise every soul that has known the Lord yearns for Him and cries, "Where art thou, O Lord? Where art Thou, my Light? What hinders Him from dwelling in me?" This hinders Him: Christ-like humility and love for my enemies are not in me.

St. Silouan of Mt. Athos

MARTYR NECTAN OF HARTLAND. Nectan was the son of St. Brychan, the oldest of twenty-four children in sixth-century Wales. Nectan developed a desire to become a monk and imitate the life of St. Anthony the Great. He and several others left Wales by boat, determined to live wherever the boat landed. They arrived at Devonshire at Hartland and lived there several years in a thick forest. Nectan's family would visit him once each year. Later Nectan moved to a hidden valley that had a spring of water. While there, he returned a lost pig to its owner, and in gratitude, the owner gave him two cows. When two thieves took the cows, Nectan found them and tried to teach them about Jesus Christ. In anger, one of them severed the saint's head. Miraculously, Nectan picked up his head and carried it a half mile to the stream near his cell. The one thief lost his mind, and the other buried Nectan. Afterward, miracles were wrought at St. Nectan's grave.

SAINTS OF THE DAY: Joseph and Pior, disciples of St. Anthony the Great; Manuel, Sabel, and Ismael of Persia; Philoneides, Bishop of Kurion in Cyprus; Aetius the Eunuch, enlightener of Ethiopia; Isaurus, Basil, Innocent, Felix, Hermeios, and Peregrinus of Athens; Ananias the Iconographer of Novgorod; Ismael of Russia; Shalva of Akhaltsikhe, Georgia; Nectan of Hartland; Botolph of Boston (England) and Adolph the Confessor; Nicander of Yaroslavl; Hypatius of Rufinianos; Uncovering of the relics of the Alfanov Brothers of Novgorod: Nicetas, Cyril, Nicephorus, Clement, and Isaac.

 Abstain from meat and dairy products.

June 18

Romans 9:18-33; Matthew 11:2-15

The devil, who once was the carrier of the light of justice, of love and holiness, has become at once—through his rebellion against God—the absolute tool of darkness, hatred, evil, lie and everything that contributes to the disaster of death and corruption. He was, and will always be darkness, lie and perdition, with a clear purpose—to rebel against everything that comes from God and against God's providence and man in particular. He became, and will always be the heir of death and hell, having the main goal to deceit and attract on his side as many people as possible.

+Elder Joseph of Vatopedi

"BOGOLIUBSK-ZIMAROVSK" ICON OF THE MOTHER OF GOD. According to ancient tradition, this icon stood on the gates of the city of Pronsk, but during a thirteenth-century invasion by the Tatars, it was taken down and broken into pieces. However, of itself, it miraculously came back together, though one-half of it remained higher than the other. Later in the eighteenth century, a landowner named Lopukhin, who lived in Moscow, had possession of the icon. Because of its antiquity, he kept it in a storeroom. In 1779, there was a fierce plague, and one of the afflicted in Moscow had a dream to have a service held before the icon. They located the icon, and after the service, he was healed. Other similar healings were also wrought by the icon. Before he died, Lopukhin willed that the icon be sent to its own native region, to the village of Zimarovo in Ryazan. In 1840, cholera raged in this city. The inhabitants went to the icon and brought it to the city, and the threat of the danger of disease stopped.

SAINTS OF THE DAY: Marina the Virgin of Bithynia; Leontius, Hypatius, and Theodulus at Tripoli; Aetherus of Nicomedia; Leontius the Myrrh-flowing; Leontius of the Kiev Caves; Nicanor of Spas-Ruzsky; Leontius of Phoenicia; Erasmus, monk; Alena of Belgium; "Bogoliubsk-Zimarovsk" and "Piukhtitsa" Icons of the Mother of God.

 Abstain from meat and dairy products.

JUNE 19

Jude 1:1-25; John 14:21-24

Pious exercises nourish the soul with divine thoughts.

St. Basil the Great

VENERABLE ROMUALD OF CAMALDOLI. Romuald was born to an aristocratic family in Ravenna, Italy. As a youth, he indulged in the pleasures and sins common to a tenth-century nobleman. His father killed a relative in a duel over property, and this devastated Romuald. He went to the Basilica of St. Apollinare to do forty days of penance, and finally decided to become a monk there. This place was not strict enough for Romuald, and this aroused so much enmity against him that he transferred to Venice, where he lived a life of extraordinary severity under the direction of a hermit named Marinus. Romuald and Marinus built a hermitage, and Romuald lived there about ten years. After that, he spent the next thirty years going about Italy founding and reforming monasteries. Then a certain man who had seen a vision of monks dressed in white ascending into heaven gave Romuald a piece of land, and it was here that he founded the famous Camaldolese order. In his youth, Romuald became acquainted with three major schools of western monastic tradition, and he integrated these traditions to establish his own monastic order. His rule included: Empty yourself completely and sit waiting. Sit in your cell as in Paradise. Put the whole world behind you and forget it. Watch your thoughts like a good fisherman watching for fish. The path you must follow is in the Psalms—never leave it. Take every opportunity you can to sing the Psalms in your heart and to understand them with your mind. If your mind wanders as you read, do not give up; hurry back and apply your mind to the words once more.

SAINTS OF THE DAY: Holy Apostle Jude; Paisios the Great of Egypt; Paisius the Bulgarian; Mary, mother of Apostle James; Zosimas the Soldier; Macarius of Petra; John the Solitary; Romuald of Ravenna; Job of Moscow; Zeno of Egypt; Barlaam of Shenkursk; Parthenius of Russia; Asyncretus, at the Church of Holy Peace by the Sea.

JUNE 20

Romans 11:2-12; Matthew 11:20-26

It is a spiritual gift from God for a man to perceive his sins.

St. Isaac the Syrian

NICHOLAS CABASILAS OF THESSALONICA. Nicholas was born into a prestigious family. He would have seen the fall of his native Thessalonica to the Turks in the late fourteenth century. Nicholas' uncle Nilus succeeded St. Gregory Palamas as Archbishop of Thessalonica. Later Nicholas traveled to Mt. Athos with St. Gregory. Nicholas, who was still a lay person, was one of three candidates to become the new patriarch of Constantinople, which at the age of thirty shows his high intellectual and spiritual qualities. He entered the Manganon Monastery near Constantinople and was most likely ordained there. He was later elected Archbishop of Thessalonica. He is called the last of the greatest Byzantine theologians. Humanism was a concept that emerged during this time, where the human person was perceived as the center of the universe, possessing within themselves all qualities of power and virtue. Nicholas argued that a human person's true life lies in Jesus Christ, the center of the universe and the measure of all things. Nicholas was a gifted writer who influenced his contemporaries and later generations. His major theological work, *A Commentary on the Divine Liturgy*, explains the symbolism of the Divine Liturgy by St. John Chrysostom in 52 chapters. Nicholas said that the Holy Eucharist is not a mere symbol but a reality. It is the body and blood of Christ, and it transfigures humanity and all creation. St. Nicholas said that the ultimate purpose of history is the union of human beings with God.

SAINTS OF THE DAY: Callistus I, Patriarch of Constantinople; Studius, of the Studion Monastery; Methodius of Patara; Lucius the Confessor, of Brindisi; Paul, Cyriacus, Paula, Felicilana, Thomas, Felix, Martyrius, Vitaly, Crispinus, and Emilius in Tomi; Nicholas Cabasilas of Thessalonica; Nahum of Ochrid; Gleb of Vladimir; Minas of Polotsk; Finding of the relics of Raphael of Lesbos; Translation of the relics of Sts. Inna, Pinna, and Rimma; Translation of the relics of St. Gurias of Kazan.

 Abstain from meat and dairy products.

JUNE 21

Romans 11:13-24; Matthew 11:27-30

Even though we all hobble along with a limp and are filled with wounds and sins, we like to speak about others. When we visit a hospital, we will observe that all the patients have some type of illness. However, we will not see anyone criticizing another sick person. Have you ever noticed this? No one says to another patient: *"Why are you lying in bed?"* Whereas, we are all sick spiritually; and yet, we criticize one another. We have a problem with our eye, and we like to occupy ourselves with someone who has lung disease. Unfortunately, we wretched people fail to realize this.

Elder Ephraim of Arizona

MARTYR APHRODISIOS IN CILICIA. Aphrodisios was from a Christian family in Cilicia, Asia Minor. He was arrested and taken before the pagan ruler Dionysios, where he confessed his Christian faith. He withstood many tortures. Red-hot irons were placed on his back, and he was put into a vat of boiling, molten lead. Seeing that these torments did not affect him, they pulled him out and suspended him upside down. Since he remained unharmed by divine grace, the idol-worshippers threw Aphrodisios into an arena with a hungry lioness, but she did not touch him. God then caused the lioness to speak with a human voice, condemning the cruelty and harshness of the pagans. This miracle caused many spectators to jump to their feet and confess faith in Jesus Christ. Seeing this, Dionysios had them all quickly beheaded. Finally, Dionysios ordered fifty-five soldiers to split a massive boulder using wedges, shims, and chisels. When a narrow crevice in the rock had been formed, they forced St. Aphrodisios into the opening, where he surrendered his soul.

SAINTS OF THE DAY: Terence, Apostle of the Seventy; Julian of Tarsus; Theodore of Starodub; Julian of Egypt, with Anthony, Anastasius, Celsius, Basilissa, Marcianilla, 20 prison guards, and 7 brothers; Aphrodisios in Cilicia; Julius and Julian of Novara; Archil II and Laursab II, kings of Georgia; Nicetas of Nisyros; Anastasia (Anna) of Serbia.

JUNE 22

Romans 11:25-36; Matthew 12:1-8

Cease rebuking a man who has stopped sinning and who has repented. If you say that you are rebuking him in God's name, first reveal the evils in yourself.

St. Mark the Ascetic

ALBAN, PROTOMARTYR OF BRITAIN. Alban was a third-century Roman citizen, living a few miles north of London. He was not a Christian. During a time of Christian persecution, the magistrate ordered the arrest of all Christian clergy. A priest named Amphibalus sought shelter at Alban's home, so soldiers would not kill him. Alban was impressed that the priest kept constant vigil and prayer. He began questioning the priest about his beliefs, and as time passed Alban believed in Christ and asked to receive Baptism. After some time, the priest left Alban's house. But before he left, Alban exchanged clothes with the priest, allowing him to escape. When soldiers heard that the priest was at Alban's house, they went and found Alban dressed as a priest. He was arrested and taken before the magistrate, who demanded to know the priest's whereabouts. Alban was threatened with death if he did not return to idol-worship, but he confessed that he was now a Christian. He was tortured, beaten, and led to the place of execution on the other side of the river Ver. As they approached the bridge, it was crowded with people. Alban prayed, making the sign of the cross, and the river parted so they could pass. When the executioner saw this, he refused to behead Alban. However, another was found, and he beheaded them both. A monastery was founded near the place of St. Alban's execution. Miracles occurred at the saint's tomb.

SAINTS OF THE DAY: Paulinus, Bishop of Nola; Eusebius, Bishop of Samosata; Zenas and Zeno of Philadelphia in Arabia; Galacteon, Juliana, and Saturninus of Constantinople; Basil of Patalaria Monastery; Athanasius, Bishop of Chytri on Cyprus; Alban, Protomartyr of Britain; Gregory, Metropolitan of Wallachia; The 1,480 Martyrs of Samaria in Palestine; Aaron of Britain.

 Abstain from meat and dairy products.

JUNE 23

Romans 6:11-17; Matthew 8:14-23

I shall repeat again: Maintain the conviction that our disorderliness is not natural to us, and do not listen to those who say, 'It is no use talking about it, because that is just how we are made, and you cannot do anything about it.' That is not how we are made, and if we undertake to cure ourselves, then we will be able to do something about it.

St. Theophan the Recluse

NEW HIEROMARTYR MAXIMUS, BISHOP OF SERPUKHOV AND FIRST BISHOP OF THE CATACOMB CHURCH. During the time of the Bolshevik Revolution in Russia, Maximus was an exceptionally talented physician and psychiatrist. Even as a layman, Maximus became the intimate friend of Patriarch Tikhon. Tikhon blessed Maximus to secretly accept monasticism, and then if in the future the church authority betrayed Christ and conceded to Soviet power, he was to become a bishop. This came to pass, and Maximus became the first bishop of the Catacomb Church. Maximus was arrested in 1929 for his vigorous and open opposition to the Soviet Church. He was sent to the Solovki prison camp, where he continued as a physician of souls and bodies until he was shot in 1931 for failing to recognize the Soviet metropolitan Sergius.

SAINTS OF THE DAY: Eustochius, Gaius, Probus, Lollius, and Urban of Ancyra; Agrippina of Rome; Joseph, Anthony, and Ioannicius of Vologda; Dionysius of Polotsk; Bishop Leonty, Bishop Maximus, and Archbishop Mitrophan of Russia; Artemius of Verkola; Aristocles, Demetrianos, and Athanasios of Cyprus; Nicetas of Thebes, with Theodore, Gregory, and Daniel; Etheldreda of Ely; Translation of the relics of St. Michael, fool-for-Christ of Klops Monastery; Translation of the relics of St. Herman of Kazan; Synaxis of All Saints of Vladimir; Synaxis of the New Martyrs of Crete; The Meeting of the "Vladimir" Icon in memory of saving Moscow from the Invasion of Khan Achmed; Pskov "Umileniye" and "Zaonikiev" Icons of the Mother of God.

SUNDAY

Nativity of St. John the Baptist
Abstain from meat and dairy products.

Romans 13:11-14:4; Luke 1:1-25, 57-68, 76-80

JUNE 24

Understand me. It is so simple. People who do not know God, or who go against Him, are to be pitied; the heart sorrows for them and the eye weeps. Both paradise and torment are clearly visible to us: We know this through the Holy Spirit. And did not the Lord Himself say, "The kingdom of God is within you?" Thus eternal life has its beginning here in this life; and it is here that we sow the seeds of eternal torment. Where there is pride there cannot be grace, and if we lose grace we also lose both love of God and assurance in prayer. The soul is then tormented by evil thoughts and does not understand that she must humble herself and love her enemies, for there is no other way to please God.

St. Silouan of Mt. Athos

NEW MARTYR PANAGIOTES OF CAESAREA IN CAPPADOCIA. Little is known about Panagiotes. He was of Jewish descent in eighteenth-century Caesarea. The Muslims attempted to bring him over to their religion, but he refused because he was an Orthodox Christian. They tortured him, sentencing him to death in the city of Constantinople on June 24, 1765.

SAINTS OF THE DAY: Nativity of St. John the Baptist; Athanasios of Paros; John the New of Romania; Michael, Great Prince of Tver; John of Solovki; John and James of Novgorod; John the Hermit of Bohemia; Anthony of Novgorod; New Martyr Panagiotes of Caesarea; Nicetas, Bishop of Remesiana; Orentius, Pharnacius, Eros, Firmus, Firminus, Cyriacus, and Longinus, near Lazica; Gerasimus, Bishop of Astrakhan and Enotaeva; Synaxis of the Righteous Zacharias and Elizabeth, parents of St. John the Baptist; Translation of the relics of St. John the New to Suceava, Romania.

 Abstain from meat and dairy products.

JUNE 25

Romans 12:4-5, 15-21; Matthew 12:9-13

Our fasting is indispensable, because with fasting we are made free from sin, otherwise, it is worthless.

+*Elder Efstratios of Glinsk*

NEW MARTYR PROCOPIOS OF VARNA. Procopios was from a wealthy and pious family in early nineteenth-century Varna, Bulgaria. He became a monk on Mt. Athos at the Skete of the Honorable Forerunner, which is a dependency of the Monastery of Iviron. He was admired for his virtue, obedience, and patience. However, he began to have troubling thoughts about returning to the world. He did not take counsel with his elder, and as the thoughts continued to trouble him, he left the Holy Mountain for Smyrna in Turkey. Procopios became despondent. One day he went into the Ottoman civil court dressed as a layman. When asked if he wanted to become a Turk, he said yes. He freely recited the vows and was catechized. Immediately upon receiving their seal of circumcision, Procopios had a change of heart, and he desired to see a spiritual father. Finding an opportune moment, he secretly visited a friend who he knew from the Skete on Mt. Athos. The monk advised Procopius to return to Mt. Athos, for the mercy of God is boundless to sinners. Prokopios genuinely repented but said he could not return. He announced that he was prepared to die. He put on clean clothes, a monastic cap, and the two prayed together. Then Procopios presented himself to the Hagarenes. He threw down the turban and boldly rebuked their religion. He was bound, beaten, and taken to the judge. His sentence was beheading. As he stood bravely at the site of execution, no one, not even the officers, would carry out the deed. Finally, they found another who had recently renounced Christ, and he beheaded St. Procopios.

SAINTS OF THE DAY: Febronia of Nisibis; Gallicianus the Patrician; Symeon of Sinai; Nikon of Optina; Dometius and Dionysius of the Forerunner, Mt. Athos; Theoleptus of Philadelphia; Cyprian of Svyatogorsk; George of Attalia; Peter and Febronia of Murom; Procopios of Varna; Adelbert, archdeacon; Leonis, Libye, and Eutropia of Syria; Moluac of Lismore.

TUESDAY **Abstain from meat and dairy products.**

JUNE 26

Romans 14:9-18; Matthew 12:14-16, 22-30

Perfection of mind depends upon the abstinence of the belly.

St. John Cassian

VIRGIN-MARTYR PERSEVERANDA OF SPAIN. Perseveranda and her two sisters, Columba and Magrina, are saints of the Church. They were from a noble family in seventh- and eighth-century Spain. The sisters gathered other religious young women around them and led an ascetic and devotional life. However, the fame of their sanctity attracted the attention of King Oliver, who was a fierce persecutor of Christians. Columba foresaw that her sisters and their friends would become the victims of persecution, and very soon letters were brought ordering them to appear before the king. Columba told her sisters to be firm in the faith, and she traveled to King Oliver who told her to renounce her faith to avoid being harmed. While she was still before the king, a bystander said that the other two sisters were even more beautiful than Columba. He immediately ordered guards to seize the other women, swearing that they would be his slaves. But Perseveranda and Magrina were warned in a dream and fled. After seven days, Perseveranda died from exhaustion and hunger. Christians who happened upon that spot saw a dove surrounded by a celestial light, hovering over her body. They buried Perseveranda with honor. When the messengers returned to the king telling him they could not find the maidens, he set off in search of them. When one of his men found the body of St. Perseveranda, he attempted to bring it to the king, but he was struck blind.

SAINTS OF THE DAY: David of Thessalonica; John, Bishop of the Goths; Dionysius, Archbishop of Suzdal; New Martyr David of St. Anne's Skete; Anthion, monk; Perseveranda of Spain; Translation of the relics of Nilus of Stolobny and Tikhon of Lukhov; Brannock of Braunton, England; Appearance of the "Tikhvin" Icon of the Mother of God; "Of the Seven Lakes," "Neamts," and "Lydda" Icons of the Mother of God.

JUNE 27

Romans 15:7-16; Matthew 12:38-45

Be the Shepherd of those who have gone astray, the Guide and Light of unbelievers, the Teacher of the foolish, the Father of orphans, the Helper of the oppressed, the Healer of the sick, the Comforter of the downtrodden. And lead us all to our desired end: to Thee, our Haven and blessed Rest.

St. Parthenius of Kiev Pechersk

VENERABLE SAMPSON THE HOSPITABLE OF CONSTANTINOPLE. Sampson was a descendent of Emperor Constantine. He was the son of wealthy Roman parents in the sixth century. He received an excellent education and became a physician. When his parents died, he gave away their wealth to the poor. He desired to go into the wilderness, but God sent him to Constantinople. He settled in a small house and took in the homeless, the poor, and the sick, and he attended to them. He healed the sick physically and spiritually. God granted him the gift of wonderworking. News about Sampson spread quickly, and when the patriarch summoned him, he ordained Sampson to the priesthood. When Emperor Justinian became incurably ill, it was revealed to him that he could receive healing from Sampson. When Sampson prayed, the emperor was healed. Declining a financial reward, Sampson asked the emperor to build a shelter for the poor and wandering. After a short illness, St. Sampson died peacefully in old age. Many healings were wrought at his grave.

SAINTS OF THE DAY: Joanna the Myrrh-bearer; Sampson the Hospitable of Constantinople; Kirion II, Catholicos-Patriarch of All Georgia; Crescens, Maximus, and Theonest, Bishops of Mainz (Germany); Martin of Turov; Anectus of Caesarea; Severus of Interocrea in Italy; Martin of Turov; Pierios of Antioch; Gregory Nikolsky of Kuban; Serapion of Kozha Lake; George of Mt. Athos and Georgia; Martyrs Marcia and Mark; Martyrdom of Luke (Mukhaidze) of Holy Cross Monastery in Jerusalem; Uncovering of the relics of the Optina Elders: Leonid, Macarius, Hilarion, Ambrose, Anatole I, Barsanuphius, and Anatole II.

 Abstain from meat and dairy products.

JUNE 28

Romans 15:17-29; Matthew 12:46-13:3

You mustn't wage your Christian struggle with sermons and arguments, but with true secret love. When we argue, others react. When we love people, they are moved and we win them over. When we love, we think that we offer something to others, but in reality we are the first to benefit.

St. Porphyrios the Kapsokalivite

SERGIOS THE MAGISTRATE OF PAPHLAGONIA. Sergios was from the ninth-century town of Niketia, close to the city of Amastris on the coast of the Black Sea. He was related to the iconophile Empress Theodora, who was the wife of Emperor Theophilos the Iconomach, and mother of Emperor Michael III. When the emperor died, she restored the holy icons. On one occasion, the Spanish Arabs conquered the island of Crete, and this left the Aegean Sea and Mt. Athos vulnerable to subsequent raids from Crete. Sergios, the magistrate, was selected by Emperor Michael III to lead the fight to regain Crete. He was described as a man of genius and was put in charge of all the armed forces and the imperial fleet. However, when he landed on Crete, Sergios was killed, and the effort failed. St. Sergios was buried in a Cretan monastery, known as the Monastery of the Magistros.

SAINTS OF THE DAY: Paul the Physician of Corinth; Sennuphius the Standard-bearer of Egypt; Sergius and Herman of Valaam; Serenus, Plutarchus, Heraclides, Heron, Raiso and others in Alexandria; Venerable Magnus; Sergios the Magistrate of Paphlagonia; Xenophon of Novgorod; Donatus of Libya; Austell of Cornwall; Three Martyrs of Galatia; Seventy Martyrs of Scythopolis; Moses the Anchorite; Martyr Pappias; Heliodorus of Glinsk Hermitage; Martyr Macedonius; Translation of the relics of Sts. Cyrus and John the Unmercenaries; "Of the Three Hands" Icon of the Mother of God.

Friday

June 29

Holy Apostles Peter and Paul
Abstain from meat and dairy products.
2 Corinthians 11:21-12:9; Matthew 16:13-19

From God comes grace, but from us comes labor. Therefore, let no one even think that the Holy Apostles relied solely on the God-given grace, or that it was easy for them, or that they performed their great work in the world without effort...so it was that the Apostles did not rely on grace alone, but also put forth nearly superhuman effort to show themselves worthy of God's grace.

St. Nikolai Velimirovich

MARY, MOTHER OF JOHN-MARK, AT JERUSALEM. The Apostle Mark the Evangelist wrote the second Gospel. His mother Mary was probably the aunt or sister of Barnabas, the companion of St. Paul. She was a woman of admirable qualities and was loyal to her Christian beliefs. The leadership of the church at that time gathered in her large home. It became a well-known center of Christian life and worship. She later gave up her Jerusalem home to be used as an infant church. Christians were a persecuted sect, yet Mary was not hesitant to offer her home, sacrifice her time, effort and money to serve the Lord. Peter had an affection for Mary's home, and it was here that Peter found his way after his miraculous escape. He knew that a company of believers had gathered there to pray for his release.

SAINTS OF THE DAY: Holy and All-Praised Apostles Peter and Paul; Peter, Prince of the Tatar Horde, wonderworker of Rostov; Mary, mother of John-Mark, nephew of Apostle Barnabas, at Jerusalem; Uncovering of the relics of St. Nicander of Pskov; "Kasperov" Icon of the Mother of God.

Saturday

Synaxis of the Twelve Holy Apostles
Fast-free

June 30

1 Corinthians 4:9-16; Matthew 9:36, 10:1-8

If from one burning lamp someone lights another, then another from that one, and so on in succession, he has light continuously. In the same way, through the Apostles ordaining their successors, and these successors ordaining others, and so on, the grace of the Holy Spirit is handed down through all generations and enlightens all who obey their shepherds and teachers.

St. Gregory Palamas

GELASIUS OF RIMET. Gelasius lived as a hermit near Rimet creek. He was granted the grace of working miracles. He became the abbot of the Rimet Monastery in Transylvania. He fasted on weekdays, eating only on Saturday and Sunday, and his only food was the Holy Eucharist. During the day, he fulfilled his monastic duties, and at night he kept vigil. He was the spiritual father of many hermits of Rimet Mountain and visited them during Great Lent. He healed the sick and cast out demons. It is said that a spring of water appeared through his prayers. Gelasius later became a bishop. After many labors on behalf of his flock, he died peacefully.

SAINTS OF THE DAY: Synaxis of the Holy Twelve Apostles: Peter, Andrew, James and John the sons of Zebedee, Philip, Bartholomew, Thomas, Matthew, James the son of Alphaeus, Jude the brother of James, Simon the Zealot, and Matthias; Basilides the Soldier at Alexandria; Stephen of Omsk; Gelasius of Rimet; Peter of Synope; Frentrude of Salzburg; Andrew, Prince of Bogoliubsk; Neomartyr Michael Paknanas the Gardener, of Athens; Martial, Bishop of Limoges; Dinar, Queen of Khereti (Georgia); Nicander of Yaroslavl; Theogenes of Kazakhstan; Milan Popovic of Rmanj; Alexander of Munich; Peter the Prince of Ordinsk, Rostov; Martyr Meleton; Glorification of St. Sophronius, Bishop of Irkutsk and All Siberia; "Balikin" Icon of the Mother of God.

Fifth Sunday of Matthew
Fast-free

JULY 1

1 Corinthians 12:27-13:8; Matthew 8:28-9:1

When a carnal thought jumps out at you, strike back. Cut up the image of the person that scandalizes you. Drive it away and erase it from your imagination as you would wipe out something with a sponge. Erase the image and hold on to the prayer—and that's that. When you feel like being lazy and the thoughts tell you to sleep in, fight back and say, 'No! Why should I sleep in?' When a judgmental thought comes and whispers to you, 'Say such-and-such a thing about him,' resist and say to yourself, 'No! I won't say it!' This is how the war is waged.

Elder Ephraim of Arizona

NEOMARTYR CONSTANTINE THE WONDERWORKER OF CYPRUS AND THOSE WITH HIM. In the fourth century, Constantine assembled a missionary group of three hundred strong to spread the gospel of Jesus Christ. They went first to the Holy Sepulcher, then to a monastery for a stay. Afterward, they traveled extensively planting the Word and converting many. After several years, they boarded a ship for Cyprus intent on further success. En route, they encountered a fierce sea that threatened to sink their craft. Constantine prayed, and the sea grew calm. After several months on Cyprus, they had canvassed the island. However, the island ruler, Savinos, was an idol-worshipper and he reacted strongly by charging the group with treason. Most of the group escaped to the hills while Constantine and a few aides remained in the city. The four were captured, tried, and beheaded. Their remains were buried in the town of Hormidias, and the grave produced a miraculous healing spring.

SAINTS OF THE DAY: Cosmas and Damian the Unmercenary Physicians, at Rome; Potitus at Naples; Peter the Patrician; Gallus of Clermont; Eparchius the Recluse of Gaul; Basil of the Deep Stream in Cappadocia; 25 Martyrs in Nicomedia; Leo the Hermit; Nicodemus of Svyatogorsk; Leontius of Radauti in Moldavia; Servanus (Serf), apostle of Western Fife; Julius and Aaron of Wales; Constantine of Cyprus, and those with him.

JULY 2

Hebrews 9:1-7; Luke 1:39-49, 56

The human soul conceals much good in its depths. One must only search for it.

St. Leo of Optina

OUDOCEUS, BISHOP OF LLANDAFF. Oudoceus' father took his pregnant wife and all his family to Armorica and took the throne as king. Oudoceus, who had been commended to God, was born there, and from his infancy, he began to excel in learning and eloquence. There came to that country a dreaded disease, yellow pestilence, that killed both the sick and the physicians. By the prayers of Oudoceus' uncle, St. Teilo, and the holy men of Britain, the disease ceased. A divine voice directed Teilo to go to his nephew Oudoceus, who had increased in goodness and knowledge. The clergy and people elected Oudoceus bishop of Llandaff, and peace reigned. An intrigue arose, and the king expelled Oudoceus from the country. Oudoceus and some of his attendants left there, carrying with them some holy relics, including those of St. Teilo. As they traveled, some bandits attacked them, taking their gold and silver. But when they held their lances against Oudoceus, they lost their sight, and their arms became stiff. He prayed for them, and the bandits acknowledged their crime and asked pardon. Their sight and senses were restored, and they promised to fast and pray, give alms, and give perpetual obedience to Oudoceus, his successors, and the Church. Once, when Oudoceus was thirsty, he went to a fountain where he found some women washing butter. Having no cup to drink from, Oudoceus formed one out of butter, and he drank. It remained in that form and appeared as gold to those who beheld it. It is said that by touching it, health is given to the diseased.

SAINTS OF THE DAY: Placing of the Honorable Robe of the Most Holy Theotokos at Blachernae; John Maximovitch of Shanghai and San Francisco; Juvenal of Jerusalem; Juvenal of America; Photius of Kiev; Quintus of Phrygia; Basil of Jerusalem; Stephen the Great of Moldavia; Lampros of Makri; Monegunde of Gaul.

 Fast-free

JULY 3

1 Corinthians 1:1-9; Matthew 13:24-30

The proud man is unable to forgive.

+Elder Sampson of Russia

MARTYR GERASIMOS THE NEW. Until the age of twelve, George, as he was known then, was a Christian. He was born to godly and pious parents in the city of Carpenision. When he went to Constantinople, he was taken in by a Turkish family. After two months, George was tricked and persuaded to accept circumcision. For the next ten years, he was a Muslim. At the age of twenty-two, the handsome George left that home because the Ottoman husband feared that his wife might fall into sin with George. When George returned to his homeland, he began to regret his conversion to Islam. With the help of the village priest, he begged forgiveness. For the next three years, he followed the path of Christian spirituality. While praying in a chapel one day, some children mistook him for a monk. George felt that this was a sign from God, so he informed his mother about his intention, but she wanted him to marry instead. George secretly traveled to Mt. Athos with a monk Gerasimos, to the Skete of St. Panteleimon. Within two years, George was tonsured a monk, taking the name Gerasimos. He soon began to seek permission to go forward to martyrdom, but his elder feared for him. Several years passed, but Gerasimos still desired martyrdom, so he left Mt. Athos. He visited the Turkish family that had adopted him, but the Ottoman father had Gerasimos arrested for treason. Refusing to renounce Christ, St. Gerasimos was beheaded in the early nineteenth century.

SAINTS OF THE DAY: Hyacinth of Caesarea, and Theodotus and Theodota; Diomedes, Eulampius, Asclepiodotos, and Golinduc; Anatolios of Constantinople; Anatolios of Laodicea, and Eusebius; Symeon the Stylite; Anatolius of the Near Caves; Anatolius of the Far Caves; Isaiah the Solitary; Martyrs Mark and Mocius; Alexander of the Unsleeping Ones; John and Longinus of Yarenga; Basil and Constantine of Yaroslavl; Gerasimos of Carpenision; Nicodemus of Kozha Lake; John "Iron Cap" of Moscow.

JULY 4

1 Corinthians 2:9-3:8; Matthew 13:31-36

We should always be on the lookout to compare ourselves with the Saints and the lights who have gone before us. If we do, we will discover that we have scarcely begun the ascetic life, that we have hardly kept our vow in a holy manner, and that our thinking is still rooted in the world.

St. John Climacus

MARTYR EUGENE THE PASSION-BEARER. Eugene was the son of the court physician Sergey Botkin. He studied medicine at the University of St. Petersburg and the universities of Berlin and Heidelberg. He was appointed the chief physician at St. Georgievsky Hospital in St. Petersburg. He also served aboard the hospital train during the Russo-Japanese War. He was appointed court physician in 1908, like his father. He married and had four children, but the marriage broke up because of Eugene's long hours of service at the court. Later, Eugene was devastated when his two older sons died during the first World War. He became increasingly religious and developed an abhorrence for the flesh. His brother said that Eugene had an extraordinary soul and a horror for any kind of struggle or fight. He chose medicine to soothe and heal without end. Eugene was a friend of Tsar Nicholas II, and he felt a duty to accompany the Romanov family into exile. The entire family, with their servants and Eugene, were murdered a short time later.

SAINTS OF THE DAY: Theodore of Cyrene, with Cyprilla, Aroa, and Lucia; Donatus of Libya; Theophilus and Theodotus; Righteous Menignos; Andrew of Crete; Sabbas of Gornji Karlovac and George Bogich; Holy Royal Martyrs: Tsar Nicholas II, Empress Alexandra, Alexis, Olga, Tatiana, Maria, and Anastasia, and others; Eugene Botkin, the Passion-bearer; Asclepias the Wonderworker; Martha, mother of St. Symeon Stylites the Younger; Innocent and Sabbatios and 30 others; Andrew the Russian; Euthymius of Suzdal; Nilus of Poltava; Andrew of Bogoliubsk; Michael Choniates of Athens; Andrew Rublev of Moscow

JULY 5

Galatians 5:22-6:2; Matthew 11:27-30

My child, evil thoughts don't attack all at once; the passions don't rise against you all at the same time. They come one-by-one, and so you deal with them as they come.

+Elder Joseph the Hesychast

VENERABLE ATHANASIOS AND HIS SIX DISCIPLES. Athanasios founded the Great Lavra in the tenth century, the first monastery on Mt. Athos. He was orphaned early and was raised by a pious nun. He copied her habits of fasting and prayer. He went to Constantinople and enrolled as a student under the rhetorician Athanasias, and eventually became a teacher. Athanasios was befriended by Nicephoros Phokas, a renown military officer, and future emperor, and they became lifelong friends. After his schooling, Athanasios became a monk in Bithynia. Desiring more solitude, he moved to Mt. Athos and attracted many disciples. Seeing the need for a monastery, he went to Emperor Nicephoros, who financed the construction. Mt. Athos became the heart of Orthodox monasticism. A famine once occurred that scattered the monks of the Lavra. As Athanasios was leaving, he beheld a woman beneath a veil, and she asked him where he was going. But he asked her who she was, and she responded, "I am the Mother of your Lord." She told him to strike his staff upon a certain rock, and suddenly a holy spring sprang forth, which exists to this day. When he returned to the Lavra, the bins were full of grain and construction work continued. One day as Athanasios and six brethren were overlooking the work, the top of the church collapsed, and they were found dead. The coffin housing St. Athanasios' wonderworking relics can be seen today at the Great Lavra.

SAINTS OF THE DAY: Athanasios of Mt. Athos and 6 disciples; Cyprian of Koutloumousiou; Stephen of Rhegium, and Suerus, Agnes, Felicitas, and Perpetua; Anna at Rome; Athanasius, disciple of Sergius of Radonezh; Theodosius of Cherepovets; Athanasius of Jerusalem; Lampados of Hirenopolis; Elizabeth Romanova, with Barbara, John, Igor, Constantine, Sergius, Vladimir, and Theodore; Agapitus of Optina.

JULY 6

1 Corinthians 4:5-8; Matthew 13:44-54

There are times when it seems as if we cannot truly love people and also love God: People have too many needs; they are too demanding. If one is called to love God with all of one's heart, soul, and strength, what is there left over? Yet, reading the Scriptures and listening to the teachings of all those who have spoken of God through the ages, we know that we cannot truly love God unless we love our neighbor. It's not an "either/or" proposition, but a "both/and."

Mother Raphaela, "Growing in Christ"

VENERABLE MONENNA OF KILLEEVY MONASTERY. Monenna is one of Ireland's early female saints. She was born in the fifth-century area of County Down. Her father was king of the territory, and her mother was a daughter of one of the northern kings. It was said that St. Patrick baptized Monenna, and he predicted that her name would be remembered throughout time. She founded a number of convents in Scotland and England. Her community eventually settled at Killeevy, which means "church of the mountain." It initially consisted of eight virgins and a widow with a baby boy, named Luger. The nuns lovingly raised him and in time became a bishop. The number of nuns eventually grew to more than 150. Monenna died peacefully and was buried at Killeevy.

SAINTS OF THE DAY: Synaxis of the Apostles Archippos, Philemon, and Onesimus; Sisoes the Great of Egypt; Marinus and Martha at Rome, and their children Audifax and Abbacum, and those with them at Rome—Cyrinus, Valentine, and Asterius; Astius, Bishop of Dyrrachium; Lucy at Rome, and 24 companion martyrs; Cyril of Hilander; Simon of Ufa; Sisoes of the Kiev Caves; Isaurus, Innocent, Felix, Hermias, Basil, Peregrinus, Rufus, and Rufinus of Apollonia; Martyrs Alexander, Epimachos, and Apollonius; Theodore (Bogoyavlensky) of Moscow; Euthymius of Optina; Barnabas of Gethsemane Skete; Monenna of Ireland; Goar, missionary along the Rhine.

JULY 7

Galatians 3:23-4:5; Mark 5:24-34

Praise God continually with spiritual hymns and always remain in meditation and in this way you will be able to bear the burden of the temptations that come upon you. A traveler who is carrying a heavy load pauses from time to time and draws in deep breaths; it makes the journey easier and the burden lighter.

St. Hyperechius of the Desert

EUPHROSYNE, GRAND-DUCHESS OF MOSCOW. Euphrosyne was a princess in fourteenth-century Suzdal. She married the Moscow Great Prince Dimitri Donskoi. They had a happy marriage and raised five sons. St. Sergius of Radonezh and St. Demetrius of Priluki baptized two of their sons. Together with St. Alexis, Metropolitan of Moscow, they had a great influence on Euphrosyne. She built churches and founded the Kremlin Ascension women's monastery, where she later became a nun. During the invasion of Tamerlane into southern Russia, Euphrosyne had the miraculous Vladimir icon of the Mother of God transferred to Moscow, and it defended the Russian land. As an ascetic labor during Lent, the princess wore chains underneath her royal clothes. She commissioned the writing of the famous icon of Archangel Michael, that became the patron icon of the Kremlin Archangel Cathedral. St. Euphrosyne died peacefully and was buried in the Ascension monastery that she founded.

SAINTS OF THE DAY: Kyriake of Nicomedia; Acacius of Sinai, mentioned in *The Ladder*; Hieromartyr Eustathius; Epictetos, presbyter, and Astion in Scythia; Peregrinus, Lucian, Pompeius, Hesychius, Pappias, Saturninus, and Germanus, in Macedonia; Pantaenus the Confessor of Alexandria; Thomas of Mt. Maleon; Evangelus, Bishop of Tomi in Romania; Euphrosyne (Eudocia), grand duchess of Moscow; New Martyr Polycarp; Willibald, Bishop of Eichstatt; Hedda, Bishop of the West Saxons; Maelruin of Tallaght; Translation of the "Blachernae" Icon of the Mother of God.

Sunday

July 8

Sixth Sunday of Matthew
Fast-free
Romans 12:6-14; Matthew 9:1-8

There never was and there never will be a place on earth free from sorrows. The only sorrowless place possible is the heart, when the Lord is present there.

St. Nikon of Optina

NEW MARTYR ANASTASIOS AT CONSTANTINOPLE. Anastasios was from the eighteenth-century village of Saint Blaise, near Ioannina. He was a parish priest in a church outside of Constantinople. Anastasios had watched the martyrdom of the priest Constantius the Russian, and pleaded with God day and night to also grant him this end. One day he saw a blind, elderly priest-monk from Cyprus who left the faith and became a Muslim. He taught Islamic legends to the Hagarenes in the courtyard of the mosque, for which he earned money. It hurt Anastasios to watch this man who had fallen from grace. The Moslems badgered Anastasios also to abandon the priesthood. Rather than be defensive, Anastasios attacked their delusion, asking why they allowed a putrid man whom God had abandoned to instruct them in their religion, saying that their lack of knowledge was to their shame. The Turks ran at Anastasios and took him before the judge and then the vizier, where he was sentenced to exile. Unhappy with this sentence, Anastasios was brought before the vizier again. In an effort to anger him, Anastasios accused him of being unwilling to hear the truth, and instead resorting to hard-hearted blind men for instruction. He then began to instruct the vizier about the Holy Trinity. The Turks were at a loss for words. St. Anastasios was beheaded. That night a holy light appeared over his relics.

SAINTS OF THE DAY: Procopius of Caesarea, with Theodosia, Antiochus, Nicostratus, and 12 women; Anastasios at Constantinople; Theophilus the Myrrh-gusher; Mirdat of Kartli; Procopius of Ustiug; Procopius, fool-for-Christ of Usya; Martyr Abdas; Edgar the Peaceable; Sunniva and others on Selje Island, Norway; Hieritha of Chittlehampton; Translation of the relics of St. Demetrius of Basarabov.

JULY 9

1 Corinthians 5:9-6:11; Matthew 13:54-58

The nurturing of a child begins with pregnancy. If the pregnant mother is agitated and worried, the [child] she is carrying in her womb is agitated. If a mother prays and lives a spiritual life, the child in her womb is sanctified. This is the reason why a pregnant woman should say the Jesus Prayer, study the Gospel, chant hymns and not be anxious; while others should also be careful not to upset her. Then, the child born will be blessed; and the parents will have no problems—neither when the child is young nor when the child is older.

St. Paisios the Athonite

MARTYRS PATERMUTHIOS, COPRES, AND ALEXANDER THE SOLDIER, IN EGYPT. Patermuthios and Copres were Christians from Egypt. They were brought before the pagan Emperor Julian the Apostate in the fourth century. Julian convinced the forty-five-year-old Copres, the younger of the two saints, to worship the idols. Copres proclaimed that he was now Julian's, not Christ's. The aged Patermuthios, who was then seventy-five years old, chastised Copres with the fear of being tormented in hell for eternity. Again, Copres cried out, but this time saying that he was Christ's. The emperor gave orders to behead Sts. Copres and Patermuthios. The soldier Alexander upon witnessing the saints' courage and suffering, became a Christian. He was beheaded.

SAINTS OF THE DAY: Pancratius, Bishop of Taormina; Cyril, Bishop of Gortyna in Crete; Dionysius the Rhetorician and Metrophanes of Mt. Athos; Patermuthios, Copres, and Alexander the soldier, in Egypt; Photios, founder of Akapniou Monastery in Thessalonica; Methodius, Bishop of Lappa on Crete; Peter of Vologda; Martyrs Andrew and Probus; Theodosius, Stylite of Edessa; Euthymius of Karelia; Everilda of Northumbria; Killian, Colman, and Totman, at Wurzburg; Uncovering of the relics of St. Gabriel, of St. Elias Skete, Mt. Athos; "Cyprus" and "Koloch" Icons of the Mother of God.

JULY 10

1 Corinthians 6:20-7:12; Matthew 14:1-13

The surest rule and standard for a well-disciplined life is this: one must be indifferent to either pleasure or pain of flesh, but one must not be immoderate in either direction, so that the body will become neither disordered by obesity nor so sickly that it cannot carry out commands.

St. Basil the Great

MARTYR APOLLONIOS OF SARDIS. Apollonios was a Christian from the third-century city of Sardis. He was taken before Perinios, the governor at Iconium of Pisidia, who ordered Apollonios to swear an oath in the name of the emperor. Apollonios said that as a Christian he was not permitted to swear in the name of a mortal man. He said that Christ commanded us not to swear by the heaven, nor earth, nor Jerusalem, nor by our head, for we cannot make one hair black or white. Also, we are instructed to let our "yes" be "yes," and "no" be "no," and anything more than this is from the Evil One. Finally, he said, "So then, it certainly is improper to swear by a man who is ignorant of the Creator and Fashioner of all." The governor condemned St. Apollonios to death on the cross.

SAINTS OF THE DAY: Deposition of the Precious Robe of the Lord at Moscow; Holy 45 Martyrs at Nicopolis in Armenia; The 10,000 Fathers of the desert and caves of Scetis; Anthony of the Kiev Caves; Bianor and Silvanus of Pisidia; Apollonios of Sardis; Silouan of the Far Caves in Kiev; Gregory, Bishop of Assos, near Ephesus; Eumenius and Parthenius of Crete; Joseph of Damascus, and companions; Synaxis of All Saints of Vatopedi, Mt. Athos; Synaxis of St. John the Theologian in Beatus; "Konevits" Icon of the Mother of God.

JULY 11

2 Corinthians 6:1-10; Luke 7:36-50

Be at peace with others, have humility, remember Christ and imitate His humility, obedience, and love for all—without which you cannot be saved, without which the other virtues are of no avail.

St. Arsenios of Paros

DROSTAN OF OLD DEER AND ABERDEEN. Drostan lived in the late sixth to early seventh-century Ireland. He was a close friend of St. Columba of Iona, Enlightener of Scotland. Drostan became one of the founders and first abbot of the great monastery of Deer, which grew into a significant monastic and missionary center. It gained royal support, and it flourished for several centuries. With Drostan's influence, a large number of churches were built near the coast in northeastern Scotland. Many years later Drostan felt a calling to lead a solitary life. He left for the far north to Glen Esk. Soon the poor, the sick, and the needy began to flock to the saint on whom God had bestowed the gift of performing miracles. Drostan died peacefully. Some called him one of the apostles of Scotland. He is buried in the village of New Aberdeen, in the church that was originally built by Sts. Columba and Drostan. Many miracles occurred there.

SAINTS OF THE DAY: Euphemia the All-praised of Chalcedon; Olga, Equal-to-the-Apostles, Princess of Russia, called Helen; Cindeos of Pamphylia; Januarius and Pelagia of Nicopolis; Nicodemus of Elbasan and Mt. Athos; Nicodemos of Hilander and Vatopedi, Mt. Athos; Arcadius of Vyazemsk; Nectarios of St. Anne's Skete, Mt. Athos; Cyril of Paros; Leo, monk of Mandra; Drostan of Old Deer and Aberdeen; New Hieromartyrs of Serbia (1941-1945); "Rudensk" Icon of the Mother of God.

 Fast-free

JULY 12

1 Corinthians 7:24-35; Matthew 15:12-21

Satan hates monasteries the most. He is able to engage the whole world against you, not to enter the monastery. When you decide to go, do not look back!

+Elder Arsenie Papacioc of Romania

RIGHTEOUS VERONICA. According to tradition, Veronica was the woman with the issue of blood who received healing by touching the hem of the robe of Christ. According to the Gospel of St. Mark: "Now a certain woman had a flow of blood for twelve years, and had suffered many things from many physicians. She had spent all that she had and was no better, but rather grew worse. When she heard about Jesus, she came behind Him in the crowd and touched His garment." For she had said within herself, "If only I may touch His clothes, I shall be made well (Mk. 5:25-28)." And Jesus said, "Daughter, your faith has made you well. Go in peace, and be healed of your affliction (Mk. 5:34)." As a way of giving thanks for this miracle, Veronica commissioned a bronze statue of Jesus, and she would pray before it. It was preserved until the time of Julian the Apostate, who seized it and broke it into pieces. Veronica gave the Lord a veil, with which the Lord wiped His face as He carried His Cross to Golgotha. The image of His face was miraculously left upon the cloth. In France, Emperor Tiberius was healed of a terminal disease when he looked at it. This cloth, also known as Veronica's Veil, is housed at the Vatican.

SAINTS OF THE DAY: Proclus and Hilary of Ancyra; Andrew the Commander, Heraclius, Taustus, Menas, and others; Mamas, near Sigmata; Serapion, Bishop of Vladimir; Serapion the New, at Alexandria; Veronica, who was healed by the Lord; Michael of Maleinus; Arsenius of Novgorod; Simon, founder of Volomsk Monastery (Vologda); Theodore and John of Kiev; John and Gabriel of Mt. Athos; Paisios the New of Mt. Athos; Translation of the relics of Momcilo Grgurevic of Serbia; Translation of the relics of St. Anthony, founder of Leokhnovo Monastery; "Of the Three Hands" Icon of the Mother of God of Hilander, Mt. Athos.

JULY 13

Hebrews 2:2-10; Matthew 15:29-31

Enemies have taught me to know what hardly anyone knows, that a person has no enemies in the world except himself.

St. Nikolai Velimirovich

VENERABLE SARAH OF SEEDS IN LIBYA. In fourth-century Egypt, the young woman Sarah entered a convent along the Nile River, not far from Alexandria. For thirteen years, she successfully guarded her thoughts and heart against the whispering attacks of the demon of fornication. She never stopped fighting, but called on Christ saying, "God, give me strength!" The demon then appeared to her in bodily form, saying, "Thou hast vanquished me, O Sarah!" But the humble saint answered, "I did not conquer thee, but my Master Christ!" In order to wither the passions of her body, she prayed fervently and ate very plain food. Whenever she put her foot outside her cell, she would always keep the remembrance of death before her eyes. She said, "It is good for one to give alms, even if it is done before others with a view to please; for, by this, one shall come to do it for God." By her example, she led many women to the monastic life. St. Sarah spent sixty years in asceticism and died peacefully.

SAINTS OF THE DAY: Synaxis of the Holy Archangel Gabriel; Stephen of St. Sabbas' Monastery; Sarah of Seeds in Libya; Mary (Golinduc) of Persia; Julian, Bishop of Cenomanis in Gaul; New Martyr Constantine Oprisan of Romania; Martyr Serapion, under Severus; Marcian of Iconium; Alamannia in Cyprus; Heliophotus, Epaphrodites, Ammon, Auxouthenius, and Euthenius, of Cyprus; Mildred, abbess of Minster Convent in Thanet; Juthwara of Cornwall; Just, monk in Cornwall; Synaxis of Hilander Saints, Mt. Athos.

JULY 14

Romans 16:1-16; Matthew 10:37-11:1

When we nurture evil thoughts, we become evil. We may think that we are good, but evil is in us… We, however, have Divine power, Divine life, and Divine energy. On the day of the Final Judgment we shall have to give an answer for the way we have used this Divine power, life, and energy which have been given to us: whether we have contributed to the harmony in the universe, or have sown disharmony.

+*Elder Thaddeus of Vitovnica*

VENERABLE ONESIMOS OF MAGNESIA. Onesimos was born in the early fourth century during the reign of Emperor Diocletian. His parents received divine Baptism from an angel of God and the news that they would give birth to a holy child whom they were to name Onesimos. They took him at an early age to the monastery in Ephesus, where there were eight hundred monks. His parents were saddened to such an extent at leaving Onesimos that they wept to the point of blindness. When Diocletian began a persecution of Christians, all the monks departed the monastery. Onesimos visited the home of his parents, but they did not recognize him. However, he left them a brief letter of explanation about himself and went off to Magnesia where he established a monastery. He invited his parents to visit him there, and through his prayers, he healed their eyes.

SAINTS OF THE DAY: Apostle Aquila of the Seventy, and St. Priscilla; Justus at Rome; Joseph, Archbishop of Thessalonica; Heraclius, Patriarch of Alexandria; Onesimos of Magnesia; Hellius of Egypt; John of Merv; Marcellinus of Utrecht; Nicodemos of Mt. Athos; Stephen of Makhrishche Monastery; Martyr Aquila; Longinus of Svyatogorsk Monastery; New Martyr Constantine Oprisan of Jilava, Romania; Procopius of Sazava in Bohemia; Uncovering of the relics of St. Theophilos of Kiev.

SUNDAY

Sunday of the Holy Fathers
Fast-free

JULY 15

Titus 3:8-15; Matthew 5:14-19

It is impossible for us who have fallen into the pit of iniquities ever to be drawn out of it, unless we sink into the abyss of the humility of the repentant.

St. John Climacus

MARTYRS KYRIKOS AND HIS MOTHER JULITTA OF TARSUS. Julitta was a young Christian widow with a three-year-old son named Kyrikos. They lived in Asia Minor in the city of Iconium. Julitta was descended from a royal family. She was a Christian and widowed early on. She instructed Kyrikos in the faith and baptized him at an early age. During the third-century persecution of Christians by Emperor Diocletian, Julitta took her child and two servants and departed the city, leaving behind her home, servants, and property. They were captured in Tarsus and brought to trial before the governor. Julitta fearlessly confessed her faith in Christ. The governor gave orders to beat her with canes, and as Kyrikos saw his mother being tortured, he began to cry. The governor picked up the boy and began hugging him to torment Julitta further. Kyrikos struck the governor and shouted, "Let me go to my mother, I am a Christian." Filled with wrath, the governor hurled the child down the stone steps, and there Kyrikos died. After more cruel tortures, Julitta was beheaded. A monastery was built near Constantinople in honor of Sts. Julitta and Kyrikos. They are prayed to for family happiness and the restoring of health to sick children.

SAINTS OF THE DAY: Julitta and Kyrikos of Tarsus; Equal-to-the-Apostles Great Prince Vladimir, enlightener of Russia; Abudimus of the isle of Tenedos; Donald of Ogilvy, and his nine virgin daughters, nuns of Abernathy (Scotland); Asiya of Tanis in Syria; Zosima of Alexandrov (Vladimir); Job of Malaya Ugolka; Rumon of Tavistock; Martyr Lollianus; Finding of the head of St. Matrona of Chios; Translation of the relics of St. Swithun, Bishop of Winchester.

JULY 16

1 Corinthians 9:13-18; Matthew 16:1-6

Therefore, do not say, 'I cannot bear to come near those that hate me', but say … 'Hate me as much as you may, I will not stop loving you', and then you will humble his hostility, and cast out all coldness. …This is the language of Christ's disciple, as the other is that of the devil. This makes men honorable and glorious, as the other makes one shameful and ridiculous. It is on this ground we feel admiration for Moses, because even when God said, 'Let Me alone, that I may destroy them in Mine anger' (Ex. 32: 10), he could not bear to despise those who had so often shown aversion to him; but said, 'If thou wilt forgive their sin, forgive it; if not, blot out me also' (ibid. vs. 32). This was because he was a friend of God, and an imitator of Him.

St. John Chrysostom

MARTYR FAUSTUS. In the year 250, Emperor Decius carried out a Christian persecution. Faustus was arrested and charged with being a Christian. He boldly and openly confessed Christ. His punishment for such an allegiance was crucifixion on the cross, which was carried out by the state executioners. Faustus happily accepted his sentence. He was nailed to a cross, then shot by archers. He survived on the cross for five days until he surrendered his soul to God.

SAINTS OF THE DAY: Athenogenes, Bishop of Heracleopolis, and his ten disciples; Antiochus, physician of Sebaste; The 15,000 Martyrs of Pisidia; Julia of Carthage; Ardalion (Ponamarev) of Kasli; New Martyr John of Turnovo; Theodotus of Glinsk Hermitage; Seraphim, Theognostus, and others of Alma-Ata; Helier of Jersey; James, Archbishop of Barnaul, and with him: Peter, John, Theodore, and John; Matrona Belyakova of Anemnyasevo; Magdalena of New Tikhvin Convent in Siberia; Martyr Athenogenes; Martyr Faustus, under Decius; Commemoration of the Fourth Ecumenical Council.

JULY 17

Galatians 3:23-4:5; Mark 5:24-34

Behold, for years and generations, the way of God has been leveled by the cross and by death. How is this with thee, that thou seest the afflictions of the way as if they were out of the way? Doest not thou wish to follow the steps of the saints? Or doest thou wish to go a way which is especially for thee, without suffering? The way unto God is a daily cross. No one can ascend unto heaven with comfort, we know where the way of comfort leads.

St. Isaac the Syrian

VENERABLE IRENARCHUS, ABBOT OF SOLOVETSK. Irenarchus lived during the seventeenth century and was tonsured at the Solovetsk monastery in imitation of Sts. Zosima and Savvatii. After the death of the abbot, Irenarchus became his successor. During this time, northern Russia was under attack by the Swedes and Danes. The Solovetsk monastery was significant in Russia's defense. Irenarchus fortified the monastery physically and spiritually. He had deep ditches dug around the monastery, and a stone wall with turrets was constructed. Irenarchus guided his monks meekly and humbly. He constantly thought of God. Under his guidance, Irenarchus produced many worthy ascetics. He gave his blessing to his friend Monk Eleazer to establish a skete monastery on Anzersk Island. St. Irenarchus spent the last two years of his life in silent prayer.

SAINTS OF THE DAY: Marina of Antioch; Scillitan Martyrs: Speratus, Cittinus, Narzalis, Felix, Veturius, Acyllinus, Laetantius, Januaria, Generosa, Donata, Secunda, and Vestina; Timothy, fool-for-Christ of Svyatogorsk; Euphrasius of Ionopolis; Sabbas, Bishop of Gornji Karlovac; Irenarchus of Solovetsk; Leonid of Ust-Neduma; Kenelm of Wales; Marcellina, sister of St. Ambrose; Translation of the relics of St. Lazarus of Mt. Galesion; Translation of the relics of St. Gabriel of Seven Lakes Monastery (Kazan); "Svyatogorsk" Icon of the Mother of God.

JULY 18

1 Corinthians 10:12-22; Matthew 16:20-24

Just as in Paradise, God walks in the Holy Scriptures, seeking man.

St. Ambrose of Milan

MARTYR FREDERICH, BISHOP OF UTRECHT. Frederich was the great grandson of Radbod, King of Friesland, before the French conquered it. He was trained up in piety and sacred literature among the clergy of the church of Utrecht. His fasts and other austerities were excessive, and he fervently prayed. He was ordained to the priesthood and charged with instructing the catechumens in the early eighth century. When the bishop died, the clergy and all the people chose Frederich as their bishop, even though Frederich, with many tears, declared his incapacity and unworthiness. But the emperor compelled him to submit. Frederich immediately applied himself to establish the best order and sent zealous laborers into the northern parts to root out idolatry. With the change of rulers, the new queen was adulterous, and great scandals ensued. This stirred up Frederich, who now acted the part of a second John the Baptist. Frederich charged her with incest and adultery, and he drew her fury like a second Jezebel. One day when Frederich came from the altar, as he was going to kneel in prayer, two assassins employed by the queen stabbed him. He died in a few minutes while reciting the 114th Psalm.

SAINTS OF THE DAY: Hyacinth of Amastris; Martyrs Dasius and Maron; Paul, Chionia (Thea), and Valentina in Caesarea of Palestine; Emilian of Silistra in Bulgaria; Athanasius of Klysma, Egypt; Stephen, Archbishop of Constantinople; Pambo, hermit of Egypt; Cozmas of Georgia; John the Confessor, Metropolitan of Chalcedon; Pambo, recluse of the Kiev Caves; Apollinarius (Mosalitinov) of Verkhoturye; Leontius, abbot of Karikhov (Novgorod); Barlaam of Bald Mountain, near Antioch in Syria; Frederich, Bishop of Utrecht; John the Long-suffering of the Kiev Caves; Martyr Marcellus; "Tolga" Icon of the Mother of God.

JULY 19

1 Corinthians 10:28-11:8; Matthew 16:24-28

The mind of the soul which lives in the fear of God, in both word and deed, no matter what it may be, is with God.

St. Diocles of Egypt

VENERABLE ABBA DIOCLES THE ANCHORITE OF EGYPT. Before he became a monk, at the age of twenty-eight, Diocles studied grammar and became highly proficient. He then moved on to the study of philosophy. He became one of the hermits that lived near the bank of the Nile River, close to the Thebaid. He lived thirty-five years in the caves. Abba Dorotheos, a priest who lived in a cave, was once given five hundred gold coins. He kept three and gave the 497 to Diocles saying, "Thou art wiser than I. I am not equal to spending these coins." Diocles sought out those who were in need and dispersed the coins. Diocles said to the fathers that the mind that removes itself from the meditation of God becomes a devil or a beast and falls into lust and that lust is savage, animal, and bestial. He also said that feelings of wrath are from the devil.

SAINTS OF THE DAY: Macrina, sister of Sts. Basil the Great and Gregory of Nyssa; Theodore, Bishop of Edessa; Abba Diocles of *The Paradise;* Dius, abbot of Antioch; Paisius of the Kiev Caves; Victor, Bishop of Glazov; Militsa (Eugenia in schema), Princess of Serbia; Stephen Lazarevic, King of Serbia; Romanus Olegovich, Prince of Ryazan; Sophronius of Svyatogorsk Monastery; Synaxis of All Saints of Kursk; Uncovering of the relics of St. Seraphim of Sarov; The Seraphim-Diveevsk "Tenderness" Icon of the Mother, before which St. Seraphim reposed.

FRIDAY

Abstain from meat and dairy products, and fish.
James 5:10-20; Luke 4:22-30

JULY 20

God is a fire that warms and kindles the heart and inward parts. Hence, if we feel in our hearts the cold which comes from the devil—for the devil is cold—let us call on the Lord. He will come to warm our hearts with perfect love, not only for Him but also for our neighbor, and the cold of him who hates the good will flee before the heat of His countenance.

St. Seraphim of Sarov

MARTYR ELIAS CHAVCHAVADZE OF GEORGIA. Elias was born in Kakheti, nineteenth-century Georgia. He was a poet and leader of the religious and civil life, even though Orthodox spirituality was under the control of the Russian government. Elias chastised the government for whitewashing the ancient icons. He worked towards returning the country to its Orthodox roots, for a restored Georgian episcopacy, as well as the return of chants and the native language that had been suppressed. He was often heard saying, "We, the Georgian people, have inherited three divine gifts from our ancestors: our motherland, our language, and our faith. If we fail to protect these gifts, what merit will we have as men?" His energies helped to begin a spiritual and literary revival. But these deeds were a threat to those who followed the new atheist ideology, so he was assassinated by the secret police in 1907. The things that Ilia believed in and fought for have finally begun to be implemented. St. Elias was canonized in 1988.

SAINTS OF THE DAY: Elias (Elijah) the Prophet; Elias, Patriarch of Jerusalem; Flavian, Patriarch of Antioch; Lydia, Alexis, and Cyril of Russia; Elias Chavachavadze of Georgia; Philosoph Omalsky, and those with him; Salome of Jerusalem; Abramius of Galich; Deacon Juvenal; Alexis of Ugine, France; Elias Fondaminsky, Demetrius Klepinine, George Skobtsov, and Nun Maria Skobtsova of Paris; Tikhon, George, Cosmas, John, Sergius, Theodore, Alexander, George, Euthymius, and Peter, at Voronezh; Ethelwida, widow of King Alfred the Great.

July 21

Romans 13:1-10; Matthew 12:30-37

The enemy is always prepared to attack. And since his missiles which steal upon us secretly are more frequent and his casting of them more concealed and clandestine, and to the extent that this is not perceived, this attack is the more effectual and more frequent to our injury… Among these is the devil of jealousy and envy. If anyone should look deeply into this, he will discover that nothing should be avoided more by a Christian, nothing provided for more cautiously than that one be not caught by envy and malice, that one, being entangled in the blind snares of a deceitful enemy, when brother by envy turns to hatred of brother, not himself unwittingly perish by his own sword. That we may be able to gather this more fully and perceive it more clearly, let us recur to its source and origin. Let us see from what jealousy begins, both when and how. For more easily will so pernicious an evil be avoided, if both the origin and magnitude of the same is known.

St. Cyprian of Carthage

MARTYRS THEOPHILOS AND TROPHIMOS, AND 13 MARTYRS WHO SUFFERED AT ROME. These confessors of the faith were brought to trial in the year 305, which was the final year of the persecuting reign of Emperor Diocletian. When they could not be coerced to deny Jesus Christ, their skin was lacerated and scraped, and stoning broke their bones. After these tortures, they were cast into a roaring fire, but the flames did not harm them. Finally, they were beheaded.

SAINTS OF THE DAY: Symeon of Emesa and John; Parthenius of Radobysdios; Acacius of Constantinople; Eleutherius of "Dry Hill"; Martyrs Justus, Matthew, and Eugene; Victor of Marseilles; Bargabdesian at Arbela; Paul and John, near Edessa; Raphael and Parthenius of Old Agapia; Onuphrius the Silent; Zoticus of Comana; Onesimus of the Kiev Caves; Three Martyrs of Melitene; Simo, Milan, and Milan of Serbia; Praxedes, at Rome.

Eighth Sunday of Matthew
Fast-free

JULY 22

1 Corinthians 10-17; Matthew 14:14-22

Oh, what great happiness and bliss, what exaltation it is to address oneself to the Eternal Father. Always, without fail, value this joy which has been accorded to you by God's infinite grace and do not forget it during your prayers; God, the angels and God's holy men listen to you.

+*Elder Joseph the Hesychast*

WANDREGISILUS OF CAUX. In the seventh-century kingdom of Austrasia, the youthful Wandregislus was made a count of the palace. He was humble and mortified amidst pleasures. To save himself from the dissipation of hurry and much conversation, he frequently retired into his closet and there conversed much with God in prayer. In compliance with the will of his parents, he took a wife who was virtuous and noble. But on the very day of his marriage, he obtained her consent that they should both consecrate their virginity to God. Later, Wandregislus took the monastic habit and built a monastery on his own estate in order to perfect himself in the most approved rules of an ascetic. About seventeen years later, he founded the famous monastery of Fontenelle and became the abbot of 300 monks. His life was austere; he slept little, was clad in sackcloth, and was exact in all the exercises of monastic life. At ninety-six years of age, St. Wandregislus died peacefully.

SAINTS OF THE DAY: Myrrh-bearer and Equal-to-the-Apostles Mary Magdalene; Cyril I, Patriarch of Antioch; Marcella of Chios; Cyprian, fool-for-Christ of Suzdal; Cornelius of Pereyaslavl; Wandregislus of Caux (Gaul); Translation of the relics of St. Phocas, Bishop of Sinope.

JULY 23

1 Corinthians 11:31-12:6; Matthew 18:1-11

It is better to be despised than to despise. It is better to be insulted than to insult another.

+Elder Justin Parvu of Romania

TWO-HUNDRED FIFTY MARTYRS KILLED BY THE BULGARIANS. These Byzantine Christian soldiers served under Emperor Nicephoros I in the ninth century. St. Theophanes the Confessor said that Emperor Nicephoros was tyrannical, evil, and heretical. He was also known for his greed, licentiousness, and barbaric cruelty. He employed magic and incantations to destroy his enemies, and he defended a false hermit who blasphemed the holy icons. In many ways, the emperor mistreated and misused his Christian subjects. St. Theophanes wrote, "At no time did Christians have the misfortune of experiencing a rule more grievous than his." In 811 A.D., the emperor attacked Bulgaria. Khan Krum led the Bulgarian army. He did not want the conflict and asked for peace, but Nicephoros sacked the city. He also plundered Krum's palace, laying claim to Khan's treasure, and setting fire to his court. When Nicephoros left, Krum quickly built wooden barricades to cut off their retreat. Three days later, he trapped the Byzantine army in a mountain pass, killing Nicephoros, his commanders, and a throng of Christian soldiers. Many Christian widows and orphans were left that day. Those who survived were captured and tortured. They were coerced to renounce Christ, and when they refused, they were executed by beheading, hanging, pierced with arrows, and starved in prison.

SAINTS OF THE DAY: Ezekiel the Prophet; Trophimos, Theophilos, and 13 others; Anna (Hannah), mother of Prophet Samuel; Eight Martyrs of Carthage; Nectarius of Yaransk; Anna of Leucadia; Apollonius at Rome; 250 Martyrs killed by the Bulgarians; John (Jacob) of Neamts; Apollinarius of Ravenna; Theodore Ushakov; Pelagia of Tinos; Repose of John Cassian the Roman; Translation of the relics of St. Herman of Kazan; "The Joy of All Who Sorrow" and "Pochaev" Icons of the Mother of God.

July 24

1 Corinthians 12:12-26
Matthew 18:18-22, 19:1-2, 13-15

A pre-disposition to self-deception is thinking you are somebody, and showing others that you're doing something important. It's imagining that you have reached spiritual heights, because you believe—let's say—that you have self-discipline; as opposed to *'these others here, who haven't yet even begun to understand the meaning of spiritual life.'* Behaving in such a proud manner is clearly a disposition to deception.

St. Paisios the Athonite

DECLAN, BISHOP OF ARDMORE. As a young boy at the beginning of fifth-century Ireland, Declan was sent to fosterage with a certain Dimma, who was a foreigner and a Christian. Under Dimma's guardianship, Declan was converted and baptized. He left for Rome where he studied for the priesthood and was later consecrated a bishop. On his return to Ireland, Declan established a monastic community. He was an active missionary in Ireland before the arrival of St. Patrick, the great organizer of Irish Christianity. Many miracles are credited to Declan. By his prayers and fasting, a severe plague was arrested. The waters of St. Declan's well are said to possess miraculous powers of healing from sprains, injuries, and rheumatism.

SAINTS OF THE DAY: Christina of Tyre; Boris and Gleb of Russia; Pachomius, abbot; Hilarion of Tvali; Bernulphus, Bishop of Utrecht; Theophilos of Zakynthos, at Chios; Athanasius of Nicaea; Polycarp of the Kiev Caves; John Kalinin of Olenevka; Bogolep, child schemamonk of Cherny Yar; Declan, Bishop of Ardmore (Ireland); Seventeen New Martyrs of Mgarsk Monastery (Poltava); Alexander of Bolshaya Rechka; Martyrs Capito and Hymenaeus; Martyr Hermogenes; Serbian New Martyrs of Prebilovci (Herzegovina).

WEDNESDAY

JULY 25

Dormition of St. Anna, Mother of the Theotokos
Abstain from meat and dairy products, and fish.
Galatians 4:22-27; Luke 8:16-21

Tending the sick is one of the most powerful means of preserving purity.

St. Macarius of Optina

VENERABLE MACARIUS, ABBOT OF ZHELTOVOD AND UNZHA. Macarius was born into a pious family in fourteenth-century Nizhni-Novgorod. He secretly left home at age twelve and took monastic tonsure at the Nizhegorodsk Pechersk monastery, under the elder St. Dionysios. Macarius distinguished himself with his strict fasting and carefully following his monastic-rule. He left the world so completely that he would not even see his father who had come to see him, saying they would see each other in the next life. With his prayers, Macarius once healed a blind and demon-possessed girl. As his fame spread, he went to live alone near Lake Zhelta. By his ascetic endeavors, patience, and determination, he overcame demonic abuse. Others began to gather around him, and at the age of eighty-six, he organized a monastery. He also taught the surrounding peoples and baptized them in the lake. Four years later, the Kazan Tartars destroyed the monastery, taking Macarius captive. Out of respect for his piety and love, the Khan released Macarius and four hundred Christians. Macarius buried the dead from his monastery and traveled a great distance to Lake Unzha on the Galich border. Through his prayers, all those with him were miraculously fed during their travels. Macarius built a new monastery and lived there five more years. He died peacefully in the fifteenth century, at the age of ninety-five. In the seventeenth century, more than fifty miraculous healings were reported at the site of the saint's relics. When the Tartars attacked the monastery to destroy the silver reliquary where the holy relics of St. Macarius were kept, they were blinded. They fled in fright, many of them drowning in the Unzha River.

SAINTS OF THE DAY: Sanctus, Maturus, and others; Olympias the Deaconess; Eupraxia of Tabenna; Vukosav and Rodoljub of Serbia; Theodore of Lovets; Gregory of Thessalonica; Synaxis of the Holy 165 Fathers of the Fifth Ecumenical Council.

JULY 26

Galatians 3:23-4:5; Mark 5:24-34

Let not one think, my fellow Christian, that only priests and monks need to pray without ceasing and not laymen. No, no; every Christian without exception ought to dwell always in prayer.

St. Gregory Palamas

VENERABLE MOSES THE HUNGARIAN OF PECHERSK. Moses and his two brothers, Ephraim and George, became saints of the Church. Moses became a prisoner of Poland. A rich widow desired the handsome Moses, and she paid his ransom hoping to marry him, but he refused, wanting instead to become a monk. She tried to entice him with banquets and riches, but he still refused, saying that he would not trade spiritual riches for perishable things of this world. Passing through the area was a hieromonk from Mt. Athos, and he gave Moses monastic tonsure. The Polish widow had Moses stretched on the ground and beaten with rods. After this, she had him put in bed, and she tried to seduce him but failed. She gave orders to give Moses one hundred lashes a day, and then to emasculate him. Even so, God gave Moses strength in his suffering. Finally, the woman was killed during a revolt in Poland. When he recovered from his wounds, Moses went to live at the Pechersk monastery. Once, a monk who had impure passions went to Moses for advice. Moses told him never to speak to a woman again and struck the fellow monk in the chest with his staff. Immediately, the brother was quickly cured of his temptation. Moses lived there ten years before dying peacefully. Any monk who venerated the relics of St. Moses was cured of fleshly temptations.

SAINTS OF THE DAY: Paraskeva of Rome; Jerusalem of Byzantium; Hermolaus, Hermippos, and Hermocrates at Nicomedia; Oriozela of Reuma; Ignatius of Mt. Stirion; Sava III, Archbishop of Serbia; Gerontios of the Skete of St. Anne; Ioannicius the New of Muscel (Romania); Theodosius of the Caucasus; Isaac of Svyatogorsk Monastery; Moses the Hungarian of the Kiev Caves; Jacob, Enlightener of the peoples of Alaska; "Emvolon" Icon of the Mother of God, in Constantinople.

FRIDAY

JULY 27

Abstain from meat and dairy products, and fish.
2 Timothy 2:1-10; John 15:17-16:2

Those who possess the fear of God are the furthest from telling lies, because they have an honest judge, their own conscience.

St. John Climacus

RIGHTEOUS ANTHOUSA, ABBESS OF MANTINEA IN ASIA MINOR. As a young girl, Anthousa chose to live in caves and wander in the mountains of eighth-century Asia Minor. She sought St. Sisinios, a renowned clairvoyant elder, and became his obedient spiritual child. He foretold that she would one day create a convent for ninety nuns. Living alone, Anthousa wore chains and a hair shirt to subdue her body. She received monastic tonsure from Sisinios and gave the blessing to build a church dedicated to St. Anna, and there the ninety nuns gathered around her. When Emperor Constantine Copronymos fell under the influence of the occult, he banned the veneration of holy icons. For not obeying his orders, Anthousa was brought before the emperor and flogged for four days, while charcoal was burned under her feet and icons burned over her head. By God's grace, she remained unharmed. When the emperor arrived to continue the torture, God blinded him. The emperor's heart softened when Anthousa's prayer healed him. Knowing that Anthousa was clairvoyant, he asked about the outcome of his wife's pregnancy. She told him that his wife would bear twins, a boy, and a girl, and this was fulfilled. Anthousa was set free. She returned to her convent and died in extreme old age.

SAINTS OF THE DAY: Great Martyr and Healer Panteleimon; Clement of Ochrid, and Angelarius, Gorazd, Nahum, and Sabbas, disciples of Sts. Cyril and Methodios; Anthousa of Mantinea in Asia Minor, and her 90 sisters; The blind man who confessed Christ and was healed by St. Panteleimon; The 853 Martyrs of Thrace who were drowned; Christodulus of Cassandra; Ambrose (Gudko), Bishop of Sarapul; Joasaph, Metropolitan of Moscow; Nicholas Kochanov of Novgorod, fool-for-Christ; Righteous Manuel; Aurelius, Sabigotha (Natalia), Felix, Liliosa, and George the Sabbaite, at Cordoba; Glorification of St. Herman of Alaska.

JULY 28

Acts 6:1-7; Matthew 15:32-39

It happens, I do not know how, that most of the proud never really discover their true selves. They think they have conquered their passions and they find out how poor they really are only after they die.

St. John Climacus

SAMSON, BISHOP OF DOL IN BRITTANY. Samson was from fifth-century Wales. He was one of the greatest missionaries ever to come from Britain. His parents dedicated him to the service of God because of their promise from prolonged childlessness. He was raised in a monastery where St. Illtyd was abbot. Later, Samson was ordained deacon and priest, and for a while, he lived as a hermit. Afterward, he was consecrated bishop and abbot of a monastery. He began his work as a missionary, traveling throughout Cornwall. He founded monasteries and churches and gathered to himself disciples, several of which became saints themselves. Finally, Samson went to Brittany where he was given land to build a monastery, and this became the spiritual center of Britain. Once again Samson established numerous monasteries. When he felt that the end of his life was nearing, he embarked on an extensive journey accompanied by seven monks, seven disciples, and seven escorts. He traveled from parish to parish, often stopping to preach and celebrate the Divine Offerings. He did this until death brought this mission to an end. Many miracles were attributed to him. St. Samson is depicted with a cross or staff together with a dove and book.

SAINTS OF THE DAY: Prochorus, Nicanor, Timon, and Parmenas, of the Seventy; Paul of Xeropotamou; Julian of Dalmatia; Eustathius the Soldier; Acacius of Apamea; Irene Chrysovolantou of Cappadocia; Ursus and Leobatius of Gaul; Anastasius of Ancyra; Anthony of Rostov; George the Builder of Iveron; Pitirim of Tambov; Samson of Dol; Basil of Sarov Monastery; Ignatius of Jablechna (Poland); Moses of the Kiev Caves; Synaxis of All Saints of Tambov.

SUNDAY

Ninth Sunday of Matthew
Fast-free

JULY 29

1 Corinthians 3:9-17; Matthew 14:22-34

Shut all the gates of your soul, that is the senses, so as to not be lured astray. When the nous sees that it is not dominated by anything, it prepares itself for immortality, gathering its senses together and forming them into one body.

St. Isaiah the Anchorite

MARTYR KALLINIKOS OF GANGRA IN ASIA MINOR. Kallinikos, a missionary, was a powerful speaker for Christianity in the third century. Trained by monks, he was compelled by the clergy to take the message of Jesus Christ to the pagan cities and villages. He converted idol-worshippers in such large numbers that the governor of Ancyra challenged him to a public debate. When Kallinikos shredded the arguments of the governor, he was threatened with martyrdom and death if he did not worship the idols. Kallinikos told him that he was not afraid of martyrdom. Because of his popularity, the governor would not execute Kallinikos, but sent him instead on a sixty-mile march to Gangra, shod in iron shoes with sharp nails within. When there was no water for the thirsty soldiers, they implored Kallinikos to ask God for water. Having pity on his tormentors, he prayed, and a spring of water miraculously drew forth from a stone. The soldiers wanted to set Kallinikos free, but they feared execution. In Gangra, Kallinikos gave thanks to the Lord and entered the blazing bonfire where he gave up his soul. His body remained unharmed and was reverently buried by Christians.

SAINTS OF THE DAY: Kallinikos of Gangra; Theodota and her three sons, in Bithynia; Theodota of Asia Minor; Benjamin and Berius of Constantinople; Constantine I, Patriarch of Constantinople; Seraphima of Antioch; Bessarion of Bulgaria; John the Soldier; Constantine and Cosmas of Kosinsk; Mamas in Darii; Romanus of Kirzhach; Eustathius of Mtskheta; Lupus of Troyes; Theodosius the New; Basiliscus the Elder; Bogolep of Black Ravine; Olaf of Norway; Anatole of the Caucasus Mountains; Seraphim and Theognostus, at Kazakhstan.

JULY 30

Acts 15:35-41; Matthew 21:28-22

What God wants is not golden chalices, but golden souls.

St. John Chrysostom

TSOTNE DADIANI THE CONFESSOR. Tsotne was the prince of Egrisi and the military leader in the thirteenth-century country of Georgia. During this time of Mongol domination, they began to extort large payments from the Georgian princes and demanded military service from Georgian subjects. Rulers from all over Georgia planned an all-out rebellion. They gathered all their troops at Mt. Kokhta for a single front attack. Tsotne and the ruler of Racha were the first to do so. However, there were traitors, and they informed the Mongols. They surrounded the Georgians and arrested everyone, except for Tsotne and the other ruler who were led away to the Mongol ruler. All the prisoners denied the proposed attack, saying that they had all gathered to collect the money that the Mongol authorities demanded of them. Infuriated by this lie, the Mongols stripped the Georgians, smeared them with honey, and left them bound in the hot sun for days. Tsotne was deeply saddened when he heard this. Out of love and devotion for his men, he took the blame upon himself. He traveled to this site, disrobed, bound himself, and lay down next to his men. When the Mongol ruler was informed of this, he summoned Tsotne, demanding an explanation. Tsotne reiterated what his men said, and if his countrymen were being punished for collecting the tribute, then he wanted to share in their lot. This so impressed the Mongols that they set everyone free.

SAINTS OF THE DAY: Silas, Silvanos, Crescens, Epenetos, and Andronikos, of the Seventy; Julitta at Caesarea; Valentine, Proculus, Ephebus, Apollonius, and Abundius; Polychronius of Babylon and Parmenius, Helimenas, Chrysotelus, Luke, Mocius, Abdon, Sennen, Maximus, and Olympius; Stephen Vladislav of Serbia; Anatole II of Optina; Alexander the Chanter; Angelina Brancovich of Serbia; Tsotne Dadiani of Mingrelia; Uncovering of the relics of St. Herman of Solovki; Synaxis of the Saints of Samara; "Okonsk" Icon of the Mother of God.

TUESDAY

Forefeast of the Precious Cross
Fast-free

JULY 31

1 Corinthians 15:29-38; Matthew 21:23-27

The value of fasting is so great, that even if it had not been instituted by the Church, she would have to institute is now. How much less then should we seek to abolish or alter an institution already established centuries ago, which has manifested so many Saints.

+Elder Epiphanios Theodoropoulos of Athens

ARSENIUS, BISHOP OF NINOTSMINDA IN GEORGIA. Arsenius was tonsured a monk in Jerusalem in the eleventh century. He was later consecrated bishop of Ninotsminda in the country of Georgia. However, he desired to live a life of solitude. He asked King Davit Kuropalates for permission to resign his post to settle in a monastery. The king honored his request, so Arsenius and Ioane Grdzeslidze, who was known as a man of letters, set off on their journey. When this news reached the Iveron Monastery on Mt. Athos, Sts. John and Ekvtime invited them to Iveron. When they arrived the following year, they helped St. Ekvtime translate many theological books, as well as the Holy Scriptures. Arsenius became known as an excellent translator, calligrapher, writer, and theologian. He was one of the most respected Church figures of his era, as was his friend John. St. Arsenius worked at his craft many years on Mt. Athos and died peacefully at an advanced age.

SAINTS OF THE DAY: Joseph of Arimathea; Julitta, at Caesarea in Cappadocia; Eudokimos of Cappadocia; John the Exarch of Bulgaria; Germanus, Bishop of Auxerre; Twelve Martyrs of Rome; Dionysius of Vatopedi, Mt. Athos; Benjamin, Sergius, George, and John of Petrograd; Basil of Kineshma; Neot, hermit in Cornwall; Arsenius, Bishop of Ninotsminda; Consecration of the Church of the Most Holy Theotokos of Blachernae; Translation of the relics of Apostle Philip to Cyprus.

If you feel sweetness or compunction at some word of your prayer, dwell on it; for then our guardian angel is praying with us.

St. John Climacus

Wednesday

August 1

Procession of the Precious Cross
Dormition Fast Begins—Strict Fast
Hebrews 11:33-12:2; Matthew 10:16-22

Do not restrict the goodness of fasting only in abstaining from food. For, true fasting is to avoid injustices.

St. Basil the Great

MARTYR ALMEDHA OF WALES. Almedha was one of the many daughters of King Brychan in South Wales, who embraced the new faith of Christianity. Almedha also became a Christian at a young age. When a pagan prince made advances, she ran away, like many women of her time, to avoid being forced into a relationship. She traveled from town to town, trying to find refuge, but time and again she was ousted by the inhabitants on the pretext of thievery. She did not find peace until she arrived at Slwch Tump, where the local lord gave her protection. But Almedha's pursuer found her. When she ran from him, he chased her downhill and beheaded her. Her head rolled down the hill and hit a stone. A healing spring burst forth from that spot. St. Almedha's well was associated with healings and other miracles.

SAINTS OF THE DAY: Holy Seven Maccabees: Abimus, Antonius, Gurias, Eleazar, Eusebonus, Alimus, and Marcellus, and their mother Solomonia, and their teacher Eleazar; Nine Martyrs of Perga: Leontius, Attius, Alexander, Cindeus, Minsitheus, Cyriacus, Menaeus, Catanus, and Eucleus; Timothy, Archbishop of Priconissus; Nicholas, enlightener of Japan; Eusebius, Bishop of Verceil (Italy); Basil, Archbishop of Chernigov; Elessa of Cythera; Papas the New; Martyr Eleazar; Martyrs Theodore and Polyeuctus; Menas, Menais, and others of England; Sidwell of Exeter; Ethelwold, Bishop of Winchester; Cennydd of Llangenydd (Wales); Almedha of Wales; Alexander (Urodov) of Sanaxar and Seven Lakes.

 Strict Fast

AUGUST 2

Acts 6:8-15, 7:1-5, 47-60; Matthew 12:1-12

The death of the body is grievous and fearful, even terrifying to those who have remained all their lives in love with their own flesh.

St. John Chrysostom

JUSTINIAN THE EMPEROR. Justinian reigned as emperor of sixth-century Byzantium for thirty-eight years. He was brought to Constantinople to be educated by his uncle, Justin I, who was head of the personal guard for the emperor. Justinian was then assigned to the emperor's guard and was later promoted to lead the armies in the east. He became the force behind his uncle's government, who was now the emperor. Justinian married Theodora who proved to be his closest and most trusted advisor. When Justin was close to death, he appointed Justinian co-emperor, and Theodora became his co-ruler. Emperor Justinian worked to establish the unity of Church and State. He healed the Akakian schism between Rome and Constantinople and attacked the Monophysite heresy and the Origenists. He lived like an ascetic, fasting often, and working with only a few hours' sleep. He was humble and accessible. He reconstructed and built more than thirty churches in Constantinople alone, including the construction of the church of St. Sophia. When rioters attacked, Theodora counseled him to act decisively, and Justinian crushed the revolt. Justinian and Theodora endowed churches, monasteries, orphanages, hospitals, and rehabilitated former prostitutes. They built poorhouses, hospices, homes for the aged, and reservoirs. Free bread was given to the poor and disabled. Justinian compiled a complete compendium of Roman laws into an orderly system. He made a tremendous effort to root out paganism. St. Justinian died on November 14, 565.

SAINTS OF THE DAY: Translation of the relics of Protomartyr Stephen; Theodore of the Dardanelles; Friardus of Gaul; Basil of Moscow; Marco of Belavinsk; Emperor Justinian and Theodora; Stephen, Pope of Rome; Martyr Phocas; Basil of Kuben Lake.

Strict Fast

AUGUST 3

2 Corinthians 1:12-20; Matthew 22:23-33

If one wishes to do something but cannot, in the sight of God, Who knows men's hearts, it is as if he had done it. This principal is to be understood as applying both to good and bad actions. The mind can do many things, both good and bad, without the body. However, without the mind, the body can do neither good nor evil; because the law of freedom exists in the mind prior to any action.

St. Mark the Ascetic

VIRGIN TREA OF ARDTREA. When St. Patrick entered the northern part of the Ulster province, he encountered opposition from a dynasty. There were two brothers, Carthenn the Elder, a wicked man and a pagan, and Carthenn the Younger, who was banished by his older brother. Likewise, Carthenn the Elder banished St. Patrick. The saint went from town to town. He baptized the virtuous and kindly Carthenn the Younger with his wife and family. After a time, his wife Mugania gave birth to a daughter, Trea. At the baptismal font, St. Patrick prophesied that she was destined to a life of grace. When she grew up, she became one of the many holy virgins St. Patrick veiled. When she stood before St. Patrick, an angel was seen descending from heaven and placing a veil on her head. It completely covered her eyes. St. Patrick attempted to lift it so that Trea might see better, but she said, "O pious father, why cannot the veil remain as it has been placed in its right position?" St. Patrick replied that it could. It was as if the veil were glued to the noble lady's face, and it covered her dove-like eyes and soft cheeks through the remaining term of her life.

SAINTS OF THE DAY: Isaac, Dalmatius, and Faustus of the Dalmatian Monastery; Holy Myrrh-bearer Salome; John of Patalaria; Theodora of Thessalonica; Cosmas of Palestine; Anthony the Roman; Theocleto of Optimaton; Rajden of Tsromi; Nine Kherkheulidze brothers, with their sister and mother and 9,000 martyrs of Georgia; Trea of Ardtrea.

SATURDAY

Abstain from meat and dairy products, and fish.

Romans 15:30-33; Matthew 17:24-18:4

AUGUST 4

Temptations and trials show what hides in the heart of a man. Temptation is similar to the medicine called an emetic. An emetic reveals what is hidden inside the stomach. So temptations and trials make manifest what is hidden inside a man. The Holy Word of God and other Christian books point out the corruption of our nature, but we recognize it by actual experience or deed in temptations and trials. Thus vainglory becomes evident through deprivation of glory, avarice through deprivation of riches, envy through success of one's neighbor, and anger through disappointment. If, then, you fall into various temptations, O Christian, this all happens by God's permission for your great benefit, that you may thereby know what is hidden in your heart, and so knowing it, you may correct yourself.

St. Tikhon of Zadonsk

MARTYR IA AND 9,000 WITH HER IN PERSIA. Ia was a Christian living in Persia during the reign of the emperor Sapor II. She was one of 9,000 Christians who was arrested and taken to the city of Bisada. The chief of the Persian sorcerers demanded that Ia renounce Christ. When she refused, she was repeatedly tortured, imprisoned, and finally beheaded. According to tradition, the sun darkened at the hour of her beheading, and a sweet fragrance filled the air.

SAINTS OF THE DAY: Holy Seven Youths of Ephesus ("Seven Sleepers"): Maximilian, Jamblicus, Martinian, John, Dionysius, Exacustodian (Constantine), and Antoninus; Ia and 9,000 with her in Persia; Eleutherius of Constantinople; Michael (Zhuk) of Staroye Zubarevo (Mordovia); Martyr Thathuil; Molua of Killaloe (Ireland); Eudocia of Persia; Consecration of the Church of Jesus Christ the Pantocrator in Constantinople.

SUNDAY

Tenth Sunday of Matthew
Forefeast of the Transfiguration
Abstain from meat and dairy products, and fish.

AUGUST 5

1 Corinthians 4:9-16; Matthew 17:14-23

Fear evil like fire. Don't let it touch your heart, even if it seems just or righteous.

St. John of Kronstadt

EUDOCIA OF PUZO AND MARIA, DARIA, AND DARIA. When Eudocia was nine years old, she befriended a girl named Maria, and they were inseparable for three years. When Eudocia was seventeen, she fell seriously ill and could only walk with a stick. Later, at the age of twenty, her condition worsened, and she burst out, saying, "I'm dying, I'm on fire." From that day, she never got up again. She was chained to her bed for about thirty-five years, and several families took constant care of her. She lived in extreme poverty, wearing the same few clothes and never cutting her hair or nails. The Russian people had a special veneration for her great suffering. People came from great distances seeking spiritual edification. Eudocia was granted the gift of clairvoyance, and she more than once prophesied her own death. She read well but was unable to write. She read the lives of the saints most of all. She had a good voice and could recite the Psalter and chant verses and hymns by heart. However, during the Russian Revolution, Eudocia and three other virgins who cared for her, were arrested, interrogated, and beaten. There was a mock trial, and they were sentenced to execution. Just before their death, some women who were tending their flocks saw four columns of light rising from the cemetery to heaven. The four virgins received the Holy Mysteries, and this gave them joy. One of the soldiers saw a white dove with outstretched wings hovering above the martyrs, protecting them. He would not shoot, but the others did. A grave was dug, and the martyrs were placed therein. There was a rumor that some people brought coffins by night and transferred the saints into them, giving them an Orthodox burial.

SAINTS OF THE DAY: Eusignius of Antioch; Pontius at Cimella; Nonna, mother of St. Gregory the Theologian; John Jacob of Neamt; Job the Gorge-dweller; Eugenius of Anatolia.

MONDAY

Holy Transfiguration
Abstain from meat and dairy products.
2 Peter 1:10-19; Matthew 17:1-9

AUGUST 6

When man fell, he not only fell below his dignity, he also accepted internally some principles foreign to his proper nature, the seeds, as it were, of every kind of evil. Consequently, in fallen man we must differentiate what is proper to his nature and what is alien to it, although this, too, is found in man. All constraining rules and measures, prescribed and established by God, are exclusively aimed against these alien and evil seeds, in order to crush them, to suffocate them, and thereby to set at liberty man's true nature.

St. Theophan the Recluse

THEOCTISTUS, BISHOP OF CHERNIGOV. Before becoming a bishop, Theoctistus was a monk at the Kiev-Pechersk Monastery in the late eleventh century. He had the gift of wonderworking, and by his prayers, he once healed St. Nikita, the future bishop of Novgorod. In 1103, Theoctistus became the abbot of the monastery, and five years later, through the generosity of Prince Gleb, he built a stone dining hall. Two years later, a heavenly pillar of fire rose from the ground to the sky, lighting up the earth. It stood over the dining hall and moved over the church, settling over the grave of St. Theodosius, and disappearing to the east. St. Nestor the Chronicler wrote that this was a manifestation of an angel of God. In 1113, Theoctistus was consecrated bishop of Chernigov. He participated in the transfer of the relics of Sts. Boris and Gleb. Later he consecrated a church in their names. St. Theoctistus died peacefully, and it is said that he was buried at the Pechersk Monastery.

SAINTS OF THE DAY: Theoctistus, Bishop of Chernigov; Abbacum of Thessalonica; New Martyrs Dimitri (Lyubimov), Archbishop of Gdov, and Nicholas Prozorov, Andrew Zimin, Sergius Tikhomirov, Domnik, Lidia, and Mary Zimin, of Russia; New Virgin-martyr Eudocia, near Sarov.

AUGUST 7

2 Corinthians 2:14-3:3; Mark 9:2-9

We cannot be saved if we love the pleasures of the world.

+*Elder Paisius of Sihla*

VENERABLE HORUS OF THE THEBAID. From his youth, Horus lived in the fourth-century Thebaid wilderness in solitude and asceticism. After many years, an angel of God visited him, announcing that many people would come to him for guidance. Horus accepted everyone who came to him for advice and help. Eventually, a large monastery formed around him, and he became the abbot. God granted him the gift of reading Holy Scripture, even though he never learned to read and write. He taught the monks by telling stories about the desert monks and the temptations of living in solitude. Everyone knew that Horus knew these monks personally. Horus would not eat in the dining hall, nor eat at all on the day that he communed the Holy Mysteries. One time, when Pascha was approaching, he stood for three days outside with arms outstretched in prayer. He told a disciple that on every feast day and during Pascha, one should keep his mind only on God and not on earthly things. Horus knew all the thoughts and deeds of his disciples, and no one dared to lie to him. By the time of his death, at the age of ninety, St. Horus had established several monasteries, with as many as one thousand monastics.

SAINTS OF THE DAY: Holy 10,000 Ascetics of Thebes; Narcissus, Patriarch of Jerusalem; Marinus and Asterius the Senator at Caesarea; Sozon of Nicomedia; Horus of the Thebaid; Nicanor of Mt. Callistratus; Hyperechius of *The Paradise;* Potamia of Alexandria; Dometius of Persia and two disciples; Mercurius of Smolensk; Dometius of Philotheou; Theodora of Sihla; Anthony of Optina; Pimen the Much-ailing of the Kiev Caves; Theodosius the New; Pimen, faster of the Kiev Caves; Joseph of Kapsa; Victricius of Rouen; Irene and Pulcheria of Constantinople; Alexander, Peter, Michael, John, Demetrius, Alexei, Elisha, and Athanasius, of Moscow; Uncovering of the relics of St. Metrophanes of Voronezh; "Valamo" Icon of the Mother of God in Heinavesi, Finland.

AUGUST 8

2 Corinthians 3:4-11; Matthew 23:29-39

To be a Christian is to affirm God as Creator of the universe; and when a Christian looks at the beauty and glory of what God has made, praise and thanksgiving pour form the lips.

St. John Chrysostom

VENERABLE GREGORY THE SINAITE. Gregory was born near the city of Smyrna in the thirteenth century. He was taken into captivity by the Hagarenes and sent to Laodicea. When he gained his freedom, he went to the island of Cyprus, where he took monastic tonsure. He went to Mount Sinai in Egypt, where Moses spoke with God. He received the great schema and fulfilled his obediences of cook, baker, and copyist of Scripture. He led a strict life of fasting, prayer, vigil, and psalmody. He visited Jerusalem and Crete, and afterward Mt. Athos to learn more about mental prayer and contemplation. However, this type of asceticism was not common yet on Athos. Gregory finally found the only monk on Mt. Athos who was experienced and perfect in his practice of this type of prayer, St. Maximus of Kapsokalyvia. Gregory became his student, and when he had mastered the art, he settled in a solitary place for silence and mental prayer. Gregory founded several cells on Mt. Athos, and four monasteries in Thrace. His teaching about the inner life can be found in *The Philokalia*, a collection of 1,100 years of wisdom of the Church Fathers. St. Gregory is also a renowned Hymnographer. He wrote the hymn "It is Truly Meet" and a Canon to the Mother of God, which is read at Sunday Vigil. He died peacefully.

SAINTS OF THE DAY: Gregory of Sinai; Myron of Crete; Eleutherius and Leonides of Constantinople, with many infants; Emilian the Confessor; Gormizdas of Persia; Gregory of Sinai; Gregory of the Kiev Caves; Gregory of the Kiev Caves; Anastasius of Radovishte; Philaret of Ivanovo; 12 Ascetics of Egypt; Euthymius of Georgia; Triandaphillos of Zagora; 2 Martyrs of Tyre; Zosimas the Sinaite; Martyr Styracius; Joseph of Tolga; Nicholas of Pokrovskoye; Nicodemus of Kostroma.

AUGUST 9

Acts 1:12-17, 21-26; Matthew 24:13-28

One who does not have a Spiritual Father—as an advisor on his spiritual journey—will get confused, weary, delayed; and will find it hard to reach his destination. No matter how wise he may be, if he comes up with solutions to his problems on his own, he will remain in darkness; for he proceeds with self-confidence and pride. But one who is humble goes to his Spiritual Father and asks his opinion and guidance, and is greatly helped. God will certainly enlighten the Spiritual father to provide the right answer.

St. Paisios the Athonite

MARTYR ANTHONY OF ALEXANDRIA. During the persecutions in Alexandria, Anthony was arrested. He would not hide or deny his Christian faith but freely confessed it. In an attempt to force Anthony to deny Jesus Christ, he was tied to a tree and flogged. He was sentenced to burning. A fire was prepared, and he was cast in. From within the flames, Anthony taught the people standing about who were witnessing his martyrdom. He implored them not to give thought to the body but to the soul, which was given by God. The flames soon consumed St. Anthony, but his body remained unharmed.

SAINTS OF THE DAY: Apostle Matthias; Julian, Marcian, John, James, Alexius, Demetrius, Photius, Peter, Leontius, Mary, and others, of Constantinople; Psoes of Egypt; Anthony of Alexandria; Macarius of Oredezh Monastery; Philaret Humilevsky of Chernigov; Felim of Kilmore; Nathy of Achonry; Synaxis of the Saints of Solovki.

August 10

2 Corinthians 4:13-18; Matthew 24:13-28

The believer has to have a Spiritual Father, be guided by his advice and be helped through the Mystery of Repentance and Confession. This is the only way for one to live an Orthodox Christian life, and be certain that he is on the right path. Of course, one should choose a spiritual guide carefully; and not entrust his soul to just anyone. Just as one seeks the best doctor for his physical health, he should also seek out a good Spiritual Father for his spiritual health; and go to him, the doctor of his soul, on a regular basis.

St. Paisios the Athonite

BLAINE OF THE ISLE OF BUTE. Blaine was from sixth-century Scotland, born on the Isle of Bute. His uncle was St. Cathan, who saw to Blaine's education in Ireland under the tutelage of Sts. Comgall and Kenneth. Blaine later became a monk and went to Scotland, where he eventually became a bishop. Several miracles are related to him, including the restoration of a dead boy to life. St. Blaine was buried at his church at Kingarth, Bute.

SAINTS OF THE DAY: Archdeacon Lawrence and Pope Sixtus, Felicissimus, and Agapitus, deacons, and others with them; Hippolytus of Rome and 18 Martyrs with him, including Concordia, Irenaeus, and Abundius; Romanus, soldier of Rome; Six Martyrs of Bizin; Bertram, King of Mercia; Lawrence, fool-for-Christ at Kaluga; Blaine of the Isle of Bute; Heron the Philosopher; Synaxis of New Martyrs and Confessors of Solovki.

SATURDAY

Abstain from meat and dairy products, and fish.

1 Corinthians 1:3-9; Matthew 19:3-12

AUGUST 11

Observe and you will see unholy vanity abounding even to the very grave in fine clothes, oils, servants, perfumes, and such... A vain person is a true idolater; he seems to honor God, but in reality he wishes to please men, not God.

St. John Climacus

HOLY MARTYR AND ARCHDEACON EUPLUS OF CATANIA. During the early fourth-century persecutions, Emperor Diocletian sent a soldier to the Sicilian city of Catania to kill any Christians he found, but they all hid. Euplus regularly preached to the pagans about Christ, always carrying the gospel with him. One time as he was explaining the gospel to a crowd, he was arrested and taken to the governor of the city. He confessed himself a Christian and denounced idol-worship. After being tortured, Euplus was imprisoned and starved for a week. During this time, the Lord caused a spring of water to come forth into the prison to quench the saint's thirst. When Euplus was brought to trial a second time, he again confessed his faith in Christ, and the judge ordered more torture. He was flogged with an iron-tipped whip, but Euplus scoffed at the flogging. His ears were severed, and he was taken to his beheading with the gospel tied around his neck. Before he died, he read the Bible to those assembled and converted many. Miracles have been wrought at the site of St. Euplus' relics near Naples, Italy.

SAINTS OF THE DAY: Euplus of Catania; Niphon, Patriarch of Constantinople; Theodore and Basil of the Kiev Caves; Taurinus, first Bishop of Evreux, Gaul; Virgin-martyr Susanna, and with her: Gaius, Pope of Rome; Gabinus, his brother and father of Susanna; Maximus, Claudius and his wife, Praepedigna, and their sons Alexander and Cuthias; Anastasius of Asomaton in Asia Minor, and Demetrius of Lesbos; Theodore (Theodosius), Prince of Ostrog; John, recluse of Svyatogorsk Monastery; Passarion of Palestine; Martyrs Neophytus, Zeno, Gaius, Mark, Macarius, and Gaianus; Commemoration of the miracle of St. Spyridon on Corfu.

SUNDAY

Eleventh Sunday of Matthew
Abstain from meat and dairy products, and fish.

AUGUST 12

1 Corinthians 9:2-12; Matthew 18:23-35

When one is following the will of God, no insurmountable obstacles will stand in the way.

St. Leo of Optina

HIEROMARTYR ALEXANDER, BISHOP OF COMANA. Alexander lived during the third century near Neocaesarea. He studied the Holy Scripture and took upon himself the ascetic discipline of a holy fool. He suffered in poverty, dressing in rags and selling coal in the city square. When the bishop of Comana died, a council under the leadership of St. Gregory the Wonderworker was assembled to select a new bishop. The group focused on the outward appearance and actions of the candidates and was unable to agree on a selection. Gregory advised that they should focus instead on the inner qualities of the men. One man jokingly said that they might as well consider Alexander, who acted like a fool. Gregory considered this the Providence of God that Alexander's name was mentioned, and he sent for him. Gregory asked Alexander to tell him truthfully who he was. Alexander revealed that he was formerly a philosopher, and had studied Holy Scripture, but for the sake of God humbly suffered in poverty. Gregory had him bathed and dressed, and before the assembly questioned him on Holy Scripture. Everyone was astonished at his knowledge and humility. Gregory ordained him to the priesthood and later bishop. Under Emperor Diocletian, Alexander confessed Christ and refused to worship idols. He was tortured and thrown into a fire, where he gave up his spirit.

SAINTS OF THE DAY: Alexander, Bishop of Comana; Pallamon of Egypt; Martyrs Pamphilus and Capito; 12 soldiers of Crete; Sergius and Stephen, monks; Anicetus and Photius of Nicomedia; Gerontius, Serapion, Germanus, Bessarion, Michael, Simeon, and Otar of Garesja; Molaise of Devenish; Jambert of Canterbury; Seigine of Iona; Muredach (Murtagh) of Killala; Barlaam, Anthony, Sergius, Elijah, Vyacheslav, Ioasaph, John, Micah, Bessarion, Euthymius, and others – of the Belogorsk St. Nicholas Monastery (Perm).

AUGUST 13

2 Corinthians 5:10-15; Mark 1:9-15

Enemies have made me a stranger in worldly realms and an extraneous inhabitant of the world. Just as a hunted animal finds safer shelter than an un-hunted animal does, so have I, persecuted by enemies, found the safest sanctuary, having ensconced myself beneath your tabernacle, where neither friends nor enemies can slay my soul.

St. Nikolai Velimirovich

EMPRESS IRENE (XENIA) OF HUNGARY AND CONSTANTINOPLE. Irene was the pious daughter of the king of Hungary. She married the son of the Emperor of Byzantium, John II Komnenos. They had eight children while living in Constantinople. She beseeched the king on behalf of the poor and became the benefactor of widows, orphans, and monasteries. Considering her station in life, she still lived the life of an ascetic through meekness, self-control, and charity. As empress, she built the Monastery of the Pantocrator in Constantinople. She also had built old age homes, hospitals, and a church. She tearfully begged her husband to continue to finance the monastery, and he agreed to as much as possible. Shortly after this time, she was tonsured a nun, taking the name Xenia. A mosaic of St. Xenia-Irene and her husband is in Hagia Sophia in Constantinople.

SAINTS OF THE DAY: Tikhon, Bishop of Voronezh, wonderworker of Zadonsk; Dorotheos of Gaza; Maximos the Confessor; Xenia-Irene of Hungary and Constantinople; Dositheus of Thawatha; Eudocia the Empress, wife of Theodosius the Younger; Seridus, abbot of Gaza; Radegunde of Poitiers; Wigbert, abbot of Hersfeld; Seraphim (Zvezdinsky), Bishop of Dmitrov; Uncovering of the relics of St. Maximus of Moscow, fool-for-Christ; "Of the Passion," "Minsk," "Of the Seven Arrows," and "The Softening of Evil Hearts" Icons of the Mother of God.

TUESDAY

Forefeast of the Dormition
Strict Fast

AUGUST 14

2 Corinthians 5:15-21; Mark 1:16-22

All the Saints are our helpers, but above all is the Panagia. She has the riches of great compassion. She has great love for mankind, especially for sinners. For this reason she never ceases to mediate to her Son, and the Son takes great joy when His mother intercedes on behalf of mankind. For this reason He brought us His mother and granted her to us that we may have her as a source of salvation.

St. Anthimos of Chios

FACHANAN, ABBOT OF ROSS CARBERY, IRELAND. Fachanan was a pupil of St. Ita and founded the monastery of Molana on an island in the Blackwater. However, his great achievement was the establishment of the monastic school of Ross, which was one of the most famous schools in Ireland that flourished for 300 years until the invading Normans destroyed it. For a time, Fachanan suffered from blindness, but he recovered at the intercession of St. Ita's sister, who was about to give birth to St. Mochoemog. Fachanan was revered as a wise and upright man, with the gift of preaching. He was generous and steadfast, fond of preaching, never saying anything that was base or displeasing to God.

SAINTS OF THE DAY: Prophet Micah; Ursicius at Nicomedia; Nazarius, Herman, Hierotheus, Simon, and Bessarion, of Georgia; Marcellus, Bishop of Apamea; Symeon of Trebizond; Luke the Soldier; Basil, Archbishop of Chernigov, and with him, Matthew and Alexis; Fachanan, abbot of Ross Carbery, Ireland; Matthew and Eleutherius of Holy Trinity Monastery (Smolensk); Eve (Pavlova), abbess of Holy Trinity Convent in Penza; Synaxis of the New Martyrs of Georgia who suffered under the Atheist Yoke; Translation of the relics of Arcadius of Novotorsk and Theodosius of the Kiev Caves; "Narva" and "Converser" Icons of the Mother of God.

Dormition of the Mother of God
Abstain from meat and dairy products.

AUGUST 15

Philippians 2:5-11
Luke 10:38-42, 11:27-28

The Panagia is the only mother of all Christians. And who does not call upon her? Because the sufferings of mankind are many in this vain world, nowhere else can we all find relief, except in the Panagia.

St. Anthimos of Chios

NEW MARTYRS FATHER PAUL SZWAJKO AND PRESBYTERA JOANNA OF GRABOVIEC. Father Paul was born in 1893. The majority of the population in Paul's district was likely Ukrainian Catholic, but Father Paul dedicated himself to Orthodoxy which is at the heart of the Ukrainian Catholic confession. He attended seminary and graduated in 1918. In 1923 he married an Economics graduate named Joanna. Father Paul was ordained a deacon, and soon after, a priest in 1920. His first parish was in Poland, where many Lemkos were returning to the Orthodox faith of their ancestors. But the work of Father Paul was viewed with profound suspicion and hostility by the Polish government. In 1938, great pressure was put upon the Lemkos to forsake Orthodoxy and accept allegiance to the Church of Rome. One day after the celebration of the Liturgy and the Baptism of the daughter of a brother priest, Paul and Joanna were attacked by a Polish partisan group. On the Feast of the Dormition in 1943, they were tortured for about an hour. Presbytera Joanna died from a loss of blood and Father Paul was shot.

SAINTS OF THE DAY: Chrestos of Ioannina; New Martyr Alexis, archpriest of Petrograd; Stephen, elder of Vyatka; New Martyrs Priest Paul Szwajko and Presbytera Joanna of Graboviec (Poland); Macarius the Roman and his disciple Chariton of Novgorod; Remembrance of the Love of God for Mankind; "Diasozousa" and "Chajnicke" Icons of the Mother of God.

THURSDAY **Translation of the Image of Our Lord**
Fast-free

AUGUST 16

1 Timothy 3:13-4:5
Luke 9:51-57, 10:22-24, 13:22

If you want to become a servant of Christ, you ought to accept everything He suffered for our sake; scorn, insults, humiliations, and even being spit upon and beaten! If you endure all these things, then you are bearing a small cross and following Christ. With comfort and empty honor and courteous talk, there is no progress or salvation.

+Elder Joseph the Hesychast

NEW MARTYR STAMATIOS OF VOLOS, THESSALY. Stamatios lived in seventeenth-century Greece, in the village of St. George in Volos. This was during the time of Turkish oppression and excessive taxation on agriculture. Stamatios organized a group and went off to the capital to present their case to the sultan. They were frustrated by the inaccessibility of the sultan, so they gave up and went home, that is, all except Stamatios who produced a list of grievances and was intent on seeing the sultan. He was quickly tried and sent to jail for many weeks of brainwashing. He was tortured and bribed to become a Muslim, but he refused. St. Stamatios was beheaded at the door of Hagia Sophia in Constantinople.

SAINTS OF THE DAY: Translation of the Image "Not-Made-by-Hands" of Our Lord Jesus Christ from Edessa to Constantinople; Diomedes the Physician; Anthony the Stylite of Georgia; Cherimon of Egypt; Romanus the Sinaite of Serbia; Nicodemus of Meteora; The 33 Martyrs of Palestine; Timothy of Euripos, founder of Pendeli; Apostolos of St. Lawrence; Gerasimos of Cephalonia; Eustathius II of Serbia; Stamatios of Volos; Martyr Alcibiades; Raphael of Banat; Nilus, brother of Emperor Laskaris; Christopher of Guria; Joachim of Osogovo; Constantine Brancoveanu of Wallachia and his sons Constantine, Stephen, Radu, and Matthew, and counselor Ioannicius; Joseph of Varatec Monastery (Romania); Translation of the relics of Sts. Seraphim, Dorotheus, James, Demetrius, Basil, and Sarantis of Megaris; "Feodorovskaya" of Kostroma and "Triumph of Holy Theotokos" of Port Arthur Icons of the Mother of God.

AUGUST 17

2 Corinthians 7:10-16; Mark 2:18-22

Do not think that you have a right to complain when your prayers are not answered. God fulfills your desires in a manner that you do not know.

St. Nectarios of Aegina

MARTYR MYRON OF CYZICUS. Myron lived in the perilous times of Emperor Diocletian in the third century. He was a priest in Achaeia who had inherited a vast estate from his father in Patras. He used this money to help the poor, to build churches, hospitals, and orphanages. He was well known throughout the empire as a spiritual leader and a converter of idol-worshippers. One time, during the Feast of the Nativity of Christ, the local governor Antipater and his soldiers entered the church to arrest those praying there and to torture them. Myron pleaded for his flock, but the saint was delivered to torture. He was tied to a post in the town square and repeatedly cut with knives. Myron prayed and showed no sign of pain. He was thrown into a red-hot oven, but God preserved him unharmed. At that same moment, 150 men at a nearby pagan temple were scorched by the oven fire. The governor demanded that Myron worship the idols, but he firmly refused. Then he gave orders to throw Myron to wild beasts, but they would not touch him. St. Myron was beheaded by the sword.

SAINTS OF THE DAY: Straton, Philip, Eutychian, and Cyprian of Nicomedia; Paul and Juliana of Syria; Patroclus of Troyes; Myron of Cyzicus; Thyrsus, Leucius, and Coronatus, with others at Caesarea; Alypius the Iconographer of the Kiev Caves; James the Deacon; Agapius at Thermes; Elias the Younger of Calabria; Demetrius of Samarina in Epirus; Macarius of Mt. St. Auxentius; Theodoretus, enlightener of the Laps; Tbeli Abuseridze of Georgia; Archilleus of Stavropol; Pimen of Ugresh; Philip of Vologda; Jeroen at Noordwijk; "Armatia" and "Svensk" Icons of the Mother of God.

AUGUST 18

1 Corinthians 1:26-2:5
Matthew 20:29-34

Just as anyone who climbs a rotten ladder risks his life, so are honors and power a danger for humility.

St. John Climacus

NEW MARTYRS AUGUSTINE OF ORANS MONASTERY AND NICHOLAS OF NIZHNI-NOVGOROD, AND 15 PEOPLE WITH THEM. In 1918, Augustine became embroiled with the authorities. He was arrested and charged with counter-revolutionary activity agitation among the peasants who surrounded the monastery settlement. Archimandrite Augustine and Archpriest Nicholas of the Nizhegorod Kazan Church concelebrated their final Liturgy in prison. Together with another fifteen people, they appeared before the military-revolutionary tribunal and were condemned to be shot on a nearby island. The prisoners were put on a steamship moving toward Mochalny Island, and they were all in an elated mood, hoping that they would die for their faith. On the way, they served a Pannikhida for themselves. The group was arranged in a manner convenient for the executioners, and Augustine stood looking fearlessly at the Red Army soldiers. They fired three separate volleys at him, yet he did not fall. On the fourth volley of shots, he finally fell dead. St. Augustine began appearing in dreams to many of the monks of Orans Monastery, usually appearing ready for Divine Services.

SAINTS OF THE DAY: John of Rila; Christodoulos the Philosopher of Georgia; Florus and Laurus of Illyria, and with them a multitude of paupers; Sophronius of St. Anne's Skete, Mt. Athos; Juliana, near Strobilus; Leo, drowned near Myra in Lycia; Hermes, Serapion, and Polyaenus of Rome; Emilian, Bishop of Trebia, with Hilarion, Dionysius, Hermippus, and 1,000 others, in Italy; Barnabas and Sophronius of Mt. Mela near Trebizond; Christopher of Mt. Mela; Demetrius the Vlach, of Samarina; John and George, Patriarchs of Constantinople; Arsenius the New of Paros; Augustine of Orans Monastery, Nicholas of Nizhni-Novgorod, and 15 people with them; "Sumela" Icon of the Mother of God.

Twelfth Sunday of Matthew
Fast-free

August 19

1 Corinthians 15:1-11; Matthew 19:16-26

It seems that from my childhood I had a great desire to help those suffering, especially those whose souls are in pain…We must rise from the mournful earth to Heaven and rejoice with the angels over the salvation of a single saved soul, over a single cup of cold water given in the Name of the Lord.

St. Elizabeth the New Martyr

MOCHTA OF BRITAIN. Mochta was a native of sixth-century Britain. One account relates that he was brought to Ireland as a child, along with his parents, by a druid named Hoam. Mochta went to Rome to continue his studies, and the pope consecrated him bishop and sent him back to Ireland with twelve companions. The first church Mochta founded was at Kilmore. From there, he left all his possessions to the monks and followed the stream, which later became the river Fane. He is said to have founded a monastery in Louth, Ireland, which was originally the site of a shrine to the Celtic god Lugh. This monastery gained a nationwide reputation. Mochta was an accomplished scholar, especially learned in sacred Scripture, and he wrote a rule for monks. One account has Mochta restoring life to the daughter of the druid Hoam. She later became a nun who made vestments and altar clothes. In his old age, St. Patrick spent some time with Mochta. St. Mochta died around the age of ninety. It is believed that he was the last of St. Patrick's disciples.

SAINTS OF THE DAY: Andrew Stratelates and 2,593 soldiers with him in Cilicia; Timothy, Agapius, and Thecla of Palestine; Pitirim, Bishop of Perm; Theophanes, wonderworker of Macedonia (Mt. Athos); Credan, abbot of Evesham; Mochta of Britain; Namadia of France; Uncovering of the relics of St. Gennadius, abbot of Kostroma; "Of the Don" Icon of the Mother of God.

August 20

2 Corinthians 8:7-15; Mark 3:6-12

It is God's task to administer the world and the soul's task to guide the body.

St. Thalassios the Libyan

MARTYRS SEVEROS AND MEMNON. Severos was a Christian from Side of Pamphylia, which had a large pagan population. His father thought that the family should move to Philippopolis since there was a significant Christian presence, but when they arrived, they found that Governor Apellianos had just martyred a group of Christians. Severos' parents quickly left, but Severos decided to stay and make a stand for his faith. He prayed for guidance, and Jesus appeared to him telling him to go to the eastern gate of the city. A centurion named Memnon met Severos at the gate and asked him to state his business. Severos took this opportunity to point out the error of idolatry and explained to him the life of Christ. Memnon listened attentively, and Severos went on to speak to others as well. These activities were reported to the governor who had Severos brought to him to worship the idols. When he refused, he was put in the custody of the centurion Memnon. The next morning, before the judgment seat, they both confessed and preached Christ. Apellianos was so filled with rage that he immediately ordered their torture. Memnon was flogged, his hands and feet cut, his skin flayed, and was burned alive. Then a voice was heard welcoming him into the choir of martyrs. Disregarding this heavenly voice, Apellianos had the flesh of Severos torn. Once again, the voice was heard, and everyone was bewildered. Unmoved, Apellianos gave orders to saw off Severos' limbs. With all their might, the soldiers were not able to separate the limbs from the body. Finally, the governor ordered the beheading of St. Severos.

SAINTS OF THE DAY: Samuel the Prophet; Philip of Heraclea; Severos, and Memnon, in Thrace; Lucius of Cyprus; Heliodorus and Dosa in Persia; Photina, at Blachernae; Hierotheus of Hungary; Stephen I, King of Hungary; Theocharis of Neopolis; Oswin of Deira; Philibert of Jumieges.

August 21

2 Corinthians 8:16-9:5; Mark 3:13-21

The more one takes pleasure in lower things, the more he is separated from heavenly love.

St. Gregory the Great

VENERABLE ABRAMIUS OF SMOLENSK. Abramius was born in mid twelfth-century Smolensk. His parents had twelve daughters, and they beseeched God for a son. After the death of his parents, he gave away all his wealth to monasteries, churches, and the destitute. He took monastic tonsure and strove to emulate the strict disciplines of the early desert fathers—fasting, prayer, and vigil. He bravely fought temptations from demons. Abramius occupied himself with the copying of books. After thirty years, he was ordained to the priesthood, and every day served the Divine Liturgy. He constantly preached in church and to those who visited him in his cell. He was strict both with himself and his spiritual children. Soon Abramius became well known, and this aroused the envy of some of the brethren who slandered Abramius to the bishop and the prince. They accused him of heresy, reading forbidden books, and tempting his spiritual children. They proposed that Abramius be drowned or burned. He was brought to trial and answered all the false accusations, but still, he was forbidden to serve as a priest. Shortly after that, a terrible drought struck the Smolensk lands. Not until the bishop pardoned Abramius, permitting him to serve and preach, did the rains begin to fall again. The bishop built a new monastery and appointed Abramius abbot. St. Abramius died peacefully, having spent fifty years in monasticism.

SAINTS OF THE DAY: Holy Forefathers Abraham, Isaac, and Jacob; Thaddeus, Apostle of the Seventy; Bassa of Edessa, and Theognios, Agapios, and Pistos; Avitus of Clermont; Theocleta of Asia Minor; Sarmean of Georgia; Symeon of Samokovo; Isaiah of Mt. Athos; Donatus, Romulus, Silvanus, and Venustus of Romania; Abramius of Smolensk, and Ephraim; Abramius of the Kiev Caves; Cornelius of Paleostrov, and Abramius; Raphael of Sisatovac; Ignatius of Optina; Martha of Diveyevo.

AUGUST 22

2 Corinthians 9:12-15, 10:1-7
Mark 3:20-27

Of course, every good deed done for Christ's sake gives us the grace of the Holy Spirit, but prayer gives us this grace most of all, for it is always at hand, as an instrument for acquiring the grace of the Spirit. For instance, you would like to go to church, but there is no church or the service is over; you would like to give alms to a beggar, but there isn't one, or you have nothing to give; you would like to preserve your virginity, but you have not the strength to do so because of your temperament, or because of the violence of the wiles of the enemy which because of your human weakness you cannot withstand; you would like to do some other good deed for Christ's sake, but either you have not the strength or the opportunity is lacking. This certainly does not apply to prayer. Prayer is always possible for everyone, rich and poor, noble and humble, strong and weak, healthy and sick, righteous and sinful.

St. Seraphim of Sarov

SYNAXIS OF THE ICON OF THE MOTHER OF GOD OF PROUSA. This icon is commemorated today because of the many miracles that the Mother of God wrought through it. The iconoclasts once tried to destroy the icon in the ninth century, but a nobleman from Prousa secretly took it to Greece. However, he lost the icon, but it miraculously appeared in a cave in the area of Litza and Agrapha. Later, a shrine and a monastery were built there that still exist today.

SAINTS OF THE DAY: Agathonicus of Nicomedia and his companions: Zotikos, Theoprepios, Acindynos, Severian, Zeno, and others; Eulalia of Barcelona; Athanasius, Bishop of Tarsus; Anthousa of Syria, with Charesimos and Neophytos; Bogolep of Uglich; Isaac I of Optina; Macarius of Orel, with Andrew, Alexis, Theodore, John, Hierotheus, John, Hilarion, and Gorazd; Martyrs Irenaeus, Deacon, Or, and Oropsus; Symphorian of Autun; Sigfrid, abbot of Wearmouth; "Prousa" and "Georgian" Icons of the Mother of God.

THURSDAY

Leave-taking of the Dormition
Fast-free

AUGUST 23

Philippians 2:5-11
Luke 10:38-42, 11:27-28

Where love is, there is Christ—Love—and where humility exists, the Grace of God takes up permanent residence, God reigns, and the earth is ultimately transformed into Paradise. Where love and humility are absent, there the devil—the enemy—takes up his abode and people live in hell with the devil already in this life, continually worsening their place in the next life, in the eternal fire.

St. Paisios the Athonite

NEW HIEROMARTYRS EPHRAIM, BISHOP OF SELENGINSK, AND ARCHPRIEST JOHN VOSTORGOV OF MOSCOW. Ephraim was born in 1876 in a family of Cossacks. He was orphaned in early childhood. A local priest noticed the shepherd boy and made him a reader in church. Later the priest sent Ephraim to theological school and then the theological seminary. He was ordained to the priesthood and then entered the Kazan Theological Academy. Ephraim served in the Trans-Baikal spiritual mission situated in Chita, becoming its head in 1904. He converted many Mongols, Buryats, and especially Koreans to Orthodoxy. He founded a parish for the Koreans in Chita. Later, he was raised to the rank of proto-priest and then archimandrite. He was a fiery preacher and beloved by the people. He was consecrated Bishop of Selenginsk. At the beginning of the Russian Revolution, he was arrested twice and released both times. Then in 1918 he was detained in Moscow together with Father John Vostorgov and cast into prison. Bishop Ephraim and Father John were shot to death.

SAINTS OF THE DAY: Irenaeus of Lyons; Irenaeus of Sirmium; Callinicus, Patriarch of Constantinople; Pothinus of Lyons; Victor of Marseilles; Eutychius and Florentius of Nursia; Nicholas the Sicilian; The 38 Martyrs of Thrace; Lupus, slave of Demetrios of Thessalonica; Anthony of Sardis; Ebba the Younger, and her companions; Ephraim (Kuznetsov) of Selenginsk, John Vostorgov of Moscow, and Nicholas Varzhansky.

August 24

2 Corinthians 11:5-21; Mark 4:1-9

If you continue your almsgiving, offering to the poor out of the little that you have, not only will you not be in want, but the Lord will bless and increase what you have. And for the few things which you will give here, in this temporary life, you will receive a thousand fold, ten thousand fold, more in the eternal life; and you will hear the Lord saying to you: "I was hungry, and ye gave me food." And when you say to Him: "Lord, when did we see Thee hungry and fed Thee?", He shall say: "Yes ye did not see me, but ye did see my poor brethren, the hungry. The bread which ye gave unto them, it is the same as if ye gave unto me. So now I grant unto you the eternal Heavenly Kingdom; and whatever goods I have, ye shall have also and all those who fed the poor, the hungry, and showed mercy unto them."

St. Arsenios of Paros

HIEROMARTYR EUTYCHIOS. Eutychios was a disciple of the holy Apostles Paul and John the Theologian. He was called a disciple even though he was not included among the Seventy Disciples. Eutychios lived in first-century Sebasteia. He traveled and preached with Apostle Paul during his early missionary travels. He was made a bishop and had as his traveling companion an angel of God. In his times of travail, God was also with him. In prison, an angel of God fed him. When he was thrown into a fire, and to wild animals, he was not harmed. Finally, he was beheaded.

SAINTS OF THE DAY: Cosmas of Aitolia; George Limniotes of Mt. Olympus; Eutychios, disciple of St. John the Theologian; Serapion of St. John the Baptist Monastery; Dionysius of Zakynthos; Cyra of Persia; Arsenius of Komel; Tation at Claudiopolis; Maxim Sandovich of the Lemkos; Ouen of Rouen; Athanasius II, Patriarch of Jerusalem; Seraphim of Grodno; Aristocleus of Moscow; Martyrius of Novgorod; Commemoration of the appearance of the Most Holy Theotokos to St. Sergius of Radonezh; "Petrovskaya" (Of St. Peter) Icon of the Mother of God.

AUGUST 25

Titus 1:1-5, 2:15, 3:1-2, 12-15
Matthew 5:14-19

So come, let us rise up, as many of us as wish to escape this slavery of the passions, and run to Christ, the true Master, so that we may acquire the title of His servants. Let us also strive to become such men as our discourse has just enumerated. Let us not, therefore, hold our salvation in contempt, nor fool ourselves and make excuses for our sins by saying, 'It is impossible for a man of the present generation ever to become such a person.' Neither let us philosophize against our own salvation, nor argue against our very souls. Because it is indeed possible, if we will it so, and so much so that free will alone can carry us up to that height. For where, as St. Basil says, there is a ready will, there is nothing to hinder.

St. Symeon the New Theologian

GENNADIOS, PATRIARCH OF CONSTANTINOPLE. Gennadios was a role model of how a gentle person can also be effective and decisive in a position of leadership. During his thirteen years as patriarch, the famous Studion Monastery was built in Constantinople, as well as the church of St. John the Baptist. The builder was the Roman senator Studios, hence the name Studion. Gennadios also led the council that eradicated simony, the buying and selling of ecclesiastical pardons. Gennadios, who was very strict with his own abstinence, only ordained priests who knew the entire Psalter by heart, which covered 117 pages. God granted Gennadios the gift to work miracles. He had foreknowledge of his death, which was revealed to him in a vision.

SAINTS OF THE DAY: Apostle Titus of the Seventy; Menas, Patriarch of Constantinople; John the Cappadocian and Epiphanius, Patriarchs of Constantinople; Gennadios, Patriarch of Constantinople; Barses and Eulogius of Edessa; Protogenes of Carrhae; Gregory of Utrecht; John of Karpathos; Aredius of Limousin; Genesius of Arles; Ebba the Elder; Moses of Solovki; Lucilla and Nemesius, at Rome; Synaxis of the Hierarchs of Crete; Translation of the relics of Apostle Bartholomew from Anastasiopolis to Lipari.

SUNDAY

Thirteenth Sunday of Matthew
Fast-free

AUGUST 26

1 Corinthians 16:13-24
Matthew 21:33-42

Live every day as if dying.

St. Anthony the Great

NEW HIEROMARTYR NECTARIUS, BISHOP OF YARANSK. Nectarius was born into the family of a priest in the village of Yatsek, Kiev province, in the late nineteenth century. At the age of three, he was orphaned and raised by the priest of the local church and his family. At twelve, he entered the Kiev theological seminary, and at nineteen he was ordained to the diaconate and priesthood. He later graduated from the Kiev Theological Academy and was tonsured in the Kiev Caves Lavra. He soon joined the army as the priest of the rifle regiment. Beginning in 1918, Nectarius was arrested several times. He was sentenced to hard labor for one year, accused of being a counter-revolutionary agitator. In 1923, he was appointed the dean of the monasteries of Petrograd, and in 1924 it is said that Patriarch Tikhon consecrated him Bishop of Vitebsk. He later was named Bishop of Yaransk. Nectarius entered into battle with the Renovationists. He also went out into the neighboring villages and assumed the authority of the Renovationist churches. He was soon looking after more than forty parishes of the true Orthodox Christians. He demanded that the Soviet power repent, stop repressions, and radically change its politics towards the Church. He said, "I reject the God-hated Renovationist movement and anathematize it." In 1925, the GPU arrested Nectarius. He was sentenced to three years on Solovki, where he worked as a fisherman and janitor.

SAINTS OF THE DAY: Adrian, Natalia, and 23 companions of Nicomedia; Tithoes of the Thebaid; Ibestion the Confessor; Adrian of Ondrusovsk; Cyprian of Storozhev; Zer-Jacob of Ethiopia; Maria of Diveyevo, fool-for-Christ; Nectarius Trezvinsky of Yaransk; Roman Medved of Moscow; Ioasaph, Prince of India; Adrian of Poshekhonye; Bassian of Alatyr; Abenner the King; Martyr Adrian; Commemoration of the Meeting of the Vladimir Icon of the Mother of God.

AUGUST 27

2 Corinthians 12:10-19; Mark 4:10-23

He who avoids physical work, cannot succeed in his spiritual work because the second is born from the first.

+Elder Efstratios of Glinsk

VENERABLE POEMEN THE GREAT. As a boy living in Egypt, he went from one ascetic to another gathering wisdom. When he became a monk, he encouraged his two brothers to follow him, so the three left the world and lived together. Life was very structured. They slept only four hours, then they read the Psalter for another four hours, and did manual labor for four hours. In this way, they passed the night. Morning to noon they worked and prayed, and noon to Vespers was spent reading. When their mother came to visit, they would not come out of their cells to see her. They asked her if she would prefer to see them in this world or the one to come. Hearing this, she was humbled and returned home. Poemen was a quiet man. One time a certain judge wanted to speak with him, but Poemen would not because he thought if one dignitary visits, then assuredly many more people will come and disturb the quiet. The judge arrested Poemen's nephew, hoping that the saint would entreat the judge for the boy's release. Even with his sister's pleas, Poemen could not be moved. Some of the other elders pressured Poemen to help, so he sent a message to the judge saying, "Examine and consider his case according to the law. If he is worthy of death, let him die. Thus, by temporal execution, he might be delivered from everlasting punishment. If he is not deserving of punishment, then do as thou dost please." Seeing the righteousness and justice of the elder, the judge released the boy. St. Poemen died at the age of 110.

SAINTS OF THE DAY: Poemen the Great; Sabbas of Benephali; Hosius the Confessor; Martyr Anthusa; Liberius of Rome; Caesarius of Arles; Kuksha, Pimen, and Nicon of the Kiev Caves; Phanurios the Newly-Revealed; Poemen of Palestine; Michael Voskresensky with 28 others; Stephen Nemkov with 18 others, of Nizhni-Novgorod; Methodius of Sukovo; Praulius of Jerusalem; Djan Darada, the Ethiopian eunuch of Queen Candace.

August 28

2 Corinthians 12:20-13:2; Mark 4:24-34

Please put this commandment into practice: Cultivate love towards the Person of Christ to such an extent that, when you pronounce His name, tears fall from your eyes. Your heart must really be aflame. Then He will become your teacher. He will be your Guide, your Brother, your Father, and your Geron (Elder).

+Elder Amphilochios Makris of Patmos

UNCOVERING OF THE RELICS OF VENERABLE JOB OF POCHAEV. Job was born into a pious Orthodox Christian family in the mid-sixteenth century. At the age of ten, he went to live at the Goritsky Monastery in the Carpathian Mountains. He was tonsured a monk at age twelve and a hieromonk at age twenty-nine. He was known for his meekness and humility. Prince Ostrozhky asked Job to be the abbot of the monastery in Dubno, where he printed and widely distributed Orthodox spiritual and liturgical books. Much later, he moved to the mountain of Pochaev and again was made abbot. He printed and distributed many Orthodox books there, and the monastery flourished. This became the center of Orthodoxy in the western Ukraine. At the age of one hundred, Job received the Great Schema and was given the name John. He died peacefully. In 1833, the relics of St. Job were opened for veneration.

SAINTS OF THE DAY: Hezekiah, King of Judah; Anna the Prophetess, daughter of Phanuel; Moses the Black of Scetis; Queen Shushaniki (Susanna) of Georgia; Martyrs Diomedes and Laurence; Amphilochius, Bishop of Vladimir; The 33 Martyrs of Nicomedia; Theodore, Prince of Ostrog; Sergius Zaytsev of Zilantov Monastery of Kazan, with Laurence, Seraphim, Theodosius, Leontius, Stephen, Gregory, Hylarion, John, and Sergius; Acacius of Miletus; Savva, abbot of Krypetsk; Synaxis of the Venerable Fathers of the Far Caves in Kiev; Uncovering of the relics of St. Job of Pochaev.

Beheading of the Prophet, John the Baptist
Strict Fast

AUGUST 29

Acts 13:25-33; Mark 6:14-30

Brethren, the Holy Forerunner encompassed within himself, within his person, all of the virtues of Heaven, all of the virtues in all of the Prophets, all of the Apostles, all of the Martyrs, all of the Angels of Heaven, all of the Confessors.

St. Justin Popovich

THE BEHEADING OF THE GLORIOUS PROPHET, ST. JOHN THE BAPTIST. The true date of St. John's beheading was in the spring. However, this date was chosen for commemoration since it was when the church was built and consecrated over St. John's relics and those of his disciples. Herod Antipas was the son of Herod the Great who killed the children up to two years of age in search of Jesus. He took his brother Philip's wife Herodias, while Philip was yet alive, and put away his own wife, who was the daughter of the Arabian king Aretas. St. John severely criticized him for this, so he was imprisoned. Even though Herod "wanted to put him to death, he feared the multitude, because they counted him as a prophet" (Matthew 14:5). During a feast, Salome, Herod's niece, asked for the head of John on a platter. "And the king was sorry; nevertheless, because of the oaths and because of those who sat with him, he commanded it" (Matthew 14:9). St. John's disciples took his body by night and buried it at Sebasteia. Salome ordered that John's head be buried deep in the earth in an unclean place, for she feared that he would come back to life. However, the pious woman Joanna, the wife of Herod's steward, buried it in an earthen vessel on the Mount of Olives. The Arabian king made war on Herod and was defeated. Salome was decapitated when she fell into the frozen River Sikoris. Her head was brought to Herod and Herodias. The Roman emperor Caligula exiled Herod and Herodias to Gaul, and then to Spain.

SAINTS OF THE DAY: Arcadius of Arsinoe; Candida and Gelasia of Constantinople; Peter of Russia; Alexander of Voche; Anastasius of Bulgaria; Theodora of Thessalonica; Sebbi of the East Saxons.

 Fast-free

AUGUST 30

Galatians 1:1-3, 20-24, 2:1-5
Mark 5:1-20

As long as the soul loves its body it cannot love God, because the Lord said: *He that loves his life shall lose it; and he that hates his life in this world shall keep it unto life eternal* (Jn. 12:25).

St. Sarah of the Nile

NEW MARTYR THEODORE OF TOBOLSK. Theodore Ivanov was from a poor family with many children in late nineteenth-century Tobolsk. As a child, he served in the city's cathedral where it was cold, and he often caught a cold after spending a night there. At thirteen years of age, he fell ill with rheumatism, and a year later, became paralyzed from the waist down. For the first several years, he would scream from pain, but when he venerated the relics of St. John of Tobolsk, the pain subsided. Many would visit him and find support and comfort for themselves. Even monks, priests, and hierarchs visited. In 1937, at the age of forty-two, Theodore, who had been bedridden for almost thirty years, was arrested by the NKVD of Moscow, under charges that he was a religious fanatic who was preparing for an armed uprising against the Soviet authorities. He was taken to prison on a stretcher. Theodore told his sister at the time of the arrest, "Pray. Don't cry for me and don't look for me!" He also said, "Don't worry, worrying is harmful." Theodore was shot in prison, as were tens of thousands of feeble, defenseless, and helpless people. These physically handicapped inmates were not able to work, so they were killed to make room for the newly-arrested people.

SAINTS OF THE DAY: Alexander, John, and Paul the New, Patriarchs; Felix of Thibiuca; Martyrs Fortunatus, Septimius, and Januarius; Fantinus of Calabria; 16 Martyrs of Thebes; 6 Martyrs of Melitene; Sarmata of Egypt; Bryaene of Nisibis; Eulalius of Cyprus; Alexander of Svir; Barlaam of Moldavia; John of Rasca; Alexander of Voch; Christopher of Palestine; Fiacrius of Breuil; Ignatius of Moscow; Peter of Smolensk; Theodore of Tobolsk; Synaxis of the Serbian Hierarchs; Uncovering of the relics of St. Daniel of Moscow; Translation of the relics of St. Alexander Nevsky.

FRIDAY

AUGUST 31

The Venerable Sash of the Mother of God
Abstain from meat and dairy products, and fish.
Hebrews 9:1-7; Luke 10:38-42, 11:27-28

If a man is unable to check the unnecessary desires of the appetite, how will he be able to extinguish the fire of carnal lust?

St. John Cassian

THE PLACING OF THE CINCTURE (SASH) OF THE MOST HOLY THEOTOKOS. Initially, the Theotokos gave Her belt to the Apostle Thomas after Her Dormition. She had made it herself out of camel hair. It was later kept in the protection of devout Christians in Jerusalem. During the reign of the emperor Arcadius in the fifth century, the Belt of the Most Holy Mother of God was placed in the Constantinople Blachernae Church, together with the holy Robe. By Divine revelation, the Robe of the Theotokos was found by two reformed Arians, Candios and Galvios. The two holy relics were kept in a sealed vessel. During the reign of Emperor Leo the Wise, in the late-ninth to early-tenth century, his wife Empress Zoe suffered from an unclean spirit. The Empress had a vision that she would be healed when the Belt of the Mother of God was placed upon her. Emperor Leo asked the patriarch to open the vessel. The holy relic was completely whole and undamaged by time. The patriarch placed the belt on Zoe, and she was immediately healed. In gratitude, Empress Zoe embroidered the holy belt with gold thread. Today's feast was established in commemoration of this miracle and the Placing of the Holy Belt. Parts of the Holy Belt can be found in the Vatopedi Monastery on Mt. Athos, in Trier Monastery, and in Georgia.

SAINTS OF THE DAY: Cyprian of Carthage; Four Martyrs of Perga; Gennadius, Patriarch of Constantinople; Paulinus of Trier; 7 Virgin-martyrs of Gaza; 366 Martyrs of Nicomedia; John of Kiev; Aidan of Lindisfarne; Martyrs Menas, Faustus, Andrew, Heraclius, Phileortus, and Diadochus; Eanswythe of Folkestone; New Martyrs of Jasenovac (Serbia).

If you believe in Christ, have hope in Him, love Him with all your soul and heart, whatever you seek from Him with faith and is to your benefit He will give you. Seek above all the kingdom of Heaven. When you love Him and do His commandments, He too will love you, and you will be united with Him. "God is love; and he that dwelleth in love dwelleth in God, and God in him."

St. Arsenios of Paros

Ecclesiastical New Year
Fast-free
1 Timothy 2:1-7; Luke 4:16-22

September 1

When the children are traumatized and hurt on account of some serious situation, don't let it affect you when they react negatively and speak rudely. In reality they don't want to, but can't help themselves at difficult times. They are remorseful afterwards. But if you become irritated and enraged, you become one with the evil spirit and it makes a mockery of you all.

St. Porphyrios the Kapsokalivite

HAIDO OF STANOS. Haido was from nineteenth-century Stanos in Halkidiki. After the Revolution of 1821, she left for Thasos with her mother. However, a Turkish ruler sought her hand in marriage, and because she did not want to convert to his religion from Christianity, she was tortured. She still refused to renounce Christ and her heritage. With the help of the village priest and some men, she escaped. Haido then entered a monastery in Kallirachi, while caring for her mother until her repose. She acquired spiritual illumination, and once for two days she was caught up into Paradise. Upon her return, she related this experience to Hieromonk Gerasimos. But while still young, Haido succumbed to sickness due to her austere way of life, and she died peacefully. Before her death, she told those with her not to change her clothes before her burial. When they disobeyed her, an earthquake occurred, and a voice was heard saying to put her old clothes back on. When this was done, there was stillness. St. Haido's relics began to exude a beautiful fragrance.

SAINTS OF THE DAY: Symeon Stylites, and his mother Martha; Holy 40 Women Martyrs, and Martyr Ammon; Venerable Evanthia; Nicholas of Courtaliatis; Joshua the son of Nun; Callista, Evodus, and Hermogenes at Nicomedia; Angelis of Constantinople; Meletios the Younger; Symeon of Lesbos; Verena of Zurzach; Haido of Stanos; Aegidius, along the Rhine; Dionysius Exiguus of Rome; Commemoration of the Great Fire at Constantinople about AD 470; Synaxis of the Most Holy Theotokos in Miasena Monastery; "Avgustovskaya" Icon of the Mother of God.

SUNDAY

Fourteenth Sunday of Matthew
Fast-free

SEPTEMBER 2

2 Corinthians 1:21-2:4
Matthew 22:2-14

Being men, we sin every day, but Saint Paul consoles us by saying 'renew yourselves' from day to day. This is what we do with houses: we are constantly repairing them as they break down. You should do the same thing to yourself.

St. John Chrysostom

NEW MARTYR BARSANUPHIUS, BISHOP OF KYRILOV, AND THOSE WITH HIM. Barsanuphius finished his studies at the Novgorod Theological Seminary in 1894, at the age of twenty-one. The next year he was tonsured a monk, ordained a deacon, and appointed a missionary preacher of the Novgorod diocese. He was ordained to the priesthood when he was twenty-four, and in 1911, he was made the abbot of the Kazan Monastery. In 1917, Barsanuphius was consecrated the bishop of Kyrilov, a jurisdiction of the Novgorod diocese. The following year he was arrested by the Red Army during the Russian Communist Revolution and was sent to his execution with the Abbess Seraphima and four laymen. However, none of the firing squad's bullets could hit Barsanuphius until they had finished praying. In frustration and fury, the Red Army soldiers lunged at him with bayonets and killed him. St. Barsanuphius was buried not far from the St. Cyril-White Lake Monastery. Many years later a pigsty was built over his burial site.

SAINTS OF THE DAY: Mamas of Caesarea, and his parents, Theodotus and Rufina; John the Faster, Patriarch of Constantinople; Eleazar, son of Aaron, and Righteous Phineas; Martyrs Philadelphus, Melanippus, and Parthagape; Anthony and Theodosius of the Kiev Caves; Martyrs Diomedes, Julian, Philip, Eftychian, Hesychios, and others; Barsanuphius, Bishop of Kyrilov, John Ivanov, and Seraphima of Therapontov Convent, and Anatole, Nicholas, Michael, and Philip; Damascene, Bishop of Starodub, Herman, Bishop of Vyaznikov, and Stephen Yaroshevich; Aeithalas and Ammon of Thrace; Hieu, abbess of Tadcaster; "Kaluga" Icon of the Mother of God.

SEPTEMBER 3

Galatians 2:11-16; Mark 5:24-34

How can there be instruction without exercise or progress without practice?

St. Ambrose of Milan

VENERABLE NEOFIT, ON MOUNT SAVAGE. Neofit was tonsured at the sixteenth-century Cozia Monastery in Romania. Desiring a more perfect life, he received a blessing to live in solitude. He dug a cell on the western side of Mount Savage, above the Cozia Monastery. He would spend the week in fasting and prayer, where he received the gift of tears and prayer for the world. He would go down to the monastery occasionally to confess to St. Daniil and to receive Holy Communion. After thirty years in the wilderness, suffering harsh winters in poverty, nakedness, and enduring severe demonic temptations, he died in his cave, unbeknownst to anyone. Finally, St. Neofit's body was discovered by a monk who would take food to the hermits. The monk took the body to the monastery for burial, but St. Neofit scolded him in a dream, telling him to return his body to his cave. The abbot also saw the same vision. However, the next morning when two monks returned St. Neofit's body to his cave, one of the monks angrily cried out with impious words, "With the bears he lived and with the bears he can stay." Because of this, the monk's head immediately turned around to the back, and with great cries, he returned to the monastery, where he confessed his sin. The fathers of the monastery prayed to St. Neofit to forgive him, and the monk was immediately healed. News of this miracle spread quickly, and many faithful began to visit the cave for healing, and still do to this day.

SAINTS OF THE DAY: Anthimus, Bishop of Nicomedia, and those with him; Aristion of Alexandria; Emperor Constantine the New; Ioannicius II, first patriarch of Serbia; Basilissa of Nicomedia; Theoctistus of Palestine; John "the Hairy," fool-for-Christ; Phoebe, at Cenchreae; Remaclus of Maastricht; Polydorus of Cyprus; Aigulphus of Provence; Pimen of Vernensk, and Meletius of Issyk-Kul; Neofit and Meletie of Romania.

SEPTEMBER 4

Galatians 2:21-3:7; Mark 6:1-7

Everything in this life passes away—only God remains, only He is worth struggling towards. We have a choice: to follow the way of this world, of the society that surrounds us, and thereby find ourselves outside of God; or to choose the way of life, to choose God Who calls us and for Whom our heart is searching.

+ *Fr. Seraphim Rose*

SYMEON, ABBOT AND WONDERWORKER OF GARESJA. Symeon was a simple monk for most of his life at the Davit-Gareji Monastery in the eighteenth-century. Toward the end of his life, he was made the abbot. Because of his humility and virtues, he was granted the gift of miracle-working. When death approached, he became terribly sick, and for one hour he appeared lifeless. Then he arose and gave all his possessions to the monks of the monastery so that they might keep remembrance of him. His disciple, St. Serapion, who was also endowed with the gift of prophecy, rushed to his elder's side to comfort him. Serapion had hoped that his elder would bury him since he knew that he was about to die. He told Symeon that he would shortly follow him in death. Exactly one week after his deathly illness, St. Symeon reposed in peace.

SAINTS OF THE DAY: Prophet Moses the God-seer, and Aaron the Priest; Babylas of Antioch and Urban, Prilidian, Epolonius, and Christodoula; Babylas of Nicomedia and 84 children; 3,628 Martyrs in Nicomedia; Sarbelus (Thathuil) and Bebaia of Edessa; Hermione, daughter of Apostle Philip the Deacon; Theotimos and Theodoulos the executioners; Charitina of Amisus; Symeon of Garesja; Martyr Sarbelus; Jerusalem of Berroia; Theodore, Ammianus, Julian, Kion (Oceanus), and Centurionus of Nicomedia; Petronius of Egypt; Anthimus of Cephalonia; Peter of Dabro-Bosnia; Parthenius of Kiziltash; Gregory of Shliserburg, Sergius of Narva, and Stephen of Nikolskoye; Uncovering of the relics of St. Ioasaph of Belgorod and St. Metrophanes of Voronezh; Synaxis of the Saints of Voronezh; "The Unburnt Bush" Icon of the Mother of God.

SEPTEMBER 5

Galatians 3:15-22; Matthew 24:13-28

Generally it seems that evil prevails in the world today. Some believe the cause of evil is God. They believe Him to be with human passions—evil, a punisher, an avenger. Why does He allow it? Why does He give it license? Why doesn't He remove it, since it afflicts His creatures so much? As is known, man is completely free to choose evil or good. For the choice of evil, God is not responsible. We cannot blame God for making us perfectly free. God is goodness, and never made anyone evil.

Monk Moses the Athonite

MARTYR ATHANASIUS OF BRETSK. Athanasius was raised in a pious Christian family in late sixteenth-century Belorussia. In his youth, he was a teacher in the houses of Polish merchants. He accepted monastic tonsure at the Vilensk monastery of the Holy Spirit. When he was ordained to the priesthood, he became the abbot of the Dubovsk monastery, and later abbot of the Bretsk Simeonov monastery. He went about restoring Orthodoxy in Russian territories that had been taken over by the Polish Reche. However, over a ten-year period, the Uniates and even the civil authorities persecuted Athanasius for his work. Three times they imprisoned him. He was sent off to Kiev to appear before a religious tribunal, but he was acquitted and returned to his monastery. Once again, he went to trial for cursing the Unia and was sentenced to death. St. Athanasius was executed in 1648.

SAINTS OF THE DAY: Holy Prophet Zacharias and Righteous Elizabeth, parents of St. John the Forerunner; Urban, Theodore, Medimnus, and 77 companions at Nicomedia; Abdas, Hormizd, and Sunin of Persia; Athanasius of Bretsk; Juventinus and Maximinus at Antioch; Gleb of Russia, in Holy Baptism David; Alexis Belkovsky, Archbishop of Great Ustiug; Appearance of Apostle Peter to Emperor Justinian at Athira, near Constantinople.

SEPTEMBER 6

Hebrews 2:2-10; Luke 10:16-21

We are not asked merely to call ourselves Christians; we are asked to be Christians through our deeds.

St. Ignatius of Antioch

COMMEMORATION OF THE MIRACLE OF THE ARCHANGEL MICHAEL AT CHONAE. Not far from the city of Hieropolis, in a place called Kherotopis, there was a great snake caged in a temple that was worshiped by all. The holy Apostles John the Theologian, Philip, and Bartholomew, destroyed it by prayer. They prophesied that Archangel Michael would also work miracles there. A spring of miracle-working water soon gushed forth. All who drank from this spring and washed in it were healed and baptized. A man whose daughter was healed there built a church over the stream. After ninety years, a ten-year-old child named Archippos moved into the church. He lived there as an ascetic for sixty years. Out of fear that the healings would continue to discredit their gods, the pagans often attacked Archippos, tearing out his hair and beard, but he would not leave the holy church. They arrived at a plan to divert two rivers and drown the ascetic. They dammed the rivers for ten days while Archippos begged Archangel Michael to preserve the place. The rivers were released, and the waters roared down upon the church. The archangel appeared and made the sign of the cross, saying, "Halt here," and the waters obeyed. He then struck a huge rock near the altar, and it split open. He said to the water, "Enter into this crevice," and it did so from that day. The enemies watched all this in terror. Archangel Michael blessed the waters, saying, "May every adverse power be cast out from here! May deliverance from every ill be granted to all who draw near with faith." Then he ascended into heaven.

SAINTS OF THE DAY: Romulus and 11,000, in Armenia; Eudoxius, Zeno, Macarius, and 1,104, in Melitene; David and Archippus of Hermopolis; Cyriacus, Faustus, Abibus, and 11 others, at Alexandria; Calodote, Macarius, Andrew, and others, in Egypt.

Forefeast of the Nativity of the Virgin Mary
Strict Fast

SEPTEMBER 7

Galatians 4:8-21; Mark 6:45-53

Happiness is a pure heart, for such a heart becomes the throne of God.

St. Nectarios of Aegina

MARTYR SOZON OF CILICIA. In the year 288, in the Roman city of Pompeiopolis, Governor Maximian offered sacrifices to the idols of polytheism. Sozon was a shepherd from Lycaonia. He always read the Holy Scriptures and shared his knowledge with other shepherds. One night, as he sat under an oak tree, he had a vision that he was called to be a martyr. He set off for Pompeiopolis, leaving behind his bow and three arrows as a reminder of the vision. Sozon went into a pagan temple and broke off the hand of a golden idol, giving the gold to the poor. This caused a great commotion in the city, and many were being interrogated and tortured. Not wanting to be the cause of suffering, Sozon went to Maximian and declared that he broke the hand of the idol. When asked why he had done this, Sozon said, "So that ye might see the lack of power of your god, which offered me no resistance. It is not a god, but rather a deaf and dumb idol." The emperor gave orders to torture Sozon. He was suspended from a tree and beaten with iron rods until his bones broke. His body was scraped with iron claws and his feet shod with iron boots and nails, and he was dragged through the streets. From these tortures, Sozon died. The emperor had slaves set a large fire to burn the martyr, but suddenly lightning flashed with loud thunder, and a heavy rain poured down on the flames. The onlookers fled. By night, the faithful Christians took the body of St. Sozon and gave it burial. Many healings took place at the saint's grave.

SAINTS OF THE DAY: Evodus and Onesiphorus of the Seventy; Sozon of Cilicia; Cassiane the Hymnographer; Macarius of Optina; Eupsychius of Caesarea; Luke and Peter of Deep Stream; Symeon and Amphilochius of Pangarati; John of Verkhne-Poltavka; Alexander and Andrew, disciples; Macarius of Kanevsk; John of Novgorod.

Saturday

Nativity of the Mother of God
Fast-free

September 8

Philippians 2:5-11
Luke 10:38-42, 11:27-28

Death came through Eve; life has come through Mary.

St. Jerome

THE KURSK-ROOT ICON OF THE MOTHER OF GOD, NAMED THE "SIGN" ("ZNAMENIE"). The Kursk Sign Icon of the Mother of God is one of the most ancient icons of the Russian Church. In the eighth century, the Tatars invaded Russia, and the ravaged country fell into extreme hardship. The city of Kursk became desolate. One day a hunter happened upon an icon that was lying face down upon the root of a tree. When he picked it up, he noticed that the image was similar to the Novgorod "Znamenie" Icon. Immediately a miracle occurred. As soon as he lifted the holy icon, a spring of pure water gushed from the ground. The hunter took the icon and placed it in a small ancient chapel. As soon as the people from the city of Ryla heard about the discovery, they began to visit the place of the appearance to venerate the icon. The holy icon was transferred to Ryla and placed in a new church, but the icon disappeared and was found back in its original place of appearance. The people persisted in returning it to the new church, but the icon always returned to its former location. Finally, everyone realized that the Mother of God preferred her image to be where it was originally found. The help granted through this icon is said to have influenced the liberation of the Russian nation during the Polish-Lithuanian invasion in 1612, and the Fatherland war in 1812.

SAINTS OF THE DAY: Sophronius of Achtalea; Martyrs Rufus and Rufianus; Martyrs Severus and Artemidorus; Lucian of Alexandrov; Athanasius of Thessalonica; Serapion of Pskov; Arsenius of Konevits; Ioane and Giorgi-Ioane of Georgia; Ina of Wessex and Ethelburga; Alexander Jacobson, at Solovki; Icon of Sophia, the Wisdom of God (Kiev); "Kursk-Root," "Pochaev," "Glinsk," "Lukianov," "Syamsk," "Kholmsk," "Isaakov," "Lesna," and "Domnitsk" Icons of the Mother of God.

Sunday before the Elevation
Fast-free
Galatians 6:11-18; John 3:13-17

SEPTEMBER 9

He who believes from the heart is informed that Christ came not to judge but to save him, and this not by works nor by toil nor by perspiration, but only by faith in Him.

St. Symeon the New Theologian

OMER, BISHOP OF THEROUANNE. Omer was born to wealthy and noble parents in late sixth-century France. They paid close attention to his education, but more so they strove to inspire him with a love of virtue. When Omer's mother died, he persuaded his father to enter a monastery with him. They sold their worldly goods and distributed them to the poor. Because of Omer's humility, mildness, obedience, and purity of intention in every action, he distinguished himself at the monastery of Luxeuil. Not long afterward he was chosen to take charge of the government of the ancient diocese of the Church in Therouanne, where most of the inhabitants were pagan. The few remaining Christians had fallen away due to the lack of priests. With much zeal and in a short time, Omer's diocese became one of the most flourishing in seventh-century France. A pagan overlord who had once persecuted the Christians could not resist Omer's exhortations. After his Baptism, he gave generous grants to the church, and Omer built a monastery in honor of the Mother of God. After thirty years of service as their bishop, Omer lost his sight, but this did not lessen his concern for his flock. He died while on a pastoral visit.

SAINTS OF THE DAY: Holy Ancestors of God Joachim and Anna; Severian of Sebaste; Theophanes of Mt. Diabenos; Martyrs Chariton and Straton; Nicetas the Hidden of Constantinople; Joseph of Volokolamsk; Joachim of Opochka; Joachim of Suzdal; Onuphrius of Voronsk; Omer of Therouanne; Kieran of Clonmacnois; Bettelin of Crowland; Wulfhilda of Barking; Cyriacus of Tazlau; Zachariah of Voronezh and Andronicus of Moscow; Commemoration of the Third Ecumenical Council; Uncovering of the relics of St. Theodosius of Chernigov; Chrysostom, Metropolitan of Smyrna (celebrated on Sunday before the Elevation).

SEPTEMBER 10

Galatians 4:28-5:10; John 3:16-21

Blessed, plainly, is that life which is not valued at the estimation of outsiders, but is known, as judge of itself, by its own inner feelings. It needs no popular opinions as its reward in any way; nor has it any fear of punishments. Thus the less it strives for glory, the more it rises above it. For to those who seek for glory, that reward in the shape of present things is but a shadow of future ones, and is a hindrance to eternal life, as it is written in the Scriptures: 'Truly I say to you, they have received their reward.'

St. Ambrose of Milan

SYNAXIS OF THE HOLY APOSTLES APELLES, LUKE, AND CLEMENT OF THE SEVENTY. The Apostle Paul mentions Apelles in his Epistle to the Romans (16:10), saying, "Greet Apelles, who is approved in Christ." When Apostle Paul used the word 'approved,' this indicates that Apostle Apelles must have overcome some trial in the name of Christ. It appears that he went from Jerusalem to Rome, and then to Smyrna, where he illuminated with the light of the gospel. St. Paul also mentions Luke in his Second Epistle to Timothy (4:11), saying, "Only Luke is with me." Apostle Luke was the first Bishop of Laodicea in Syria, where he shepherded the flock well. Finally, St. Paul mentions Clement in his Epistle to the Philippians (4:3), saying, "...along with Clement and the rest of my co-workers, whose names are in the Book of Life." Apostle Clement was the Bishop of Sardis and died after suffering wounds for Christ.

SAINTS OF THE DAY: Menodora, Metrodora, and Nymphodora at Nicomedia; Pulcheria of Greece; Barypsabas in Dalmatia; Salvius of Albi; Ioasaph of Kubensk; Three Holy Women of Constantinople; Theodoritus of Ryazan; Peter and Paul, Bishops of Nicaea; Paul the Obedient of the Kiev Caves; Cassian of Spaso-Kamenny, and Cyril of White Lake; Finian of Ulster; Theodaard of Maastricht; Meletius Fedyunev of Kuzhba, Gabriel Yatsik of Donskoy Monastery, and Warus of Lipetsk; Synaxis of the Holy Apostles Apelles, Lucius, and Clement of the Seventy.

SEPTEMBER 11

Galatians 5:11-21; John 12:19-36

Light does not fail because men have blinded themselves; it remains, with its own properties, while the blinded are plunged in darkness through their own fault… Therefore, all who revolt from the Father's light, and who transgress the law of liberty, have removed themselves through their own fault, since they were created free and self-determining.

St. Irenaeus of Lyons

VENERABLE DEINIOL, BISHOP OF BANGOR IN WALES. Deiniol was famous for establishing two monasteries in Wales with the name Bangor. The first was called Bangor Fawr, which became one of the greatest monastic centers with 2,000 monks living in it. The other was called Bangor Iscoed. The name "Bangor" means a settlement within a wattle fence. The monasteries were built in low-lying areas to prevent raids from pagan pirates. Many disciples gathered around Deiniol, and they went out and evangelized the surrounding region. Others came to live together with their families within the monastery's territory. Deiniol was the abbot of these monasteries and the first bishop of the Bangor diocese. Many miracles are associated with the saint. One time, robbers stole oxen from a ploughman. At Deiniol's command, stags started working in the fields instead of the lost oxen. St. Deiniol died peacefully in the sixth century and is buried on the island of Bardsey, where according to tradition 20,000 saints of God rest in peace.

SAINTS OF THE DAY: Demetrius, Euanthia, and Demetrian at Skepsis; Ia of Persia and 9,000 martyrs with her; Theodora of Alexandria; Diodorus, Didymus, and Diomedes of Laodicea; Euphrosynus the Cook of Alexandria; Paphnutius the Confessor; Elias the Cave-dweller of Calabria; John of Svyatogorsk Monastery; Theodora of Vasta; Joseph of Zaonikieva; Deiniol, Bishop of Bangor; Translation of the relics of Sts. Sergius and Herman of Valaam; Glorification of St. Xenia of St. Petersburg, fool-for-Christ; "Kaplunovka" Weeping Kazan Icon of the Mother of God.

SEPTEMBER 12

Galatians 6:2-10; John 11:47-54

The Christian religion transforms people and heals them. The most important precondition, however, for someone to recognize and discern the truth is humility. Egotism darkens a person's mind, it confuses him, it leads him astray, to heresy. It is important for a person to understand the truth.

St. Porphyrios the Kapsokalivite

VENERABLE BASSIAN OF TOTEMSK. Bassian was a tailor from the sixteenth-century village of Strelitsa, near the city of Totma. He left his family and became a disciple of St. Theodosios of Totemsk, at the Sumorinsk monastery, where he spent several years in obedience. He resettled near a church in honor of St. Nicholas, by the River Tiksna. He lived for a while in the church portico until he built a cell near the church, and he attended every service. For thirty years, he wore a heavy chain on his shoulders, an iron cap, and an iron belt as an ascetic discipline. He lived in solitude within his cell, seeing no one but his spiritual father. He lived on the alms that people left by his window. Bassian died peacefully, and only then did anyone see the hardship he endured. Twenty-three years after his death, a deadly plague struck the land, and many sick people received healing at the place of St. Bassian's burial.

SAINTS OF THE DAY: Coronatus, Bishop of Nicomedia (Iconium); Autonomos, bishop in Italy; Julian of Galatia, and 40 martyrs with him; Andronicus of Atroa; Macedonius in Phrygia, and with him Tatian and Theodulus; Daniel of Thasos; Martyr Okeanos; Sacerdos, Bishop of Lyons in Gaul; Dositheus of Tbilisi, Georgia; Bassian of Totemsk; Theodore, Archbishop of Alexandria; Alexis, fool-for-Christ of Elnat and Zharki; Athanasius, disciple of Sergius of Radonezh, and his disciple Athanasius; Ailbhe (Elvis) of Emly; Translation of the relics of St. Symeon of Verkhoturye.

THURSDAY

Forefeast of the Elevation
Fast-free

SEPTEMBER 13

Hebrews 3:1-4; John 12:25-36

It is useless to accuse those around us and those who live with us of somehow interfering with or being an impediment to our salvation and spiritual perfection... Spiritual or emotional dissatisfaction comes from within ourselves, from inexperience and from poorly conceived opinions we do not want to abandon, but which bring on doubt, embarrassment, and misunderstanding. All of this tires and burdens us, and brings us to a sorry state. We would do well to comprehend the Holy Fathers' simple advice: If we will humble ourselves, we will find tranquility anywhere, without having to mentally wander about many other places, where we might have the same, or even worse, experiences.

St. Ambrose of Optina

VENERABLE JOHN OF PRISLOP. John grew up near the Prislop Monastery in southwestern Romania at the turn of the sixteenth century. Later, he became a monk there. After several years, he went into the mountains to lead a solitary ascetical life, struggling against the assaults of the demons. One day while John was making a window in his cell, he was shot and killed by a hunter who mistook him for a wild animal.

SAINTS OF THE DAY: Cornelius the Centurion; Seleucus of Galatia; Straton of Nicomedia; Cronides, Leontius, and Serapion of Alexandria; Theodotus of Alexandria; Hierotheos of Kalamata; Ketevan, Queen of Kakheti, Georgia; Elias, Zoticus, Lucian, Valerian, Macrobius, and Gordian at Tomis in Moesia; Peter at Atroe; John of Prislop (Romania); Litorius, Bishop of Tours; Cornelius of Padan-Olonets, and with him Dionysius and Misael; Commemoration of the Founding of the Church of the Resurrection (the Holy Sepulcher) at Jerusalem.

Elevation of the Holy Cross
Strict Fast

SEPTEMBER 14

1 Corinthians 1:18-24
John 19:6-11, 13-20, 25-28, 30-35

Glory, O Lord, to the power of Thy Cross, which never fails! When the enemy oppresses me with a sinful thought or feeling, and I, lacking freedom in my heart, make the sign of the Cross several times with faith, suddenly my sins falls away from me, the compulsion vanishes, and I find myself free... For the faithful the Cross is a mighty power which delivers from all evils, from the malice of the invisible foe.

St. John of Kronstadt

LESNA ICON OF THE MOTHER OF GOD. In 1683, a herdsman saw a small icon among the branches of a pear tree. A halo of light surrounded it. In terror, he fell on his knees and prayed, then ran away without the icon. When he told his friend what he had seen, the two of them told the priest and the people of their village of the miraculous appearance. The icon was taken to the house of a local landowner, where many pilgrims came to venerate it. However, the Roman Catholics gained possession of the icon and placed it in their newly-built church in Lesna. Many years later, in 1863, the Roman Catholic church was closed and turned over to the local Orthodox community. By the turn of the century, the holy icon wrought more than 500 miracles.

SAINTS OF THE DAY: Repose of St. John Chrysostom; Placilla the Empress, wife of Theodosius the Great; New Martyr Ioasaph of Thessalonica; Child-martyr Valerian; Martyr Theocles; Maria of Tarsus; Cyprian, Bishop of Carthage; New Martyr Macarios of Thessalonica; Papas of Lycaonia; Commemoration of the Holy Fathers of the Sixth Ecumenical Council; Uncovering of the relics of Sts. Alexandra, Martha, and Helen of Diveyevo; "Lesna" Icon of the Mother of God.

Saturday after the Elevation
Fast-free

September 15

1 Corinthians 1:26-2:5
John 8:21-30

Destroy within you the devil's rule over you; destroy all his influence over you; acquire spiritual freedom. The foundation of your struggle is the grace of Holy Baptism; your weapon is the prayer of Jesus.

St. Ignatius Brianchaninov

JOSEPH, BISHOP OF ALAVERDI IN GEORGIA. From his early years, Joseph chose monasticism and settled in the barren Alaverdian steppes, in the sixth century. He pursued asceticism under the guidance of St. John Zedazni. Through prayer and fasting, Joseph's spiritual strength became so great that wild beasts would not harm him, and deer came to him to nourish him with their milk. One day a noble man from that area happened upon the saint while hunting. He was so impressed seeing Joseph standing at prayer, that he remained there and became a monk. Reports of this spread and people who felt a need for piety in their lives made a pilgrimage to the Alaverdian steppes. A monastery began there, and a church was built dedicated to Great Martyr George. Joseph became the abbot and guided the monks with a paternal love. He also traveled from the monastery to teach the pagans in the surrounding areas. When they saw Joseph's holiness and sincerity, they abandoned their customs and accepted the gospel teaching. Towards the end of his life, he went into complete seclusion in a small cell. St. Joseph died peacefully and was buried next to the altar in the church of St. George in Alaverdi.

SAINTS OF THE DAY: Nicetas the Goth; Martyr Maximus; Bessarion I and Bessarion II, Metropolitans of Larissa; Symeon of Thessalonica; Gerasimus of Sourvia; Philotheus of Asia Minor; Joseph of Alaverdi; Porphyrios the Mime; Joseph the New of Paros; Two maidens slain by the sword; John of Crete; Nicetas, disciple of St. Sergius of Radonezh; Ignatius Biryukov of Aleksievo-Akatov; Dimitry Ignatenko of Melitopol; Mirin of Paisley; Uncovering of the relics of the Holy Protomartyr Stephen; Uncovering of the relics of St. Acacius the Confessor of Melitene.

Sunday after the Elevation
Fast-free

SEPTEMBER 16

Galatians 2:16-20; Mark 8:34-9:1

Every action of Christ glorifies the Church, but the cross is the glory above all glory. Paul understood that well when he said: "I will glory in nothing else but the cross of Christ."

St. Cyril of Jerusalem

KUSHKA THE CONFESSOR OF ODESSA. At the age of twenty-one, Kushka was received as a prospective monk at the Russian monastery of St. Panteleimon on Mt. Athos. Seventeen years later, he became a resident of the Kiev Caves Holy Dormition Lavra, and at the age of fifty-six, he received his tonsure into the schema. In 1934, the Kiev Caves Lavra was shut down due to Communist persecution. Still, Kushka showed great courage to continue serving as a priest. Then he entered an eight-year struggle as a confessor. He was labeled a "minister of the cult" and sentenced to five years in the prison camps and then three years in exile. Upon his release, people were drawn to him as they are to a lighted lamp at night. Kushka was constantly watched and persecuted. Even towards the end of his life, in the 1960's, a new generation of militant atheist rulers shut down churches, monasteries, and religious schools. At the Holy Dormition Monastery in Odessa, Kushka would get up very early, read his prayer rule, commune every day, and especially loved to serve the early Liturgy, which he said was for spiritual strugglers. When St. Kushka died, the authorities feared that his funeral would draw an enormous flood of people, so they set a two-hour time limit in which to bury him.

SAINTS OF THE DAY: Euphemia the All-praised of Chalcedon; Victor and Sosthenes at Chalcedon; Dorotheus, hermit of Egypt; Ninian, Bishop of Whithorn; Ludmilla, grandmother of St. Wenceslaus, Prince of the Czechs; Melitina of Marcianopolis; Isaac and Joseph at Karnu, Georgia; Kushka of Odessa; Cyprian of Serbia; Procopius, abbot of Sazava in Bohemia; Cyprian, Metropolitan of Kiev; Edith of Wilton; "Support of the Humble" Icon of the Mother of God.

September 17

Ephesians 1:22-2:3; Luke 3:19-22

A mother should not be satisfied by giving her child a physical caress, but should also coddle it with the caress of prayer. In the depths of its soul the child senses the spiritual caress that its mother conveys to it and is drawn to her. It feels security and certainty when its mother mystically embraces it with constant, intense and fervent prayer and releases it from whatever is oppressing it.

St. Porphyrios the Kapsokalivite

MARTYRS MAXIMOS, ASCLEPIODOTOS, AND THEODOTOS. Maximos and Asclepiodotos were prominent citizens from fourth-century Marcianopolis during the persecutions of Emperor Maximian. They lived a pious life, and by their example attracted many to the faith. They were arrested by the governor Tiris of Thrace and ordered to deny their faith. When they refused, they were cruelly beaten. Witnessing this inhumanity, a pious man named Theodotos reproached Tiris. The angry governor gave orders to hang him on a tree and tear his flesh with iron hooks. Then the three saints were taken to the city of Adrianopolis, where they received more torture. Their bodies were burned with molten metal, but a voice from heaven gave them comfort and strength. A few days later, they were sent to the arena to be devoured by wild beasts, but they would not touch them. Asclepiodotos was tied to a bull, but it would not move. Finally, the three martyrs were beheaded. Sometime later, a bolt of lightning struck Tiris as he sat on the judgment seat.

SAINTS OF THE DAY: Sophia and her daughters, Faith, Hope, and Love, at Rome; Heraclides and Myron, bishops of Cyprus; Maximos, Asclepiodotos, and Theodotos of Marcianopolis; Theodota at Nicaea, and Agathoklea; Lucy and her son Geminian of Rome; Innocent of Glinsk; Anastasius of Perioteron; Eusipius of Cyprus; Lambert of Maastricht; Joachim, Patriarch of Alexandria; 100 Martyrs of Egypt; 156 Martyrs of Palestine; Paul, Theodosius, Nicodemus, and Seraphim of Koryazha Monastery; Martyrs Haralampus, Panteleon, and others.

SEPTEMBER 18

Ephesians 2:19-3:7; Luke 3:23-4:1

We attain freedom from sin in six ways: by preserving the purity of the five senses and of the spoken word.

St. Elijah the Priest

VENERABLE HILARION OF OPTINA. Hilarion was born on the night of Pascha in the town of Kluch, Russia, in the early nineteenth century. From his youth, he had a desire to become a monk. He learned his father's trade as a tailor, thinking that this would be useful in the monastery. Through his study of the Holy Scriptures and the writings of the holy Fathers, the desire to become a monk was rekindled. He visited many monasteries and decided on Optina. He was thirty-six years old. Hilarion was placed in a cell next to Father Barlaam, the retired abbot of Valaam Monastery. He instructed Hilarion in the Jesus Prayer and told him to examine his thoughts and heart often. For thirty-nine years, Hilarion served as the cell attendant to the elder St. Macarius. He also tended the gardens, baked, and served as the beekeeper. He progressed spiritually but kept this hidden from men. Upon the death of St. Macarius, Hilarion became the abbot and confessor of the monastery. He also confessed the nuns who lived nearby and the many pilgrims who came to him. His advice would come from the Scriptures or the writings of the Fathers, and this advice was effective because he had experienced what he taught. He led people to an awareness of their sins and to feel sorry for them, in order to heal their spiritual infirmities. His prayers also healed their physical or mental illness. Towards the end of his life, he became seriously ill for two years. He did not ask God to let him recover, but for patience and endurance. During his final days, St. Macarius appeared to him many times in his dreams. St. Hilarion was buried next to his Elder St. Macarius.

SAINTS OF THE DAY: Ariadne of Phrygia; Eumenius of Gortyna; Sophia and Irene of Egypt; Castor of Alexandria; Arcadius of Novgorod; Bidzina, Shalva, and Elizbar of Georgia; Romulus the Sinaite; Hilarion of Optina; Amphilochius of Krasnoyarsk.

SEPTEMBER 19

Ephesians 3:8-21; Luke 4:1-15

The tongue of a back-biting soul is three-pronged: it injures the speaker, the listener and sometimes the person being maligned.

St. Thalassios the Libyan

HIEROMARTYR CONSTANTINE GOLUBEV OF BOGORODSK, AND TWO OTHERS WITH HIM. At the age of twenty-four, Constantine felt called to missionary service. He was assigned to the Brotherhood of the Holy Cross in the village of Baranovka. Recognizing his success, Bishop Tikhon assigned him as an anti-sectarian and anti-schismatic missionary for the Saratov Diocese. Constantine was ordained to the priesthood at the age of forty-three. He became involved in activities to benefit the incarcerated and conducted Divine Services for them. He also addressed religious education, the enlightenment of women, and the battle against alcoholism. He also saw that his seven children were strictly raised in an Orthodox spirit. Constantine was arrested in 1918, during the Bolshevik Revolution. Without legal proceedings, he was sentenced to death. When he was taken to the place of execution, an enormous crowd followed him. The firing squad only wounded him, then threw him, still alive, into a shallow pit and buried him. According to some eyewitnesses, the ground still "breathed" for some time. Executed with Constantine was a woman who fearlessly tried to protect him, and a member of the Red Army who refused to carry out the death sentence. The murderer was tortured by his conscience. Several times St. Constantine appeared to him. He soon shot his wife who he mistook for the martyr, and then he killed himself. St. Constantine's relics were later found incorrupt.

SAINTS OF THE DAY: Trophimus, Sabbatius, and Dorymedon of Synnada; Seguanus of Gaul; Theodore, Prince of Smolensk and Yaroslavl, and his sons David and Constantine; Alexis of Zosima Hermitage; Zosimas, hermit of Cilicia; Theodore of Tarsus, Archbishop of Canterbury; Igor-George, Prince of Chernigov; Constantine Golubev of Bogorodsk, and two martyrs with him.

SEPTEMBER 20

Ephesians 6:10-17; Luke 21:12-19

The key to the kingdom of Heaven is prayer.

St. Elijah the Priest

MICHAEL THE WONDERWORKER AND HIS COUNCILOR THEODORE. Michael was the prince of thirteenth-century Chernigov. As a child, he was pious and mild mannered, but in poor health. He asked for the prayers of St. Nikita the Stylite and was healed. In 1238, the Mongol-Tatars had destroyed many territories and were moving towards southern Russia and Kiev, but Michael would not negotiate a surrender. Instead, he rode to the Hungarian king to organize allied forces to resist the enemy and tried to recruit Poland and Germany. But before Michael could accomplish this, the Mongols had devastated Russia, Hungary, and Poland. With Kiev in ruins, Michael still worked towards a united Christian Europe against the Mongols; however, this effort also failed. Finally, the Mongols demanded that Michael journey to their realm. Michael knew they would challenge his Christian faith. When Michael and his friend, the Boyar Theodore, arrived, they were ordered to walk through a bonfire to cleanse their evil intents, and to worship the sun and fire. Michael replied, "A Christian worships only God, the Creator of the world, and not creatures." The Tatars fiercely beat him until the ground was red with his blood. Then he was beheaded. Theodore was beheaded after fierce torments. The martyrs were thrown to dogs to be devoured, but miraculously they were protected for several days. Christians secretly buried them with reverence. Persuaded by the keeping of the Orthodox faith and their willingness to die for Christ, the Tatar khans ceased demanding Russian Christians in the Horde to fulfill pagan rituals. However, the Russian Church continued to struggle for a long time against the Mongol Yoke.

SAINTS OF THE DAY: Eustathius Placidas, Theopistes, Agapius and Theopistus, of Rome; Theodore, Euprepius, and two named Anastasius; Hilarion the Cretan; Michael and Theodore of Chernigov; John of Crete; Eustathius of Thessalonica; John of Putivl (Ukraine).

SEPTEMBER 21

Ephesians 4:17-25; Luke 4:22-30

Love dominates all rules and laws. Love everyone; if you can't, at least show a goodwill. How to love the evil man? Hate the evil, but love those who do evil. Who knows maybe one day they will repent their sins by the powers of prayer, tears and confession and become like an angel.

St. Gabriel Urgebadze

NEW HIEROMARTYR THEOPHAN, METROPOLITAN OF LIPETSK AND BELORUSSIA. From his youth, Theophan wanted to serve the Church in a priestly-monastic office. He received his Bachelor of Theology degree in 1889. When he wanted to enter the monastic life, Bishop Theophan the Recluse wrote to him saying that he should not have the ulterior motive of becoming a bishop, but only to save his own soul and to gain a spiritually wise understanding. He also said that the rank of hierarch ought to correspond to spiritual perfection. Over the next fifteen years, Theophan's desire to become a hierarch faded. Finally, he received the metropolitan's blessing to enter the St. Alexander Nevsky Lavra. As a novice, this period was the happiest and most joyful in his life. Several years later, he was consecrated bishop, then archbishop, and raised to the rank of metropolitan. But in 1937, there were massive arrests of clergy and laymen. Theophan was arrested, interrogated, and subjected to cruel tortures. They housed him in a basement cell which they flooded with water. He and the Orthodox were accused of imaginary political crimes, counter-revolutionary activity, the overthrow of Soviet authority, and the restoration of capitalism in the USSR. The Soviets burned collective farms, stockpiled timber and forests, and standing crops. Metropolitan Theophan was executed by firing squad.

SAINTS OF THE DAY: Quadratus of the Seventy; Jonah the Sabbaite; Eusebios, Nestabus, Zeno, and Nestor of Gaza; Eusebius of Phoenicia; Priscus of Phrygia; Isaacius and Meletius of Cyprus; Daniel of Shugh Hill; Theophan of Lipetsk, and Maurice of Yuriev-Polsky; Joseph of Zaonikiev.

SEPTEMBER 22

1 Corinthians 14:20-25
Luke 4:31-36

Innocence is greater than genius.

+Elder Amphilochios Makris of Patmos

VENERABLE COSMAS OF ZOGRAPHOU. Cosmas was a learned and enlightened young man from fourteenth-century Bulgaria. He studied Holy Scripture in his native Bulgarian and Greek. He avoided quarrelsome boys, observed the fasts, and spent time with his studies and prayers. He was accepted to live at Zographou Monastery on Mt. Athos. Cosmas was soon ordained to deacon and then presbyter. He prayed fervently to the Mother of God for guidance and heard Her voice coming forth from Her holy icon, and She asked Jesus, "How wilt Cosma be saved?" The answer of the Lord was, "Let him withdraw from the monastery into silence." Cosmas received the blessing of his elder to withdraw into the wilderness, to a cave that was cut into a cliff, and there he acquired the virtues and the gift of clairvoyance. Once two monks went to visit him, but along the way, they hid a gourd of wine. As they were leaving, Cosmas told them to break the gourd because a poisonous snake had crawled in, and this proved to be so. On another occasion, he saw the soul of the abbot of Hilander being tortured by demons. He sent word to the monks to pray for their abbot who had just died. At the end of his days, Cosmas was granted a vision of Christ, Who informed him that before his death he would be beaten by Satan himself and his demons. Cosmas bravely endured furious beatings, and on the third day, he gave up his soul. At the time of the burial, a multitude of beasts and birds flocked to his cave. After forty days, when the relics of Cosmas were to be transferred, they were mysteriously missing.

SAINTS OF THE DAY: Phocas.of Sinope; Peter the Tax Collector; 26 Martyrs of Zographou; Jonah the Presbyter; Phocas the Gardener; Macarius of Zhabyn; Theophanes the Silent; Theodosius of Brazsk; Parasceva of Diveyevo; Emmeram, in Gaul; Jonah of Yashezersk; Benjamin of Romanov; Maurice and the Theban Legion.

SUNDAY

First Sunday of Luke
Conception of St. John the Baptist
Fast-free

SEPTEMBER 23

Galatians 4:22-27; Luke 5:1-11

God never abandons a soul that puts its trust in Him, even though it is overpowered by temptations, for He is aware of all weaknesses. A man knows the weight that can be placed on the back of an ass, a mule or a camel, and burdens each beast with as much as it can carry; the potter knows how long he must keep his clay in the fire, for if he exposes it too long to the flames, the pot will crack, and if he does not bake it long enough, it will not be fit for use. Now if a man has judgment as precise as this, how infinitely greater is the wisdom of God in judging the degree of temptation which a soul is able to bear?

St. Nilus of Sora

VIRGIN-MARTYR RHAIS OF ALEXANDRIA. Rhais was the daughter of a priest living in Egypt. She became a nun at the age of twelve. One day she saw a ship at the shore with a large group of men, women, clergy, monks, and nuns. They were all chained for their confession of the Christian faith. Rhais voluntarily joined them, even though a guard warned her to go away. When the ship arrived in the city of Antipolis, she stood before the governor and ridiculed his gods. St. Rhais was tortured and beheaded. After her, the other Christians confessed their faith in Christ and were martyred.

SAINTS OF THE DAY: Conception of St. John the Baptist; Xanthippa and Polyxena of Spain; Rhais of Alexandria; Andrew, John, Peter, and Antoninus of Syracuse, martyred in Africa; New Martyr Nicholas Pantopolis at Constantinople; New Martyr John of Epirus; New Martyr Arsenius of Russia; Adamnan, abbot of Iona; Glorification of St. Innocent, Metropolitan of Moscow, enlightener of Alaska and Siberia; "Slovensk" Icon of the Mother of God.

September 24

2 Timothy 3:10-15; Luke 5:12-16

It may be that a man seems to be silent, but if his heart judges others, then he is always speaking.

St. Poimen the Great

GALACTEON OF VOLOGDA. Galacteon was the son of Prince Belsky. Family members hid away the seven-year-old boy out of fear that Tsar Ivan the Terrible would cause him harm. When he grew up, he became a shoemaker in Vologda. He married and had a child, but his wife soon died, leaving Galacteon to raise their infant daughter. The adversities that he endured strengthened him to devote himself to God. He dug himself a hole and built a cell near a church. He took monastic vows and began to pray and fast. He continued his craft as a shoemaker, and from his earnings, he gave one-third to the poor, one-third for his sustenance, and one-third he dedicated to God. He chained himself to the wall in his cell, and Christians would bring him dry bread and water through a window. People soon began to come for guidance because his words were filled with spiritual power. Once during a terrible drought, he prayed with the bishop, and the rains replenished the earth. Another time, he had a vision that the Poles and Lithuanians would overrun Vologda because of the people's sins. He emerged from his cell in chains, telling everyone to pray and fast in preparation and to build a church in honor of the Znamenie Icon of the Mother of God. He also said that several churches would be burned, but a church would be founded and a monastery would be built over his cell. This prophecy was fulfilled. In 1612, the Poles and Lithuanians stormed Vologda, plundered the churches, set fire to the city, and killed many people, including Galacteon. Christians buried him in his cell, and many miraculous healings began to occur there. Beginning in 1627, a church dedicated to the Znamenie Icon of the Mother of God was built over St. Galacteon's relics, and a monastery was founded.

SAINTS OF THE DAY: Silouan the Athonite; Coprius of Palestine; Thecla of Iconium; Stephen of Serbia; Dorothea of Kashin.

SEPTEMBER 25

Ephesians 5:20-25; Luke 5:12-16

Hence it is very clear that disturbing urges are not always aroused in us by other people's faults. Rather, we are to blame—we who have stored up within ourselves the causes of our offenses and the seeds of our vices that, when the rain shower of temptation drenches our mind, at once break forth into buds and fruits.

St. John Cassian

MARTYR PAPHNUTIOS AND 546 COMPANIONS IN EGYPT. During the third-century persecutions of Diocletian, the governor Adrian called for the arrest of Paphnutios from out of the Egyptian wilderness. Not waiting for his captors, Paphnutios went directly to Adrian, confessed his faith, and was put to torture. The power of God preserved him to the point that the two soldiers who tortured him came to believe in Jesus Christ, and they were beheaded. After this, Paphnutios was imprisoned. He converted forty prisoners to Christianity. These forty were burned alive, but Paphnutios was set free. A Christian named Nestorios took him in. He and all his family were strengthened in the faith, and they ultimately were martyred. Paphnutios is credited with strengthening 546 men in Christ, and they were all martyred. Some were burned and others killed by the sword. Paphnutios was thrown into a river with a heavy stone around his neck, but he miraculously floated to shore. Finally, St. Paphnutios was sent to the emperor who gave orders to crucify him on a date tree.

SAINTS OF THE DAY: Paphnutios and 546 companions in Egypt; Euphrosyne of Alexandria, and her father Paphnutius; Euphrosyne of Suzdal; Paul and Tatta, and their children Sabinian, Maximus, Rufus, and Eugene; Dosithea the Recluse of Kiev; Paraskeva of Kostroma; Arsenius the Great of Georgia; Finbar (Barry) of Cork; Cadoc of Llancarfan; Ceolfrith (Geoffrey) of Wearmouth-Jarrow; Translation of the relics of St. Herman, Archbishop of Kazan; Repose of St. Sergius, abbot of Radonezh; Commemoration of the Deliverance from the Great Earthquake in Constantinople in 447, and the child who heard the "Trisagion."

Wednesday

Translation of St. John the Theologian
Abstain from meat and dairy products, and fish.

September 26

1 John 4:12-19
John 19:25-27, 21:24-25

On days when a Saint is celebrated, Christians ought to pray more ardently, with contrition and love, and entreat the Saint to intercede with God for the salvation of their soul. The feast day of every Saint is for Christians a serious reminder of the great sufferings which the Saints experienced for the sake of Christ's faith. They were glorified by God and with glory they received a place in the kingdom of Heaven.

St. Raphael of Lesvos

VENERABLE NILOS OF ROSSANO. Two of the greatest commandments are to love God with all our mind, heart, and strength, and to love our neighbor as ourselves. Nilos would undergo long journeys just to save another person some trouble. He was an ascetic who founded many monasteries. His prayers wrought miracles, and he was a defender of the purity of Orthodoxy in the face of heresies. He lived during the latter part of the tenth century among the Greeks of Rossano, also known as Calabria. Among his many disciples was St. Bartholomew, who wrote many Canons for the Church.

SAINTS OF THE DAY: Repose of the Holy Apostle and Evangelist John the Theologian; Gideon, judge of Israel; Martyr Heras; Five Virgin-martyrs and Monastrion; Ephraim, wonderworker of Novgorod; Nilos the Younger of Rossano; Neagoe Basarab, Prince of Wallachia; Glorification of St. Tikhon (Bellavin), Patriarch of Moscow and All Russia; Arrival of the Iveron Icon of the Mother of God in Georgia.

September 27

Ephesians 5:33-6:9; Luke 6:12-19

It is not the same to eat your meal with a blessing and to eat it without a blessing. Every meal is the table of God, which God Himself has set for us. This is why it is necessary as a householder to thank God and to beg for His blessings. Blessed food is more tasty and more satisfying while unblessed food is untasty, unsatisfying and unhealthy.

St. Paisios the Athonite

NEW HIEROMARTYR HERMAN, BISHOP OF VOLSK. While Herman was a student at the St. Petersburg Theological Academy, he was tonsured and ordained to the diaconate. He was ordained to the priesthood and graduated from the academy in 1906. Over the ensuing years, he was appointed an assistant inspector of four different theological schools. In 1916, he became rector of the Vladimir theological seminary. There are varied accounts of how he died: He was killed in Saratov as a hostage after the attempt on the life of Lenin; he was condemned to fifteen years' imprisonment by the Saratov revolutionary tribunal, released on amnesty, arrested again and shot in 1919.

SAINTS OF THE DAY: Apostles Mark, Aristarchus, and Zenas of the Seventy; Callistratus and 49 Martyrs of Carthage; Sabbatius of Solovki; Flavian I, Archbishop of Antioch; Martyrs Philemon and Fortunatus; Epicharis of Rome; Martyr Gaiana; Aquilina of Thessalonica; Ignatius, abbot of the Deep Stream; Anthimus the Georgian of Wallachia; Archippus of Glinsk Hermitage; Herman Kosolapov, Bishop of Volsk; Fifteen Martyrs drowned at sea; Sigebert, King of the East Angles; Barry, disciple of St. Cadoc; Dimitri the New of Basarab; Rachel of Borodino Convent; Peter Polyansky, Metropolitan of Krutitsa.

SEPTEMBER 28

2 Corinthians 4:6-15
Luke 6:17-23

When we reach the grave we cannot even say, 'Lord, have mercy' or do any good deed.

+Elder Gabriel of Koutloumosiou

VENERABLE CHARITON THE CONFESSOR OF PALESTINE. Chariton lived under the Christian persecutions of Emperor Aurelian. He denounced the pagan gods and confessed faith in Jesus Christ. He was fiercely beaten, but God healed his wounds in prison. When the emperor died, Chariton and all the prisoners were released, and Christians came out of hiding. On his way to Jerusalem, Chariton was set upon by thieves who meant to kill him. While he waited to die, a venomous snake crawled into the cave where Chariton was and poisoned the robbers' wine. When they returned to the cave and began drinking the wine, they all perished. Chariton distributed the plundered gold to the poor and the monasteries. At the robber's cave, he built a church, and a monastery formed, attracting many disciples. This monastery is the famous Tharan Lavra in Palestine. The monastery followed a strict rule that Chariton implemented. Yearning solitude, he went further into the wilderness. Since he could heal sickness and drive out demons, people would find him, and he founded yet two more monasteries. Towards the end of his life, he pursued asceticism in a cave not far from one of his monasteries. At the time of his death, he asked to be buried in the Tharan monastery in the church built on the robbers' cave.

SAINTS OF THE DAY: Prophet Baruch; Chariton the Confessor; Mark the Shepherd, and Alexander, Zosimas, Alphius, Nicon, Neon, Heliodorus, and 24 others; Eustace of Rome; Cyril and Maria, parents of Sergius of Radonezh; Chariton of Vologda; Herodion of Iloezersk; Faustus of Riez; Hilarion of Petushki, and Michaela of Aksinyino (Moscow); Juliana, Princess of Olshansk; Annemund of Lyons; Martyr Alexander; Wenceslaus, Prince of the Czechs; Wenceslaus of Zenkovka; Auxentius the Alaman; Leoba of Bischofsheim; Translation of the relics of St. Neophytus the Recluse of Cyprus.

SEPTEMBER 29

1 Corinthians 15:39-45
Luke 5:17-26

God abandons no one. For Him all are children. None are stepchildren. And the hard occasions and situations—all is sent for our benefit.

St. Theophan the Recluse

MARTYRS DADA, GABDELAS, AND CASDOA OF PERSIA. During the persecutions of Persian Emperor Sapor, Dada was appointed chief court-steward. When it was discovered that he was a Christian, he was sentenced to be burned at the stake. However, when he signed himself with the cross, the fire went out. When Sapor's son Gabdelas witnessed this miracle, he believed in Christ and confessed his faith. The judge reported this to the emperor, and he commanded that his son be fiercely tortured. An angel of God comforted Gabdelas and restored him to health after each torment. Upon seeing these miracles, many others in prison became Christians. Gabdelas' sister Casdoa watched as a volley of arrows was shot at her brother and the arrows bounced off him and struck the archers instead. Casdoa confessed herself a Christian and her father had her terribly beaten and imprisoned. Gabdelas prayed for his sister and assured her that she would suffer no more torture. The following day Gabdelas asked two priests to baptize him. At that moment, a cloud overshadowed the martyr, and water and oil poured forth from it, and a voice was heard, "Servant of God, thou hast already received Baptism." His face became radiant, and a fragrance filled the air. Finally, he was run through with spears and died shortly afterward. His body and that of Martyr Dada, who was terribly tortured, were cut into pieces, and the priests buried their relics. At midnight, Gabdelas appeared to a priest and gave him a vessel with oil, asking him to anoint her with oil and commune her the Holy Mysteries. He did this, and she gave up her spirit.

SAINTS OF THE DAY: Theophanes the Merciful; Cyriacus the Hermit of Palestine; Gudelia of Persia; Mary of Palestine; 80 Holy Martyrs of Byzantium.

SUNDAY

Second Sunday of Luke
Fast-free

SEPTEMBER 30

2 Corinthians 9:6-11
Luke 6:31-36

Looking at what came to pass, believe what is to come. No one in the future will be able to prevail against the Church. If they did not manage to crush her when she numbered but a few members, when her teaching seemed novel and strange, when so many terrible wars and so many persecutions were raised against her from everywhere, much more they will not manage to injure her today, when she has spread in the whole world, and increased her dominion among all nations, abolishing their pagan altars and idols, their festivals and celebrations, the smoke and the smell of their abominable sacrifices. How did the Apostles achieve such a great, such an important task, after so many obstacles? Surely, it was by the divine and unconquerable power of Him, who prophesied about the creation and triumph of His Church. No one can deny this, unless he is mindless and completely unable to think.

St. John Chrysostom

MICHAEL, FIRST METROPOLITAN OF KIEV. Michael was sent by the Patriarch of Constantinople to establish Christianity in tenth-century Russia, an imposing assignment for one man. However, in just four years, Michael baptized many people in the cities of Novgorod, Kiev, Rostov, and other towns. He ordained priests, bishops, and created churches. He established a monastery in Kiev and even sent missionaries to other peoples, especially the Tatars and the Bulgars. He died peacefully. His relics can be found at the Monastery of the Caves.

SAINTS OF THE DAY: Gregory, Bishop of Greater Armenia; Rhipsimia, Gaiana, and companions, in Armenia; Michael, Great Prince of Tver; Meletius, Patriarch of Alexandria; Honorius of Canterbury; Seraphim of Kharkov; Martyr Mardonius; Martyr Stratonicus; 1,000 Martyrs slain by the sword; 2 female Martyrs; 70 male Martyrs; Gregory of Pelshma; Alexandra of Moscow; Translation of the relics of St. Michael of Kiev.

The

2019

Daily Lives, Miracles, and Wisdom of the Saints & Fasting Calendar

Take pride in the title of "woman," take pride in the fact that you were born not a man, but a woman, for the Lord has given you a heart much better than that of men, a heart receptive to all that is holy, a heart soft as wax, feeling the truth of Christ. You live not by a cold mind, as do men, but you live by the sense of the heart, for the human heart, together with the mind, is an organ of perception. And the perception of the heart is higher than that of the mind.

St. Luke of Simferopol

Protection of the Mother of God
Fast-free

OCTOBER 1

Acts 9:10-19; Luke 6:24-30

To have faith in Christ means more than simply despising the delights of this life. It means we should bear all our daily trials that may bring us sorrow, distress, or unhappiness, and bear them patiently for as long as God wishes and until He comes to visit us. For it is said, 'I waited on the Lord and He came to me.'

St. Symeon the New Theologian

APOSTLE ANANIAS OF THE SEVENTY. Apostle Ananias was one of the Seventy Disciples and bishop of Damascus. Jesus appeared to him, telling him to baptize Saul of Tarsus. Ananias said that Saul had the authority to persecute all who called on Him in Damascus, but Jesus said that He would show Saul all that he must suffer and do for Him. Ananias went to Saul, put his hands on him, and said that he would receive his sight and be filled with the Holy Spirit. Ananias continued to preach the gospel to the Jews and pagans. He healed many in Eleutheropolis. The governor there tried to persuade him to offer sacrifice to the idols, but he boldly confessed Christ. Orders were given to torture the saint, but these did not sway Ananias. He was led out of the city and stoned to death. His relics were transferred to Constantinople.

SAINTS OF THE DAY: Apostle Ananias of the Seventy; Romanus the Melodist of Constantinople; John Kukuzelis the Singer of Mt. Athos; Gregory the Singer of Mt. Athos; Sabbas, abbot of Vyshera; Bavo of Haarlem; Domninus of Thessalonica; King Mirian and Queen Nana, and Abiathar of Mtskheta, and Sidonia, disciple of St. Nina; Michael, abbot of Zovia Monastery, and 36 Fathers with him; Remigius of Rheims, apostle to the Franks; Bavo of Ghent; Mylor of Brittany; Melchizedek I, Catholicos-Patriarch of All Georgia; Alexis Stavrovsky of Petrograd; Ismael Rozhdestvensky of Strelna; Joseph of Bisericani Monastery (Moldavia); Miracle of the Pillar with the Robe of the Lord under it at Mtskheta, Georgia; "Quick to Hear" and "Pokrov" (Pskov) Icons of the Mother of God.

OCTOBER 2

1 Timothy 1:12-17; Luke 6:37-45

Do not cast off brotherly love lightly, for there remains no other way of salvation for human beings. Observe yourself with care, and see if the evil, which separates you from your brother, has its cause, not in him, but in you; and make haste to be reconciled with him, lest you transgress the commandment of love. Do not despise the commandment of love, because—through it—you will become a son of God; whereas, when you transgress it, you become a son of Gehenna.

St. Maximos the Confessor

VENERABLE DAMARIS OF ATHENS. Damaris is mentioned in the Acts of the Apostles as the first woman of Athens who, along with Dionysius the Areopagite and others, came to believe in the gospel preached by the Apostle Paul on Mars Hill in 52 A.D. Since ancient times the Church has almost universally associated Damaris as the wife of Dionysius. St. John Chrysostom and St. Ambrose of Milan mention this. According to tradition, Damaris remained in Athens and served the needs of the Church, as did Dionysius who was made the bishop of Athens. There is also a service composed in her honor.

SAINTS OF THE DAY: Cyprian and Justina of Nicomedia of Antioch, and Martyr Theoctistus, at Nicomedia; Cassian the Greek of Uglich; Theophilus the Confessor; Anna, Princess of Kashin; Theodore (Gavra) of Atran in Chaldia of Pontus; David and Constantine, princes of Argveti, Georgia; Damaris of Athens; Andrew, fool-for-Christ of Constantinople; Cyprian of Suzdal, fool-for-Christ; Hadji George of Philadelphia in Asia Minor; Theodore Ushakov, admiral of the Russian Navy; Leodegarius (Leger), Bishop of Autun.

OCTOBER 3

Acts 17:16-34; Luke 6:46-7:1

One must not accept the following two thoughts: fornication and judgment of one's neighbor. When the enemy presents one of these we must rise up and pray; and pray again, with tears to God, and God will deliver us.

St. Sarah of Egypt

HIEROMARTYRS HEWALD THE WHITE AND HEWALD THE BLACK, AT COLOGNE. These two saints spent several years together in schools in Ireland and were companions later in life. They were renowned for their holiness. They set out for seventh-century Old Saxony in an attempt to convert their cousins to Christianity. They stayed in the home of the steward of a certain ealdorman. The steward promised to take them to the chieftain, who the Hewalds intended to convert. However, the pagans suspected that their overlord would be converted and their temples destroyed, so both priests were seized. Hewald the White was killed with the sword and Hewald the Black was tortured and torn limb from limb. Their bodies were thrown into the Rhine River. When the ealdorman heard what had happened, he killed the murderers and burned their village. Miracles followed the death of the martyrs, including their bodies being carried upstream for forty miles to the steward's home, with a heavenly light shining on them. One of the Hewalds appeared in a vision to a monk, telling him where to find their relics, and he interred them with the honor due martyrs. A spring of water is said to have gushed forth in the place of their martyrdom.

SAINTS OF THE DAY: Dionysius the Areopagite, with Rusticus and Eleutherius; John the Chozevite, Bishop of Caesarea; Dionysius, Bishop of Alexandria and 8 Martyrs with him; Agathangelus, Metropolitan of Yaroslavl; Dionysius, recluse of the Kiev Caves; Jerome of Aegina; Martyrs Theoctistus, Theogenes, and Theotecnus; Hesychius the Silent of Mt. Horeb; Hewald the White and Hewald the Black, at Cologne; Uncovering of the relics of St. Joseph, elder of Optina Monastery.

OCTOBER 4

Philippians 1:20-27; Luke 7:17-30

Everything that we give with our hands will be what we will have in the afterlife.

+Elder Gabriel of Koutloumosiou

JOHN LAMBADISTOS THE WONDERWORKER OF CYPRUS. John was the only son of wealthy Christian parents in tenth-century Lambadistos, Cyprus. As a boy, he showed the qualities of modesty, purity, and reverence for God. At the age of four, he was sent to learn how to read and write through the study of Holy Scripture. As he grew, he proved to have a sharp intellect and excelled, continually focusing and reflecting on his lessons. When he became a young man, his parents were adamant that he marry a certain girl; however, he was not at all in agreement with this. Instead, he had a sincere desire to devote his life to Jesus Christ. Hearing this, the prospective bride's parents, who had already made the marriage arrangements, turned to sorcery, causing John to lose his eyesight. He was not dejected or frightened, saying that he still had spiritual eyes to see the glory of God. John and his servant went to a quiet place and lived a harsh ascetic life in the wilderness. He fasted continuously and only ate every three or four days. John lived like this for twelve years, thankful for his blindness and working to attain the virtues. The Holy Spirit dwelled with John, and he was granted the gift to work miracles, to alleviate suffering, and to cast out unclean spirits. John recovered his sight three days before his death. He saw three eagles flying over him, and he realized that it was time to leave the world. St. John died at the age of twenty-two.

SAINTS OF THE DAY: Peter of Capitolia; Hierotheus of Athens; Domnina of Syria, with Bernice and Prosdoce; Ammon of Egypt; Theodore of Tamassos; Adauctus and Callisthene of Ephesus; Gaius, Faustus, Eusebius, and Chaeremon of Alexandria; Jonah and Nectarius of Kazan; John Lambadistos of Cyprus; Helladius and Onesimus of the Near Caves; Ammon of the Far Caves; Peter of Kuznetsk; Vladimir and Anna of Novgorod; Evdemoz of Georgia; Stephen and Helen of Serbia.

OCTOBER 5

Philippians 1:27-2:4; Luke 7:31-35

Dear friend, obey the commandments of God which are contained in the Decalogue and in the holy Gospel. Do them all with simplicity without exceptions. The Lord commanded that we observe all that he has commanded. We must not observe some and neglect others.

St. Nicodemus the Hagiorite

VENERABLES DANIIL AND MISAIL OF TURNU MONASTERY. In 2016, the Romanian Orthodox Church canonized the hermits Daniil and Misail. They were born during the second half of the sixteenth century. They entered the Cozia Monastery as brothers and received tonsure shortly after that. Daniil, who studied the Holy Scriptures and teachings of the Fathers, was ordained to the priesthood and elected as the monastery confessor. Misail was Daniil's disciple. He was full of good works and became an example to all. With the blessing of their abbot, they went into the mountains around the monastery and dug cells near springs of water. A small community of brothers gathered around them, and they struggled in unceasing prayer, vigils, fasting, and reading soul-profiting books. They also built a wooden church to serve their needs. On Sundays and feast days, they came down to the Turnu Hermitage to confess and celebrate the Divine Liturgy. Foreseeing his end, Daniil left his disciple Misail in charge. After their death in the first half of the seventeenth century, they were buried by the altar in their little church. Later, the metropolitan of Romania built a new stone church and placed their relics at the foundation of the new altar.

SAINTS OF THE DAY: Peter, Alexis, Jonah, Macarius, Philip, Hermogenes, Philaret, Innocent, and Tikhon, of Moscow; Charitina of Amisus; Gregory of Chandzoe; Methodia of Cimola; Damian the Healer, and Jeremiah and Matthew, of the Kiev Caves; Cosmas, in Bithynia; Charitina of Lithuania; John of Euchaita; Mamelta of Persia; Varlaam of Chikoysk; Sabbas of Vatopedi; Seraphim of Glinsk; Gabriel of Melekess.

OCTOBER 6

1 Corinthians 4:9-16; John 20:19-31

Almsgiving should be in secret, for God alone to know.

St. Sophia of Kleisoura

HOLY APOSTLE THOMAS. Thomas founded the Christian church in India. There was a merchant named Abbanes, who was commanded by King Gundafor to find a carpenter to build him a palace. Jesus appeared to Abbanes and sold him His slave Thomas for three pounds of silver. King Gundafor marveled at Thomas' drawings and gave him much gold, promising to return in three years to live in the palace. But Thomas gave the gold to the poor and spent two years teaching, converting, and working miracles. Upon his return, the king learned about the deception and imprisoned Thomas, but Thomas told him that he had built him a mansion in heaven. The next day, Gundafor's brother, Gad, died. An angel of the Lord took the soul of Gad to heaven and showed him his brother's mansion that was built with the gold given to Thomas. The angel returned Gad's soul to his body, and he quickly told his brother about his mansion. Immediately, the king sent his servants to the prison to bring forth Thomas. Shortly after, Thomas baptized Gundafor and Gad. While Thomas was in India, the Dormition of the Mother of God took place. All the Apostles from the various lands were caught up by clouds and taken to Her in Gethsemane. Thomas did not arrive until the third day after the burial. He was caught up in a cloud, and he beheld Her body ascending to heaven. She removed her belt and gave it to him, saying, "Receive this, my friend." When Thomas arrived at Her tomb, he asked the others to open it, and they found that She had vanished. In the city of Melipur, Apostle Thomas converted the wife and son of the governor. For this he was imprisoned, tortured, and finally pierced with five spears, giving up his soul. A part of his relics are in India, Hungary, and on Mt. Athos.

SAINTS OF THE DAY: Holy Apostle Thomas; Martyr Eroteis; Macarius of St. Anne's Skete; Cindeus of Cyprus; "Hawaiian Iveron" and "O All-hymned Mother" Icons of the Mother of God.

Third Sunday of Luke
Fast-free

October 7

2 Corinthians 11:31-12:9
Luke 7:11-16

We are called to do good deeds, but it is not through good deeds that we are saved. If we were to be saved by our deeds, then it would not have been necessary for the Lord to come down and save us. We are saved only by the mercy of God. It is the Grace of God that saves. The Lord saves. We can get a reward for our good deeds, but salvation is from God.

+Elder Thaddeus of Vitovnica

VENERABLE JOSEPH, ELDER OF KHEVI AND WONDER-WORKER OF GEORGIA. Little is known about Joseph who was a priest in the eighteenth-century village of Khevi. The people there had a reputation for being great warriors and devout Christians. Mount Kazbegi rises 13,000 feet above the village and is known for its ice-capped peaks. The Trinity Monastery sits on the slope of this mountain, and above it, on the ice-covered cliff of Mount Kazbegi, is a cave hermitage called the Bethlehem Cave. The only way to reach this hermitage is by climbing chains that are let down from the cave. Sacred objects and Church treasures have been stored here for centuries, including the tent of Patriarch Abraham and the manger of Christ. Joseph, who was known for his clairvoyance, miracle working, and love of holy objects, once climbed that mountain and brought down a piece of Abraham's tent to present to King Erekle. St. Joseph died peacefully.

SAINTS OF THE DAY: Sergius and Bacchus, in Syria; Polychronius of Gamphanitus; Julian, Caesarius, Eusebius, and Felix, at Terracina; Leontius the Consul; The 99 Fathers of Crete; Sergius, founder of Nurma Monastery (Vologda); Jonah, Bishop of Hankou, Manchuria; Joseph the Elder of Khevi, Georgia; Sergius the Obedient of the Kiev Caves; Abdon of Persia; Olympiades of Persia; Osyth, Princess of Chich (England); Dubtach, Bishop of Armagh (Ireland); Valentine Sventsitsky of Moscow; Uncovering of the relics of St. Martinian, abbot, of Belozersk.

OCTOBER 8

Philippians 2:12-15; Luke 7:36-50

The Lord does not show Himself to a proud soul. The proud soul, no matter how many books it reads, will never know God, since by its pride it does not give place for the grace of the Holy Spirit, while God is known only by the humble soul.

St. Silouan the Athonite

TRIDUANA, NUN OF RESTALRIG. Triduana was a Christian woman from Scotland. She was born in the Greek city of Colossae and traveled from Constantinople with St. Rule, who brought the bones of St. Andrew to Scotland in the fourth century. She settled at Rescobie, but her beauty attracted the attention of King Nectan of the Picts. To stall these unwanted attentions, Triduana tore out her own eyes and gave them to Nectan. She spent her later years in Restalrig and healed the blind who came to her. It was there in Restalrig, in the twelfth century, that the Earl of Orkney punished the bishop John of Caithness, by having him blinded. John prayed to St. Triduana, and later regained his sight when he was brought to her resting place. The seventeenth-century Acta Sanctorum records a story of a blind English woman who was miraculously cured by St. Triduana. The saint appeared to her in a dream, instructing her to travel to Restalrig, to her tomb, and there she regained her sight. The woman's daughter was later cured of blindness after praying to St. Triduana. Restalrig is now part of Edinburgh.

SAINTS OF THE DAY: Taisia (Thais) of Egypt; Pelagia the Penitent of the Mount of Olives; Virgin-martyr Pelagia of Antioch; Tryphon of Vyatka; Dositheus, abbot of Verkneostrov (Pskov); Anthony, Archbishop of Novgorod; Ignatius of Bulgaria and Mt. Athos; Jonah Lazarev, Bishop of Nevel (Pskov); Demetrius Dobroserdov, Archbishop of Mozhaisk, Ambrose Astakhov of Aksinyino, Pachomius Turkevich of Moscow, and John Khrenov, deacon, and with them Barlaam, Tatiana, Nicholas, Maria, and Nadezhda; Iwi of Lindisfarne; Triduana of Restalrig; Keyene, hermitess of Cornwall; Synaxis of the Saints of Vyatka.

Fast-free

October 9

1 Corinthians 4:9-16
Matthew 9:36-10:8

No one spits on you, no one even strikes you, no one crowns you with thorns, and the rest. Christ the Lord endured all these things with great meekness and long-suffering. For whom? For me and for you, His unworthy servants. And not only did He endure all this, but He also prayed for His enemies, *Father, forgive them,* (Luke 23:34). Look on this patience as in a mirror and consider, and you will no doubt forgive your neighbor.

St. Tikhon of Zadonsk

PUBLIA THE CONFESSOR OF ANTIOCH. Publia was married in the fourth century and had a son who became a worthy priest. When her husband died, she organized a monastery in her home. She guided widows and young women wanting to devote their lives to Christ. During the persecution of the emperor Julian the Apostate, he required that everyone sacrifice to his gods. As he walked past Publia's house, he heard them chanting the 113th Psalm, denouncing idol-worship. Greatly angered, the soldiers burst into the home and forbade them to chant anymore. However, at Publia's direction, they continued. She was dragged into the street and fiercely beaten. She was imprisoned and threatened with death. The emperor was killed during a battle with the Persians. St. Publia was released but died a short while later.

SAINTS OF THE DAY: Holy Apostle James, son of Alphaeus; Andronicos and Athanasia of Egypt; Forefather Abraham and his nephew Righteous Lot; Demetrius, Bishop of Alexandria; Publia the Confessor of Antioch; Peter of Galatia; Maximos of Persia; Stephen the Blind, King of Serbia; Stephen Lazarevic, King of Serbia; Dionysius of Paris; Uncovering of the relics of St. Sebastian (Fomin) of Optina and Karaganda; "Korsun" (Kherson) Icon of the Mother of God.

OCTOBER 10

Philippians 2:24-30; Luke 8:22-25

Provided they live a worthy life, both those who choose to dwell in the midst of noise and hubbub and those who dwell in monasteries, mountains and caves can achieve salvation. Solely because of their faith in Him God bestows great blessings on them. Hence those who because of their laziness have failed to attain salvation will have no excuse to offer on the day of judgment. For He who promised to grant us salvation simply on account of our faith in Him is not a liar.

St. Symeon the New Theologian

SYNAXIS OF THE SAINTS OF VOLHYNIA. The city of Volhynia is one of the most ancient domains of Christian Russia, and now part of Ukraine. The Orthodox faith was brought there in the time of Grand Prince Vladimir. The city had been ravaged by the Mongol Hordes, occupied by Poland-Lithuania, then absorbed back into the Russian empire under Catherine the Great. After World War II, it became a part of the Soviet Union. Today it is predominantly Orthodox Christian. One of the most revered monasteries of Russian and Ukrainian Orthodoxy is the Holy Dormition Pochaev Lavra in Volhynia. Although many saints have come from Volhynia, the ones commemorated by name on this feast are Sts. Job of Pochaev, Juliana of Olshansk, Macarius of Kanev, Stephen, Bishop of Vladimir, Theodosius, and Yaropolk, prince of Vladimir.

SAINTS OF THE DAY: Eulampius and Eulampia at Nicomedia with 200 Martyrs; Bassian of Constantinople; Theotecnus of Antioch; Pinytus of Knossos; Theophilus the Confessor of Bulgaria; Innocent of Penza; Andrew of Totma, fool-for-Christ; Paulinus of York; Ambrose of Optina; 26 Martyrs of Zographou Monastery on Mt. Athos by the Latins; Theodore Pozdeyevsky of Volokolamsk; Synaxis of the Saints of Volhynia: Job of Pochaev, Macarius of Kanev, Yaropolk-Peter of Vladimir, Theodore of Ostrog, Stephen and Amphilocius of Vladimir, and Juliana Olshanskaya; "Of the Akathist" Zographou Icon of the Mother of God.

Fast-free

OCTOBER 11

Acts 8:26-39; Luke 9:7-11

Put up with that person who grieves you and creates temptations. Put up with him joyfully. Pray for him every day. Always try to do good to him, to commend him, to speak to him with love, and God will work His miracle and he will reform. Then our Christ will be glorified, and the devil, who sets up all the stumbling-blocks, will be foiled. Force yourself especially to stop criticizing and lying.

Elder Ephraim of Arizona

ARSAKIOS AND SISINIOS, PATRIARCHS. Arsakios was the brother of Patriarch Nectarios, who is also celebrated today. In the early fifth century, Arsakios was consecrated after the unlawful exile of St. John Chrysostom. The elderly and meek priest tried in vain to stop the imperial authorities from persecuting John. Even after he was made Patriarch, many refused to recognize or serve with him. Patriarch Arsakios died after one year. Attikos, one of the chief accusers of St. Chrysostom, became the next patriarch. He served for nineteen years and eventually restored St. John Chrysostom's name. When Patriarch Attikos died, the office was vacant for one year due to a lack of consensus. Then the highly esteemed Sisinios I, known for his piety and love of the poor, became Patriarch. However, two years later, Nestorios followed him, spreading his evil heresy.

SAINTS OF THE DAY: Apostle Philip of the Seventy; Nectarius, Arsakios, and Sisinios, Archbishops of Constantinople; Theophanes Graptus the Confessor; Zenais and Philonilla of Tarsus; Kenneth of Aghaboe (Ireland); Theophanes the Faster of the Kiev Caves; Ethelburga of Barking (England); Cainnech (Kenneth) of Aghaboe (Ireland); Gommar of Lier; Synaxis of the Elders of Optina: Leonid, Macarius, Moses, Anthony, Hilarion, Ambrose, Anatole I, Isaac I, Joseph, Barsanuphius, Anatole II, Nektary, Nikon, and Isaac II; Commemoration of the miracle from the Icon of our Lord Jesus Christ in Beirut.

October 12

Philippians 3:8-19; Luke 9:12-18

Where there is no prayer and fasting, there are the demons.

St. Theophan the Recluse

VENERABLE THEOSEVIOS THE GOD-BEARER OF ARSINOE IN CYPRUS. Theosevios was born in the late fourth-century village of Melandra in Arsinoe. He was the brother of St. Arcadios, Bishop of Arsinoe. Arcadios went to Constantinople to study, and Theosevios was a shepherd of his parents' sheep. He married a pious girl from the village of Philousa, and they agreed to live as brother and sister. He found a cave where he tended the sheep, and there he would fast, pray, and keep all-night vigil. He always gave some of his bread to the poor, and when he could find none, he fed the birds to continue his almsgiving. By divine revelation, he knew the end of his life was coming. A few days later, after much prayer, he died in his cave. Several days later, his dog gathered the sheep and brought them back to the saint's home, and quickly returned to the cave. For three days, his parents and wife's parents and relatives searched for him. When they heard the dog barking, they found the cave and the body of Theosevios, who was fresh and fragrant. When they tried to take him back to Melandra to have his funeral, he was immovable. That evening Theosevios appeared to his father in a dream, saying that he wished to be buried in his cave, and this was done. A church was built there in his name. St. Theosevios has cured many blind and deaf people.

SAINTS OF THE DAY: Juventius and Maximus at Antioch; Martin of Tours; Symeon the New Theologian; Domnina of Anazarbus and Anastasia of Rome; Probus, Tarachus, and Andronicus, at Tarsus; Maximilian of Noricum; Theodotus of Ephesus; Jason of Damascus; Euphrosyne the Faster; Amphilochius, Macarius, Tarasius, and Theodosius of Glushitsa; Theosevios the God-bearer of Arsinoe; Martyrs Andromachos and Diodoros; Arsenius of Svyatogorsk; Juvenal of Ryazan; Lawrence of Optina; Martyrs Malfethos and Anthea; 70 Martyrs beheaded; Nicholas of Alma-Ata; Edwin, King of Northumbria; Wilfrid of York.

October 13

2 Corinthians 1:8-11; Luke 6:1-10

What toil we must endure, what fatigue, while we are attempting to climb hills and the summits of mountains! What, that we may ascend to heaven! If you consider the promised reward, what you endure is less. Immortality is given to the one who perseveres; everlasting life is offered; the Lord promises His kingdom.

St. Cyprian of Carthage

GREAT MARTYR ZLATA (CHRYSE) OF MEGLIN, BULGARIA, AND SERBIA. Zlata was a Christian girl from an impoverished family in Meglin, Bulgaria, during the late eighteenth century. At this time, Bulgaria was under the Turkish Yoke. She had a firm faith in Christ, a strong character, and was chaste and beautiful. A Turk there wanted to marry her, but only if she converted to Islam. The man seized her and carried her to his house where he stated his intentions. He repeatedly tried to persuade her and threaten her, but Zlata refused to leave her Christian faith. Then he gave her over to a group of Muslim women, hoping in vain that they would convince her. He threatened her family and demanded that they convince her, but Zlata would not relent. Finally, she was imprisoned and tortured for three months. St. Zlata was hanged from a pear tree and cut into tiny pieces.

SAINTS OF THE DAY: Carpus, Papylus, Agathodorus, and Agathonica at Pergamus; Zlata (Chryse) of Meglin, Bulgaria and Serbia; Dioscorus of Egypt; Nicetas the Confessor of Paphlagonia; Florentius of Thessalonica; Benjamin, deacon, of Persia; Venantius of Tours; Benjamin of the Kiev Caves; Jacob of Hamatoura Monastery (Lebanon); Anthony of Chkondidi and his disciple James the Elder; Martyr Antingonus; Luke of Demena, Sicily; Cogman, abbot of Lochaish; Uncovering of the relics of St. Thaddeus Uspensky, Archbishop of Tver; Translation into Moscow of the "Iveron" Icon of the Mother of God; "Of the Seven Lakes" Icon of the Mother of God.

SUNDAY

Sunday of the Seventh Ecumenical Council
Fast-free

OCTOBER 14

Titus 3:8-15; Luke 8:5-15

Before doing anything, pray and think: would this be wise and pleasing to God?

St. Nikon of Optina

THE MIRACLE WROUGHT BY ST. PARASKEVE FOR THE ISLAND OF CHIOS. On the island of Chios in the fifteenth century, a divine wrath fell upon the island, on account of the sins and lawlessness of the residents. A tremendous rainstorm began that was described as a river pouring down. Hieromonk Ambrose was serving Vespers at the Church of St. Paraskeve when this began. When he finished, the downpour prevented him from leaving the church. He realized that God's wrath had come upon the island and the severe rain would soon submerge the island. Throughout the night he prayed and begged God to save the island. Then he fell into a light sleep and saw the roof of the church opened, and a woman on a cloud of light with her hands lifted up in fervent prayer. Ambrose was terrified, and he heard a voice, saying, "Ambrose, cease fearing. I am the holy Martyr Paraskeve; thy homeland is preserved." The next day people from the lowlands arrived, saying that the sea had overreached her bounds, and they confessed that it was on account of their sins. Ambrose told them about his vision, and this helped to ease their fears. The people began to pray to God and St. Paraskeve. They formed a procession with her icon, and implored her to preserve the island. The storms ended, the sea settled down, and the citizens gave glory and thanks to God and St. Paraskeve. They began to live in a more becoming manner, according to the precepts of God. A church was built by the sea dedicated to St. Paraskeve so that she might protect them from future occurrences. The sea never surpassed its bounds again.

SAINTS OF THE DAY: Cosmas the Hymnographer; Silvanus of Gaza, with 40 Martyrs; Nazarius, Gervasius, Protasius, and Celsius of Milan; Ignatius of Mithymna; Cosmas of Yakhromsk; Peter Apselamus of Eleutheropolis; Nikola, Prince of Chernigov; Parasceva of Epibatima.

OCTOBER 15

Philippians 4:10-23; Luke 9:18-22

The yoke of Christ and His commandments seem difficult for immature minds. They imagine that it is not entirely necessary to follow what God and His Holy Church commands. It seems to them that they can serve both God and the world at the same time. They say, *'We are already strong enough to withstand destructive temptations and attractions. We can, by ourselves, hold on to the truth and the correct teachings. Allow us to improve our minds by many kinds of knowledge. Let us strengthen our wills amid temptations and pitfalls. Through experience, our senses will be convinced of the foulness of vice!'* Such desires are not better than the ill-considered request of the younger son to his father: *'Father, give me the portion of goods that falleth to me.'*

St. John Maximovitch

AURELIA OF STRASBURG. In the fourth-century, Aurelia accompanied St. Ursula on her trip to Rome with eleven thousand virgins. They started out in Roman Britain and got as far as Cologne, Germany, where they stopped to rest from their tiring journey. The bishop of Cologne blessed them and sent them on their way with their new supplies. The group walked south to Basel, Switzerland, but many of the women suffered from fevers and other illnesses along the way. Aurelia died there and was buried by three of her friends. Many years later, these three friends were buried next to St. Aurelia. A long time later, a man dug up the grave and found the four bodies that had not decayed.

SAINTS OF THE DAY: Sabinus, Bishop of Catania; Barses the Confessor; Lucian of Greater Antioch; Lucian of the Kiev Caves; John, Bishop of Suzdal; Dionysius, Archbishop of Suzdal; Euthymius the New of Thessalonica; Aurelia of Strasburg; Thecla of Ochsenfurt (Germany); Valerian Novitsky of Telyadovich; Athanasius, Bishop of Kovrov; Synaxis of the New Hieromartyrs of Belorussia; "Prosperess of Loaves" (Multiplier of Wheat) Icon of the Mother of God.

October 16

Colossians 1:1-3, 7-11
Matthew 27:33-54

As the body is capable of fornication with the body of a woman, the mind can also fornicate with the thought of the woman, through the imagination of that same body. A man imagines in his mind the form of his own body to be united with the form of the woman's body. The same is true with the other sins as well. Those things which the body does actively in the physical world, the mind also does in the world of thoughts. But why do I say that you must guard the imagination as you do the external senses? Actually, we must take greater care in guarding our imagination than our senses.

St. Maximos the Confessor

VENERABLE LONGINOS THE GATEKEEPER OF THE KIEV CAVES. Longinos was a monk at the Kiev-Pechersk monastery in the eleventh century, and his monastic obedience was the gatekeeper. He was pure, humble, and filled with the Holy Spirit. God rewarded him with the gift of clairvoyance. Longinos knew the disposition of each person that entered or left the gates of the monastery. He died peacefully, and his miracle-working relics are buried in the Farther Caves.

SAINTS OF THE DAY: Longinos the Centurion, who stood at the Cross of the Lord; Isaurus and Aphrodisius, who suffered with St. Longinus; Longinos the Gate-keeper of the Kiev Caves; Martyrs Dometius, Leontios, Terence, and Domninus; Malus the Hermit; John and Longinus of Yaranga, monks of Solovki; Eupraxia of Pskov; Gall, enlightener of Switzerland; Longinus of Koryazhemka; Domna, fool-for-Christ of Tomsk.

 Strict Fast

OCTOBER 17

Romans 9:18-33; Luke 9:44-50

Orthodox asceticism is not only for monasteries, but also for the world.

St. Porphyrios the Kapsokalivite

MARTYRS ETHELRED AND ETHELBERT. Ethelred and Ethelbert were the sons of King Ermenred of Kent and Queen Oslaf. While still young, they were committed to the care of their cousin King Egbert, in the mid seventh century. Because of their innocence and holiness of life, they offended Thunar, one of the king's counts. Thunar feared that the brothers would supplant him in the king's favor. He accused them before the king and asked permission to kill them. But Ethelred and Ethelbert were family, and they were dear to the king. Nevertheless, Thunar killed the boys and hid them under the king's throne. In the morning, the king saw a beam of light shining up through the roof of the hall, up to heaven, and he asked Thunar what he had done with his cousins. When Thunar told him, the king summoned his counselors and the princes' sister, St. Ermenburga. He asked her to fix the compensation for their murder, and she chose land on the Isle of Thanet. When he was asked which part of the land she wanted, she replied as much land as her deer, which always ran in front of her when she traveled. The murderer Thunar complained, saying to the king, "Sir, how long will you listen to this dumb animal, which will run round the whole of this land? Will you give it all to the queen?" At that moment, the earth opened up and swallowed Thunar. The king founded a monastery there, and St. Ermenburga became the first abbess.

SAINTS OF THE DAY: Hosea the Prophet; Unmercenaries Cosmas and Damian in Cilicia, with Leontius, Anthimus, and Eutropius; Alexander of Semipalatinsk; Anthony of Novgorod; Jacinthus and Callistus of Verkhoturye; Queen Shushanik (Susanna) of Georgia; Andrew of Crete; Cosmas of Arabia; Joseph, Catholicos of Georgia; Ethelred and Ethelbert of Kent; Translation of the relics of St. Lazarus (of the Four Days in the tomb).

OCTOBER 18

Colossians 4:5-11, 14-18
Luke 10:16-21

May God hear you. He is able to do more than we ask or understand.

St. Augustine of Hippo

NEW MARTYRS GABRIEL AND CIRMIDOL OF EGYPT. Gabriel and Cirmidol were twenty-year-old youths in sixteenth-century Egypt. They were raised with good morals and were skilled in their professions as secretaries of noblemen. One day, two Turks lied to the authorities, saying that Gabriel and Cirmidol were defiling their house of worship by throwing rubbish and unclean things upon it. Soldiers were dispatched to bring them in. At first, they were flattered, then threatened to deny their Christian faith and join the Hagarene religion. Gabriel and Cirmidol were fearless and steadfast, saying, "We are Christians and believe in Jesus Christ." They were sent to the judge, and again they confessed their faith with a sense of joy and firmness. By now, a crowd of people gathered to watch, and they became incensed with these responses. Cirmidol's mother arrived and encouraged her son to remain strong, but the crowd beat her, ripped her clothing, and threw her out of that place. Gabriel told the judges that neither wealth, nor tortures, nor death could separate him from Jesus Christ, and he offered his neck for beheading. Cirmidol announced himself in like manner. The enraged crowd murdered them. Cirmidol was stabbed in the chest and pummeled. A large stone split his head, and his eyes were gouged out. Soldiers stabbed Gabriel and beheaded him. For two days, they tried to burn the saints' bodies, but could not. Finally, they threw them into a blazing bonfire. Patriarch Joachim anointed the relics, laid them in a chest, and buried them in the Church of St. Nicholas. Many miracles have occurred for those who venerated them with faith.

SAINTS OF THE DAY: Apostle and Evangelist Luke; Marinus the Elder at Anazarbus; Mnason of Cyprus; Julian the Hermit; Gabriel and Cirmidol of Egypt; David of Serpukhov; Symeon, Theodore, and Euphrosyne; Joseph of Volokolamsk; Peter of Cetinje; 40 Children Martyrs.

OCTOBER 19

Acts 2:14-21; Luke 10:1-15

If I prayed God that all men should approve of my conduct, I should find myself a penitent at the door of each one, but I shall rather pray that my heart may be pure towards all

St. Sarah of the Nile

TRANSLATION OF THE RELICS OF VENERABLE JOHN OF RILA. John was born in the ninth-century village of Skrino in Bulgaria. He left his native village and pursued asceticism on a barren hill. One night, robbers attacked John and drove him out. He found a desolate cave and lived there for twelve years. Then he resettled in the Rila wilderness, living inside the hollow of a tree. He fasted and prayed, incessantly wept, and ate only grass. Seeing his endurance, God had beans grow in the wilderness. Shepherds discovered him one day, and they, in turn, told others who brought the sick and those afflicted with unclean spirits, which John healed by prayer. He became so well known that he fled from there and settled on a high and difficult to reach rock crag. He dwelled there for seven years under the open sky. Later on, he attracted disciples, and together they built a church and a monastery in the cave, and John tended his flock. He died peacefully at the age of seventy. In the late tenth century, during the struggle between Bulgaria and Byzantium, St. John appeared to his disciples, telling them to transfer his relics to Sofia. Later, the right hand of St. John was transferred to the city of Rila. His incorrupt and fragrant relics were housed in a church built in his honor, and his prayers continued to heal and work miracles there. His precious relics were later moved two more times because other rulers valued their holy power. Eventually, the holy relics of St. John of Rila were returned to the Rila monastery in 1469, where they remain to the present day, granting help to all those who believe.

SAINTS OF THE DAY: John of Kronstadt; Prophet Joel; Warus and 7 others in Egypt; Sadoc (Sadoth) of Persia, with 128 Martyrs; Leontius the Philosopher; Gabriel of St. Elias Skete; Demetrius of Moscow.

OCTOBER 20

2 Corinthians 3:12-18; Luke 7:1-10

You will not be able to perceive the face of virtue so long as you still look on vice with a feeling of pleasure. But vice will appear hateful to you when you hunger for the taste of virtue and avert your gaze from every form of evil.

St. Elijah the Priest

VENERABLE GERASIMOS THE NEW OF CEPHALONIA. Gerasimos was born in the village of Trikala in the Peloponnesus. His parents raised him in piety, and he studied the writings of the holy Fathers. After he had left his home, he traveled to the island of Zakina and then Mt. Athos. Here he studied with the ascetics. With the blessing of the monastery elders, he set off to worship at the holy places in Jerusalem, Mt. Sinai, Antioch, Damascus, Alexandria, and Egypt. When he returned to Jerusalem, he became a candle lighter at the Sepulcher of the Lord. He was ordained to the diaconate and then to the priesthood by the patriarch of Jerusalem. He withdrew to Jordan to live a life of silence. For five years he lived alone, eating only vegetation. Finally, he went to the island of Cephalonia and then to Omal. Gerasimos restored an old church and founded a women's monastery. He labored there for thirty years in vigil, prayer, and constant toil. God granted him the gift to heal the sick and cast out evil spirits. Having foreknowledge of his death, he blessed the nuns and peacefully gave up his spirit, at seventy-one years of age, in the year 1579. St. John's fragrant incorrupt relics remain there for the sanctification of the faithful.

SAINTS OF THE DAY: Artemios at Antioch; Aborsam and Senoe of Persia; Zebinas of Caesarea, and Martyrs Germanos, Nicephorus, and Anthony; Gerasimos the New of Cephalonia; Matrona of Chios; Manatho in Caesarea; Nicholas (Liubomudrov) of Latskoye village, Yaroslavl; Artemius of Verkola; Herman Kokel, Bishop of Alatyr; Gabriel Urgebadze of Mtskheta, Georgia; Theodosius of Svyatogorsk; Acca, Bishop of Hexham (England); Uncovering of the relics of St. Nikodim Kononov, Bishop of Belgorod; Translation of the relics of St. Ignatius of Bulgaria.

Sixth Sunday of Luke
Fast-free
Galatians 2:16-20; Luke 8:26-39

OCTOBER 21

It is easier to measure the entire sea with a tiny cup than to grasp the ineffable greatness of God with the human mind.

St. Basil the Great

VENERABLE FINTAN MUNNU, ABBOT OF TAGHMON. Fintan was from sixth-century Ireland. According to tradition, he was trained in monastic life under St. Comgall. Fintan lived in great piety and was brilliantly versed in the Holy Scriptures. He once decided to move to St. Columba's monastery in Scotland, but before his arrival, St. Columba prophesied that when Fintan arrived, he should not be admitted as a monk but told to return to Ireland where he would found a monastery and labor for the salvation of many souls. Fintan believed these words without hesitation and sailed back to Ireland. The land was bestowed to him by Dimma, a local pious ruler, and the Monastery of Taghmon (formerly called Tech Munnu) in Leinster was founded. Dimma later joined the monastery and became a clergyman. Fintan became famous as a wise abbot, mentor, and inspiring preacher, with a fine knowledge of theology. The monastery flourished with around 150 monks. Fintan was also famous for his close friendship with wild animals. Even as a boy, wolves served him, guarding his father's sheep. Throughout his life, angels appeared to him. He was noted for his gifts of clairvoyance, prophecy, and healing. He even raised two people from the dead by his prayers. In his final years, St. Fintan suffered much from what was most likely leprosy, with great humility enduring the painful illness until his death in 634.

SAINTS OF THE DAY: Hilarion the Great; Dasius, Gaius, and Zoticus at Nicomedia; Hilarion of Kiev; Hilarion of Pskov; Hilarion of Meglin; Hilarion of the Kiev Caves; Philotheus of Mt. Athos; Socrates and Theodote of Ancyra; John of Monemvasia; Bessarion and Sophronius of Ciorara; Oprea of Salistie; John of Gales and Moses of Sibiel; Theophilus and James of Omutch; Azes, Eucratus, Zachariah, Andrew, Stephen, Paul, and Peter; Baruch, monk; Ursula of Cologne and others; Condedus of Fontenelle.

OCTOBER 22

Colossians 2:13-20; Luke 10:22-24

Let a man respect his bishop. For whoever is sent by the Master to run His house, we ought to receive him as we would receive the Master Himself.

St. Ignatius of Antioch

VENERABLES PAUL AND THEODORE OF ROSTOV. In the fourteenth century, Theodore went to the River Ust, near Rostov, to establish a monastery. Three years later Paul arrived to pursue the life of an ascetic. When St. Sergius of Radonezh returned to his native homeland of Rostov, Theodore and Paul traveled to him for spiritual counsel. St. Sergius visited their wilderness monastery and pointed out the place where they should build a church dedicated to the Passion-Bearers Sts. Boris & Gleb. During the construction, monks began gathering there to struggle in asceticism with the abbot Theodore and with Paul. Theodore accepted them, and soon built a second church dedicated to the Most Holy Mother of God. When this monastery was in order, Theodore entrusted it to Paul. With several disciples, Theodore withdrew into the Vologda forest at White Lake. He founded another monastery, and after several years, Theodore appointed an abbot to take over. Having received a revelation that he would soon die, he returned to the Sts. Boris and Gleb monastery. Paul directed both monasteries for the remainder of his life.

SAINTS OF THE DAY: Lot of Egypt; Holy Seven Youths of Ephesus; Abercius of Hierapolis; Alexander, Heraclius, Anna, Elizabeth, Theodota, and Glyceria, at Adrianople; Paul and Theodore of Rostov; Rufus of The Paradise; Martyr Zachariah; Alexander of Cherkassy; Mellon of Rouen; James of Luga and Omutch; George the New Confessor of Drama; Seraphim of Uglich, Menas Shelaev, Herman Polyansky, Alexander Lebedev, Vladimir Sobolev, Basil Bogoyavlensky, and Alexander Andreyev, priests; "Kazan" and "Andronicus" Icons of the Mother of God.

OCTOBER 23

Galatians 1:11-19; Matthew 13:54-58

Under no circumstances should you become despondent or hopeless; this is worse than any sin. Such states lead one to spiritual death and even suicide. 'There is no sin that cannot be forgiven, except the sin which is not repented of." ... You have no reason to despair... 'Separate yourself from the world and draw closer to the Lord,' and He will console you here and in the life to come.

+Abbot Nikon Vorobiev

VENERABLE ODA OF SCOTLAND. Oda was born blind. Her father sent her on a pilgrimage to Liege to visit St. Lambert's grave. As she was praying there, she was miraculously cured. She vowed to dedicate her life to God and returned to Scotland. However, her father wanted her to marry, so she fled across the North Sea. Oda prayed in various villages in the Netherlands and Belgium, where she was disturbed by magpies. When she fled from them, birds led her to an open space in the forest, now known as Sint Oedenrode. Oda planted some bushes around her shelter to protect it from rain, snow, wind, and hail. By the following day, they had already grown into a thick hedge. Oda's father tried to find her, and he was able to locate her from her use of coins from her homeland. However, when he tried to approach her, the magpies repeatedly drove him off, so he gave up and returned home.

SAINTS OF THE DAY: Holy Apostle James, the Brother of the Lord; Ignatius, Patriarch of Constantinople; Petronius of Egypt, disciple of St. Pachomius the Great; Nicephorus of Constantinople; Macarius the Roman of Mesopotamia; Elisha of Lavrishevo, Belorussia; Eusebius Rozhdestvensky, Archbishop of Shadrinsk, and Vladimir Ambartsumov of Moscow; Oda of Scotland; Ethelfleda of Romsey; Translation of the relics of St. James of Borovichi (Novgorod).

OCTOBER 24

Blessed is the one who considers those who sleep in their coffins in graves and has rejected every foul-smelling desire, for he will rise in glory when the heavenly trumpet sounds, rousing all the children of humankind from sleep.

St. Ephraim the Syrian

NEW HIEROMARTYR LAURENCE, BISHOP OF BALAKHNA. Laurence came from a priest's family and graduated from St. Petersburg Theological Academy in 1902. Then he went on to serve as rector, teacher, and inspector of theological seminaries. He was modest, quiet, and beloved by teachers and students. He practiced the Jesus Prayer. He was tonsured a monk and ordained to the priesthood, and in 1917, in Moscow, he was consecrated Bishop of Balakhna. When the Russian Revolution began, he said, "Now I must become spiritual, now the Church is in need, and I must serve her." His last three sermons ended with the words: "Beloved brothers and sisters, we are living through a quite special time, before us all there stands the feat of confession, and for some—martyrdom." In 1918, he was arrested, and his relatives would send him food. Once, Laurence sent back a worn out prayer rope, asking for a new one. Laurence served liturgies in prison. He was sentenced to be shot but was offered clemency if he renounced the priesthood, which he refused. Having the Holy Gifts with him, Laurence communed himself. He was calm and joyful, and he said, "We must rejoice, I'm ready!" Before the firing squad, he raised his arms and prayed a fiery prayer. The Russian soldiers refused to shoot because they said they heard the chanting of the Cherubic Hymn, so others were summoned to carry out the sentence.

SAINTS OF THE DAY: Arethas of Omir, with 4,299 Martyrs; Syncletica and two daughters; Elesbaan of Ethiopia; Theophilus, Arethas, and Sisoes, of the Kiev Caves; Sebastiana at Heraclea; Acacius of Armenia; John of the Pskov Caves; Zosimas of Siberia; Athanasius, Patriarch of Constantinople; Laurence of Balakhna, Alexis Porfiriev, and Alexis Neidhardt.

 Fast-free

OCTOBER 25

Colossians 4:2-9; Luke 11:14-23

If we desire to be in good things after the death of this body, let us take every care that our soul does not become glued to the body, nor mingled with it, staggering around as if drunk with the passions of the body, trusting itself to bodily pleasures.

St. Ambrose of Milan

TABITHA OF JOPPA. Tabitha was a model Christian woman in the church of Joppa. She was full of good works and charitable deeds. At one point, she became sick and died. The women washed her, prepared her for burial, and laid her in an upper room. The disciples sent two men to Apostle Peter, who was preaching at Lydda, asking him to come quickly. When he arrived, the widows met him, showing him the clothes that Tabitha had made them. Peter was left alone in the room with Tabitha, and on bended knee, he prayed to the Lord. He approached Tabitha's bed and called out, "Tabitha, arise!" Immediately, she got up and was completely healed. Many people came to believe in Jesus Christ.

SAINTS OF THE DAY: Tabitha (Dorcas) of Joppa, the widow raised from the dead by Apostle Peter; Anastasius the Fuller at Salona in Dalmatia; George, Bishop of Amastris; Marcian and Martyrius the Notaries; Macarius, Bishop of Paphos on Cyprus; Crispinus and Crispinianus, Romans martyred under Diocletian, at Soissons; Two Martyrs of Thrace; Martyrius the Deacon and Martyrius the Recluse of the Kiev Caves; Matrona the Confessor of Diveyevo; Martyrs Wallerios and Chrysaphus; Martyr Savinos; Philadelphus and Polycarp; Martyrs Nikephoros and Stephen; Martyrs Faustus, Basil, and Lucian; Martyrs Pappias, Diodorus, and Claudianus, of Pamphylia; Martyr Waros; Martyr Wallerinos; Front, Bishop of Perigueux; Miniatus of Florence.

OCTOBER 26

2 Timothy 2:1-10; John 15:17-16:2

Heaven is full of repentant sinners.

+Elder Arsenie Papacioc of Romania

TRANSLATION OF THE ICON OF ST. DEMETRIOS THE MYRRH-GUSHER OF THESSALONICA. The holy icon of St. Demetrios rested on his myrrh-gushing reliquary in Thessalonica until the year 1149. St. Demetrios is portrayed standing straight with his hands lifted to heaven. It happened that Emperor Manuel Komnenos was on his way to war in Sicily. Abbot Joseph from the Pantocrator Monastery in Constantinople went to meet the emperor about some important matter. They met in a small village about two days' travel from Thessalonica. During their conversation, the abbot reminded Manuel that a promise had been made long before that the icon would one day reside at the monastery. He requested the transfer so the saint might be a great adornment and guardian of the Pantocrator Monastery; for the protection from barbarians, heathens, and invisible enemies; to guard the cities of the realm; and that the saint might be a helper to Emperor Manuel and his successors. The emperor wrote a letter to the commander of Thessalonica asking that a new icon be made to replace the icon on the reliquary of St. Demetrios, and the ancient icon be transferred to the Pantocrator Monastery. The new icon was made with gold and silver and was larger and more beautiful than the first one. When the icon and the traveling party were about seven miles from the city, a throng of clergy, monastics, senators, and the lay people met them. The icon was escorted to the monastery with hymns, lamps, and incense. For three days, people from the capital and all the outlying areas came to venerate the icon in uninterrupted lines.

SAINTS OF THE DAY: Demetrius the Myrrh-gusher of Thessalonica, and his slave Lupus; Athanasius of Medikion; Anthony of Vologda; Theophilus of the Kiev Caves; Demetrius of Basarabov; Alexander of Guria; Ioasaph of Mt. Athos; Cedd of Lastingham; Eata of Hexham; Commemoration of the Great Earthquake at Constantinople in 740.

OCTOBER 27

2 Corinthians 5:1-10; Luke 8:16-21

"Him that cometh to Me I will in no wise cast out," (John 6:37). The Lord rejoices over every person who longs for Him immeasurably more than a mother rejoices over displays of love from her own child. For this reason, do not fear the future. God is with us—today, tomorrow and always. Fear only to grieve Him through some form of sin. If, in our weakness, we fall into some wrong, let us repent and the Lord will forgive us as long as we do not consciously choose evil, attempt to justify ourselves or murmur against God. Fear nothing. Be bold to bring to the Lord all your troubles, confusion, fears, hurts from the demons and people. He both desires and knows how to relieve you of these and to free you from them when this will be most beneficial for you.

+Abbot Nikon Vorobiev

PROCLA, WIFE OF PONTIUS PILATE. When Pilate was about to judge Christ, Procla sent a message to him, saying, "Have nothing to do with that just Man, for I have suffered many things today in a dream because of Him (Mt. 27:19)." Pilate washed his hands and said to those assembled, "I am innocent of the blood of this just Person (Mt. 27:24)." But Pilate ignored her warning. Later, she became a disciple of the Lord and was baptized. She suffered much for her Christian faith. St. Procla died peacefully.

SAINTS OF THE DAY: Alexander, Bishop of Guria and Samegrelo; Nestor of Thessalonica; Mark of the isle of Thasos; Procla, wife of Pontius Pilate; Cyriacus, Patriarch of Constantinople; Capitolina and Eroteis of Cappadocia; Nestor the Chronicler of the Kiev Caves; Demetrius of Basarbov in Bulgaria; Sergius Chernukhin of Danilov Monastery; Ia, virgin of Cornwall; Uncovering of the relics of St. Andrew, Prince of Smolensk.

SUNDAY

Seventh Sunday of Luke
Fast-free

OCTOBER 28

Galatians 6:11-18; Luke 8:41-56

Having God, fear nothing, but cast all of your care upon Him, and He will take care of you. Believe undoubtingly, and God will help you according to His mercy.

St. Barsanuphius the Great

VENERABLE STEPHEN THE HYMNOGRAPHER. Stephen was from eighth-century Damascus. He was the nephew of St. John of Damascus. From his youth, he desired the monastic life. He entered the Lavra of St. Savvas the Sanctified near Jerusalem, and spent his entire life there. He was exemplary in obedience and silence. He was a simple man, courteous and affable, with good judgment. Stephen always preferred the solitude of the wilderness, and this is where he was often found. God bestowed upon him the gift of miracle-working and perspicacity. Through his prayers he tamed wild animals, cast out demons, and brought forth water from the ground with the tap of his staff. Stephen became known as an ecclesiastical poet. Sts. John and Cosmas the Hymnographers also resided at the Lavra. Stephen worked together with the holy monk Andrew the Blind. They composed hymns for Great Lent and special hymns for services between the Sunday of the Publican and Palm Sunday. The theme of the hymns glorify and praise fasting as a remedy for the suffering soul. St. Stephen died peacefully in the ninth century.

SAINTS OF THE DAY: Parasceva of Iconium; Cyriacus, Patriarch of Jerusalem, and his mother Anna; Athanasius I, Patriarch of Constantinople; Terence, Africanus, Maximus, Pompeius, and 36 others, at Carthage; Stephen the Hymnographer; Terence and Neonilla of Syria, and their children: Sarbelus, Photus, Theodulus, Hierax, Nitus, Bele, and Eunice; Febronia, daughter of Emperor Heraclius; Arsenius I of Srem; Firmilian of Caesarea, and Malchion; Neophytus of Urbnisi; Parasceva of Pirimin; Angelis, Manuel, George, and Nicholas of Crete; Job of Pochaev; Michael of Kuban; Arsenius of Cappadocia; Constantine Dyakov of Kiev; Demetrius of Rostov; Nestor of the Kiev Caves; Theophilus of Kiev.

October 29

1 Thessalonians 1:1-5
Luke 11:29-33

He who seeks the forgiveness of his sins loves humility. But he who judges another strengthens his own evil deeds against himself.

St. Mark the Ascetic

VENERABLE ANNA OF CONSTANTINOPLE, KNOWN AS EPHEMIANOS. Anna was from eighth-century Constantinople. When her parents died, her grandmother forced her to marry a pious man, and they had two children. After some time, her uncle, a clairvoyant monk of Mount Olympos, visited her and perceived that she would become a nun. He told Anna, who was expecting her second child that her husband would soon die. Six months later this came to pass, and she lamented his death bitterly. When Anna's son was born, she entrusted him to another uncle. She kept her older child with her, and together they secretly began ascetic labors. Her uncle revisited her, telling her that the afflictions of the righteous are many and that the Lord would take her children. Shortly after that, her children reposed, and Anna wailed for them. She distributed all her goods to the poor and was tonsured a nun. She dressed as a man and traveled to a place on Mount Olympos. She gave herself the name Ephemianos. She went to the first monastery she saw, and the abbot thought she was a eunuch. She told him that by living a life of solitude, she hoped to find favor in the Day of Judgment. She was a model of humility, prayer, and virtue, and for this God granted her the gift to work miracles. This attracted many to the monastery who wanted to become monks. Soon the monastery quarters became tight, so the Patriarch of Constantinople gifted the abbot a large property for another monastery, which soon filled to capacity. Seeking solitude, Anna departed the monastery and went to a quiet place where she lived out the remainder of her life in peace.

SAINTS OF THE DAY: Anastasia of Rome; Abramius the Recluse and his niece Mary; Anna (Ephemianos) of Mt. Olympus; Melitena of Marcianopolis; Athanasius of Sparta; Timothy of Esphigmenou.

 Fast-free

OCTOBER 30

1 Thessalonians 1:6-10
Luke 11:34-41

Scripture does not prohibit any of the things given to us by God for our use, but it castigates immoderation and corrects restlessness. For example, it does not forbid us to eat, to have money, or to manage it properly; but it does forbid gluttony, avarice, and the like. It does not even forbid us to think of these things, for this is why they were made; what it does forbid is to think of them in a passionate way.

St. Maximos the Confessor

MARTYRS ALEXANDER, CRONION, JULIAN, MACARIOS, AND THEIR 30 COMPANIONS AT ALEXANDRIA. During the persecutions of Emperor Decius in Alexandria, Alexander was called to a tribunal. Since he suffered from gout, he was unable to stand on his feet, so Cronion accompanied him. When they would not deny their Christian faith, they were suspended and beaten. Lime was poured over them, and then they were boiled. Alexander and Cronion gave up their souls. Julian and Macarios also refused to deny Christ. They underwent various tortures and were beheaded. The thirty companions were either tortured, torn into pieces, burned to death, or beheaded. They all refused to deny Christ.

SAINTS OF THE DAY: Apostles Tertius, Mark, Justus, and Artemas of the Seventy; Apostle Cleopas of the Seventy; Zenobios and Zenobia of Aegae, Cilicia; Alexander, Cronion, Julian, Macarios, and 30 companions at Alexandria; Eutropia of Alexandria; Asterius, Claudius, Neon, and Neonilla of Cilicia; Asterius, Metropolitan of Amasea; Joseph I, Patriarch of Constantinople; Marcian, Bishop of Syracuse; Dometius of Phrygia; Martyr Manuel; King Milutin, King of Serbia, his brother Dragutin, and their mother Helen; Nine martyred by fire; Jotham Zedghinidze, near Lake Paravani (Georgia); Varnava (Nastic), Bishop of Hvosno; Finding of the relics of Stephen-Urosh III of Decani, Serbia; Uncovering of the relics of St. Eutropia of Kherson; "Ozeryansk" Icon of the Mother of God.

OCTOBER 31

Romans 16:1-16; Luke 11:42-46

Prepare your heart for your departure. If you are wise, you will expect it every hour. Every day say to yourself: "See, the messenger who comes to fetch me is already at the door. Why am I sitting idle? I must depart for ever. I cannot come back again." Go to sleep with these thoughts every night, and reflect on them throughout the day. And when the time of departure comes, go joyfully to meet it, saying, "Come in peace. I knew you would come, and I have not neglected anything that could help me on my journey."

St. Isaac the Syrian

APOSTLES STACHYS, APELLOS, AMPLIAS, URBANUS, ARISTOVOULOS, AND NARCISSUS OF THE SEVENTY. The holy Disciples were all members of the Seventy Apostles. The holy Apostle Andrew the First-called consecrated them bishops. Stachys was the first bishop of Byzantium. He died peacefully after serving sixteen years as bishop. Aristovoulos was the brother of the Apostle Barnabus, and he was the bishop of Britain. Although they were a wild people, they never beat him. He died peacefully. Amplias was the bishop of Odyssopoulos in Macedonia. He suffered death by martyrdom because of his destruction of the idols. Urbanus was the bishop of all Macedonia. He was tortured by the pagans and was put to death. Narcissus was the bishop of Athens, and he was martyred for teaching the truth of the gospel. Apellos was the bishop of Herakleia in Thrace. He was an outstanding orator and brought many to the faith. He died peacefully.

SAINTS COMMEMORATED: Apostles Stachys, Apelles, Amplias, Urbanus, Aristovoulos, and Narcissus; Spyridon and Nicodemus the Prosphora-bakers; Maura of Constantinople; Epimachus of Pelusium; James of Mygdonia; Epimachus the Roman and Gordian; Anatolius of the Kiev Caves; Nicholas the New of Chios; Foillan of Burgh Castle; John (Kochurov) of Chicago; Seleucius and Stratonica; Martyr Pais; Leonid of Vologda, Euphrosynus of Kazan, Anatole of Tver, and Innocent of Volokolamsk.

The rose does not speak, but puts forth a strong fragrance. We too, should put forth fragrance, pour forth spiritual fragrance, the fragrance of Christ. The fragrance of our deeds should be heard from far around: good, pure, and righteous deeds, full of love. Only thus can the kingdom of God appear within our hearts, appearing not through words, but with power. Amen.

St. Luke of Simferopol

NOVEMBER 1

1 Corinthians 12:27-13:8
Matthew 10:1, 5-8

Man must give his love to the woman! Forget her name and always call her: 'my love'!

+Elder Joseph of Vatopedi

VENERABLE DAVID OF EVIA. David was born at the beginning of the sixteenth century. At the age of three, he had a vision of St. John the Baptist. He remained standing before St. John's icon for six days. At the age of fifteen, he left home in search of a spiritual father and found Hieromonk Akakios, and David was tonsured a monk. He embraced humble-mindedness, silence, and solitude, never filling his stomach or wearing fine clothes. He was led to the Great Lavra on Mt. Athos. He was ordained to the priesthood and was made abbot of the Monastery of the Mother of God near Nafpaktos. However, there was a conflict with the monks there because of David's strict spiritual demands, so he left and settled in a barren place near Parnassos. The Turks arrested him, and he was charged with sheltering a runaway slave. He was tortured but then freed when the faithful living in the area paid a ransom. David left in search of a new hermitage on the island of Evia. He founded a monastery with a group of disciples who gathered there to share his way of life. David continued his almsgiving, in addition to feeding and clothing the impoverished, Christian and Muslim alike. His prayers caused a troublesome swarm of mosquitoes to flee and drown in the sea. Once while traveling by ship, it sank, and David was cast overboard. After nine hours, he was seen in the ocean lying on his back as though he were asleep. David knew in advance the day of his death. He gathered his disciples and told them to love one another, to pray for their enemies, to shun evil thoughts, to meditate on death, and to make Confession to correct thoughts and deeds. After St. David's death, many miracles occurred at his grave.

SAINTS OF THE DAY: Unmercenaries Cosmas and Damian, and Theodota; Cyrenia and Juliana in Cilicia; Helen of Sinope; David of Evia; John and James, in Persia; Caesarius, Hermeningilda the Goth; James of Mt. Athos.

 Strict Fast

NOVEMBER 2

1 Thessalonians 2:14-20
Luke 12:2-12

The newspapers present us daily with the Calvary of suffering humanity. Reading them should inspire us to compassion and prayer.

+Elder Sergei of Vanves

GABRIEL URGEBADZE, CONFESSOR OF GEORGIA. Gabriel was a well-known spiritual guide and wonderworker in Georgia. He was visited by hundreds of pilgrims every day from around the world, but a great many from Georgia. He was reputed to have the ability to answer his guests' questions before they could ask. He was extraordinarily harsh to himself but was very kind and gentle towards other. The elder opposed the Communist regime in Soviet Georgia and was persecuted by the government for many years. He was arrested by Soviet police in 1965 after he burned down a huge portrait of Lenin during the parade in Tbilisi. He was tortured by the KGB for several months and was eventually released from prison. During his last years, he lived in the Samtavro Convent in the King Miran Tower that was built in the fourth century. According to witnesses, the oil from the vigil lamp which constantly burns at the grave of the saint has healing powers from diseases like cancer, cerebral palsy, hydrocephalus, and others. St. Gabriel is buried at the Samtavro Transfiguration Orthodox Church.

SAINTS OF THE DAY: Acindynus, Pegasius, Anempodistus, Elpithephorus, Aphthonius, and those with them, of Persia; Anthony the Confessor, Archbishop of Thessalonica; Atticus, Eudoxius, Agapius, Carterius, Istucarius, Pactobius (Tobias), Nictopolion, and companions, at Sebaste; Marcian of Cyrrhus in Syria; Martyrs Domna, Domnina, and Cyriaca; Cyprian of Storozhev, former outlaw; Bishop Victorin and Basil Luzgin, of Glazomicha; Erc, Bishop of Slane, Ireland; Gabriel Urgebadze of Georgia; Martyrs of senatorial rank beheaded under Marcus Aurelius; "Shuisk-Smolensk" Icon of the Mother of God.

NOVEMBER 3

2 Corinthians 8:1-5; Luke 9:1-6

Beware the mother of evil, self-love! For this is an irrational love for the flesh; from it are born the three basic and seemingly irresistible passions of gluttony, lust, and vanity, with the excuse that these are natural bodily needs, thus giving birth to a whole swarm of passions.

St. Maximos the Confessor

NEW MARTYR GEORGE OF NEAPOLIS, ASIA MINOR. George was a priest in Neapolis, Asia Minor, in the eighteenth century. The Greeks were under Turkish domination during this time. George's distinguishable characteristics were meekness, humbleness, forbearance, and affection to his neighbor. When George heard that the priest in a neighboring village was driven out, he traveled there to conduct the liturgy. However, during his journey, he was killed by a group of Ottoman Turks. Christians found his body and hastily buried it. The grave was marked with the inscription, "Priest George." Many years later, a devout Christian widow had repeated dreams that the relics of Father George should be unearthed and moved to a church. The village priest organized a group, and they went with a coffin to exhume the body. The saint's relics were found whole, incorrupt, and fragrant. The Christians venerated them, and they were placed in a wooden chest. Numerous miraculous healings were reported. Later, when the Orthodox people were forced to leave Asia Minor in 1922, the wonderworking relics of St. George were transferred to the church of St. Efstathios in New Neapolis. To this day, the relics are a fountain of divine grace for those who hasten with faith to the saint.

SAINTS OF THE DAY: Achaemonides (Hormisdas), of Persia; Theodore of Ancyra; Snandulia of Persia; Pimen of Zographou; Acepsimas, Joseph, and Aeithalas of Persia; Elias of Egypt; Hubert of Liege; George the Younger of Neapolis; Nicholas, Radiant Star of Georgia; Acepsimas of Cyrrhus; Pirmin of Germany; Anna, Princess of Kiev; 9 Martyrs slain by the sword; 28 Martyrs slain by fire; Winifred of Wales.

Fifth Sunday of Luke
Fast-free

NOVEMBER 4

Ephesians 2:4-10; Luke 16:19-31

The saints are like the Lord, but so are all people who keep the commandments of Christ; but those who live according to their own passions and do not repent are like the devil. I think that if this mystery were revealed to the world, then they would stop serving the devil, and everyone would strive to serve the Lord with all his strength, and to be like Him.

St. Silouan the Athonite

SYLVIA, MOTHER OF ST. GREGORY THE DIALOGIST. Sylvia was from a distinguished family in sixth-century Sicily. She was the mother of St. Gregory the Great. Her husband and three sister-in-laws are all venerated as saints. Sylvia was noted for her great piety. She gave Gregory and his brother an excellent education. After the death of her husband, Sylvia devoted herself entirely to her religion at the "New Cell by the gate of blessed Paul." She also had a chapel built in her house. More than fifty years after her death, monks from the monastery of Mar Saba in Palestine settled there. Sylvia was portrayed sitting in full view. It is said that the wrinkles of age could not hide her beauty, and she appears gracious and animated. St. Sylvia is invoked by pregnant women for a safe delivery.

SAINTS OF THE DAY: Ioannicios the Great of Bithynia; Nicander, Bishop of Myra, and Hermas the priest; Sylvia, mother of Gregory the Dialogist; Porphyrios the Mime of Caesarea; Mercurius the Faster of the Far Caves in Kiev; Luke, Bishop of Novgorod; Nicander, founder of Gorodnoezersk Monastery, Novgorod; Paul, Metropolitan of Tobolsk; Simon of Yurievets and Zharki, fool-for-Christ; John III Doukas Vataxis the Merciful, Emperor of Nicaea; George Karslides of Drama; Ioane, Stephen, and Isaiah the Georgians; Clether of Cornwall; Birnstan of Winchester.

November 5

1 Thessalonians 2:20-3:8
Luke 12:13-15, 22-31

Some are most careful about the food they take in but negligent about the words they give out.

St. Elijah the Priest

MARTYRS GALACTION AND EPISTIMIA. Galaction's parents were pagans in the third-century Phoenician city of Edessa. They were childless for a long time, and they prayed to all the pagan gods but remained childless. A certain monk named Onuphrios concealed his priestly clothes with beggar's rags and walked from house to house seeking alms. Wherever he saw the possibility to turn people away from their pagan ways, he preached Christ. When he went to the home of Galaction's parents, he converted and baptized her. A few days later she conceived, and her husband received Baptism as well. When Galaction was twenty-four years old, his father arranged a marriage with a ten-year-old girl, Epistimia, who was from a pagan family. Galaction converted her, and they agreed to retain their virginity and devote themselves to the monastic life. They gave away their goods and went to Mount Publion, where there was a monastery for men and one for women. They lived apart for six years, struggling in prayer, labor, obedience, and humility. When the pagans learned about the monasteries, soldiers were sent to capture the monastics. Many nuns and monks hid, but Galaction would not flee, and he was arrested. When Epistimia saw him being led away, she received permission to suffer with him. Together they endured terrible tortures. Galaction told the judge that Christ had dignified him with the name "Christian." As Galaction was being whipped, Epistimia encouraged the judge to beat her as well. She rebuked him for having disrobed her as if she were a murderess. Suddenly, all those watching went blind. Epistimia healed them, and they believed in Christ. Finally, Sts. Galaction and Episteme were beheaded.

SAINTS OF THE DAY: Hermas, Patrobus, Linus, Gaius, and Philologus, of the Seventy; Gregory of Alexandria; Jonah of Novgorod; Silvanus of Gaza; Gregory of Cassano.

November 6

Hebrews 8:1-6; Luke 12:8-12

Everyone must bear with gratitude what comes to him in the course of events. The more a person descends into humility, the more progress he makes and the more he succeeds.

St. Ignatius Brianchaninov

LEONARD OF NOBLAC. According to legend, Leonard was from a noble Frankish family, and St. Remy of Reims was his godfather. Leonard secured from the king the release of a great number of prisoners. Through prayer, he also obtained a safe delivery from confinement for the queen of the Franks. King Clovis gifted him a domain at Noblac, near Limoges, where he founded a monastery. After the eleventh century, little by little churches were dedicated to St. Leonard in France, England, Belgium, Spain, Italy, Switzerland, Germany, Bavaria, and Poland. Many pilgrims, including kings and princes, flocked to Noblac due to the numerous miracles attributed to Leonard. From the fourteenth to the eighteenth century, there are records of about four thousand favors granted through the saint's intercessions. He wrought the delivery of captives, women in confinement, those possessed by an evil spirit, and people and beasts afflicted with a disease. St. Leonard is portrayed holding chains in his hands.

SAINTS OF THE DAY: Paul the Confessor; Herman, Archbishop of Kazan; Gregory the Cross-bearer of Russia; Luke of Taormina (Sicily); Winnoc of Flanders; Luke of the Kiev Caves; Demetrianus, Bishop of Cytheria; Barlaam of Keret (Karelia); Barlaam of Khutyn Monastery; Paul of Corinth, fool-for-Christ; Martyr Nicander; Nicetas Delektorsky, Bishop of Orekhovo-Zuevsk; Barlaam Nikolsky of Andreyevskoe (Moscow); Gabriel Vladimirov of St. Michael Skovorodsky Monastery; Gabriel (Gur) of Lytkarino (Moscow); Illtyd of Llanilltyd Fawr, Wales; Leonard of Noblac (Gaul); Cowey of Portaferry; Synaxis of the New Martyrs of Sarov: Anatole, Basil, Hierotheus, Isaac, and Rufinus; Commemoration of the falling of ash from the sky in 472 AD.

NOVEMBER 7

1 Thessalonians 4:1-12
Luke 12:48-59

Some people by the word freedom understand the ability to do whatever one wants… People who have the more allowed themselves to come into slavery to sins, passions, and defilements more often than others appear as zealots of external freedom, wanting to broaden the laws as much as possible. But such a man uses external freedom only to more severely burden himself with inner slavery. True freedom is the active ability of a man who is not enslaved to sin, who is not pricked by a condemning conscience, to choose the better in the light of God's truth, and to bring it into actuality with the help of the gracious power of God.

St. Philaret of Moscow

MARTYRS AUCTUS, TAURION, AND THESSALONICA AT AMPHIPOLIS IN MACEDONIA. Thessalonica was the daughter of Cleonas, a wealthy and well-known pagan priest in Amphipolis. However, she was a Christian, and she took no pride in her father's status. Cleonas tried desperately to separate his daughter from the Christian faith, but she would not deny Christ. She was beaten with rawhide by four men, her sides beaten with clubs, and she was thrown out of the house. When Auctus and Taurion openly condemned Cleonas, they were arrested. They were stoned and thrown into a blazing furnace, but God preserved them by divine grace, and they walked out of the flames unharmed. Having confessed their faith in Christ, they were beheaded. St. Thessalonica died from her wounds, and she was reverently buried together with Sts. Auctus and Taurion.

SAINTS OF THE DAY: Holy 33 Martyrs of Melitene; Auctus, Taurion, and Thessalonica, at Amphipolis; Cassina and Melasippus, their son Antoninus, and 40 children, at Ancyra; Theodotus of Ancyra; Alexander of Thessalonica; Gregory, brother of St. Gregory the Wonderworker; Lazarus of Mt. Galesion; Zosimas of the Annunciation Monastery; Willibrord of Utrecht; Martyr Athenodoros; Cyril Smirnov, Metropolitan of Kazan; Michael of Diveyevo; Joseph Petrovykh of Petrograd.

Thursday

Synaxis of the Archangels
Fast-free

November 8

Hebrews 2:2-10; Luke 10:16-21

Don't be troubled if you don't feel the love of God in yourself, but think about the Lord, that He is merciful, and guard yourself from sins, and the grace of God will teach you.

St. Silouan the Athonite

SYNAXIS OF THE ARCHANGEL MICHAEL AND THE OTHER BODILESS POWERS: ARCHANGELS GABRIEL, RAPHAEL, URIEL, SALAPHIEL, JEGUDIEL, BARACHIEL, AND JEREMIEL. In the fourth century, Pope Sylvester and Patriarch Alexander established this day to celebrate the nine orders of angels. According to a Church Canon of the fourth-century Council of Laodicea, angels are not to be worshipped. Each angel has his particular service, but all are equal in honor. The hierarchy of the nine orders is six-winged seraphim, many-eyed cherubim, godly thrones, dominions, virtues, powers, principalities, archangels, and angels. Archangel Michael is the leader of the angelic army. His name means, "Who is like God." When Lucifer and his followers were cast from heaven, Archangel Michael said, "Let us give heed! Let us stand aright! Let us stand with fear!" Archangel Michael defends the Garden of Eden, told Abraham not to sacrifice Isaac, told Lot to flee Sodom, protected Jacob from Esau, took the soul of Moses from the devil, and changed the course of a river in Asia Minor to protect a holy spring in a church. In Orthodox churches, the image of Archangel Michael is situated on the left side of the icon screen, and Archangel Gabriel is on the right. The name Gabriel means "The power of God." Archangel Gabriel announces the mysteries of God.

SAINTS OF THE DAY: Synaxis of the Archangels Michael, Gabriel, Raphael, Uriel, Salaphiel, Jegudiel, Barachiel, and Jeremiel and the other Bodiless Powers; Maria (Martha), Princess of Pskov; Michael the Blessed of Chernigov; Willihad, Bishop of Bremen (Germany); Tyssilio, abbot of Meifod.

NOVEMBER 9

1 Thessalonians 5:9-13, 5:24-28
Luke 13:31-35

A Christian must be courteous to all. His words and deeds should breath with the grace of the Holy Spirit, which abides in his soul, so that in this way he might glorify the name of God. He who regulates all of his speech also regulates all of his actions. He who keeps watch over the words he is about to say also keeps watch over the deeds he intends to do, and he never goes out of the bounds of good and benevolent conduct.

St. Nectarios of Aegina

MARTYR ANTHONY OF SYRIA. Anthony was a stone cutter from fifth-century Syria. One day as he watched the Greek pagans worshipping the idols, he advised them to end the senselessness. When they refused, he departed for the wilderness. When he arrived, he met an elder named Timothy. Anthony continued there for three years in ascetical pursuits. With his elder's blessing, he returned to his former village, only to arrive when they were celebrating a feast to the demons. Anthony walked into the temple and smashed the idols. The pagan townspeople gave him a severe beating, but he escaped and went to the city of Apamea. With the blessing of the bishop of Apamea, Anthony built a church in honor of the Holy Trinity. When the pagans learned this, they came upon St. Anthony by night and murdered him with a sword.

SAINTS OF THE DAY: Nectarios, Metropolitan of Pentapolis; Onesiphoros and Porphyrios of Ephesus; Eustolia and Sosipatra of Constantinople; John the Short of Egypt; Matrona of Constantinople; Symeon Metaphrastes of Constantinople; Onesiphorus of the Kiev Caves; Anthony of Apamea; Theoctista of Lesbos; Claudius, Castor, Sempronian, and Nicostratus of Pannonia; Parthenius of Ananyevsk; Alexis of Yaroslavl; Martyrs Christopher and Maura; Euthymius and Neophytus the Serbians; Martyrs Narses and Artemonos; Helladius, monk; Benignus of Armagh; "The Quick Hearer of Mt. Athos" Icon of the Mother of God.

NOVEMBER 10

1 Corinthians 4:9-16
Luke 9:37-43

It is through the Jesus Prayer that we can better concentrate during the liturgical services of the Church and better assimilate them into ourselves.

+Elder Sergei of Vanves

HIEROMARTYR MILOS AND HIS DISCIPLES. Milos was a Christian from fourth-century Persia. He studied theology and the Holy Scriptures and lived for several years in a remote area of Babylon. Bishop Gennadios appointed Milos the Bishop of Babylon. He found the people to be especially unreceptive because of the prevailing mood of sin and sloth. In vain, Milos tried to restore a sense of decency. At last, he prophesied that he would leave and not return until a disaster had come upon them. After two years, the king of Babylon had many people killed because of their disobedience. To wreak further destruction, he caused a stampede of several hundred elephants through the city. When Milos heard this, he returned from Jerusalem and brought many to Christ. Babylon enjoyed a Christian revival. However, the king had Milos and his four disciples arrested. The disciples were stoned to death, and Milos was tortured and killed with arrows by the king and his brother. Before he died, Milos prophesied that they would die in like manner. The prophecy came to pass when during a hunt, the king and his brother accidentally shot each other.

SAINTS OF THE DAY: Erastus, Olympas, Herodion, Sosipater, Quartus, and Tertius, of the Seventy; Arsenios of Cappadocia; Orestes of Cappadocia; Nonnus of Heliopolis; Milos, in Persia, with Aborsam and Senoe; Eucharius of Trier; Constantine-Kakhi of Kartli; Theocteristus of Symbola; Justus of Canterbury; 10 Martyrs of Gaza; Orion, Niros, and Calliopios; Augustine of Kaluga, with Ioannicius, Niphon, John, and others; Nicholas, Anna, Olga, and Theoctista; Procopius of Kherson; Seraphim of Optina; Translation of the relics of St. Gregory of Assos; Commemoration of the torture of Great Martyr St. George in 303 (Georgian).

Eighth Sunday of Luke
Fast-free

NOVEMBER 11

2 Corinthians 4:6-15
Luke 10:25-37

You do not know when the Lord will come and visit you; be impartial to all, kind to all, sincere and hospitable.

St. John of Kronstadt

GREAT MARTYR MENAS OF EGYPT. Menas was a Roman soldier in the late third century during the persecutions of Emperor Maximian. He was stationed in the Egyptian desert, where only the finest troops were sent to control the barbarian desert-dwellers. He resigned from the military at a young age and became a monk in that desert. Even though there was little organization among the desert monastics, Menas became well known and was sought out by the crowds to hear him speak of the faith. He converted Nomads as well as Roman soldiers. Hearing this, the prefect Pyrros arrested him, scarcely believing that a Roman soldier would join what he considered to be a weak element of society. However, Menas would not obey the prefect's order to disavow Christ. When torture could not persuade him, he was beheaded and burned. His remains were buried in the desert and later installed in a church in his name. This site became known as El Alamein. It was here, 1,700 years later, that the tanks of German commander Rommel, also known as the Desert Fox, mysteriously ground to a halt, allowing the Allies to regroup and turn the tide of one of the most crucial battles of World War II.

SAINTS OF THE DAY: Menas of Egypt; Theodore the Confessor, abbot of the Studion; Stephen-Urosh III of Decani, Serbia; Euthymius and Nestor of Decani; Maximus of Moscow, fool-for-Christ; Vincent of Spain; Martyrius, founder of Zelenets Monastery; Neophytus and Stephen Urosica of Serbia; Victor and Stephanida, at Damascus; Nicodemus the Younger of Beroea in Macedonia; Bartholomew the Younger of Rossano, Calabria; Drakonas of Arauraka in Armenia; Milica (Eugenia), Princess of Serbia; Synaxis of the Saints of Decani; Myrrh-streaming "Montreal" Iveron Icon of the Mother of God.

November 12

2 Corinthians 9:6-11
Matthew 5:14-19

What does it mean to walk in truth (3 John 1:4)? It means to accept truth in your heart, to abide in such thoughts and feelings as the truth requires. In this way, it is the truth that God is everywhere and sees everything. He who accepts this truth with his heart and begins to keep himself both inwardly and outwardly as if God Himself is before him and is seeing everything within him, is walking in this truth.

St. Theophan the Recluse

MACHAR, BISHOP OF ABERDEEN. Machar was a disciple of St. Columba in Iona, where they labored together in the sixth century. Machar converted many souls to Christ and performed miracles, including the healing of seven lepers. He eradicated the cults of pagan gods and destroyed many idols. Later, he went to northeast Scotland to evangelize the Picts, which was successful, but he needed good interpreters. He built many churches in the current city of Aberdeen and the famous cathedral at Old Aberdeen. Aberdeen, a seaport and center for the North Sea oil industry, is the center of veneration of St. Machar. Water from a holy well of St. Machar near his cathedral was formerly used for baptisms.

SAINTS OF THE DAY: Martin the Merciful, Bishop of Tours; Prophet Achias of Silom; John the Merciful, Patriarch of Alexandria; Nilus the Faster of Sinai; Nilus the Myrrh-gusher of Mt. Athos; Leontius, Patriarch of Constantinople; Emilian of Vergegio in Spain; Blessed John "the Hairy," fool-for-Christ, of Rostov; Nicholas of Marmaran, at Constantinople; Sabbas Nigdea in Asia Minor, at Constantinople; Martyr Arsakius; Sinell of Cleenish, Ireland; Machar, Bishop of Aberdeen; Cadwaladr, king of the Welsh; Lubuinus, missionary to Friesland; New Martyrs and Confessors of Nasaud, Romania: Athanasius Todoran, Basil Dumitru, Gregory Manu, and Basil Oichi; Synaxis of the Russian New Martyrs of Optina: Anatolius, Barnabas, Dositheus, Nectarius, Panteleimon, and Vincent; "The Merciful" Icon of the Mother of God.

November 13

Hebrews 7:26-8:2
John 10:9-16

Did not the Lord Jesus Himself begin His divine ministry of the salvation of mankind with a long, forty day fast? And did not He, in this way, clearly show that we must make a serious beginning to our life as Christians with fasting? First, the fast, and then all the rest comes together with, and through, the fast. By His own example, the Lord showed us how great a weapon fasting is. With this weapon, He vanquished Satan in the wilderness, and with it was victorious over the three chief satanic passions with which Satan tempted Him: love of ease, love of praise, and love of money. These are three destructive greeds, the three greatest traps into which the evil enemy of the human race lures Christ's soldiers.

St. Nikolai Velimirovich

LEONARDO OF VIENNA. Leonardo is an Orthodox and Roman Catholic saint. He was from fifth-century Pannonia, current-day Hungary. The Burgundians later took him prisoner and took him back to Autun. But when Leonardo was freed, he locked himself in a cell where he would talk with people, but they could not see him. Later, he went to Vienna and again went into seclusion. He attracted a large number of people who settled in the vicinity of his cell. It was customary there for the bishop to choose a holy man who would devote himself to seclusion within the city to mediate between heaven and the city. Leonardo governed a few dozen monks, and together they founded the Abbey of St. Peter in Vienna with the support of a wealthy duke. Sometime later, the two created the abbey of Saint-Andre-le-Haut for women, in Vienna. It housed about sixty nuns. Leonardo died in that city and was buried in what was once the church of the Apostles, and became the abbey of St. Peter.

SAINTS OF THE DAY: John Chrysostom, Archbishop of Constantinople; Euphrasius of Clermont; Quintianus of Clermont; Bricius of Tours; Damascene of the Great Lavra; Leonardo of Vienne.

WEDNESDAY

Nativity Fast Begins
Abstain from meat and dairy products.

NOVEMBER 14

1 Corinthians 4:9-16
John 1:43-51

To fast is to do violence to nature. It is to do away with whatever pleases the palate. Fasting ends lust, roots out bad thoughts, frees one from evil dreams. Fasting makes for purity of prayer, an enlightened soul, a watchful mind, a deliverance from blindness.

St. John Climacus

DYFRIG OF WALES. Dyfrig was one of the founders of Orthodox monasticism in late-fifth, early-sixth-century Wales. He was a founder of many monastic communities, and about 2,000 monks lived in the monasteries established by him. According to tradition, while still a boy, Dyfrig healed his grandfather, the king, from epilepsy. When he was a young man, he was sent to a monastery. He was considered one of the most diligent and able students. He became a theologian and learned in the various sciences and the law. An angel of God once helped him find a location for a monastery. He told Dyfrig to find a white sow with piglets and to build a monastery on that site in honor of the Holy Trinity. On the following day, he saw a sow in the bushes, and he built on that spot. It was called "Moch-Ross," meaning the hog's place. Both the learned and uneducated came to Dyfrig for instruction. He was also a great wonderworker, laying his hands on the sick and possessed, and healing them. Many saints of the sixth century were students under Dyfrig. Later, when his relics were transferred to another location, a seven-week drought ended, and it started to rain hard. For over fifty years, St. Dyfrig unceasingly labored to spread the Church of Christ and monasticism in various regions of Wales.

SAINTS OF THE DAY: Holy Apostle Philip; Gregory Palamas, Archbishop of Thessalonica; Philip of Irap; Fantinus the Younger, of Calabria; Panteleimon the Youth of Asia Minor; Alberik of Utrecht; Virgin-martyrs of Emesa (Syria); Constantine of Hydra; Aristarchus of Peshnosha (Moscow); Malo (Machulus) of Brittany; Dyfrig, in Hereford; Gwent of Bardsey Island; Repose of St. Alexander Nevsky of Novgorod.

 Abstain from meat and dairy products.

NOVEMBER 15

2 Thessalonians 2:13-3:5
Luke 16:1-9

Ah, this flame of love has not yet entered into any of you! If it is kindled and blazes up in your heart, you will never again be moved by the vain things of this world. I pray that God may burn your hearts with His love!

St. Paisios the Athonite

MARTYRS ELPIDIOS, MARKELLOS, AND EFSTOCHIOS. Elpidios was a member of the imperial court, entrusted with secrets of the state during the reign of Julian the Apostate in the fourth century. He was brought before Julian on charges of being a Christian. The executioners were ordered to disrobe him and rip his flesh with a sharp stone necklace that he was wearing. Then boiling water was poured on his body, followed by tar and animal fat, and he was burned with torches. Having survived the torture, Elpidios was brought together with the confessors Markellos and Efstochios. They were tied to bulls by their hair and their feet tied to wild horses. But by divine power, the animals stood motionless. Finally, they were untied, and their limbs were shattered with rods. They were thrown into a fire, where they gave up their souls. When their relics were buried on Mount Carmel, thunder was heard, and lightning struck. Jesus Christ appeared with a host of angels and embraced the three martyrs. Jesus translated Markellos and Efstochios to another place but resurrected Elpidios for a second martyrdom. When Julian heard that Elpidios was alive, he had him beaten. Salt and vinegar were poured into his wounds, and he was stretched out on red-hot coals that covered his head. He was beaten with a sharp iron but remained unharmed. Many unbelievers came to the Christian faith and destroyed the idols. Finally, St. Elpidios was thrown into a burning furnace and surrendered his soul.

SAINTS OF THE DAY: Gurias, Samonas, and Abibus of Edessa; Herman of Alaska; Martyrs Elpidios, Markellos, and Efstochios; Justinian the Emperor, and Theodora; Philip of Rabang; Paisius Velichkovsky of Moldavia; Thomas the New of Constantinople; Demetrius of Thrace.

FRIDAY

Abstain from meat and dairy products, and fish.

Romans 10:11-11:2
Matthew 9:9-13

NOVEMBER 16

Of all the afflictions that burden the human race, there is not one, whether spiritual or bodily, that cannot be healed by the Holy Scriptures.

St. John Chrysostom

NEW HIEROMARTYR PANTELEIMON OF OPTINA. Panteleimon came from a poor family, and as a boy of twelve, he had to help his father who worked hard as the village shepherd. But whenever he had the chance, Panteleimon would go to the Optina Monastery to pray. Later, when he was called to active military service, he was trained as the company paramedic. When he was released from duty, he worked in the Zhytomyr province hospital until he decided that monasticism should be his life's path. He spent seven years as a novice at Optina until he was tonsured. His obedience was paramedic of the monastery. After fifteen years, in 1918, Optina and many monasteries were closed by the Soviet government. One day, there were mass arrests by the government at an open-air market. Panteleimon was accused of leading a monastic-monarchical group and was sent to prison for five years. After serving his sentence, he was relentlessly persecuted another two years, then was again arrested. He complained that all the peasants were forced onto collective farms where the animals and people were all dying of starvation. In a sermon, he had said that the government was leading mankind to hell, to the joy of the Antichrist. St. Panteleimon was shot by a firing squad and buried in a common unknown grave.

SAINTS OF THE DAY: Holy Apostle and Evangelist Matthew; Fulvianus, Prince of Ethiopia; Sergius, abbot of Malopinega; Otmar, abbot and monastic founder in Switzerland; Eucherius of Lyons; Panteleimon Arzhanykh, abbot of Optina Monastery; Philoumenus of the monastery at Jacob's Well (Nablus).

 Abstain from meat and dairy products.

NOVEMBER 17

1 Corinthians 12:7-11
Luke 9:57-62

The husband and wife should be like the hand and eyes. When the arm hurts, the eyes cry. And when eyes cry—hands wipe away tears.

St. John Chrysostom

GENNADIOS, PATRIARCH OF CONSTANTINOPLE. Gennadios was from fifth-century Constantinople. He received a good education and was noted for his excellent memory. He was ordained to the priesthood under Patriarch Anatolios, and when he died, Gennadios was elevated to the throne. Gennadios ordained no one unless they knew the Psalter by heart. He made certain that the priests of each church distribute through him anything offered to each church, and not for the Great Church of Constantinople to take everything. Patriarch Gennadios condemned simony, which was the act of buying or selling an ecclesiastical office. He once healed a painter whose hand withered when he inaccurately painted Christ to look like Zeus, with long hair and a full beard. Another time he told a priest who was leading a chaotic life, that if he did not correct himself, his life would be shortened. The priest died the next day. Gennadios once happened upon a demon that said as long as the patriarch lived, the demon would be unable to carry out his destructive designs. St. Gennadios died peacefully. St. Neophytos of Cyprus gave a eulogy on St. Gennadios, comparing him to St. Andrew the Fool-for-Christ and St. Daniel the Stylite.

SAINTS OF THE DAY: Gennadios and Maximos, Patriarchs of Constantinople; Gregory of Neo-Caesarea; Gregory, Victor, and Geminus of Heracleon in Thrace; Basil of Hamah; Longinus of Egypt; 150 philosophers converted by St. Catherine; Zacharias and John, at Constantinople; Gregory of Tours; Gennadius of Vatopedi; Vulfolaic, Stylite of Trier; John the Cobbler of Olumba; Zachariah the Cobbler and Mary; Nicon of Radonezh; Righteous Justin; Lazarus the Iconographer of Constantinople; Gobron and 133 soldiers, of Georgia; Hilda of Whitby.

SUNDAY

Ninth Sunday of Luke
Abstain from meat and dairy products.

NOVEMBER 18

Ephesians 4:1-7; Luke 12:16-21

The first and most essential means of making peace with those who offend and persecute us is to pray for them, according to the commandment of Christ.

St. Leo of Optina

MARTYR PLATON OF ANCYRA. Platon lived in third-century Galatia. From his youth, he was an exemplary Christian. He berated the idol-worshippers for their subservience to dead things. He was arrested and brought to trial to the temple of Zeus before Governor Agrippina. The judge tried to flatter him to renounce Christ, but Platon refused. He eloquently explained his beliefs. He said that each person has two lives and two deaths. One life is transitory, and the other never ends; one death is temporal and the other eternal. The governor threatened him with torture and death, but Platon said he preferred temporal death for the sake of eternal life. Agrippina gave orders to beat and imprison Platon. As he was led to prison, he told the people who had gathered at the temple not to forsake the Christian faith. Red-hot balls of iron were placed on his body, and he was cut with knives. Seven days later, he was brought again to trial before Agrippina. The judge offered him a choice to either offer sacrifice or be tortured. He refused once again and was sent to prison. For eighteen days, he was without food and water. Finally, the holy Martyr Platon was beheaded.

SAINTS OF THE DAY: Platon of Ancyra; Zacchaeus the Deacon and Alphaeus the Reader, of Caesarea; Romanus of Caesarea in Palestine; Barulas of Antioch; Romanus, who suffered under Maximian at Antioch; Daniel of Corfu; Anastasios of Paramythia in Epirus; Odo, abbot of Cluny; Mabyn, nun of Cornwall; Mawes, bishop in Cornwall and Brittany; Helen, abbess of Novodevichy Convent (Moscow); Synaxis of All Saints of Estonia.

 Abstain from meat and dairy products.

NOVEMBER 19

1 Timothy 1:1-7; Luke 17:20-25

Be true to yourself, and no one can harm you.

St. John Chrysostom

VENERABLES BARLAAM AND IOASAPH. Ioasaph was the heir to King Abenner of India. When Ioasaph was born, one of the emperor's stargazers predicted that he would accept Christianity. Therefore, the emperor commanded that a separate palace be built for his son so that he would never hear a word about Christ. When Ioasaph became a young man, he asked to leave the palace. He saw suffering, sickness, old age and death, and this caused him to think seriously about the vanity of life. By divine insight, the desert ascetic Monk Barlaam learned that Prince Ioasaph was searching for truth. He visited the prince, in the guise of a merchant, and taught him the faith and baptized him. Barlaam returned to the desert where he lived a total of seventy years. When the king heard that his son had accepted Christianity, he became angry and arranged for a debate about the faith of the Christians and pagans. The emperor employed the cunning of a magician, who disguised himself as Barlaam. However, in a vision, Ioasaph learned about the deception. Not only was Ioasaph able to convert the wizard, but after some time his father also converted. The king spent the remaining four years of his life in deep repentance. Ioasaph restored Christianity in the lands and built churches. When King Abenner died, Ioasaph abdicated the throne, and went into the wilderness, to Monk Barlaam. When Barlaam approached death, he served the Divine Liturgy, communed, and gave up his soul, at the age of one hundred. He lived in the wilderness for seventy years. Ioasaph spent thirty-five years in the cave and died at the age of sixty. With the help of a hermit, the Emperor Barachias found the cave with the undecayed and fragrant relics of Sts. Barlaam and Ioasaph, and took them back for burial in a church that was built by St. Ioasaph.

SAINTS OF THE DAY: Obadiah the Prophet; Azes of Isauria and 150 soldiers; Heliodorus in Pamphylia; Barlaam of Caesarea; Simon of Calabria.

TUESDAY **Forefeast of the Entry of the Mother of God**
Abstain from meat and dairy products.

NOVEMBER 20

1 Timothy 1:8-14
Luke 17:26-18:8

There are certain kinds of trees which never bear fruit as long as their branches stay up straight, but if stones are hung on the branches to bend them down they begin to bear fruit. So it is with the soul. When it is humbled it begins to bear fruit and the more fruit it bears the lowlier it becomes. So also the saints: the nearer they get to God, the more they see themselves as sinners.

St. Dorotheos of Gaza

HIEROMARTYRS BISHOP NIRSES AND JOSEPH HIS DISCIPLE, OF PERSIA. In fourth-century Persia during the great persecutions of Emperor Shapur II, Bishop Nirses and his disciple Joseph were brought before Shapur who was a sun worshipper. Shapur was inclined to spare them, asking only that they worship his deity. Nirses said that they could not be flattered or deceived and that he had served Jesus Christ from his youth and would not betray Him by worshipping things created and not the Creator. When Shapur threatened them with death, Nirses replied that seven deaths would not deter them. The two were led to the execution site followed by a crowd of people. Nirses told Joseph that he had now broken the snares of the world and had entered the narrow path to the kingdom of heaven. Sts. Nirses and Joseph were beheaded.

SAINTS OF THE DAY: Gregory Decapolites; Proclus, Archbishop of Constantinople; Dasius of Dorostolum in Moesia; Azades the Eunuch; Sozomen of Cyprus; Eustace, Thespesius, and Anatolius of Nicaea; Nirses, Bishop of Shahrqart, and his disciple Joseph, and those with them in Persia: John, Isaac, and Shapur, bishops of Seit Selok; Guhshtazad, Mari, Sasan, Tima, Noah, and Zaun, of Lashom, and Bautha, Denachis, Thecla, Dinaq, Tatun, Mama, Mazakya, Ana, Abyat, and Hatay; Isaac, Catholicos of Armenia; Theoctistus the Confessor of Constantinople; Edmund, King of East Anglia; Macarius Karmazin, Bishop of Dnepropetrovsk, Arsenius Dmitriev, Eutychius Kachur, and Hilarion Pisarets; Ioannikia Kozhevnikova of the Convent of the Entry of the Theotokos (Tikhvin).

WEDNESDAY **The Entry of the Theotokos into the Temple**
Abstain from meat and dairy products.

NOVEMBER 21

Hebrews 9:1-7
Luke 10:38-42, 11:27-28

For a man's complete sanctification, the body of the servant of the Lord must be united with the Body of Christ, and this is accomplished in the Mystery of Holy Communion. The true Body and the true Blood of Christ which we receive become part of the great Body of Christ. Of course, for union with Christ, the mere conjoining of our body with the Body of Christ does not suffice. The consumption of the Body of Christ becomes beneficial when in spirit we strive towards Him and unite ourselves with Him. Receiving the Body of Christ, while turning away from Him in spirit, is like the contact with Christ which they had who struck Him and mocked and crucified Him. Their contact with Him served not for their salvation and healing, but for their condemnation. But those who partake with piety, love and readiness to serve Him, closely unite themselves with Him and become instruments of His Divine will.

St. John Maximovitch

VENERABLE COLUMBANUS OF BOBBIO, ABBOT AND FOUNDER OF LUXEUIL ABBEY. Columbanus was a scholar from seventh-century Ireland. He became a monk and was known for his excellent writings on the monastic coenobitic life. He went to Gaul to evangelize, where he founded and served as abbot of the Luxeuil Abbey. He converted so many people to Christianity that the king of Burgundy gave him land for a monastery. Columbanus attracted many disciples, and two more monasteries were founded. He was a father and intercessor before God for each of his several hundred monks. Later, when he fell out of favor with the rulers of Burgundy, he left there and continued his missionary work in other areas of Gaul, Germany, and Italy. St. Columbanus spent the remainder of his life spreading the word of Christ.

SAINTS OF THE DAY: Columbanus of Bobbio, abbot and founder of Luxeuil Abbey; "Everlasting Hope" Icon of the Mother of God.

 Abstain from meat and dairy products.

November 22

Philemon 1:1-25; Luke 18:31-34

Christians will not be asked how they began but, rather, how they finished. St. Paul began badly, but finished well. Judas's beginning was praiseworthy, but his end was despicable.

St. Jerome of Stridon

MARTYR MENIGNOS THE FULLER AT PARIUM. Menignos was a fuller, someone who cleanses wool, in the third-century city of Parion in Hellespont. Twice he heard a voice from heaven, saying, "Menignos, come to Me, that thou mightest enjoy those good things prepared for those who love My name." During the Christian persecution under Emperor Decius, Christians were tracked down, beaten, and jailed. One night these prisoners prayed that God would send an angel to loose their bonds, as He did for Apostle Peter, and to lead them out of prison. Jesus appeared, saying, "Go forth from here and proclaim My power in every place." Their bonds melted like wax, and the prison doors opened of their own accord. When Menignos heard this, he rejoiced and was filled with love for Christ. He tore the imperial decree in the city square ordering the persecution of Christians. He declared himself a Christian, and for this was arrested. His skin was flayed, and his fingers cut off. Milk flowed from his wounds. At the time of the saint's beheading, a white dove flew out of his mouth.

SAINTS OF THE DAY: Apostles of the Seventy Archippos, Philemon, Onesimus, and Apphia; Menignos the Fuller, at Parium; Cecilia, Valerian, Tiburtius, and Maximus, at Rome; Procopius the Reader at Caesarea; Stephen, Mark, and Mark at Antioch in Pisidia; Callistus II, Patriarch of Constantinople; Agabbas of Syria; Agapion of Greece, with Sisinius and Agapius; Germanus of Eikoiphinissa in Macedonia; Martyrs Thaddeus, Christopher, Ephemia, Thallelaius and Anthimus; Anthony of Izeru Skete; Yaropolk-Peter, Prince of Vladimir; Michael, Great Prince of Tver; Clement of Ochrid; Michael the Soldier of Bulgaria; Ioasaph of Mogilev, and Gerasim and Alexis; Eutychius, Abner, Sava, and Mark of Optina, with Boris.

NOVEMBER 23

1 Timothy 4:4-8; Luke 19:12-28

A good deed is never lost; he who sows courtesy reaps friendship, and he who plants kindness gathers love.

St. Basil the Great

BURIAL OF ST. ALEXANDER NEVSKY OF NOVGOROD. Alexander was born in the thirteenth-century city of Pereslavl-Zaleesk. He was the son of Prince Yaroslav Vsevolodovich and Rostislava Mstislavna, daughter of the Prince of Kiev. From a young age, Alexander accompanied his father on campaigns. At nineteen years old, he was summoned to lead the military to defend their lands from Swedish and German invaders. When the Swedish army landed on the rivers Izhora and Neva, Alexander prayed a long while, asking God to help him. A miracle happened. At dawn one of Alexander's generals saw a boat and on it were the Holy Martyrs Boris and Gleb, dressed in royal purple attire. And he heard Boris say, "Brother Gleb, guide the oar, let us help our kinsman Alexander." When the miracle was reported to Alexander, he told his troops not to speak about the miracle, and with a prayer, he urged on his army. An angel of God invisibly helped Alexander's army, and they defeated the enemy. Because of this victory at the River Neva, he was given the name "Nevsky." By his prayers, Alexander defeated the Teutonic Knights on the ice of Lake Chud. Alexander, who was always close to God, continuously did works of mercy and built many churches. He devoted his life to the service of the Russian Church. He negotiated peace with the Golden Horde, but during one of his travels to Sarai, the capital of the Horde, Alexander fell deathly ill and died on his way back to Vladimir. He was forty-three years old. Before his death, he accepted the monastic-schema. This day commemorates the moving of his relics to Vladimir.

SAINTS OF THE DAY: Gregory of Agrigentum; Sisinius the Confessor; Amphilochius of Iconium; Ischyrion, in Egypt; Metrophanes of Voronezh; Trudo of Zirkingen; Dionysius I of Constantinople; Seraphim of Moscow; Boris of Ivanovo; Eleazar of Crimea; Alexander, in Perm.

 Abstain from meat and dairy products.

NOVEMBER 24

Philippians 3:20-4:3
Luke 10:19-21

All of us, clergy, laity, monastics, must bring Christ to our minds first, as soon as we awake from our sleep. Let us offer to Him the beginning of all our thoughts like a morning sacrifice.

St. Symeon the New Theologian

HIEROMARTYR PETER, ARCHBISHOP OF ALEXANDRIA. Peter was the archbishop of Alexandria for twelve years at the beginning of the fourth century. He was a highly-educated man, a theologian, and a great champion of Orthodoxy. His most widely-known works are called the "Penitential Canons." He taught at the school of the famous Christian teacher Origen. Peter ministered to the Christians locked up in prison, helped the widows and orphans, and preached the Word of God. During this time, the heretic Arius, who denied the Divinity of Christ, was causing unrest. Peter excommunicated him from the Church. Arius asked Peter to lift the excommunication, saying that he had repented and given up on his false teachings. However, Peter had a vision of Jesus, Whose robe was torn from top to bottom. Peter asked Him who had done this, and Jesus said that it was the madman Arius, and to refuse Arius his request. Not only did Peter deny the request, but he also anathematized him in this world and the next. Emperor Maximian branded Peter an enemy of the state and had him imprisoned in Alexandria, sentencing him to death. Many Christians of Alexandria gathered at the prison gates to support Peter. Fearing bloodshed, Peter had the warden break the back wall of the jail, so that he could be taken away secretly. He was beheaded at the same spot where the holy Disciple Mark, the first patriarch of Alexandria, had been executed.

SAINTS OF THE DAY: Hermogenes of Agrigentum; Clement of Rome; Peter of Alexandria; Gregory of the Golden Rock; Alexander at Corinth; Theodore of Antioch; Mastridia of Alexandria; Mercurius of Smolensk; Mercurius of the Kiev Caves; Mercurius the Faster of the Far Caves; Luke of the Kiev Caves; Simon of Soiga; Martyr Chrysogenes and Mark Triglinos; Malchus of Chalcis; Nicodemus the Younger; Righteous Carion.

SUNDAY

Thirteenth Sunday of Luke
Abstain from meat and dairy products.

NOVEMBER 25

Galatians 3:23-4:5; Luke 18:18-27

True wealth, for me, is to see you in the kingdom of Heaven.
+*Elder Amphilochios Makris of Patmos*

GREAT MARTYR MERCURIOS OF CAESAREA. Mercurius was a popular and much sought-after third-century military officer in Rome. He was also the best swordsman in his regiment and a tactician that never lost a battle. He was secretly a Christian and highly favored by God. On the eve of a great battle, an angel of the Lord appeared to him and presented him a sword, saying, "Fear not. Go forth bravely against the enemy. And when thou art victorious, forget not the Lord thy God." Mercurios defeated the enemy and killed the leader. Emperor Decius was grateful and made him a military commander. Mercurios was just twenty years old. He was soon caught up in the glamor and tribute of this honor. The same angel of the Lord reappeared and told him not to forget by Whom the victory had been given. Mercurios repented and recalled how his father Gordian had confessed the Christian faith. Mercurios declared himself a Christian and threw his soldier's belt and mantle at Decius' feet. The saint was stretched over a fire, cut with knives, beaten with lashes, and then thrown into prison. Again the angel appeared to him, encouraging him to endure the suffering for Christ. Each time he was thrown back into prison, the Lord completely healed him. Mercurios had a vision of the Lord Himself, promising relief from his sufferings. Mercurios was sentenced to death and beheaded at Caesarea. His body exuded fragrant myrrh, and many of the sick were healed. A century later, through the prayers of St. Basil the Great, the Lord sent St. Mercurios to punish the emperor Julian the Apostate, who was killing Christians. During a Persian campaign the spear of an unknown assailant, who disappeared immediately, mortally wounded Julian. As he lay dying, he cried out, "Thou has conquered, Galilean!"

SAINTS OF THE DAY: Catherine of Alexandria and 150 rhetoricians; Faustina the Empress, Porphyrius Stratelates and 200 soldiers; Peter the Silent; Clement of Ochrid.

 Abstain from meat and dairy products.

NOVEMBER 26

1 Timothy 5:1-10; Luke 19:37-44

The mole that burrows under the earth, being blind, is unable to look up at the stars; and he who is unable to trust that God will provide him with temporal goods, is unable to trust that He will provide him with eternal goods.

St. Isaiah of Scetis

AKAKIOS THE OBEDIENT OF SINAI. Akakios was a monk in a monastery named Kellivara, located on Mount Latros. At an early age, he practiced the ascetical life, keeping a sober and proper disposition. His elder, however, was very ill-tempered. Every day he would beat and berate Akakios, sometimes leaving bruises. Akakios endured this with silence and patience. Once, St. John Climacus visited Mount Latros. He perceived that something was wrong with Akakios, and asked the monk how he was doing, but he did not tell him about the elder. However, St. John said to him to endure, and he will receive a great benefit. After nine years and much abuse, Akakios died and was buried in the cemetery. The elder went to a certain discerning father to tell him that Akakios had died. When he could not believe it, the elder took him to the cemetery to see. In disbelief, the discerning elder addressed Akakios as if he were alive, asking, Brother Akakios, hast thou died?" Akakios responded, "And how is it possible, O venerable father, for a man who is a toiler at obedience to die?" The abusive elder trembled with fear and fell to the ground and wept. He confessed to the fathers what he had done, and he retired to a cell near the grave of his disciple and prayed for repentance for the rest of his days.

SAINTS OF THE DAY: Innocent of Irkutsk; James the Solitary of Syria; Stylianos of Paphlagonia; Alypius the Stylite of Adrianople; Peter, Patriarch of Jerusalem; Silas, Bishop of Persidos; Acacius of Mt. Latros, who is mentioned in *The Ladder*; George of Chios, in Asia Minor; Athanasius and Theodosius of Cherepovets Monastery (Vologda); Nicon Metanoeite of Armenia; Tikhon Buzov of Donskoy Monastery (Moscow); Dedication of the Church of St. George at Kiev.

 Abstain from meat and dairy products.

NOVEMBER 27

1 Timothy 5:11-21
Luke 19:45-48

A humble man who lives a spiritual life, when he reads the Holy Scriptures, will relate all things to himself and not to others.

St. Mark the Ascetic

VENERABLE DIODORUS OF YUREGORSK. Diodorus went on a pilgrimage to the Solovki Monastery at the age of fifteen and decided to remain there as a novice. He was tonsured a monk four years later. He later lived with other hermits on desolate islands and then settled at Lake Vodla, where he lived for seven years. Diodorus went to Moscow and received permission from Tsar Michael to build a monastery. The Tsar's mother, the nun and Eldress Martha, gave him money for the project. Together with his disciple Prochorus, they founded a monastery on Mount Yurev in honor of the Holy Trinity. Just before he died, Diodorus found it necessary to travel to Kargopol on monastery matters. Before he left, he foretold that he would soon die. He died in 1633 and was buried at Kargopol. After two years, his incorrupt relics were transferred back to his monastery and buried.

SAINTS OF THE DAY: Pinuphrius of Egypt; James the Persian; James of Rostov; 17 Monk-martyrs in India; Theodosius of Turnovo; Diodorus of George Hill; Palladius of Thessalonica; Palladius, Bishop of Elenopolis; Nathaniel of Nitria; Andrew Ogorodnikov, fool-for-Christ, of Simbirsk; Nicholas Dobronravov, Archbishop of Vladimir; Nikon Belyaev of the Staro-Golutvin Monastery; Ioasaph Boyev of Nikolskoye Monastery; Nicholas Saltykov of St. Nicholas-Peshnosha Monastery; Apollos Fedoseyev of Moscow; Cronides, Seraphim, and Xenophont of St. Sergius Lavra; Virgil, Bishop of Salzburg; Congar, Bishop of Somerset; Fergus, Bishop of Glamis; Maximus of Riez; Uncovering of the relics of St. Vsevolod, wonderworker of Pskov; Synaxis of the New Martyrs and Confessors of Radonezh; Commemoration of the Miracle of the Weeping Icon "Of the Sign" at Novgorod; "Kursk-Root," "Of Abalak," "Of Tsarskoe Selo," and "Of Seraphimo-Ponetaev" Icons of the Mother of God.

NOVEMBER 28

1 Timothy 5:22-6:11
Luke 20:1-8

Do you believe that the devil is free? No! He's the most bound for he is not in Christ ... So do not be afraid of him. He is tolerated, not a power.

+Elder Arsenie Papacioc of Romania

MARTYR IRENARCHOS AND SEVEN WOMEN-MARTYRS AT SEBASTE. Irenarchos was from third-century Sebaste. At an early age, he became an executioner, taking orders from the emperor. During the persecution of Diocletian, seven Christian women were suffering torture at the hands of the governor of Sebaste. When the women refused to offer sacrifice to the idols, they were cast into a lake. This is the same lake where the Holy Forty Martyrs of Sebaste had suffered martyrdom. The women were tortured, then beheaded. One of the women, before she was martyred, entrusted her two children to Irenarchos. When Irenarchos witnessed this, his soul was moved by divine grace. Be boldly confessed Christ and said he was a Christian. The general had him cast into the lake. Immediately the water turned solid, and Irenarchos was able to flee with the help of an angel. When sixty-eight soldiers chased after him, the waters suddenly became liquid again. When Irenarchos reached the other shore, he met there the priest Akakios who baptized him. Shortly after, Irenarchos and Akakios were captured by the pagans. They were cast into a furnace with the two children but remained unharmed. Then they were beheaded.

SAINTS OF THE DAY: Stephen the New of Mt. St. Auxentius; Irenarchos and 7 Women-martyrs, at Sebaste; Timothy and Theodore, and Peter, John, Sergius, Theodore, Nicephorus, Basil, Thomas, Hierotheus, Daniel, Chariton, Socrates, Comasius, Eusebius, and Etymasius, at Tiberiopolis; Christos of Constantinople; Anna, Martyr for the Holy Icons; Oda of Brabant; Basil, Stephen, Gregory, Gregory, John, Andrew, Peter, Anna, and many others, who suffered with St. Stephen the New; Theodore of Rostov; Juthwara of Cornwall; Seraphim of St. Petersburg; Raphael Tyupin of Zlatoustov and Vincent Nikolsky of Optina.

 Abstain from meat and dairy products.

NOVEMBER 29

1 Timothy 6:17-21
Luke 20:9-18

It is no great thing not to judge and to be sympathetic to someone who is in trouble and falls down before you, but it is a great thing not to judge or to strike back when someone, on account of his own passions, speaks against you. Likewise, it is a great thing not to disagree when someone else is honored more than you are.

St. Dorotheos of Gaza

RADBOUD, BISHOP OF UTRECHT. Radboud spent his childhood with his uncle, Bishop Gunther of the church of Cologne. He seemed irradiated by God's grace, and everyone loved him. He managed to overcome the years of his youth by austerity, disparaging worldly affairs by comparison with heavenly affairs, putting his heart and soul to spiritual enjoyment, and keeping a distance from that which is transitory. At an early age, he possessed the character of an old man. He was appointed the bishop of Utrecht in 900 A.D. when this city was in ruins following a number of Norman raids. He devoted the majority of his life to his studies and science and consequently became a patron of Roman Catholic higher education. He was described as a teacher of charity, a friend to those in need, compassionate and merciful, and radiated joy and happiness to all who met him. The more Radboud exerted himself to remain hidden, the more people extolled his name all over the world.

SAINTS OF THE DAY: Nicholas, Archbishop of Thessalonica; Philoumenos of Ancyra, and with him Valerian and Phaedrus; Dionysius, Bishop of Corinth; Tiridates, King of Armenia; Abibus, Bishop of Nekresi in Georgia; Paramon and 370 Martyrs with him, at Bithynia; John of Persia; Urban of Macedonia; Saturninus, Bishop of Toulouse; Pitirim of Egypt; Radboud, Bishop of Utrecht; Nectarius the Obedient of the Kiev Caves; Brendan of Birr; Mardarije Uskokovic, missionary and first Serbian bishop in America; Pancosimus, monk; Six Martyrs who entered a rock which wondrously opened and received them.

FRIDAY

Andrew the First-called Apostle
Abstain from meat and dairy products, and fish.

NOVEMBER 30

1 Corinthians 4:9-16
John 1:35-51

Just as nothing is to be preferred to love, then, so also, on the other hand, nothing is to be less esteemed than rage and wrath. For everything, however beneficial and necessary it may appear, should nonetheless be put aside in order to avoid the disturbance of anger, and everything that may seem inimical should be put up with and tolerated in order to maintain unharmed the tranquility of love and peace, for it must be believed that nothing is more destructive than anger and annoyance and nothing more beneficial than love.

St. John Cassian

ANDREW SAGUNA, METROPOLITAN OF TRANSYLVANIA. Andrew's family migrated from Romania to Hungary, seeking to obtain better status. They converted to Roman Catholicism over the second-class Eastern Orthodox. Andrew later rejoined the Eastern Church and became a monk. At the same time, he became a convinced nationalist, refusing to join the Serbian Orthodox Church. Instead, he left for Transylvania in Romania and integrated with the Romanian-dominated clergy, where he became a bishop of the Romanian Orthodox Church. After the Hungarian Revolution, he sought increased rights for Romania and demanded that Transylvania become autonomous. Still, he always sought the avenue of compromise. In Austria, he asked for an institution of higher learning to be approved by their leadership and further liberties and education rights for the Romanian community. Eventually, Andrew and other Romanian leaders were forced to limit their activities to the cultural field, and he remained focused on these until his death.

SAINTS OF THE DAY: Holy Apostle Andrew the First-called; Alexander, Bishop of Methymna; Frumentius, Archbishop of Abyssinia; Peter I and Samuel I of Georgia; Vakhtang, King of Georgia; Tudwal, bishop in Wales; Andrew (Saguna), Metropolitan of Transylvania; Simeon (Stefan), Metropolitan of Belgrade; Elias of Valaam.

 Abstain from meat and dairy products.

DECEMBER 1

Galatians 5:22-6:2; Luke 12:32-40

Our prayer is public and common. When we pray, we pray not for one, but for the whole people, because we the whole people are one.

St. Cyprian of Carthage

VENERABLE ANTHONY THE NEW OF KIOS. Anthony's parents dedicated him to the spiritual life. As a young man, he helped an anchorite monk, who prophesied that Anthony would one day become a monk. Later, an admiral of the Byzantine navy took notice of Anthony and employed him in the military, where he advanced rapidly. Emperor Michael II then appointed him the governor of strategically important lands of the empire. However, as Anthony prospered along these paths and considered marriage, he received a message from the anchorite monk he had once served reminding him of the prophecy. He escaped the military, along with ambition and vainglory, and he and his servant became monks on Mt. Olympus. During the ninth-century persecutions of the icons, Emperor Theophilus had Anthony imprisoned for a time on false charges. Anthony then went to live in a monastic community as a novice, keeping secret his past public life and his ascetic endeavors. He labored humbly in the monastery vineyards and the dining room. Later he spent seven years in Constantinople, living in seclusion. Anthony was granted the gift to work miracles. He once healed the brother of Empress Theodora, General Petronas, who then became Anthony's spiritual son. With Anthony's counsel and blessings, Petronas fought the army of the emir of Melitene, lifelong enemies of the Byzantines, and destroyed them. Anthony and Petronas died peacefully at the same time, as Petronas did not want to live without his elder.

SAINTS OF THE DAY: Prophet Nahum; Onesimus of Ephesus; Ananias and Solochonus of Ephesus; Philaret the Merciful of Amnia; Anthony the New of Kios; Ananias of Persia; Theoclites of Sparta; Ioannicus of Devich; Eligius of Noyon; Tudwal of Lan Pabu; Botolph of Ikanhoe, England.

SUNDAY **Fourteenth Sunday of Luke**

Abstain from meat and dairy products.

DECEMBER 2

Ephesians 6:10-17; Luke 18:35-43

True fasting lies in rejecting evil, holding one's tongue, suppressing one's hatred, and banishing one's lust, evil words, lying, and betrayal of vows.

St. Basil the Great

MARTYR MYROPE OF CHIOS. Myrope was born in the city of Ephesus in the third century. Her father died early, and her mother raised her in the Christian faith. She lived near the tomb of St. Hermione, the daughter of the Apostle Philip. Myrope took the myrrh that flowed from the relics and healed the sick. During the persecution of Emperor Decius, Myrope and her mother went to the island of Chios. When St. Isidore was martyred, Myrope bravely took and buried the body of the saint. The soldiers who were ordered not to let anyone take the body were shackled with heavy chains and sentenced to death. Myrope had pity on them, so she confessed to the soldiers and the governor that she buried the martyr. At the trial, she confessed herself a Christian. She spoke boldly, telling the governor that she "scorned and spit on his depravity and godlessness." Filled with rage, he had her beaten mercilessly and dragged through the city by her hair. In prison at night, a heavenly light shown. St. Isidore and angels appeared, and they took up to heaven the soul of Myrope. A fragrance filled the prison. A pagan guard saw the vision and told a priest. He received Baptism and was later martyred for his confession of Christ. St. Myrope was buried next to St. Isidore, and a church was built over her relics.

SAINTS OF THE DAY: Prophet Habakkuk; John, Heraclemon, Andrew, and Theophilus, hermits of Egypt; Solomon, Archbishop of Ephesus; Cyril of Philea; Stephen-Urosh V, King of Serbia and his mother Helen; Jesse, Bishop of Tsilkani in Georgia; Athanasius "the Resurrected," recluse of the Kiev Caves; Athanasius, recluse of the Kiev Caves; Myrope of Chios; Abibus the New; Abbaum of Cyprus; Ioannicius of Devic (Serbia); Danax Kalashnikov of Arkhangelskoye and Cosmas Magda of Milyatino (Moscow); Porphyrios of Kapsokalyvia and Kallisa.

 Abstain from meat and dairy products.

DECEMBER 3

2 Timothy 2:20-26; Luke 20:27-44

How can you find out if you are living within the will of God? Here is the sign: If you are troubled about anything, this means that you have not completely given yourself over to the will of God. A person who lives in the will of God is not concerned over anything. And if he needs anything, he gives both it and himself over to God. And if he does not receive the necessary thing, he remains calm nevertheless, as if he had it. The soul which has been given over to the will of God is afraid of nothing, not of thunder nor of thieves—nothing. But whatever happens, she says, "Thus it pleases God." If she is sick, she thinks: this means that I need to be sick, or else God would not have given it to me. Thus, peace is preserved in both soul and body.

St. Silouan the Athonite

HIEROMARTYR THEODORE, ARCHBISHOP OF ALEXANDRIA. Theodore served as Archbishop of Alexandria for only three years at the very beginning of the seventh century. Many of the citizens in Alexandria were idol-worshippers. These pagans were always at odds with the Christians and sometimes oppressed them. Theodore, however, not only shepherded his flock but also educated the pagans into Christianity. This caused a public outcry against him, so they beat him. They placed a crown of thorns on his head and ridiculed and laughed at him. He was thrown into the sea but emerged unharmed. Finally, St. Theodore was beheaded.

SAINTS OF THE DAY: Prophet Zephaniah; John the Silent; Theodore, Archbishop of Alexandria; Theodulus of Constantinople; Angelos of Chios; Cosmas of St. Anne's Skete; Martyrs Mamas, Seleucus, and Agapius; Gabriel, Metropolitan of Ganos and Chora, at Prousa; Sabbas, founder of Storozhev Monastery (Zvenigorod); Gregory of Cherniksk; Nicetius, Bishop of Lyons; George of Cernica; Birinus, Bishop of Dorchester; Sola, Anglo-Saxon missionary; Lucius, King of Britain; Hilarion Grigorovich, Bishop of Krutitsa.

 Abstain from meat and dairy products.

DECEMBER 4

Galatians 3:23-4:5; Mark 5:24-34

Marriage is more than human; it is a miniature kingdom, which is the little house of the Lord.

St. Clement of Alexandria

NEW MARTYR ALEXANDER HOTOVITZKY OF RUSSIA. Alexander had a love for the Church. He received a seminary education and became a reader, and then the priest at St. Nicholas Orthodox Church in New York City, under the direction of the bishop St. Tikhon. Alexander helped to establish parishes in Philadelphia, Passaic, Yonkers, and many other cities throughout North America. These churches were comprised of cradle Orthodox, as well as converted Protestants and Carpatho-Russians brought over from the Unia. Alexander was the editor of the publication *American Orthodox Messenger*. He was instrumental in the construction of the majestic St. Nicholas Cathedral in New York City. In 1917 Alexander was transferred to Moscow as an assistant pastor, again under the guidance of St. Tikhon. During the Civil War years, they collaborated in the administration of the Moscow diocese. Alexander's writings helped to rally the Orthodox around the Church at a time when it was being attacked as outdated and superstitious. He was arrested several times by the state for holding church school for the children. In 1922, the state began confiscating church treasures, under the pretense that the money was being used to feed the starving. St. Tikhon issued statements against this practice, and many were arrested throughout Russia and sentenced to death as enemies of the state. Alexander was exiled for three years. Upon his return, he was raised to proto-presbyter and became a close assistant to the Deputy Locum Tenens of the Patriarchal Throne. It was said that his glance penetrated the heart and embraced it with affection. In 1937, St. Alexander was arrested again and martyred.

SAINTS OF THE DAY: Great Martyr Barbara and Juliana, at Heliopolis; John Damascene of St. Sabbas; Gennadius of Novgorod; Seraphim of Phanarion and Neochorion; John of Polybotum; Damascene of Glukhov.

WEDNESDAY

Abstain from meat and dairy products, and fish.

DECEMBER 5

Galatians 5:22-6:2
Matthew 11:27-30

If these beings angels guard you, they do so because they have been summoned by your prayers.

St. Ambrose of Milan

GURIAS, ARCHBISHOP OF KAZAN. Gurias was born in sixteenth-century Radonezh, near Moscow. From his youth, he was humble, pious, gentle, and chaste. His family was not wealthy, so he served Prince Ivan Penkov as steward of his estates. However, Gurias was accused of improprieties with the prince's wife and was imprisoned in an underground dungeon for two years. This adversely affected his health but increased his religious zeal. He wrote a book while in prison to teach children how to read and write, and he gave the proceeds to the poor. When he was released, he received monastic tonsure at St. Joseph Monastery, and later served for nine years as abbot. Then he resigned and remained there as a simple monk for two years. He accepted the position of abbot at the Trinity Selizharov Monastery, serving just one year. He was chosen by lot to become the bishop of Kazan. With the help of St. Barsanuphius, they collaborated in missionary activity. Over the next eight years, four new monasteries were founded, ten churches built, and the Annunciation Cathedral organized. Gurias' health deteriorated the last two years of his life to the point that he could not walk or stand. On feast days, he was carried to church, where he either sat or lay. Just before he died, Gurias received the great Schema under St. Barsanuphius. He was buried in the Saviour Transfiguration monastery. About thirty years later, the relics of both St. Gurias and St. Barsanuphius were uncovered and found incorrupt, a sign of the grace of God.

SAINTS OF THE DAY: Sabbas the Sanctified; Nicetius of Trier; Philotheus of Karyes, and Nectarius of Bitol; Gratus and Nonnus, monks; Gurias of Kazan; Cosmas of Vatopedi and the monks of Karyes; Martyrs Diogenes and Abercius; Martyr Anastasias; Carion and Zachariah of Egypt; Sabbas the New of Kalymnos; Justinian of Wales.

 Abstain from meat and dairy products.

DECEMBER 6

Hebrews 13:17-21; Luke 6:17-23

If the soul is better than the body, and if God, the Creator of the world, is incomparably superior to His creation, then a man who cares for his body more than for his soul, and prefers the world to God, its Creator, such a man is no different at all from an idol-worshipper.

St. Maximos the Confessor

BLESSED MAXIMUS, METROPOLITAN OF KIEV. Maximus was by birth a Greek. He was appointed to replace the Metropolitan of Kiev in the thirteenth century. When Maximus arrived in Kiev, he found it in ruins, having been devastated by the Mongols. He made fervent prayers to the Mother of God, and she indicated to him to go to Vladimir. Maximus set a spiritual example, and he concerned himself with his flock's spiritual growth. He established rules about fasting, for Wednesday and Friday, Great Lent, and the Lenten periods for the Apostles, Nativity, and Dormition. He encouraged Orthodox men to take wives from the Church, saying that woman is for the salvation of man. Maximus admonished that it is detrimental to cleave to a woman in promiscuity without marriage. Maximus died peacefully and was buried in the Vladimir Uspenie cathedral. The "Maximov" icon of the Mother of God hangs on the wall above his grave. It was written in 1299 following a vision to Metropolitan Maximus. A description of that vision was placed on the left side of his grave.

SAINTS OF THE DAY: Nicholas the Wonderworker, Archbishop of Myra in Lycia; Theophilus, Bishop of Antioch; Maximus, Metropolitan of Kiev; Nicholas, Bishop of Patara; Nicholas of Tobolsk; Nicholas, missionary of Moscow; Nicholas of Novo-Nikolskaya; New Martyr Nicholas of Caramania in Asia Minor; Commemoration of the divine warning of an impending earthquake.

DECEMBER 7

Titus 1:15-2:10; Luke 21:37-22:8

Our religion slays the passions, not the body.

+*Elder Amphilochios Makris of Patmos*

PHILOTHEA OF TURNOVO, THE PROTECTRESS OF ROMANIA. Philothea was born in thirteenth-century Turnovo. Her mother taught her to attend church and to do good to others. While still a child, her mother died and her father remarried. Philothea's stepmother often accused her of giving away their possessions to the poor. Still, she prayed and continued to give what she could. Each day, Philothea would take food to her father who was working in the fields. However, she would give some to the poor children who were begging in the street. When he complained to his wife that she was not sending enough food, she told him to ask his daughter. One day he saw Philothea giving away the food, and he became enraged and threw an ax at his twelve-year-old daughter. It struck her on the leg, and she died from the wound. He tried to lift Philothea's body, but it became as heavy as a rock. Filled with fear, he ran to the archbishop to confess his sin. The archbishop and his priests went with incense and candles to take her body to the cathedral, but they were also unable to lift her. They realized that Philothea did not want to be buried in Bulgaria, so they started naming cathedrals, churches, and monasteries to see where she wished to go. When the Monastery of Cortea de Argesh in Romania was said, her body lifted easily. She helps those who ask for her prayers. Each year there is a festival in her honor attended by the faithful from all over Romania.

SAINTS OF THE DAY: Ambrose of Milan; Athenodoros of Mesopotamia; 62 priests and 300 laymen martyred by the Arians in Africa; Philothea of Turnovo; Paul the Obedient of Cyprus; John the Faster of the Kiev Caves; Ignatius, near Blachernae; Nilus of Stolben Island; Ammoun of Nitria; Anthony of Siya; Holy woman martyr of Rome; Bassa of Jerusalem; Martyrs Acepsimas, Isidore, and Leo; Martyrs Gaius and Gainus; John of St. Sabbas; Gregory of Serbia.

SATURDAY

Forefeast of the Conception
Abstain from meat and dairy products.

DECEMBER 8

Ephesians 1:16-23; Luke 13:19-29

Christians are forbidden to correct the stumblings of sinners by force... It is necessary to make a man better not by force but by persuasion. We neither have authority granted us by law to restrain sinners, nor, if it were, should we know how to use it, since God gives the crown to those who are kept from evil not by force, but by choice.

St. John Chrysostom

HOLY APOSTLES OF THE SEVENTY: SOSTHENES, APOLLOS, CEPHAS, TYCHICUS, EPAPHRODITUS, CAESARIUS, AND ONESIPHORUS. The Seventy Apostles were chosen by Jesus Christ to preach. Sosthenes was the head of the Jewish synagogue in Corinth. During the riot against Apostle Paul, he suffered a beating. Paul converted him to faith in Christ, and he later became bishop of Caesarea. Apollos was a scholar from Alexandria who taught in Corinth. He converted many and became bishop of Caesarea. He preached on the island of Crete. Cephas was the bishop at Colophon in Pamphylia. Tychicus was from Asia Minor and was a disciple and companion of the Apostle Paul. When Apostle Paul was in prison, Tychicus delivered the Epistles to the Ephesians and the Colossians. He became bishop of Caesarea. Epaphroditus was also a close companion of Apostle Paul and was bishop of Adriaca. Caesarius was bishop of Dirracheia, in the Peloponnesus. They all died peacefully. Onesiphorus was the bishop at Colophon, and later in Corinth. He died a martyr in the city of Parium, near Ephesus.

SAINTS OF THE DAY: Apostles of the Seventy: Sosthenes, Apollos, Cephas, Tychicus, Epaphroditus, Caesarius, and Onesiphorus; Patapius of Thebes; Cyril, founder of Chelmogorsk Monastery (Karelia); Sophronius I, Bishop of Cyprus; Budoc, Bishop of Dol; Valerius, Bishop of Trier.

SUNDAY

Tenth Sunday of Luke
Conception of the Mother of God
Abstain from meat and dairy products.

DECEMBER 9

Galatians 4:22-27; Luke 13:10-17

God requires us to go on repenting until our last breath.

St. Isaiah of Scetis

NEW MARTYR SERGIUS MECHEV OF MOSCOW, A TRUE SPIRITUAL FATHER. Sergius received his religious training at home and in the church where he was active in a student theological circle. There he met Patriarch Tikhon who urged him to become a priest. Also inspired by the elder Anatole of Optina, Sergius was ordained to the priesthood. From his first weeks as a priest, he began acquiring spiritual children. He told them that frequent church attendance was the best school for development of a spiritual life. He wanted them to always be honest before God. He gave a moderate rule of fasting and prayer to be fulfilled without fail. He said that the Lord had given us the mysteries of Holy Baptism, Chrismation, and the Holy Eucharist, but Confession is the gift we bring to God to take away the heavy burden of sin. Without our participation, the Lord cannot help us. A particular passion possesses each person, and we must work to uproot it. It is shameful to sin, but there is no shame in wanting to be healed. He said, "Many come to Confession with cold hearts. They enumerate their sins calmly as if speaking about something foreign to them. And here a boy comes and cries and cries because he took candy away from his sister. That, my dear ones, is how one ought to confess." Sergius was arrested in 1929, falsely charged with heading a counter-revolutionary underground church. He spent three years in exile, was arrested several more times, and almost certainly executed in prison, in 1941.

SAINTS OF THE DAY: Prophetess Anna (Hannah); Stephen "the New Light" of Constantinople; Narses of Persia; Sergius Mechev of Moscow; Sositheus of Persia; Martyr Isaac; Valeria of Aquitaine; Mardarije of Libertyville, Illinois; Commemoration of the Founding of the Church of the Resurrection at Jerusalem; "Unexpected Joy" Icon of the Mother of God.

 Abstain from meat and dairy products.

December 10

Hebrews 3:5-11, 17-19
Mark 8:11-21

It is not difficult to get rid of material things if you so desire; but only with great effort will you be able to get rid of thoughts about them.

St. Thalassios the Libyan

MARTYRS MENAS THE MELODIUS, HERMOGENES, AND EUGRAPHUS OF ALEXANDRIA. Menas was a renowned orator and a high officer under Emperor Maximian. Eugraphus was the secretary to Menas. Menas was not a professed Christian but a believing one. He was sent by the Emperor from Athens to Alexandria to quell an uprising between the Christians and pagans. Instead, Menas declared himself a Christian and began preaching the Christian faith. When Maximian heard this, he sent Hermogenes to conduct a trial, and to get rid of the Christians. Menas suffered many tortures. His tongue was cut out, his feet cut off, and he was blinded. In prison, Jesus appeared to Menas and healed him. Hermogenes was amazed at the saint's endurance and the miraculous healings, and he also came to believe in Christ. Maximian then came to Alexandria himself. He had Menas and Hermogenes tortured, but they endured courageously. Eugraphus confessed that he was a Christian, and Maximian himself stabbed him. Menas and Hermogenes were beheaded. Their relics were put in an iron chest and thrown into the sea. The chest miraculously floated to Constantinople, where a bishop received foreknowledge of their arrival. Maximian was blinded by God aboard ship and complained of being beaten by invisible hands. He soon died.

SAINTS OF THE DAY: Menas the Melodius, Hermogenes, and Eugraphus, of Alexandria; Hieromartyr Theotecnos; John, King of Serbia, and his parents Stephen the Blind and Angelina Brancovich; Gemellus of Paphlagonia; Martyrs Marianus and Eugene; Thomas Defourkinos of Mt. Kyminas in Bithynia; Ioasaph, Bishop of Belgorod; Sergius Sorokin and Anna, nun-confessor, of Sreznevo (Ryazan).

 Abstain from meat and dairy products.

DECEMBER 11

Hebrews 4:1-13; Mark 8:22-26

It is only necessary to seek one thing: to be with Jesus. The man who remains with Jesus is rich, even if he is poor with regard to material things. Whoever desires the earthly more than the heavenly loses both the earthly and the heavenly. But whoever seeks the heavenly is Lord of the whole world.

St. Ignatius Brianchaninov

NEW HIEROMARTYR THEOPHANES OF SOLIKAMSK. Theophanes was born in the family of a deacon in the Saratov region. He attended the seminary and the Kazan Theological Academy. He was ordained to the priesthood at the age of thirty-one, in 1898. He was also tonsured into monasticism at the Valaam Monastery and held positions within the Church. He was elevated to the episcopate of Solikamsk. In order to know his flock, he went around his entire vicariate on foot. Theophanes was a great man of prayer and fasting. He was fearless in unmasking the falsehoods of the godless. He once led a great procession with the cross in the area of Perm to rally the believers and admonished those who dared to take Church land and property, saying that they would stand before the dread judgment of Almighty God. He was arrested in 1918 and accepted a martyr's death at the hands of the Bolsheviks. In the freezing temperature of -30°C, St. Theophanes was repeatedly dipped into a hole cut in the ice of the Kama River, after which he was drowned.

SAINTS OF THE DAY: Daniel the Stylite of Constantinople; Mirax of Egypt; Barsabas, abbot of Ishtar, and ten companions in Persia; Aeithalas and Acepsius at Arbela in Assyria; Nicon "the Dry" of the Kiev Caves; Theophanes Ilminsky, Bishop of Perm and Solikamsk, and with him two priests and five laymen; Kuksha, Hieroschemamonk of Odessa; Martyrs Terence, Vincent, Emilian, and Bebaia; Leontios of Monemvasia, in the Peloponnesus; Luke the New Stylite of Chalcedon; Synaxis of the Saints of Georgia.

Wednesday

Abstain from meat and dairy products, and fish.
Ephesians 5:8-19; John 10:9-16

December 12

Our behavior is only acceptable to God if we have the strength of purpose to complete any work we have undertaken.... The reward is not promised to the one who begins, but rather to the one who perseveres.

St. Isidore of Pelusium

JOHN, METROPOLITAN OF ZICHNE. John was orphaned at the age of two and was raised by his uncle, the priest-monk Ioannikios, who resided on Mt. Athos. He taught John to read and instilled in him a love for monasticism. John progressed spiritually through fervent prayer and abstinence of food. They took refuge on the heights of Mount Menoikion and established a small monastery. Eventually, John was ordained to the priesthood. The people of Zichne in eastern Macedonia ardently wanted John to be their bishop, and Ioannikios granted him permission on the condition that John never neglect their monastery. John gave all his energy to the absence of his own rest. He always led his flock on the path to salvation, either by example, instruction, or reprimands. Following his uncle's death, John succeeded him as abbot of St. John the Baptist Monastery. Through the generosity of emperors and kings, the monastery was enlarged. The existing chapel became a cathedral and was decorated with many beautiful icons. A new refectory was built so that the monks could eat together in the coenobitic style. A second monastery was founded in the city of Serres, and John made sure the monks lacked for nothing. From his youth, John loved silence and scorned earthly, temporal cares. Shortly before his death, he took monastic vows and returned to the monastery of St. John the Baptist. He died peacefully in 1333.

SAINTS OF THE DAY: Spyridon the Wonderworker; Alexander of Jerusalem; John of Zichne; Therapontes of Monza; John of Zedazeni; Anthus of Palestine and Amonathas of Pelusium; Synesius of Rome; Finian of Clonard; Michael of Ireland; Corentin of Quimper; Colman of Glendalough; Synaxis of the First Martyrs of the American land.

DECEMBER 13

Hebrews 7:1-6; Mark 9:10-15

God's love for the biggest sinner is greater than the love of the holiest man for God.

+Elder Arsenie Boca of Romania

VENERABLE HERMAN, WONDERWORKER OF ALASKA. St. Herman is the first canonized American saint. Herman was born in 1756 to a pious merchant family near Moscow. He entered the monastic life at the age of sixteen and lived at first at the Trinity-St. Sergius Lavra near St. Petersburg, then later at the Valaam Monastery on Lake Ladoga. He often withdrew into the wilderness for days at a time to pray. In 1795, at the age of thirty-eight, he joined seven other monks to travel to America as missionaries. They crossed Siberia, and almost a year later, arrived at Kodiak Island. They found the Aleuts receptive to the teaching of the gospel, and after one year, they had baptized 7,000 people and performed 1,500 marriages. However, many of the pagans opposed their message and stirred up the people against them. St. Herman settled on Spruce Island, near Kodiak, and pursued a hermit's life. He dwelled in a small cabin in the forest and subdued his flesh with great asceticism. He spent his days in prayer and mission work. He slept little, fasted on blackberries and vegetables, wore chains, and a 15-pound cross. He founded an orphanage and a school for the natives, built a chapel, and cared for the sick. He became known as the protector of orphans. His kindness, teaching, and the example of his life brought many to Christ, and God granted him prophetic insight and the grace to work miracles. Herman died peacefully on Spruce Island at the age of eighty-one. Some of the inhabitants nearby saw a pillar of light rising above his hermitage. Since his death in 1837, he has been a renowned wonderworker.

SAINTS OF THE DAY: Lucia (Lucy) of Syracuse; Eustratius, Auxentius, Eugene, Mardarius, and Orestes, at Sebaste; Arsenios of Mt. Latros; Ares, monk; Auberius, bishop; Columba of Terryglass; Odilia of Alsace; Innocent of Kherson; Mardarius of the Kiev Caves; Gabriel of Serbia.

DECEMBER 14

Hebrews 7:18-25; Mark 9:33-41

Let us live more simply and God will have mercy on us.

St. Ambrose of Optina

ILARION, METROPOLITAN OF SUZDAL. Ilarion was tonsured a monk, and two years later founded and built the Phlorischev wilderness monastery. He had a harsh struggle with fleshly passions. He fell down before the miraculous Vladimir Icon of the Mother of God and implored her with tears to help him, and this pacified his spirit. One evening when Ilarion was serving in the church together with a monk-deacon, robbers burst in and killed the deacon and set Ilarion on fire. They demanded Ilarion to tell them where the monastery treasure was kept. In terrible pain, Ilarion turned towards the wonderworking icon, saying, "O All-Pure Virgin Mary, Mother of our Lord Jesus Christ! If they injure me with the fire, I shall no more have the ability to always glorify Thy Son and Thee." Suddenly they heard the shouts of people outside, and the robbers fled in fear. Another time, Ilarion began building a new stone church, but later felt regret for starting it because of the disgruntled workers and the time it demanded, distracting him from prayer. He prayed to the Mother of God not to abandon him and to alleviate these worries. After his prayer, he fell asleep, and the Mother of God appeared to him. She instructed him to take her image, the Vladimir Icon, from the church and put it in the newly-made stone church, and she would be his helper. From that time, the work went well and was soon finished. At the age of fifty, Ilarion was consecrated Archbishop of Suzdal and Yuriev, and the next year was elevated to Metropolitan. He was known for his unceasing concern for the poor. St. Ilarion died peacefully at the age of seventy-four.

SAINTS OF THE DAY: Philemon, Apollonius, Arianus, Theoctychus, and four guards, at Alexandria; Thyrsus, Leucius, Callinicus, with others, in Bithynia; Folciunus of Tervas; Ilarion of Suzdal and Yuriev; Venantius of Poitiers; Hygbald, in Lincolnshire; Bassian of Tambov; Miraculous deliverance from an earthquake in the year 557, in Constantinople.

Abstain from meat and dairy products, and fish.
2 Timothy 1:8-18; Mark 2:23-3:5

DECEMBER 15

Let no man then accuse poverty as being the cause of innumerable evils, nor let him contradict Christ, who declared it to be the perfection of virtue, saying, 'If you will be perfect.' [Matthew 19:21] For this He both uttered in His words, and showed by His acts, and taught by His disciples. Let us therefore follow after poverty, it is the greatest good to the sober-minded. Perhaps some of those who hear me, avoid it as a thing of ill omen. I do not doubt it. For this disease is great among most men, and such is the tyranny of wealth, that they cannot even as far as words endure the renunciation of it, but avoid it as of ill omen. Far be this from the Christian's soul: for nothing is richer than he who chooses poverty of his own accord, and with a ready mind.

St. John Chrysostom

VENERABLE NECTARIOS OF BITOL. Nectarios was from the small Bulgarian town of Bitol in the fifteenth century. Before a Turkish invasion, his mother had a vision of the Most Holy Mother of God who told her to flee and go into hiding with her husband and children. Nectarios and his father withdrew to a monastery dedicated to the Holy Unmercenaries Cosmas and Damian. When he reached adolescence, Nectarios moved to Mt. Athos where he was tonsured a monk. He suffered for a long time from the envy and spite of another novice, yet he displayed complete humility. Nectarios was known for his charity. He distributed any money he received from his handicraft to the poor. St. Nectarios died peacefully in the year 1500.

SAINTS OF THE DAY: Susanna the Deaconess; Eleutherius of Illyricum, and Anthia, Coremonus the Eparch, and two executioners; Paul of Mt. Latros; Eleutherius of Byzantium; Pardus of Palestine; Stephen the Confessor of Surozh; Joseph of Petrograd; Hilarion of Verey; Bacchus of St. Sabbas Monastery; Tryphon of Pechenga, and Jonah; Aubertus, bishop; Nectarios of Bitol; Synaxis of the Saints of Kola.

SUNDAY

Eleventh Sunday of Luke
Abstain from meat and dairy products, and fish.

DECEMBER 16

Colossians 3:4-11; Luke 14:16-24

Grumbling is caused by misery and it can be put aside by doxology (giving praise). Grumbling begets grumbling and doxology begets doxology. When someone doesn't grumble over a problem troubling him, but rather praises God, then the devil gets frustrated and goes off to someone else who grumbles, in order to cause everything to go even worse for him. You see, the more one grumbles, the more one falls into ruin. Sometimes the devil deceives us and makes us unable to be pleased with anything; however, one can celebrate all things in a spiritual manner, with doxology, and secure God's constant blessing.

St. Paisios the Athonite

MODESTOS II, ARCHBISHOP OF JERUSALEM. Modestos was born into a Christian family in Sebaste, Asia Minor. He became a monk and later the abbot of the monastery of St. Theodosios the Great in seventh-century Palestine. He led by word and deed. When the Persians raided Syria and Palestine, they captured many Christians and Patriarch Zacharias, along with the Holy Cross of our Lord. Modestos was selected to govern the Jerusalem Church as locum tenens. With the help of the patriarch John the Merciful of Alexandria, Modestos restored the churches, including the Sepulcher of the Lord in Jerusalem. He buried the slaughtered monks of St. Savvas Monastery and rallied the Christians who had scattered. Fourteen years later, Patriarch Zacharias returned with the Holy Cross. He led for four more years before his death. Modestos was chosen to succeed him. He performed many miracles through his prayers and led the Church for only another two years. St. Modestos died peacefully at the age of ninety-seven.

SAINTS OF THE DAY: Prophet Haggai (Aggaeus); Modestos II of Jerusalem; Theophania, wife of Leo the Wise; Memnon of Ephesus; Sophia (Solomonia) of Moscow; Nicholas Chrysoberges of Constantinople; Martyrs Promus and Hilarion; Marinus of Rome; Vladimir of Okhansk.

Abstain from meat and dairy products, and fish.

Hebrews 11:33-12:2
Mark 9:42-10:1

December 17

Only through the Grace-filled authority of the Holy Fathers can we be enlightened unto salvation by God's revelation and take in and assimilate doctrines in our mind and in our heart in a correct manner. The Grace of the Holy Spirit acted in the Holy Fathers as it had in the Apostles. It revealed to them, in the deepest possible way, the whole of God's revelation, of the Old and the New Testaments, and made clear to them, on our behalf, all truths, both in the field of dogmatics as well as in the field of morality, for all time.

St. Seraphim of Sofia

NEW MARTYR NICETAS OF NYSSA. Nicetas was from late thirteenth-century Ancyra. Soon after his wedding, he went to Nyssa on business with two companions. His mother and sisters lived there. When the three Christians arrived in Nyssa, they sat down to eat, but they were arrested for breaking the law of fasting. It was the month of Ramadan. They were taken before the judge and tortured. Nicetas' two companions apostatized, but Nicetas was made strong through the test of suffering and remained unshakeable despite the pleas of his mother. Nicetas was burned alive, and his remains were placed beside the relics of St. Gregory of Nyssa. A heavenly light appeared above his tomb to reveal the glory that he had received in heaven.

SAINTS OF THE DAY: Holy Prophet Daniel and the Three Holy Youths: Ananias, Azarias, and Misael; Dionysius in Zakynthos, Archbishop of Aegina; Daniel (Stephen) the Confessor of Spain and Egypt; Patermuthius, Coprius, and Alexander the Soldier, of Egypt; Athanasius, Nicholas, and Anthony, founders of Vatopedi Monastery, Mt. Athos; New Martyr Nicetas of Nyssa; Iacchus of Triglia; New Martyr Paisius, abbot of Trnava Monastery, Cacak, and Abacum the Deacon, at Belgrade; Misael of Abalak Monastery (Irkutsk); Sturm, abbot and founder of Fulda Monastery (Germany); Sergius Florinsky of Rakvere, Estonia.

Strict Fast

December 18

Hebrews 9:8-23; Mark 10:2-12

You live a good life in vain if you do not continue it until you die.

St. Gregory the Great

NEW HIEROMARTYR THADDEUS USPENSKY. Thaddeus graduated from the Moscow Theological Academy. He often talked of becoming a monk, but he did not think himself ready. Then he had occasion to visit with St. John of Kronstadt several times. Foreboding Thaddeus' future, St. John quoted the words of the Holy Gospel, "If you love me, feed my sheep..." He was then tonsured a monk and soon ordained. Eighteen years later, in 1908, Thaddeus was ordained a bishop of Vladimir-Volyn. Patriarch Tikhon of Russia called Thaddeus a wonder of our time and a saint. After becoming a bishop, Thaddeus did not change his feats of fasting and prayer. He was a model of meekness, humility, and purity. He was arrested during the Russian Revolution along with Metropolitan Cyril. They were placed in a cell with thieves and murderers and in terrible prison conditions. Thaddeus said, "Now our souls should open for the exploit and sacrifice. Do not be discouraged. Christ is with us after all." At that moment, everything changed for Cyril, and his soul became serene and joyful. When packages of supplies and food arrived for Thaddeus, he shared them with everyone in the cell. He gave away everything he received, even his own boots. He kept nothing for himself. His exile ended in 1923. The example of his personal life was more eloquent than any words, and his moral influence on the people was huge. He had the gift of clairvoyance and healing. In 1937 St. Thaddeus was arrested again for counter-revolutionary activities and accused of being the leader of the church-monarchist organization. He was drowned in a pit of sewage.

SAINTS OF THE DAY: Sebastian at Rome, with many others; Modestus I of Jerusalem; Zacchaeus and Alphaeus of Caesarea; Florus of Amisus; Daniel of Voronet; Sebastian of Sokhotsk; Martyrs Phocas and Hermylus; Michael the Confessor; Eubotius at Cyzicus; Gatianus of Tours; Symeon of Verkhoturye; Sophia the Wonderworker; Nicholas of Great Ustiug.

DECEMBER 19

Hebrews 10:1-18; Mark 10:11-16

Come close, all of you, and tell me of your troubles as though I were alive! I'll see you, I'll hear you, and I'll come to your aid.

St. Matrona the Blind of Moscow

GEORGE THE SCRIBE AND SAVA OF KHAKHULI. George and Sava were brothers and monks at Khakhuli Monastery in eleventh-century southern Georgia. George was a spiritual adviser to the court of King Bagrat III Kuropalates, and along with the king, he produced ecclesiastical literature. Sava was a righteous and blameless man. According to St. George the Lesser, the brothers were known for their spiritual blessings and material wealth. Hearing about the piety of their nephew George, they brought him to the monastery. He later became known as St. George of the Holy Mountain. One time, a nobleman named Peris, who was married to the daughter of King Bagrat, selected the unwilling George to serve as the instructor and spiritual guide at his palace. He was responsible for all the earthly and spiritual matters. But a year later, Byzantine Emperor Basil II brought false charges against Peris and had him executed. Peris' wife and those in his court, as well as George and the young George of the Holy Mountain, were all taken to prison in Constantinople. They were held there twelve years before being released. Sts. George and Sava died peacefully.

SAINTS OF THE DAY: Boniface the Merciful, Bishop of Ferentino; Gregory (Gregentius), Archbishop of Omirits; Elias, Ares, and Probus, in Cilicia; Boniface at Tarsus in Cilicia, and Aglae of Rome; Polyeuctus at Caesarea and Timothy the Deacon, in Mauretania; George the Scribe and Sava, monks of Khakhuli Monastery; Amphilochius, wonderworker of Pochaev; Eutyches and Thessalonica, and with them 200 men and 70 women; Capito, Bishop of Kherson; Elias of Murom, wonderworker of the Kiev Caves; Martyr Tryphon; Seraphim Romantsov of Sukhumi.

Thursday

Abstain from meat and dairy products, and fish.

Hebrews 10:32-38; Mark 9:33-41

December 20

The fear of God illumines the soul, annihilates evil, weakens the passions, drives darkness from the soul and makes it pure. The fear of God is the summit of wisdom. Where it is not you will find nothing good. Whoever does not have the fear of God is open to diabolical falls.

St. Ephraim the Syrian

HIEROMARTYR IGNATIOS THE GOD-BEARER, BISHOP OF ANTIOCH. Ignatios was the child that Jesus held in the midst of his disciples, saying, "Assuredly, I say to you, unless you are converted and become as little children, you will by no means enter the kingdom of heaven (Mt. 18:3)." Ignatios later became a disciple of the holy Apostle St. John the Theologian. He was also called one of the six Apostolic Fathers because he lived among the apostles, sharing in their missionary work. He became the bishop of Antioch in the footsteps of the Apostle Peter. Ignatios was a persuasive speaker and prolific writer. His epistles to the churches were written in the format used by the Apostle Paul. He urged harmony, obedience to hierarchs, and separation from the heretics. Passing through Antioch, Emperor Trajan ordered Ignatios to sacrifice to the idols. A famous dialogue ensued, and when Ignatios refused to sacrifice, he was chained and sent to Rome to be thrown to the wild beasts. Ignatios rejoiced in the suffering for his Lord. He told the crowd gathered at the circus that he was the wheat of Jesus Christ, and when he was ground by the teeth of the wild beasts that would devour him, then he would be the pure bread of Jesus Christ. Only a few bones and the saint's heart remained. When the pagans cut open the saint's heart, they beheld within it in gold lettering "Jesus Christ." When Trajan heard about the courage of St. Ignatios, he stopped the persecution of the Christians.

SAINTS OF THE DAY: Ignatios the God-bearer; Philogonius of Antioch; Daniel II of Serbia; Ignatius of the Kiev Caves; John of the isle of Thasos; Anthony of Voronezh; Repose of St. John of Kronstadt.

DECEMBER 21

Hebrews 11:8-16; Mark 10:24-32

In truth there is only one freedom—the holy freedom of Christ, whereby He freed us from sin, from evil, from the devil. It binds us to God. All other freedoms are illusory, false, that is to say, they are all, in fact, slavery.

St. Justin Popovich

REPOSE OF PETER, METROPOLITAN OF ALL RUSSIA. Peter was only twelve years old when he became a monk in thirteenth-century Russia. He studied the Holy Scriptures and became an iconographer. He was ordained a priest-monk. After several years at the monastery, he went to a solitary place at the Rata River and began to pursue asceticism in silence. He became a renowned ascetic. Peter founded a monastery, naming it Novodvorsk. Other monks began arriving, and Peter became the abbot. He led by word and example. Later, Peter was consecrated the Metropolitan of Kiev by Patriarch Athanasius of Constantinople. He governed the Church well for eighteen years, even though he suffered greatly from the heretics and those envious of him. He built a tomb for himself in the Church of the Dormition in the Moscow Kremlin, and his relics are still there to this day. Many miracles were done through the prayers of St. Peter.

SAINTS OF THE DAY: Abel, son of Adam and first Martyr in the history of mankind; Juliana of Nicomedia, and with her 500 men and 130 women; Themistocles of Myra in Lycia; Macarius the Faster, abbot of the Khakhuli Monastery; Juliana, Princess of Vyazma; Procopius of Vyatka, fool-for-Christ; Philaret (Theodosius), Metropolitan of Kiev; Nicetas Pribytkov, Bishop of Belev; Repose of Peter, Metropolitan of Kiev and Moscow; Finding of the relics of New Monk-martyr St. Ephraim of Nea Makri.

SATURDAY

Saturday before the Nativity of Christ
Abstain from meat and dairy products, and fish.

DECEMBER 22

Galatians 3:8-12; Luke 13:19-29

Monotony and misery cannot exist where there is love. But the fire of love must be kept burning warmly & brightly with the sweet wood of sacrifice. In teaching us to cross the "I" out of life, our Lord tells us the secret of happiness; what the Saints call the ecstasy of self-forgetfulness. For divine love is always self-effacing, seeks to give rather than to receive, to serve rather than be served, to love rather than to be loved, and will sacrifice anything for the beloved. Only then does love become a clean and holy fire in the heart, and not an ugly flare of lust.

St. Seraphim of Sarov

MARTYR THEODOTA OF BITHYNIA. Theodota was from late third-century Macedonia. She was a widow with three children. She devoted her life entirely to the raising of her children and to the ministering of Christian captives during the persecutions of Diocletian. Anastasia the Great Martyr, who is also commemorated this day, stayed with Theodota and her children when she went to Macedonia. Together they washed the martyrs' wounds and loosened their bonds, helping wherever they could. Anastasia and Theodota were arrested, and together with her children, Theodota was sent to Nicetas, the governor of Bithynia. When an idol-worshipper tried to touch her body, an angel of God suddenly appeared and hit the man. Theodota and her children were thrown into a blazing furnace, where they gave up their souls.

SAINTS OF THE DAY: Great Martyr Anastasia of Rome, the Deliverer from Bonds, and her teacher Chrysogonus, and with them: Theodota, Evodias, Eutychianus, Zoilus, and others, who suffered under Diocletian; Boris Talantov of Kostroma.

Sunday before the Nativity of Christ
Genealogy Sunday
Abstain from meat and dairy products, and fish.
Hebrews 11:9-10, 32-40
Matthew 1:1-25

DECEMBER 23

Salvation exists only in Christ and His Orthodox Church.
+*Elder Arsenie Papacioc of Romania*

RIGHTEOUS SARAH. As described in the Book of Genesis, Sarah was the wife of Abraham. When God told Abraham to leave his homeland and travel to the unknown land, later known as Canaan, Sarah accompanied him. However, there was famine in that land, so they took refuge in Egypt. Because of Sarah's beauty, Abraham asked her to pose as his sister, so his life would not be in danger, but as he feared, Sarah was taken by the pharaoh who rewarded Abraham with riches. But God struck pharaoh and all his house with severe plagues until he discovered Sarah's secret. He ordered Abraham to take Sarah and depart. However, the pharaoh was so impressed with Abraham's righteousness that he sent his daughter Hagar to be Sarah's handmaiden. Because Sarah remained childless, she offered Hagar to Abraham as a concubine, and Hagar immediately conceived, and she named her son Ishmael. Later, God sent three angels disguised as men to tell Abraham, who would soon be 100 years old, that his wife Sarah, who was approaching 90, would give birth. Abraham laughed with joy, and Sarah laughed with doubt. God told Abraham to name the child Isaac, after Sarah's laughter of doubt. Sarah died in Hebron at the age of 127. Abraham bought a family burial plot, which was the Cave of Machpelah, or the Cave of the Patriarchs. It became the burial site of Abraham and Sarah, Isaac and Rebecca, and Jacob and Leah—three patriarchs and three matriarchs.

SAINTS OF THE DAY: All the Ancestors of Christ according to the flesh: including, Adam, Abel, Abraham, Isaac and Jacob, Moses, Joshua, David the King, Solomon; Prophets Elias and Daniel, Zechariah, Joachim and Anna, Joseph the Betrothed, Sarah, Rebecca, Ruth, Deborah, and others; Paul of Neo-Caesarea; Theoctistus of Novgorod; Niphon of Constantia; Ten Martyrs of Crete; David of Echmiadzin.

Eve of the Nativity of Christ
Strict Fast

December 24

Hebrews 1:1-12; Luke 2:1-20

Panaghia prays and intercedes for all people, but especially for the humble. Let us fervently ask her to grant us something of her beautiful humility. When we do, then—even if we find ourselves in an economic crisis, or in illness, or in any other difficulty or unemployment—we will have patience, hope, consolation and optimism.

+*Blessed Monk Moses*

VENERABLE ANTIOCHUS, MONK OF PALESTINE. Antiochus became a monk at the famous Lavra of St. Sabbas in Palestine in the seventh century. He became well-known for his virtue, saintliness, and his writings. At the request of the abbot of another monastery, Antiochus authored 130 chapters on the moral teachings of the Scriptures. This is known as the *Pandektes of Holy Scripture*. These chapters were written for the benefit of the monks in Galatia who were expelled by the Persians. These same Persians also carried away the Holy Cross into their country, where it remained for fourteen years. Antiochus wrote, "A proud monk is like a barren and rootless tree; he cannot withstand the force of the wind; and like a burst bubble, he vanishes. Thus does the memory of a proud man disappear after death. As the prayer of a humble man appeases God, so does the entreaty of a proud one anger the Almighty."

SAINTS OF THE DAY: Eugenia of Rome, and with her, Philip her father, Protus, Hyacinth, Basilla, and Claudia; Aphrodisius and Antiochus, monks of Palestine; Vitimonus of Scetis; New Martyr Achmed (Ahmet) the Calligrapher, at Constantinople; Nicholas the Monk of Bulgaria; Martyr Achaicus; Innocent Beda of Voronezh; Sergius Mechev of Moscow.

Nativity of Our Lord and Savior Jesus Christ
Fast-free period till January 5
Galatians 4:4-7; Matthew 2:1-12

December 25

"The Lord entered into her and became a servant; He, Who is the Word, entered and became silent within her; thunder entered her, and made no sound; there entered the Shepherd of all, and—in her—He became the Lamb… Naked and stripped there came forth from her He, Who clothes all! Praise be to Thee, to Whom all things are easy; for Thou art almighty."

St. Ephraim the Syrian

THE ADORATION OF THE MAGI: MELCHIOR, CASPAR, AND BALTHASAR. The word "Magi" is the plural of "Magus," the name that was given to one who was a philosopher and astronomer. They were also called kings. In Scripture, "Magus" was a common name given to one who ruled a single city. Melchior is depicted as an old man, with a beard and long gray hair. He brought gold to the King and Master Jesus. Caspar was young and beardless, with a ruddy complexion. His gift was frankincense to God Incarnate. Balthazar, who was bearded and very dark, presented myrrh to the Son of Man, Who would undergo death. The three Magi came from the east, from the neighboring countries of Arabia, Persia, and Ethiopia. They traveled independently with their entourage, then providentially met and joined company. It was not an ordinary star that led them, but a divine and angelic power that appeared in the form of a star. The consensus is that the star appeared in the sky at the Annunciation. Stars move from east to west, but this star moved from the east southward to Jerusalem. It shone like the sun during the day, guiding the Magi to Bethlehem. They arrived in Jerusalem on the day of the Nativity, but the star hid so others would not go to Bethlehem. When they departed the city, the star reappeared and descended near the earth, showing the exact location of the cave. It is said that the Holy Family remained in the cave for forty days, until just before the Presentation in the Temple.

SAINTS OF THE DAY: The Adoration of the Magi; Commemoration of the shepherds in Bethlehem; Jonah of Pechenga with 115 others.

Synaxis of the Mother of God
Fast-free

December 26

Hebrews 2:11-18; Matthew 2:13-23

The humble soul is blessed. The Lord loves her. The Mother of God is higher than all in humility, and therefore all races bless her on earth, while the heavenly powers serve her. And the Lord has given us this blessed Mother of His as a defender and helper.

St. Silouan the Athonite

VENERABLE EVARESTUS OF THE STUDION MONASTERY. Evarestus was from a wealthy family in ninth-century Galatia. He received a religious education, was obedient to his parents, and had a delightful disposition. He also showed generosity to strangers. He decided that he wanted to become a monk, but instead, his father got him into the employ of an ambassador to the Bulgarians. But even in this circumstance, he found a book written by St. Ephraim the Syrian on the last judgment, the reading of which caused him great compunction. Evarestus also met a monastic elder during this time and was tonsured a monk. This elder sent him to the Studion Monastery that was headed by St. Nafkratios. Evarestus fasted strictly, eating only a little barley meal and wheat germ baked into bread, and he drank juice from boiled vegetables. He wore chains as an additional ascetic struggle. When the monastery came under persecution, Evarestus and other monks founded another monastery named Kokorovion, where he became the abbot. He prayed fervently with the gift of tears, gave to the poor, and showed hospitality to all who visited the monastery. He was also granted the gift to work miracles and to prophesy. In this manner, he lived his life well and died peacefully.

SAINTS OF THE DAY: Synaxis of the Most Holy Theotokos; Commemoration of the flight into Egypt; Euthymius of Sardis; Zeno of Maiuma; Nicodemus of Tismana; Andrew of Ufa and Valentina of Russia; Archelaus of Haran; Constantine of Synnada; Constantius the Russian; Evarestus of the Studion Monastery; Tathai of Llantathan; Jarlath of Tuam (Ireland); Leonid of Mariisk, Isaac II of Optina, Basil, hieromonk, and Augusta, schemanun; "The Blessed Womb" Icon of the Mother of God.

DECEMBER 27

Acts 6:8-15, 7:1-5, 47-60
Matthew 21:33-42

If one does not start sacrificing something now, like giving up some desire or selfishness, how will he ever be able to sacrifice his life at a given time? If, even now, he thinks of the labor, and tries to avoid working a little harder than the next person, how will he ever attain the state of risking his own life to save another's? … When there is no spirit of sacrifice, everyone looks only to save himself.

St. Paisios the Athonite

HOLY PROTOMARTYR AND ARCHDEACON STEPHEN. Stephen was the first of the Seven Deacons chosen by the Apostles to minister to the poor. He was educated under the renowned rabbinical teacher Gamaliel, as was his relative Saul, who came to be known as Apostle Paul. Stephen studied Holy Scripture and debated the Jews in the temple with whom he had once studied. By his prayers, he worked miracles among the people. The Jews slandered Stephen, saying that he blasphemed against God and Moses. Stephen stood before them, his face resplendent with light, and spoke of God's works and the transgressions of the Israelites (Acts 7). When he denounced them for the murder of Jesus Christ, they drove him from the city and stoned him to death. His last words were, "Lord, do not hold this sin against them. Lord Jesus, receive my spirit." Saul, whom Jesus had not yet converted, stood by. Afar off was the Theotokos and the holy Apostle John the Theologian, who witnessed the first martyrdom for Christianity. The Theotokos prayed fervently for St. Stephen. This is believed to have happened on the first anniversary of Pentecost. The body of St. Stephen was left to be devoured by beasts, but it was secretly taken by the teacher Gamaliel and his son Habib, and given burial. Afterward, both believed in Christ and received Holy Baptism.

SAINTS OF THE DAY: Protomartyr and Archdeacon Stephen; Theodore Graptus "the Branded" and Bithynia; Maximus of Alexandria; Theodore of Constantinople; Barlaam of Tobolsk; Luke of Tryglia.

DECEMBER 28

James 2:1-13; Luke 14:25-35

Brothers and Sisters! The all-merciful God desires happiness for us both in this life and in the life to come. To this end He established His Holy Church, so that she might cleanse us from sin, sanctify us, reconcile us with Him and give us a heavenly blessing. The embrace of the Church is always open to us. Let us all hasten there more quickly, we whose consciences are burdened. Let us hasten, and the Church will lift the weight of our burdens, give us boldness before God, and fill our hearts with happiness and blessedness.

St. Nectarios of Aegina

VENERABLE IGNATIUS OF LOMSK AND YAROSLAVSK. Ignatius lived in several monasteries in sixteenth-century Russia. He went to an area near the city of Lomsk and founded a wilderness monastery. He gradually attracted disciples but withdrew to a forested skete where he pursued asceticism in silence. He earned his livelihood by plaiting shoes, which he would leave alongside the road. Those who took the shoes would leave bread. Ignatius built a church in honor of the Protection of the Most Holy Mother of God, and later a monastery was founded next to it. He died peacefully and was buried in the church.

SAINTS OF THE DAY: The 20,000 Martyrs of Nicomedia, including: Glycerius, Zeno, Theophilus, Dorotheus, Mardonius, Migdonius, Index, Gorgonius, Peter, Euthymius, and the virgins Agape, Domna, Theophila, and others; Apostle Nicanor the Deacon,. of the Seventy; Simon the Myrrh-gusher, founder of Simonopetra Monastery, Mt. Athos; Babylas of Tarsus; Ignatius, founder of Lomsk and Yaroslavl; Cornelius of Krypetsk Monastery (Pskov); Nikodim Kononov, Bishop of Belgorod, and Arcadius Reshetnikov, deacon; Martyr Secundus; Wunibald of Heidenheim (Germany).

Saturday after the Nativity of Christ
Fast-free

DECEMBER 29

1 Timothy 6:11-16
Matthew 12:15-21

There are pious people who have a bitter death, and there are sinners who have a sweet death. But the bitter death of the pious washes whatever bitter sins as a man he may have committed in his life, for no one is without sin, but God alone. While the sweet death of the sinner takes away the little right to reward for whatever good he happened to do.

St. Nephon of Constantia

VENERABLE THADDEUS, CONFESSOR OF THE STUDION. For one hundred seventeen years, between the years 725-845, the iconoclasts fought Orthodoxy, ordering the destruction of all icons. Persecutions began against the monks who were the most zealous defenders of the icons. Thaddeus was a monk and disciple of St. Theodore the Studite, and a defender of the veneration of icons. He was arrested and taken to trial. The heretics put an icon of Jesus Christ on the ground, and forcibly caused Thaddeus to trample it. After this, the judge said, "Thou hast trampled upon the icon of Christ, now join together with us." Thaddeus cursed the impiety of the iconoclasts. He was beaten with canes and dragged outside the city walls, thinking he was dead. However, Thaddeus was still alive. A Christian took him into his home and cared for him another three days, and then St. Thaddeus gave up his soul.

SAINTS OF THE DAY: The14,000 infants (Holy Innocents) slain by Herod at Bethlehem; Mark the Grave-digger of the Kiev Caves; Thaddeus of the Studion; Athenodorus, disciple of St. Pachomius the Great; George of Nicomedia; Benjamin of Nitria in Egypt; Marcellus, abbot of the monastery of the Unsleeping Ones, Constantinople; Lawrence of Chernigov; Basiliscus of Turinsk (Siberia); Theophilus and John of the Kiev Caves; Trophimus of Arles; Theophilus of Luga; Evroult of Ouche in Normandy; Job Knyaginitsky of Manyava Skete (Ukraine); Commemoration of all Orthodox Christians who have died from hunger, thirst, the sword, and freezing.

Sunday after the Nativity of Christ
Fast-free

DECEMBER 30

Galatians 1:11-19
Matthew 2:13-23

Should there be any free moments during the course of the day, use them to read attentively some chosen prayers, or some chosen portions of Scripture; and, by means of these, fortify the powers of your soul, which have become exhausted through activity in the midst of a world of vanities. Should there not be any such golden moments, it is necessary to regret their loss, as though it were the loss of a valuable treasure. What is wasted today should not be lost on the day following, because our heart conveniently gives itself up to negligence and forgetfulness, which lead to that dismal ignorance, so ruinous of Divine activity, of the activity of man's salvation.

St. Ignatius Brianchaninov

RIGHTEOUS JOSEPH THE BETROTHED. Before he was chosen to become the husband and guardian of the Most Holy Mother of God, Joseph had been married and was the father of two daughters and four sons. When his wife died, he lived a life of strict temperance. An angel of God told him of the Incarnation of Jesus through the Theotokos. Joseph was present when the Magi and the shepherds worshipped the newborn Jesus. He led the Mother of God and baby Jesus into Egypt to escape King Herod who killed fourteen thousand male children two years of age and younger. Joseph worked as a carpenter in Egypt while awaiting a safe return home. It is believed that Joseph lived to be one hundred years old.

SAINTS OF THE DAY: Sunday after the Nativity: Joseph the Betrothed, David the King, and James the Brother of the Lord; Anysia at Thessalonica; Theodora of Caesarea; Philoterus of Nicomedia, with six soldiers and one count; Magistrianus, Paulinus, Umbrius, Verus, Severus, Callistratus, Florentius, Arianus, Anthimus, Ubricius, Isidore, Euculus, Sampson, Studius, and Thespesius, under Julian the Apostate; Apostle Timon of the Seventy; Macarius of Moscow; Tryphon of Rostov.

December 31

James 2:14-26; Mark 12:13-17

Let, therefore, every devout Christian say the 'prayer' (Jesus Prayer) unceasingly with the mind and lips... Let the priests practice this prayer diligently like an apostolic mission for themselves and their rational flock, just like preaching and the celebration of the holy Sacraments. Let those who live in the world use the prayer as often as they can, because it is the seal and mark of our faith, sanctification, and the opponent of every temptation.

St. Symeon the New Theologian

VENERABLE CYRIACUS OF TAZLAU, ROMANIA. Cyriacus was from a poor family and became a monk at the Tazlau Monastery in the seventeenth century. He was found worthy of the priesthood because of his prayers, virtues, and humility. But wanting to progress even further, he went into the wilderness, where he lived for fifty years, eating only fruits and dry bread. He kept all-night vigils and shed a multitude of tears. Because of his ascetical endeavors, Cyriacus was granted the gift to cast out demons and foresee the future. Over time he attracted many disciples, who also became hesychasts living in the mountains. He died peacefully in great old age and was buried in a cave. Here his relics worked many miracles. More than a hundred years later, when infidels overran the area, the faithful divided his relics among themselves, so that the invaders would not desecrate them.

SAINTS OF THE DAY: Theophylactus, Archbishop of Ochrid; Gelasius, monk of Palestine; Dositheus, Metropolitan of Zagreb; The Ten Virgin-martyrs of Nicomedia; Zoticus the Priest of Constantinople, feeder of orphans; Melania the Younger, nun of Rome; Peter Mogila, Metropolitan of Kiev; Sabiana, abbess of Samtskhe Convent; Anysius, Bishop of Thessalonica; Cyriacus of Bisericani Monastery (Romania); Cyriacus of Tazlau Monastery (Romania); Gaius, monk; Martyr Olympiodora; Martyr Nema; Martyrs Busiris, Gaudentius, and Nemo.

DON'T FORGET TO ORDER ...

The

2019

Daily Lives, Miracles, and Wisdom of the Saints & Fasting Calendar

Place your order at
www.LivesoftheSaintsCalendar.com